The Acts of the Apostles

E.G. White

Printed for

Remnant Publications

by

Pacific Press Publishing Association
Boise, Idaho

The Desire of Ages

This edition published 1993

The bracketed numbers at the foot of each page coordinate this edition with the pagination of the standard hardback printings.

ARE YOU SEARCHING FOR TRUTH?

NEED RELIABLE ANSWERS TO URGENT QUESTIONS?

Can we know and understand the future?
What are the tests of a true prophet?
Is the development of character important?
Are there physical and spiritual laws for health and happiness?
What really happens to us after death?
Is is possible to live forever?
How can you find inner peace in a world of chaos?

Discover the answers to these and other vital questions by enrolling in our BIBLE CORRESPONDENCE COURSE. We care. We are concerned about you and interested in your welfare. A consecutive series of these thought-provoking Bible-study lessons will help stimulate you to think independently and make conscientious choices.

The first two lessons in the series are free of charge for enrolling. We ask you to include a nominal freewill offering beginning with lesson three to cover the postage and handling.

DO YOU WANT TO KNOW MORE?

Yes. Please enroll me, at no charge for the first two lessons, in the BIBLE CORRESPONDENCE COURSE.

Name_____

Address_____

City_____ State_____ Zip_____

Send to:

BIBLE CORRESPONDENCE COURSE
P.O. Box 2660
Kalispell, MT 59901

Contents

Seven Books That Will Change Your Life . . .

Patriarchs and Prophets

Where did the human race come from? Why do bad things happen to good people? Why are babies born sick, and why do so many hard-working people never seem to get ahead? If God is good, why doesn't He prevent sadness and heartbreak? And if He is all-powerful, why doesn't He do something about evil and sickness?

These questions and many more are answered in this remarkable book. **Patriarchs and Prophets** has brought peace and hope to millions throughout the world. *US$7.95

Prophets and Kings

Beginning with King Solomon, this book recounts the stories of great men and women of the Bible who lived from his reign to the first advent of Jesus Christ. Here you will read of Elijah, Daniel, Isaiah, and Jeremiah, among others—and you will find the lessons God would have us all learn from their lives. *US$7.95

The Desire of Ages

This book is about the Man who stands at the center of all human history. No one else has had such a profound influence on the people of this planet as Jesus Christ. *US$7.95

The Acts of the Apostles

This book is about power—ultimate power. The awesome power of the Holy Spirit, and what He can do in human lives when we surrender to be used by Him. When Pentecost came upon the early church, what God's people accomplished was miraculous. And all that the apostles did, God wants to do again through us today. *US$7.95

. . . FOREVER!

The Great Controversy

The world is on the verge of a stupendous crisis. Here is the authoritative answer to the confusion and despair of this tense age. Revealing God's ultimate plan for mankind, **The Great Controversy** may be the most important book you will ever read. ***US$7.95**

The Ministry of Healing

Using Jesus Christ as the example of the true Medical Missionary, this book, first written over 80 years ago, is an extraordinary example of medical-science prophecy. Many topics, such as mind cures, natural remedies, vegetarian diet, exercise, prenatal influences, and health education, are covered. The author speaks of true health and healing in conjunction with the powers of the Great Physician, Jesus Christ. ***US$5.95**

Christ's Object Lessons

Here is the most compelling book ever written on the parables of Jesus. Through familiar objects and incidents—the harvest, the shepherd, the builder, the traveler, the homemaker—Jesus linked divine truth with the common and ordinary. As you read this book, you will experience the sensation of walking through a door into a previously unseen but very real world. ***US$6.95**

*All prices include postage and handling.

**Send check or money order to:
Remnant Publications
P.O. Box 2660, Kalispell, MT 59901
Please allow up to six weeks for delivery.**

1

God's Purpose for His Church

The church is God's appointed agency for the salvation of men. It was organized for service, and its mission is to carry the gospel to the world. From the beginning it has been God's plan that through His church shall be reflected to the world His fullness and His sufficiency. The members of the church, those whom He has called out of darkness into His marvelous light, are to show forth His glory. The church is the repository of the riches of the grace of Christ; and through the church will eventually be made manifest, even to "the principalities and powers in heavenly places," the final and full display of the love of God. Ephesians 3:10.

Many and wonderful are the promises recorded in the Scriptures regarding the church. "Mine house shall be called an house of prayer for all people." Isaiah 56:7. "I will make them and the places round about My hill a blessing; and I will cause the shower to come down in his season; there shall be showers of blessing." "And I will raise up for them a plant of renown, and they shall be no more consumed with hunger in the land, neither bear the shame of the heathen any more. Thus shall they know that I the Lord their God am with them, and that they, even the house of Israel, are My people, saith the Lord God. And ye My flock, the flock of My pasture, are men, and I am your God, saith the Lord God." Ezekiel 34:26, 29-31.

"Ye are My witnesses, saith the Lord, and My servant whom I have chosen: that ye may know and believe Me, and understand that I am He: before Me there was no God formed, neither shall there be after Me. I, even I, am the Lord; and beside Me there is no Saviour. I have declared, and have saved, and I have showed, when there was no strange god among you: therefore ye are My witnesses." "I the Lord have called thee in righteousness, and will hold thine hand, and will keep thee, and give thee for a covenant of the people, for a light of the Gentiles; to open the blind eyes, to bring out the prisoners from the prison, and them that sit in darkness out of the prison house." Isaiah 43:10-12; 42:6, 7.

"In an acceptable time have I heard thee, and in a day of salvation have I helped thee: and I will preserve thee, and give thee for a covenant of the people, to establish the earth, to cause to inherit the desolate heritages; that thou mayest say to the prisoners, Go forth; to them that are in darkness, Show yourselves. They shall feed in the ways, and their pastures shall be in all high places. They shall not hunger nor thirst; neither shall the heat nor sun smite them: for He that hath mercy on them shall lead them, even by the springs of water shall He guide them. And I will make all My mountains a way, and My highways shall be exalted. . . .

"Sing, O heavens; and be joyful, O earth; and break forth into singing, O mountains: for the Lord hath comforted His people, and will have mercy upon His afflicted. But Zion said, The Lord hath forsaken me, and my Lord hath forgotten me. Can a woman forget her sucking child, that she should not have compassion on the son of her womb? yea, they may forget, yet will I not forget thee. Behold, I have graven thee upon the palms of My hands; thy walls are continually before Me." Isaiah 49:8-16.

The church is God's fortress. His city of refuge, which He holds in a revolted world. Any betrayal of the church is treachery to Him who has bought mankind with the blood of His only-begotten Son. From the beginning, faithful souls have constituted the church on earth. In every age the Lord has had His watchmen, who have borne a faithful testimony to the generation in which they lived. These sentinels gave the message of warning; and when they were called to lay off their armor, others took up the work. God brought these witnesses into covenant relation with Himself, uniting the church on earth with the church in heaven. He has sent forth His angels to minister to His church, and the gates of hell have not been able to prevail against His people.

Through centuries of persecution, conflict, and darkness, God has sustained His church. Not one cloud has fallen upon it that He has not prepared for; not one opposing force has risen to counter-work His work, that He has not foreseen. All has taken place as He predicted. He has not left His church forsaken, but has traced in prophetic declarations what would occur, and that which His Spirit inspired the prophets to foretell has been brought about. All His purposes will be fulfilled. His law is linked with His throne, and no power of evil can destroy it. Truth is inspired and guarded by God; and it will triumph over all opposition.

During ages of spiritual darkness the church of God has been as a city set on a hill. From age to age, through successive generations, the pure doctrines of heaven have been unfolding within its borders. Enfeebled and defective as it may appear, the church is the one object upon which God bestows in a special sense His supreme regard. It is the theater of His grace, in which He delights to reveal His power to transform hearts.

"Whereunto," asked Christ, "shall we liken the kingdom of God? or with what comparison shall we compare it?" Mark 4:30. He could not employ the kingdoms of the world as a similitude. In society He found nothing with which to compare it. Earthly kingdoms rule by the ascendancy of physical power; but from Christ's kingdom every carnal weapon, every instrument of coercion, is banished. This kingdom is to uplift and ennoble humanity. God's church is the court of holy life, filled with varied gifts and endowed with the Holy Spirit. The members are to find their happiness in the happiness of those whom they help and bless.

Wonderful is the work which the Lord designs to accomplish through His church, that His name may be glorified. A picture of this work is given in Ezekiel's vision of the river of healing: "These waters issue out toward the east country, and go down into the desert, and go into the sea: which being brought forth into the sea, the waters shall be healed. And it shall come to pass, that everything that liveth, which moveth, whithersoever the rivers shall come, shall live: . . . and by the river upon the bank thereof, on this side and on that side, shall grow all trees for meat, whose leaf shall not fade, neither shall the fruit thereof be consumed: it shall bring forth new fruit according to his months, because their waters they issued out of the sanctuary: and the fruit thereof shall be for meat, and the leaf thereof for medicine." Ezekiel 47:8-12.

From the beginning God has wrought through His people to bring blessing to the world. To the ancient Egyptian nation God made Joseph a fountain of life. Through the integrity of Joseph the life of that whole people was preserved. Through Daniel God saved the life of all the wise men of Babylon. And these deliverances are as object lessons; they illustrate the spiritual blessings offered to the world through connection with the God whom Joseph and Daniel worshiped. Everyone in whose heart Christ abides, everyone who will show forth His love to the world, is a worker together with God for the blessing of humanity. As he receives from the Saviour grace to impart to others, from his whole being flows forth the tide of spiritual life.

God chose Israel to reveal His character to men. He desired them to be as wells of salvation in the world. To them were committed the oracles of heaven, the revelation of God's will. In the early days of Israel the nations of the world, through corrupt practices, had lost the knowledge of God. They had once known Him; but because "they glorified Him not as God, neither were thankful; but became vain in their imaginations, . . . their foolish heart was darkened." Romans 1:21. Yet in His mercy God did not blot them out of existence. He purposed to give them an opportunity of again becoming acquainted with Him through His chosen people. Through the teachings of the sacrificial service, Christ was to be uplifted before all nations, and all who would look to Him should live. Christ was the foundation of the Jewish economy. The whole system of types and symbols was a compacted prophecy of the gospel, a presentation in which were bound up the promises of redemption.

But the people of Israel lost sight of their high privileges as God's representatives. They forgot God and failed to fulfill their holy mission. The blessings they received brought no blessing to the world. All their advantages they appropriated for their own glorification. They shut themselves away from the world in order to escape temptation. The restrictions that God had placed upon their association with idolaters as a means of preventing them from conforming to the practices of the heathen, they used to build up a wall of separation between themselves and all other nations. They robbed God of the service He required of them, and they robbed their fellow men of religious guidance and a holy example.

Priests and rulers became fixed in a rut of ceremonialism. They were satisfied with a legal religion, and it was impossible for them to give to others the living truths of heaven. They thought their own righteousness all-sufficient, and did not desire that a new element should be brought into their religion. The good will of God to men they did not accept as something apart from themselves, but connected it with their own merit because of their good works. The faith that works by love and purifies the soul could find no place for union with the religion of the Pharisees, made up of ceremonies and the injunctions of men.

Of Israel God declared: "I had planted thee a noble vine, wholly a right seed: how then art thou turned into the degenerate plant of a strange vine unto Me?" Jeremiah 2:21. "Israel is an empty vine, he bringeth forth fruit unto himself." Hosea 10:1. "And now, O inhabitants of Jerusalem, and men of Judah, judge, I pray you, betwixt Me and My vineyard. What could have been done more to My vineyard, that I have not done in it? wherefore, when I looked that it should bring forth grapes, brought it forth wild grapes?

"And now go to; I will tell you what I will do to My vineyard: I will take away the hedge thereof, and it shall be eaten up; and break down the wall thereof, and it shall be trodden down: and I will lay it waste: it shall not be pruned, nor digged; but there shall come up briers and thorns: I will also command the clouds that they rain no rain upon it. For the vineyard of the Lord of hosts is the house of Israel, and the men of Judah His pleasant plant: and He looked for judgment, but behold oppression; for righteousness, but behold a cry." Isaiah 5:3-7. "The diseased have ye not strengthened, neither have ye healed that which was sick, neither have ye bound up that which was broken, neither have ye brought again that which was driven away, neither have ye sought that which was lost; but with force and with cruelty have ye ruled them." Ezekiel 34:4.

The Jewish leaders thought themselves too wise to need instruction, too righteous to need salvation, too highly honored to need the honor that comes from Christ. The Saviour turned from them to entrust to others the privileges they had abused and the work they had slighted. God's glory must be revealed, His word established. Christ's kingdom must be set up in the world. The salvation of God must be made known in the cities of the wilderness; and the disciples were called to do the work that the Jewish leaders had failed to do.

2

The Training of the Twelve

For the carrying on of His work, Christ did not choose the learning or eloquence of the Jewish Sanhedrin or the power of Rome. Passing by the self-righteous Jewish teachers, the Master Worker chose humble, unlearned men to proclaim the truths that were to move the world. These men He purposed to train and educate as the leaders of His church. They in turn were to educate others and send them out with the gospel message. That they might have success in their work they were to be given the power of the Holy Spirit. Not by human might or human wisdom was the gospel to be proclaimed, but by the power of God.

For three years and a half the disciples were under the instruction of the greatest Teacher the world has ever known. By personal contact and association, Christ trained them for His service. Day by day they walked and talked with Him, hearing His words of cheer to the weary and heavy-laden, and seeing the manifestation of His power in behalf of the sick and the afflicted. Sometimes He taught them, sitting among them on the mountainside; sometimes beside the sea or walking by the way, He revealed the mysteries of the kingdom of God. Wherever hearts were open to receive the divine message, He unfolded the truths of the way of salvation. He did not command the disciples to do this or that, but said, "Follow Me." On His journeys through country and cities, He took them with Him, that they might see how He taught the people. They traveled with Him from place to place. They shared His frugal fare, and like Him were sometimes hungry and often weary. On the crowded streets, by the lakeside, in the lonely desert, they were with Him. They saw Him in every phase of life.

It was at the ordination of the Twelve that the first step was taken in the organization of the church that after Christ's departure was to carry on His work on the earth. Of this ordination the record says, "He goeth up into a mountain, and calleth unto Him whom He would: and they came unto Him. And He ordained twelve, that they should be with Him, and that He might send them forth to preach." Mark 3:13, 14.

Look upon the touching scene. Behold the Majesty of heaven surrounded by the Twelve whom He has chosen. He is about to set them apart for their work. By these feeble agencies, through His word and Spirit, He designs to place salvation within the reach of all.

With gladness and rejoicing, God and the angels beheld this scene. The Father knew that from these men the light of heaven would shine forth; that the words spoken by them as they witnessed for His Son, would echo from generation to generation till the close of time.

The disciples were to go forth as Christ's witnesses, to declare to the world what they had seen and heard of Him. Their office was the most important to which human beings had ever been called, second only to that of Christ Himself. They were to be workers together with God for the saving of men. As in the Old Testament the twelve patriarchs stood as representatives of Israel, so the twelve apostles stand as representatives of the gospel church.

During His earthly ministry Christ began to break down the partition wall between Jew and Gentile, and to preach salvation to all mankind. Though He was a Jew, He mingled freely with the Samaritans, setting at nought the Pharisaic customs of the Jews with regard to this despised people. He slept under their roofs, ate at their tables, and taught in their streets.

The Saviour longed to unfold to His disciples the truth regarding the breaking down of the "middle wall of partition" between Israel and the other nations—the truth that "the Gentiles should be fellow heirs" with the Jews and "partakers of His promise in Christ by the gospel." Ephesians 2:14; 3:6. This truth was revealed in part at the time when He rewarded the faith of the centurion at Capernaum, and also when He preached the gospel to the inhabitants of Sychar. Still more plainly was it revealed on the occasion of His visit to Phoenicia, when He healed the daughter of the Canaanite woman. These experiences helped the disciples to understand that among those whom many regarded as unworthy of salvation, there were souls hungering for the light of truth.

Thus Christ sought to teach the disciples the truth that in God's kingdom there are no territorial lines, no caste, no aristocracy; that they must go to all nations, bearing to them the message of a Saviour's love. But not until later did they realize in all its fullness that God "hath made of one blood all nations of men for to dwell on all the face of the earth, and hath determined the times before appointed, and the bounds of their habitation; that they should seek the Lord, if haply they might feel after Him, and find Him, though He be not far from every one of us." Acts 17:26, 27.

In these first disciples was presented marked diversity. They were to be the world's teachers, and they represented widely varied types of character. In order successfully to carry forward the work to which they had been called, these men, differing in natural characteristics and in habits of life, needed to come into unity of feeling, thought, and action. This unity it was Christ's object to secure. To this end He sought to bring them into unity with Himself. The burden of His labor for them is expressed in His prayer to His Father, "That they all may be one; as Thou, Father, art in Me, and I in Thee, that they also may be one in Us;" "that the world may know that Thou has sent Me, and hast loved them, as Thou hast loved Me." John 17:21, 23. His constant prayer for them was that they might be sanctified through the truth; and He prayed with assurance, knowing that an Almighty decree had been given before the world was made. He knew that the gospel of the kingdom would be preached to all nations for a witness; He knew that truth armed with the omnipotence of the Holy Spirit, would conquer in the battle with evil, and that the bloodstained banner would one day wave triumphantly over His followers.

As Christ's earthly ministry drew to a close, and He realized that He must soon leave His disciples to carry on the work without His personal supervision, He sought to encourage them and to prepare them for the future. He did not deceive them with false hopes. As an open book He read what was to be. He knew He was about to be separated from them, to leave them as sheep among wolves. He knew that they would suffer persecution, that they would be cast out of the synagogues, and would be thrown into prison. He knew that for witnessing to Him as the Messiah, some of them would suffer death. And something of this He told them. In speaking of their future, He was plain and definite, that in their coming trial they might remember His words and be strengthened to believe in Him as the Redeemer.

He spoke to them also words of hope and courage. "Let not your heart be troubled," He said; "ye believe in God, believe also in Me. In My Father's house are many mansions: if it were not so, I would have told you. I go to prepare a place for you. And if I go and prepare a place for you, I will come again, and receive you unto Myself; that where I am, there ye may be also. And whither I go ye know, and the way ye know." John 14:1-4. For your sake I came into the world; for you I have been working. When I go away I shall still work earnestly for you. I came to the world to reveal Myself to you, that you might believe. I go to My Father and yours to co-operate with Him in your behalf.

"Verily, verily, I say unto you, He that believeth on Me, the works that I do shall he do also; and greater works than these shall he do; because I go unto My Father." John 14:12. By this, Christ did not mean that the disciples would make more exalted exertions than He had made, but that their work would have greater magnitude. He did not refer merely to miracle working, but to all that would take place under the agency of the Holy Spirit. "When the Comforter is come," He said, "whom I will send unto you from the Father, even the Spirit of truth, which proceedeth from the Father, He shall testify of Me: and ye also shall bear witness, because ye have been with Me from the beginning." John 15:26, 27.

Wonderfully were these words fulfilled. After the descent of the Holy Spirit, the disciples were so filled with love for Him and for those for whom He died, that hearts were melted by the words they spoke and the prayers they offered. They spoke in the power of the Spirit; and under the influence of that power, thousands were converted.

As Christ's representatives the apostles were to make a decided impression on the world. The fact that they were humble men would not diminish their influence, but increase it; for the minds of their hearers would be carried from them to the Saviour, who, though unseen, was still working with them. The wonderful teaching of the apostles, their words of courage and trust, would assure all that it was not in their own power that they worked, but in the power of Christ. Humbling themselves, they would declare that He whom the Jews had crucified was the Prince of life, the Son of the living God, and that in His name they did the works that He had done.

In His parting conversation with His disciples on the night before the crucifixion the Saviour made no reference to the suffering that He had endured and must yet endure. He did not speak of the humiliation that was before Him, but sought to bring to their minds that which would strengthen their faith, leading them to look forward to the joys that await the overcomer. He rejoiced in the consciousness that He could and would do more for His followers than He had promised; that from Him would flow forth love and compassion, cleansing the soul temple, and making men like Him in character; that His truth, armed with the power of the Spirit, would go forth conquering and to conquer.

"These things I have spoken unto you," He said, "that in Me ye might have peace. In the world ye shall have tribulation: but be of good cheer; I have overcome the world." John 16:33. Christ did not fail, neither was He discouraged; and the disciples were to show a faith of the same enduring nature. They were to work as He had worked, depending on Him for strength. Though their way would be obstructed by apparent impossibilities, yet by His grace they were to go forward, despairing of nothing and hoping for everything.

Christ had finished the work that was given Him to do. He had gathered out those who were to continue His work among men. And He said: "I am glorified in them. And now I am no more in the world, but these are in the world, and I come to Thee. Holy Father, keep through Thine own name those whom Thou hast given Me, that they may be one, as We are." "Neither pray I for these alone, but for them also which shall believe on Me through their word; that they all may be one; . . . I in them and Thou in Me, that they may be made perfect in one; and that the world may know that Thou hast sent Me, and hast loved them, as Thou hast loved Me." John 17:10, 11, 20-23.

3

The Great Commission

After the death of Christ the disciples were well-nigh overcome by discouragement. Their Master had been rejected, condemned, and crucified. The priests and rulers had declared scornfully, "He saved others; Himself He cannot save. If He be the King of Israel, let Him now come down from the cross, and we will believe Him." Matthew 27:42. The sun of the disciples' hope had set, and night settled down upon their hearts. Often they repeated the words, "We trusted that it had been He which should have redeemed Israel." Luke 24:21. Lonely and sick at heart, they remembered His words, "If they do these things in a green tree, what shall be done in the dry?" Luke 23:31.

Jesus had several times attempted to open the future to His disciples, but they had not cared to think about what He said. Because of this His death had come to them as a surprise; and afterward, as they reviewed the past and saw the result of their unbelief, they were filled with sorrow. When Christ was crucified, they did not believe that He would rise. He had stated plainly that He was to rise on the third day, but they were perplexed to know what He meant. This lack of comprehension left them at the time of His death in utter hopelessness. They were bitterly disappointed. Their faith did not penetrate beyond the shadow that Satan had cast athwart their horizon. All seemed vague and mysterious to them. If they had believed the Saviour's words, how much sorrow they might have been spared!

Crushed by despondency, grief, and despair, the disciples met together in the upper chamber, and closed and fastened the doors, fearing that the fate of their beloved Teacher might be theirs. It was here that the Saviour, after His resurrection, appeared to them.

For forty days Christ remained on the earth, preparing the disciples for the work before them and explaining that which heretofore they had been unable to comprehend. He spoke of the prophecies concerning His advent, His rejection by the Jews, and His death, showing that every specification of these prophecies had been fulfilled. He told them that they were to regard this fulfillment of prophecy as an assurance of the power that would attend them in their future labors. "Then opened He their understanding," we read, "that they might understand the Scriptures, and said unto them, Thus it is written, and thus it behooved Christ to suffer, and to rise from the dead the third day: and that repentance and remission of sins should be preached in His name among all nations, beginning at Jerusalem." And He added, "Ye are witnesses of these things." Luke 24:45-48.

During these days that Christ spent with His disciples, they gained a new experience. As they heard their beloved Master explaining the Scriptures in the light of all that had happened, their faith in Him was fully established. They reached the place where they could say, "I know whom I have believed." 2 Timothy 1:12. They began to realize the nature and extent of their work, to see that they were to proclaim to the world the truths entrusted to them. The events of Christ's life, His death and resurrection, the prophecies pointing to these events, the mysteries of the plan of salvation, the power of Jesus for the remission of sins—to all these things they had been witnesses, and they were to make them known to the world. They were to proclaim the gospel of peace and salvation through repentance and the power of the Saviour.

Before ascending to heaven, Christ gave His disciples their commission. He told them that they were to be the executors of the will in which He bequeathed to the world the treasures of eternal life. You have been witnesses of My life of sacrifice in behalf of the world, He said to them. You have seen My labors for Israel. And although My people would not come to Me that they might have life, although priests and rulers have done unto Me as they listed, although they have rejected Me, they shall have still another opportunity of accepting the Son of God. You have seen that all who come to Me confessing their sins, I freely receive. Him that cometh to Me I will in no wise cast out. To you, My disciples, I commit this message of mercy. It is to be given to both Jews and Gentiles—to Israel, first, and then to all nations, tongues, and peoples. All who believe are to be gathered into one church.

The gospel commission is the great missionary charter of Christ's kingdom. The disciples were to work earnestly for souls, giving to all the invitation of mercy. They were not to wait for the people to come to them; they were to go to the people with their message.

The disciples were to carry their work forward in Christ's name. Their every word and act was to fasten attention on His name, as possessing that vital power by which sinners may be saved. Their faith was to center in Him who is the source of mercy and power. In His name they were to present their petitions to the Father, and they would receive answer. They were to baptize in the name of the Father, the Son, and the Holy Spirit. Christ's name was to be their watchword, their badge of distinction, their bond of union, the authority for their course of action, and the source of their success. Nothing was to be recognized in His kingdom that did not bear His name and superscription.

When Christ said to the disciples, Go forth in My name to gather into the church all who believe, He plainly set before them the necessity of maintaining simplicity. The less ostentation and show, the greater would be their influence for good. The disciples were to speak with the same simplicity with which Christ had spoken. They were to impress upon their hearers the lessons He had taught them.

Christ did not tell His disciples that their work would be easy. He showed them the vast confederacy of evil arrayed against them. They would have to fight "against principalities, against powers, against the rulers of the darkness of this world, against spiritual wickedness in high places." Ephesians 6:12. But they would not be left to fight alone. He assured them that He would be with them; and that if they would go forth in faith, they should move under the shield of Omnipotence. He bade them be brave and strong; for One mightier than angels would be in their ranks—the General of the armies of heaven. He made full provision for the prosecution of their work and took upon Himself the responsibility of its success. So long as they obeyed His word, and worked in connection with Him, they could not fail. Go to all nations, He bade them. Go to the farthest part of the habitable globe and be assured that My presence will be with you even there. Labor in faith and confidence; for the time will never come when I will forsake you. I will be with you always, helping you to perform your duty, guiding, comforting, sanctifying, sustaining you, giving you success in speaking words that shall draw the attention of others to heaven.

Christ's sacrifice in behalf of man was full and complete. The condition of the atonement had been fulfilled. The work for which He had come to this world had been accomplished. He had won the kingdom. He had wrested it from Satan and had become heir of all things. He was on His way to the throne of God, to be honored by the heavenly host. Clothed with boundless authority, He gave His disciples their commission, "Go ye therefore, and teach all nations, baptizing them in the name of the Father, and of the Son, and of the Holy Ghost: teaching them to observe all things whatsoever I have commanded you: and, lo, I am with you alway, even unto the end." Matthew 28:19, 20.

Just before leaving His disciples, Christ once more plainly stated the nature of His kingdom. He recalled to their remembrance things He had previously told them regarding it. He declared that it was not His purpose to establish in this world a temporal kingdom. He was not appointed to reign as an earthly monarch on David's throne. When the disciples asked Him, "Lord, wilt Thou at this time restore again the kingdom to Israel?" He answered, "It is not for you to know the times or the seasons, which the Father hath put in His own power." Acts 1:6, 7. It was not necessary for them to see farther into the future than the revelations He had made enabled them to see. Their work was to proclaim the gospel message.

Christ's visible presence was about to be withdrawn from the disciples, but a new endowment of power was to be theirs. The Holy Spirit was to be given them in its fullness, sealing them for their work. "Behold," the Saviour said, "I send the promise of My Father upon you: but tarry ye in the city of Jerusalem, until ye be endued with power from on high." Luke 24:49. "For John truly baptized with water; but ye shall be baptized with the Holy Ghost not many days hence." "Ye shall receive power, after that the Holy Ghost is come upon you: and ye shall be witnesses unto Me both in Jerusalem, and in all Judea, and in Samaria, and unto the uttermost part of the earth." Acts 1:5, 8.

The Saviour knew that no argument, however logical, would melt hard hearts or break through the crust of worldliness and selfishness. He knew that His disciples must receive the heavenly endowment; that the gospel would be effective only as it was proclaimed by hearts made warm and lips made eloquent by a living knowledge of Him who is the way, the truth, and the life. The work committed to the disciples would require great efficiency; for the tide of evil ran deep and strong against them. A vigilant, determined leader was in command of the forces of darkness, and the followers of Christ could battle for the right only through the help that God, by His Spirit, would give them.

Christ told His disciples that they were to begin their work at Jerusalem. That city had been the scene of His amazing sacrifice for the human race. There, clad in the garb of humanity, He had walked and talked with men, and few had discerned how near heaven came to earth. There He had been condemned and crucified. In Jerusalem were many who secretly believed Jesus of Nazareth to be the Messiah, and many who had been deceived by priests and rulers. To these the gospel must be proclaimed. They were to be called to repentance. The wonderful truth that through Christ alone could remission of sins be obtained, was to be made plain. And it was while all Jerusalem was stirred by the thrilling events of the past few weeks, that the preaching of the disciples would make the deepest impression.

During His ministry, Jesus had kept constantly before the disciples the fact that they were to be one with Him in His work for the recovery of the world from the slavery of sin. When He sent forth the Twelve and afterward the Seventy, to proclaim the kingdom of God, He was teaching them their duty to impart to others what He had made known to them. In all His work He was training them for individual labor, to be extended as their numbers increased, and eventually to reach to the uttermost parts of the earth. The last lesson He gave His followers was that they held in trust for the world the glad tidings of salvation.

When the time came for Christ to ascend to His Father, He led the disciples out as far as Bethany. Here He paused, and they gathered about Him. With hands outstretched in blessing, as if in assurance of His protecting care, He slowly ascended from among them. "It came to pass, while He blessed them, He was parted from them, and carried up into heaven." Luke 24:51.

While the disciples were gazing upward to catch the last glimpse of their ascending Lord, He was received into the rejoicing ranks of heavenly angels. As these angels escorted Him to the courts above, they sang in triumph, "Sing unto God, ye kingdoms of the earth; O sing praises unto the Lord, to Him that rideth upon the heavens of heavens. . . . Ascribe ye strength unto God: His excellency is over Israel, and His strength is in the heavens." Psalm 68:32-34, margin.

The disciples were still looking earnestly toward heaven when, "behold, two men stood by them in white apparel; which also said, Ye men of Galilee, why stand ye gazing up into heaven? this same Jesus, which is taken up from you into heaven, shall so come in like manner as ye have seen Him go into heaven." Acts 1:10, 11.

The promise of Christ's second coming was ever to be kept fresh in the minds of His disciples. The same Jesus whom they had seen ascending into heaven, would come again, to take to Himself those who here below give themselves to His service. The same voice that had said to them, "Lo, I am with you alway, even unto the end," would bid them welcome to His presence in the heavenly kingdom.

As in the typical service the high priest laid aside his pontifical robes and officiated in the white linen dress of an ordinary priest; so Christ laid aside His royal robes and garbed Himself with humanity and offered sacrifice, Himself the priest, Himself the victim. As the high priest, after performing his service in the holy of holies, came forth to the waiting congregation in his pontifical robes; so Christ will come the second time, clothed in garments of whitest white, "so as no fuller on earth can white them." Mark 9:3. He will come in His own glory, and in the glory of His Father, and all the angelic host will escort Him on His way.

Thus will be fulfilled Christ's promise to His disciples, "I will come again, and receive you unto Myself." John 14:3. Those who have loved Him and waited for Him, He will crown with glory and honor and immortality. The righteous dead will come forth from their graves, and those who are alive will be caught up with them to meet the Lord in the air. They will hear the voice of Jesus, sweeter than any music that ever fell on mortal ear, saying to them, Your warfare is accomplished. "Come, ye blessed of My Father, inherit the kingdom prepared for you from the foundation of the world." Matthew 25;34.

Well might the disciples rejoice in the hope of their Lord's return.

4

Pentecost

This chapter is based on Acts 2:1-39

As the disciples returned from Olivet to Jerusalem, the people looked on them, expecting to see on their faces expressions of sorrow, confusion, and defeat; but they saw there gladness and triumph. The disciples did not now mourn over disappointed hopes. They had seen the risen Saviour, and the words of His parting promise echoed constantly in their ears.

In obedience to Christ's command, they waited in Jerusalem for the promise of the Father—the outpouring of the Spirit. They did not wait in idleness. The record says that they were "continually in the temple, praising and blessing God." Luke 24:53. They also met together to present their requests to the Father in the name of Jesus. They knew that they had a Representative in heaven, an Advocate at the throne of God. In solemn awe they bowed in prayer, repeating the assurance, "Whatsoever ye shall ask the Father in My name, He will give it you. Hitherto have ye asked nothing in My name: ask, and ye shall receive, that your joy may be full." John 16:23, 24. Higher and still higher they extended the hand of faith, with the mighty argument, "It is Christ that died, yea rather, that is risen again, who is even at the right hand of God, who also maketh intercession for us." Romans 8:34.

As the disciples waited for the fulfillment of the promise, they humbled their hearts in true repentance and confessed their unbelief. As they called to remembrance the words that Christ had spoken to them before His death they understood more fully their meaning. Truths which had passed from their memory were again brought to their minds, and these they repeated to one another. They reproached themselves for their misapprehension of the Saviour. Like a procession, scene after scene of His wonderful life passed before them. As they meditated upon His pure, holy life they felt that no toil would be too hard, no sacrifice too great, if only they could bear witness in their lives to the loveliness of Christ's character. Oh, if they could but have the past three years to live over, they thought, how differently they would act! If they could only see the Master again, how earnestly they would strive to show

Him how deeply they loved Him, and how sincerely they sorrowed for having ever grieved Him by a word or an act of unbelief! But they were comforted by the thought that they were forgiven. And they determined that, so far as possible, they would atone for their unbelief by bravely confessing Him before the world.

The disciples prayed with intense earnestness for a fitness to meet men and in their daily intercourse to speak words that would lead sinners to Christ. Putting away all differences, all desire for the supremacy, they came close together in Christian fellowship. They drew nearer and nearer to God, and as they did this they realized what a privilege had been theirs in being permitted to associate so closely with Christ. Sadness filled their hearts as they thought of how many times they had grieved Him by their slowness of comprehension, their failure to understand the lessons that, for their good, He was trying to teach them.

These days of preparation were days of deep heart searching. The disciples felt their spiritual need and cried to the Lord for the holy unction that was to fit them for the work of soul saving. They did not ask for a blessing for themselves merely. They were weighted with the burden of the salvation of souls. They realized that the gospel was to be carried to the world, and they claimed the power that Christ had promised.

During the patriarchal age the influence of the Holy Spirit had often been revealed in a marked manner, but never in its fullness. Now, in obedience to the word of the Saviour, the disciples offered their supplications for this gift, and in heaven Christ added His intercession. He claimed the gift of the Spirit, that He might pour it upon His people.

"And when the Day of Pentecost was fully come, they were all with one accord in one place. And suddenly there came a sound from heaven as of a rushing mighty wind, and it filled all the house where they were sitting."

The Spirit came upon the waiting, praying disciples with a fullness that reached every heart. The Infinite One revealed Himself in power to His church. It was as if for ages this influence had been held in restraint, and now Heaven rejoiced in being able to pour out upon the church the riches of the Spirit's grace. And under the influence of the Spirit, words of penitence and confession mingled with songs of praise for sins forgiven. Words of thanksgiving and of prophecy were heard. All heaven bent low to behold and to adore the wisdom of matchless, incomprehensible love. Lost in wonder, the apostles exclaimed, "Herein is love." They grasped the imparted gift. And what followed? The sword of the Spirit, newly edged with power and bathed in the lightnings of heaven, cut its way through unbelief. Thousands were converted in a day.

"It is expedient for you that I go away," Christ had said to His disciples; "for If I go not away, the Comforter will not come unto you; but if I depart, I will send Him unto you." "When He, the Spirit of truth, is come, He will guide you into all truth: for He shall not speak of Himself; but whatsoever He shall hear, that shall He speak: and He will show you things to come." John 16:7, 13.

Christ's ascension to heaven was the signal that His followers were to receive the promised blessing. For this they were to wait before they entered upon their work. When Christ passed within the heavenly gates, He was enthroned amidst the adoration of the angels. As soon as this ceremony was completed, the Holy Spirit descended upon the disciples in rich currents, and Christ was indeed glorified, even with the glory which He had with the Father from all eternity. The Pentecostal outpouring was Heaven's communication that the Redeemer's inauguration was accomplished. According to His promise He had sent the Holy Spirit from heaven to His followers as a token that He had, as priest and king, received all authority in heaven and on earth, and was the Anointed One over His people.

"And there appeared unto them cloven tongues like as of fire, and it sat upon each of them. And they were all filled with the Holy Ghost, and began to speak with other tongues, as the Spirit gave them utterance." The Holy Spirit, assuming the form of tongues of fire, rested upon those assembled. This was an emblem of the gift then bestowed on the disciples, which enabled them to speak with fluency languages with which they had heretofore been unacquainted. The appearance of fire signified the fervent zeal with which the apostles would labor and the power that would attend their work.

"There were dwelling at Jerusalem Jews, devout men, out of every nation under heaven." During the dispersion the Jews had been scattered to almost every part of the inhabited world, and in their exile they had learned to speak various languages. Many of these Jews were on this occasion in Jerusalem, attending the religious festivals then in progress. Every known tongue was represented by those assembled. This diversity of languages would have been a great hindrance to the proclamation of the gospel; God therefore in a miraculous manner supplied the deficiency of the apostles. The Holy Spirit did for them that which they could not have accomplished for themselves in a lifetime. They could now proclaim the truths of the gospel abroad, speaking with accuracy the languages of those for whom they were laboring. This miraculous gift was a strong evidence to the world that their commission bore the signet of Heaven. From this time forth the language of the disciples was pure, simple, and accurate, whether they spoke in their native tongue or in a foreign language.

"Now when this was noised abroad, the multitude came together, and were confounded, because that every man heard them speak in his own language. And they were all amazed and marveled, saying one to another, Behold, are not all these which speak Galileans? and how hear we every man in our own tongue, wherein we were born?"

The priests and rulers were greatly enraged at this wonderful manifestation, but they dared not give way to their malice, for fear of exposing themselves to the violence of the people. They had put the Nazarene to death; but here were His servants, unlettered men of Galilee, telling in all the languages then spoken, the story of His life and ministry. The priests, determined to account for the miraculous power of the disciples in some natural way, declared that they were drunken from partaking largely of the new wine prepared for the feast. Some of the most ignorant of the people present seized upon this suggestion as the truth, but the more intelligent knew it to be false; and those who understood the different languages testified to the accuracy with which these languages were used by the disciples.

In answer to the accusation of the priests Peter showed that this demonstration was in direct fulfillment of the prophecy of Joel, wherein he foretold that such power would come upon men to fit them for a special work. "Ye men of Judea, and all ye that dwell at Jerusalem," he said, "be this known unto you, and hearken to my words: for these are not drunken, as ye suppose, seeing it is but the third hour of the day. But this is that which was spoken by the prophet Joel: And it shall come to pass in the last days, saith God, I will pour out of My Spirit upon all flesh: and your sons and your daughters shall prophesy, and your young men shall see visions, and your old men shall dream dreams: and on My servants and on My handmaidens I will pour out in those days of My Spirit; and they shall prophesy."

With clearness and power Peter bore witness of the death and resurrection of Christ: "Ye men of Israel, hear these words: Jesus of Nazareth, a man approved of God among you by miracles and wonders and signs, which God did by Him in the midst of you, as ye yourselves also know: Him . . . ye have taken, and by wicked hands have crucified and slain: whom God hath raised up, having loosed the pains of death: because it was not possible that He should be holden of it."

Peter did not refer to the teachings of Christ to prove his position, because he knew that the prejudice of his hearers was so great that his words on this subject would be of no effect. Instead, he spoke to them of David, who was regarded by the Jews as one of the patriarchs of their nation. "David speaketh concerning Him," he declared: "I foresaw the Lord always before My face, for He is on My right hand, that I should not be moved: therefore did My heart rejoice, and My tongue was glad; moreover also My flesh shall rest in hope: because Thou wilt not leave My soul in hell, neither wilt Thou suffer Thine Holy One to see corruption. . . .

"Men and brethren, let me freely speak unto you of the patriarch David, that he is both dead and buried, and his sepulcher is with us unto this day." "He . . . spake of the resurrection of Christ, that His soul was not left in hell, neither His flesh did see corruption. This Jesus hath God raised up, whereof we all are witnesses."

The scene is one full of interest. Behold the people coming from all directions to hear the disciples witness to the truth as it is in Jesus. They press in, crowding the temple. Priests and rulers are there, the dark scowl of malignity still on their faces, their hearts still filled with abiding hatred against Christ, their hands uncleansed from the blood shed when they crucified the world's Redeemer. They had thought to find the apostles cowed with fear under the strong hand of oppression and murder, but they find them lifted above all fear and filled with the Spirit, proclaiming with power the divinity of Jesus of Nazareth. They hear them declaring with boldness that the One so recently humiliated, derided, smitten by cruel hands, and crucified, is the Prince of life, now exalted to the right hand of God.

Some of those who listened to the apostles had taken an active part in the condemnation and death of Christ. Their voices had mingled with the rabble in calling for His crucifixion. When Jesus and Barabbas stood before them in the judgment hall and Pilate asked, "Whom will ye that I release unto you?" they had shouted, "Not this Man, but Barabbas!" Matthew 27:17; John 18:40. When Pilate delivered Christ to them, saying, "Take ye Him, and crucify Him: for I find no fault in Him;" "I am innocent of the blood of this just Person," they had cried, "His blood be on us, and on our children." John 19:6; Matthew 27:24, 25.

Now they heard the disciples declaring that it was the Son of God who had been crucified. Priests and rulers trembled. Conviction and anguish seized the people. "They were pricked in their heart, and said unto Peter and to the rest of the apostles, Men and brethren, what shall we do?" Among those who listened to the disciples were devout Jews, who were sincere in their belief. The power that accompanied the words of the speaker convinced them that Jesus was indeed the Messiah.

"Then Peter said unto them, Repent, and be baptized every one of you in the name of Jesus Christ for the remission of sins, and ye shall receive the gift of the Holy Ghost. For the promise is unto you, and to your children, and to all that are afar off, even as many as the Lord our God shall call."

Peter urged home upon the convicted people the fact that they had rejected Christ because they had been deceived by priests and rulers; and that if they continued to look to these men for counsel, and waited for them to acknowledge Christ before they dared to do so, they would never accept Him. These powerful men, though making a profession of godliness, were ambitious for earthly riches and glory. They were not willing to come to Christ to receive light.

Under the influence of this heavenly illumination the scriptures that Christ had explained to the disciples stood out before them with the luster of perfect truth. The veil that had prevented them from seeing to the end of that which had been abolished, was now removed, and they comprehended with perfect clearness the object of Christ's mission and the nature of His kingdom. They could speak with power of the Saviour; and as they unfolded to their hearers the plan of salvation, many were convicted and convinced. The traditions and superstitions inculcated by the priests were swept away from their minds, and the teachings of the Saviour were accepted.

"Then they that gladly received his word were baptized: and the same day there were added unto them about three thousand souls."

The Jewish leaders had supposed that the work of Christ would end with His death; but, instead of this, they witnessed the marvelous scenes of the Day of Pentecost. They heard the disciples, endowed with a power and energy hitherto unknown, preaching Christ, their words confirmed by signs and wonders. In Jerusalem, the stronghold of Judaism, thousands openly declared their faith in Jesus of Nazareth as the Messiah.

The disciples were astonished and overjoyed at the greatness of the harvest of souls. They did not regard this wonderful ingathering as the result of their own efforts; they realized that they were entering into other men's labors. Ever since the fall of Adam, Christ had been committing to chosen servants the seed of His word, to be sown in human hearts. During His life on this earth He had sown the seed of truth and had watered it with His blood. The conversions that took place on the Day of Pentecost were the result of this sowing, the harvest of Christ's work, revealing the power of His teaching.

The arguments of the apostles alone, though clear and convincing, would not have removed the prejudice that had withstood so much evidence. But the Holy Spirit sent the arguments home to hearts with divine power. The words of the apostles were as sharp arrows of the Almighty, convicting men of their terrible guilt in rejecting and crucifying the Lord of glory.

Under the training of Christ the disciples had been led to feel their need of the Spirit. Under the Spirit's teaching they received the final qualification, and went forth to their lifework. No longer were they ignorant and uncultured. No longer were they a collection of independent units or discordant, conflicting elements. No longer were their hopes set on worldly greatness. They were of "one accord," "of one heart and of one soul." Acts. 2:46; 4:32. Christ filled their thoughts; the advancement of His kingdom was their aim. In mind and character they had become like their Master, and men "took knowledge of them, that they had been with Jesus." Acts 4:13.

Pentecost brought them the heavenly illumination. The truths they could not understand while Christ was with them were now unfolded. With a faith and assurance that they had never before known, they accepted the teachings of the Sacred Word. No longer was it a matter of faith with them that Christ was the Son of God. They knew that, although clothed with humanity, He was indeed the Messiah, and they told their experience to the world with a confidence which carried with it the conviction that God was with them.

They could speak the name of Jesus with assurance; for was He not their Friend and Elder Brother? Brought into close communion with Christ, they sat with Him in heavenly places. With what burning language they clothed their ideas as they bore witness for Him! Their hearts were surcharged with a benevolence so full, so deep, so far-reaching, that it impelled them to go to the ends of the earth, testifying to the power of Christ. They were filled with an intense longing to carry forward the work He had begun. They realized the greatness of their debt to heaven and the responsibility of their work. Strengthened by the endowment of the Holy Spirit, they went forth filled with zeal to extend the triumphs of the cross. The Spirit animated them and spoke through them. The peace of Christ shone from their faces. They had consecrated their lives to Him for service, and their very features bore evidence to the surrender they had made.

5

The Gift of the Spirit

When Christ gave His disciples the promise of the Spirit, He was nearing the close of His earthly ministry. He was standing in the shadow of the cross, with a full realization of the load of guilt that was to rest upon Him as the Sin Bearer. Before offering Himself as the sacrificial victim, He instructed His disciples regarding a most essential and complete gift which He was to bestow upon His followers—the gift that would bring within their reach the boundless resources of His grace. "I will pray the Father," He said, "and He shall give you another Comforter, that He may abide with you forever; even the Spirit of truth; whom the world cannot receive, because it seeth Him not, neither knoweth Him: but ye know Him; for He dwelleth with you, and shall be in you." John 14:16, 17. The Saviour was pointing forward to the time when the Holy Spirit should come to do a mighty work as His representative. The evil that had been accumulating for centuries was to be resisted by the divine power of the Holy Spirit.

What was the result of the outpouring of the Spirit on the Day of Pentecost? The glad tidings of a risen Saviour were carried to the uttermost parts of the inhabited world. As the disciples proclaimed the message of redeeming grace, hearts yielded to the power of this message. The church beheld converts flocking to her from all directions. Backsliders were reconverted. Sinners united with believers in seeking the pearl of great price. Some who had been the bitterest opponents of the gospel became its champions. The prophecy was fulfilled, "He that is feeble. . . shall be as David; and the house of David . . . as the angel of the Lord." Zechariah 12:8. Every Christian saw in his brother a revelation of divine love and benevolence. One interest prevailed; one subject of emulation swallowed up all others. The ambition of the believers was to reveal the likeness of Christ's character and to labor for the enlargement of His kingdom.

"With great power gave the apostles witness of the resurrection of the Lord Jesus: and great grace was upon them all." Acts 4:33. Under their labors were added to the church chosen men, who, receiving the word of truth, consecrated their lives to the work of giving to others the hope that filled their hearts with peace and joy. They could not be restrained or intimidated by threatenings. The

Lord spoke through them, and as they went from place to place, the poor had the gospel preached to them, and miracles of divine grace were wrought.

So mightily can God work when men give themselves up to the control of His Spirit.

The promise of the Holy Spirit is not limited to any age or to any race. Christ declared that the divine influence of His Spirit was to be with His followers unto the end. From the Day of Pentecost to the present time, the Comforter has been sent to all who have yielded themselves fully to the Lord and to His service. To all who have accepted Christ as a personal Saviour, the Holy Spirit has come as a counselor, sanctifier, guide, and witness. The more closely believers have walked with God, the more clearly and powerfully have they testified of their Redeemer's love and of His saving grace. The men and women who through the long centuries of persecution and trial enjoyed a large measure of the presence of the Spirit in their lives, have stood as signs and wonders in the world. Before angels and men they have revealed the transforming power of redeeming love.

Those who at Pentecost were endued with power from on high, were not thereby freed from further temptation and trial. As they witnessed for truth and righteousness they were repeatedly assailed by the enemy of all truth, who sought to rob them of their Christian experience. They were compelled to strive with all their God-given powers to reach the measure of the stature of men and women in Christ Jesus. Daily they prayed for fresh supplies of grace, that they might reach higher and still higher toward perfection. Under the Holy Spirit's working even the weakest, by exercising faith in God, learned to improve their entrusted powers and to become sanctified, refined, and ennobled. As in humility they submitted to the molding influence of the Holy Spirit, they received of the fullness of the Godhead and were fashioned in the likeness of the divine.

The lapse of time has wrought no change in Christ's parting promise to send the Holy Spirit as His representative. It is not because of any restriction on the part of God that the riches of His grace do not flow earthward to men. If the fulfillment of the promise is not seen as it might be, it is because the promise is not appreciated as it should be. If all were willing, all would be filled with the Spirit. Wherever the need of the Holy Spirit is a matter little thought of, there is seen spiritual drought, spiritual darkness, spiritual declension and death. Whenever minor matters occupy the attention, the divine power which is necessary for the growth and prosperity of the church, and which would bring all other blessings in its train, is lacking, though offered in infinite plenitude.

Since this is the means by which we are to receive power, why do we not hunger and thirst for the gift of the Spirit? Why do we not talk of it, pray for it, and preach concerning it? The Lord is more willing to give the Holy Spirit to those who serve Him than parents are to give good gifts to their children. For the daily baptism of the Spirit every worker should offer his petition to God. Companies of Christian workers should gather to ask for special help, for heavenly wisdom, that they may know how to plan and execute wisely. Especially should they pray that God will baptize His chosen ambassadors in mission fields with a rich measure of His Spirit. The presence of the Spirit with God's workers will give the proclamation of truth a power that not all the honor or glory of the world could give.

With the consecrated worker for God, in whatever place he may be, the Holy Spirit abides. The words spoken to the disciples are spoken also to us. The Comforter is ours as well as theirs. The Spirit furnishes the strength that sustains striving, wrestling souls in every emergency, amidst the hatred of the world, and the realization of their own failures and mistakes. In sorrow and affliction, when the outlook seems dark and the future perplexing, and we feel helpless and alone,—these are the times when, in answer to the prayer of faith, the Holy Spirit brings comfort to the heart.

It is not a conclusive evidence that a man is a Christian because he manifests spiritual ecstasy under extraordinary circumstances. Holiness is not rapture: it is an entire surrender of the will to God; it is living by every word that proceeds from the mouth of God; it is doing the will of our heavenly Father; it is trusting God in trial, in darkness as well as in the light; it is walking by faith and not by sight; it is relying on God with unquestioning confidence, and resting in His love.

It is not essential for us to be able to define just what the Holy Spirit is. Christ tells us that the Spirit is the Comforter, "the Spirit of truth, which proceedeth from the Father." It is plainly declared regarding the Holy Spirit that, in His work of guiding men into all truth, "He shall not speak of Himself." John 15:26; 16:13.

The nature of the Holy Spirit is a mystery. Men cannot explain it, because the Lord has not revealed it to them. Men having fanciful views may bring together passages of Scripture and put a human construction on them, but the acceptance of these views will not strengthen the church. Regarding such mysteries, which are too deep for human understanding, silence is golden.

The office of the Holy Spirit is distinctly specified in the words of Christ: "When He is come, He will reprove the world of sin, and of righteousness, and of judgment." John 16:8. It is the Holy Spirit that convicts of sin. If the sinner responds to the quickening influence of the Spirit, he will be brought to repentance and aroused to the importance of obeying the divine requirements.

To the repentant sinner, hungering and thirsting for righteousness, the Holy Spirit reveals the Lamb of God that taketh away the sin of the world. "He shall receive of Mine, and shall show it unto you," Christ said. "He shall teach you all things, and bring all things to your remembrance, whatsoever I have said unto you." John 16:14; 14:26.

The Spirit is given as a regenerating agency, to make effectual the salvation wrought by the death of our Redeemer. The Spirit is constantly seeking to draw the attention of men to the great offering that was made on the cross of Calvary, to unfold to the world the love of God, and to open to the convicted soul the precious things of the Scriptures.

Having brought conviction of sin, and presented before the mind the standard of righteousness, the Holy Spirit withdraws the affections from the things of this earth and fills the soul with a desire for holiness. "He will guide you into all truth" (John 16:13), the Saviour declared. If men are willing to be molded, there will be brought about a sanctification of the whole being. The Spirit will take the things of God and stamp them on the soul. By His power the way of life will be made so plain that none need err therein.

From the beginning, God has been working by His Holy Spirit through human instrumentalities for the accomplishment of His purpose in behalf of the fallen race. This was manifest in the lives of the patriarchs. To the church in the wilderness also, in the time of Moses, God gave His "good Spirit to instruct them." Nehemiah 9:20. And in the days of the apostles He wrought mightily for His church through the agency of the Holy Spirit. The same power that sustained the patriarchs, that gave Caleb and Joshua faith and courage, and that made the work of the apostolic church effective, has upheld God's faithful children in every succeeding age. It was through the power of the Holy Spirit that during the Dark Ages the Waldensian Christians helped to prepare the way for the Reformation. It was the same power that made successful the efforts of the noble men and women who pioneered the way for the establishment of modern missions and for the translation of the Bible into the languages and dialects of all nations and peoples.

And today God is still using His church to make known His purpose in the earth. Today the heralds of the cross are going from city to city, and from land to land, preparing the way for the second advent of Christ. The standard of God's law is being exalted. The Spirit of the Almighty is moving upon men's hearts, and those who respond to its influence become witnesses for God and His truth. In many places consecrated men and women may be seen communicating to others the light that has made plain to them the way of salvation through Christ. And as they continue to let their light shine, as did those who were baptized with the Spirit on the Day of Pentecost, they receive more and still more of the Spirit's power. Thus the earth is to be lightened with the glory of God.

On the other hand, there are some who, instead of wisely improving present opportunities, are idly waiting for some special *LATTER RAIN* season of spiritual refreshing by which their ability to enlighten others will be greatly increased. They neglect present duties and privileges, and allow their light to burn dim, while they look forward to a time when, without any effort on their part, they will be made the recipients of special blessing, by which they will be transformed and fitted for service.

It is true that in the time of the end, when God's work in the earth is closing, the earnest efforts put forth by consecrated believers under the guidance of the Holy Spirit are to be accompanied by special tokens of divine favor. Under the figure of the early and the latter rain, that falls in Eastern lands at seedtime and harvest, the Hebrew prophets foretold the bestowal of spiritual grace in extraordinary measure upon God's church. The outpouring of the Spirit in the days of the apostles was the beginning of the early, or former, rain, and glorious was the result. To the end of time the presence of the Spirit is to abide with the true church.

But near the close of earth's harvest, a special bestowal of spiritual grace is promised to prepare the church for the coming of the Son of man. This outpouring of the Spirit is likened to the falling of the latter rain; and it is for this added power that Christians are to send their petitions to the Lord of the harvest "in the time of the latter rain." In response, "the Lord shall make bright clouds, and give them showers of rain." "He will cause to come down . . . the rain, the former rain, and the latter rain," Zechariah 10:1; Joel 2:23.

But unless the members of God's church today have a living connection with the Source of all spiritual growth, they will not be ready for the time of reaping. Unless they keep their lamps trimmed and burning, they will fail of receiving added grace in times of special need.

Those only who are constantly receiving fresh supplies of grace, will have power proportionate to their daily need and their ability to use that power. Instead of looking forward to some future time when, through a special endowment of spiritual power, they will receive a miraculous fitting up for soul winning, they are yielding themselves daily to God, that He may make them vessels meet for His use. Daily they are improving the opportunities for service that lie within their reach. Daily they are witnessing for the Master wherever they may be, whether in some humble sphere of labor in the home, or in a public field of usefulness.

To the consecrated worker there is wonderful consolation in the knowledge that even Christ during His life on earth sought His Father daily for fresh supplies of needed grace; and from this communion with God He went forth to strengthen and bless others. Behold the Son of God bowed in prayer to His Father! Though He is the Son of God, He strengthens His faith by prayer, and by communion with heaven gathers to Himself power to resist evil and to minister to the needs of men. As the Elder Brother of our race He knows the necessities of those who, compassed with infirmity and living in a world of sin and temptation, still desire to serve Him. He knows that the messengers whom He sees fit to send are weak, erring men; but to all who give themselves wholly to His service He promises divine aid. His own example is an assurance that earnest, persevering supplication to God in faith—faith that leads to entire dependence upon God, and unreserved consecration to His work—will avail to bring to men the Holy Spirit's aid in the battle against sin.

Every worker who follows the example of Christ will be prepared to receive and use the power that God has promised to His church for the ripening of earth's harvest. Morning by morning, as the heralds of the gospel kneel before the Lord and renew their vows of consecration to Him, He will grant them the presence of His Spirit, with its reviving, sanctifying power. As they go forth to the day's duties, they have the assurance that the unseen agency of the Holy Spirit enables them to be "laborers together with God."

6

At the Temple Gate

This chapter is based on Acts 3; 4:1-31

The disciples of Christ had a deep sense of their own ineffi-
ciency, and with humiliation and prayer they joined their
weakness to His strength, their ignorance to His wisdom,
their unworthiness to His righteousness, their poverty to His ex-
haustless wealth. Thus strengthened and equipped, they hesitated
not to press forward in the service of the Master.

A short time after the descent of the Holy Spirit, and immediately after a season of earnest prayer, Peter and John, going up to
the temple to worship, saw at the gate Beautiful a cripple, forty
years of age, whose life, from his birth, had been one of pain and
infirmity. This unfortunate man had long desired to see Jesus, that
he might be healed; but he was almost helpless, and was far
removed from the scene of the great Physician's labors. His pleadings at last induced some friends to bear him to the gate of the
temple, but upon arriving there, he found that the One upon whom
his hopes were centered, had been put to a cruel death.

His disappointment excited the sympathy of those who knew
for how long he had eagerly hoped to be healed by Jesus, and daily
they brought him to the temple, in order that passers-by might be
induced by pity to give him a trifle to relieve his wants. As Peter
and John passed, he asked an alms from them. The disciples
regarded him compassionately, and Peter said, "Look on us. And
he gave heed unto them, expecting to receive something of them.
Then Peter said, Silver and gold have I none." As Peter thus
declared his poverty, the countenance of the cripple fell; but it grew
bright with hope as the apostle continued, "But such as I have give
I thee: In the name of Jesus Christ of Nazareth rise up and walk.

"And he took him by the right hand, and lifted him up: and
immediately his feet and anklebones received strength. And he
leaping up stood, and walked, and entered with them into the
temple, walking, and leaping, and praising God. And all the people
saw him walking and praising God: and they knew that it was he
which sat for alms at the Beautiful Gate of the temple: and they

were filled with wonder and amazement at that which had happened."

"And as the lame man which was healed held Peter and John,
all the people ran together unto them in the porch that is called
Solomon's, greatly wondering." They were astonished that the
disciples could perform miracles similar to those performed by
Jesus. Yet here was this man, for forty years a helpless cripple, now
rejoicing in the full use of his limbs, free from pain, and happy in
believing in Jesus.

When the disciples saw the amazement of the people, Peter
asked, "Why marvel ye at this? or why look ye so earnestly on us,
as though by our own power or holiness we had made this man to
walk?" He assured them that the cure had been wrought in the name
and through the merits of Jesus of Nazareth, whom God had raised
from the dead. "His name through faith in His name," the apostle
declared, "hath made this man strong, whom ye see and know: yea,
the faith which is by Him hath given him this perfect soundness in
the presence of you all."

The apostles spoke plainly of the great sin of the Jews in
rejecting and putting to death the Prince of life; but they were
careful not to drive their hearers to despair. "Ye denied the Holy
One and the Just," Peter said, "and desired a murderer to be granted
unto you; and killed the Prince of life, whom God hath raised from
the dead; whereof we are witnesses." "And now, brethren, I wot
that through ignorance ye did it, as did also your rulers. But those
things, which God before had showed by the mouth of all His
prophets, that Christ should suffer, He hath so fulfilled." He
daclared that the Holy Spirit was calling upon them to repent and
be converted, and assured them that there was no hope of salvation
except through the mercy of the One whom they had crucified. Only
through faith in Him could their sins be forgiven.

"Repent ye therefore, and be converted," he cried, "that your
sins may be blotted out, when the times of refreshing shall come
from the presence of the Lord."

"Ye are the children of the prophets, and of the covenant which
God made with our fathers, saying unto Abraham, And in thy seed
shall all the kindreds of the earth be blessed. Unto you first God,
having raised up His Son Jesus, sent Him to bless you, in turning
away every one of you from his iniquities."

Thus the disciples preached the resurrection of Christ. Many
among those who listened were waiting for this testimony, and
when they heard it they believed. It brought to their minds the words

that Christ had spoken, and they took their stand in the ranks of those who accepted the gospel. The seed that the Saviour had sown sprang up and bore fruit.

While the disciples were speaking to the people, "the priests, and the captain of the temple, and the Sadducees, came upon them, being grieved that they taught the people, and preached through Jesus the resurrection from the dead,"

After Christ's resurrection the priests had spread far and near the lying report that His body had been stolen by the disciples while the Roman guard slept. It is not surprising that they were displeased when they hear Peter and John preaching the resurrection of the One they had murdered. The Sadducees especially were greatly aroused. They felt that their most cherished doctrine was in danger, and their reputation at stake.

Converts to the new faith were rapidly increasing, and both Pharisees and Sadducees agreed that if these new teachers were suffered to go unchecked, their own influence would be in greater danger than when Jesus was upon the earth. Accordingly, the captain of the temple, with the help of a number of Sadducees, arrested Peter and John, and put them in prison, as it was too late that day for them to be examined.

The enemies of the disciples could not but be convinced that Christ had risen from the dead. The evidence was too clear to be doubted. Nevertheless, they hardened their hearts, refusing to repent of the terrible deed they had committed in putting Jesus to death. Abundant evidence that the apostles were speaking and acting under divine inspiration had been given the Jewish rulers, but they firmly resisted the message of truth. Christ had not come in the manner that they expected, and though at times they had been convinced that He was the Son of God, yet they had stifled conviction, and crucified Him. In mercy God gave them still further evidence, and now another opportunity was granted them to turn to Him. He sent the disciples to tell them that they had killed the Prince of life, and in this terrible charge He gave them another call to repentance. But feeling secure in their own righteousness, the Jewish teachers refused to admit that the men charging them with crucifying Christ were speaking by the direction of the Holy Spirit.

Having committed themselves to a course of opposition to Christ, every act of resistance became to the priests an additional incentive to pursue the same course. Their obstinacy became more and more determined. It was not that they could not yield; they could, but would not. It was not alone because they were guilty and deserving of death, not alone because they had put to death the Son of God, that they were cut off from salvation; it was because they armed themselves with opposition to God. They persistently rejected light and stifled the convictions of the Spirit. The influence that controls the children of disobedience worked in them, leading them to abuse the men through whom God was working. The malignity of their rebellion was intensified by each successive act of resistance against God and the message He had given His servants to declare. Every day, in their refusal to repent, the Jewish leaders took up their rebellion afresh, preparing to reap that which they had sown.

The wrath of God is not declared against unrepentant sinners merely because of the sins they have committed, but because, when called to repent, they choose to continue in resistance, repeating the sins of the past in defiance of the light given them. If the Jewish leaders had submitted to the convicting power of the Holy Spirit, they would have been pardoned; but they were determined not to yield. In the same way, the sinner, by continued resistance, places himself where the Holy Spirit cannot influence him.

On the day following the healing of the cripple, Annas and Caiaphas, with the other dignitaries of the temple, met together for the trial, and the prisoners were brought before them. In that very room and before some of those very men, Peter had shamefully denied his Lord. This came distinctly to his mind as he appeared for his own trial. He now had an opportunity of redeeming his cowardice.

Those present who remembered the part that Peter had acted at the trial of his Master, flattered themselves that he could now be intimidated by the threat of imprisonment and death. But the Peter who denied Christ in the hour of His greatest need was impulsive and self-confident, differing widely from the Peter who was brought before the Sanhedrin for examination. Since his fall he had been converted. He was no longer proud and boastful, but modest and self-distrustful. He was filled with the Holy Spirit, and by the help of this power he was resolved to remove the stain of his apostasy by honoring the name he had once disowned.

Hitherto the priests had avoided mentioning the crucifixion or the resurrection of Jesus. But now, in fulfillment of their purpose, they were forced to inquire of the accused how the cure of the impotent man had been accomplished. "By what power, or by what name, have ye done this?" they asked.

With holy boldness and in the power of the Spirit Peter fearlessly declared: "Be it known unto you all, and to all the people of Israel, that by the name of Jesus Christ of Nazareth, whom ye crucified, whom God raised from the dead, even by Him doth this man stand here before you whole. This is the stone which was set at nought of you builders, which is become the head of the corner. Neither is there salvation in any other: for there is none other name under heaven given among men, whereby we must be saved."

This courageous defense appalled the Jewish leaders. They had supposed that the disciples would be overcome with fear and confusion when brought before the Sanhedrin. But, instead, these witnesses spoke as Christ had spoken, with a convincing power that silenced their adversaries. There was no trace of fear in Peter's voice as he declared of Christ, "This is the stone which was set at nought of you builders, which is become the head of the corner."

Peter here used a figure of speech familiar to the priests. The prophets had spoken of the rejected stone; and Christ Himself, speaking on one occasion to the priests and elders, said: "Did ye never read in the Scriptures, The stone which the builders rejected, the same is become the head of the corner: this is the Lord's doing, and it is marvelous in our eyes? Therefore say I unto you, The kingdom of God shall be taken from you, and given to a nation bringing forth the fruits thereof. And whosoever shall fall on this stone shall be broken: but on whomsoever it shall fall, it will grind him to powder." Matthew 21:42-44.

As the priests listened to the apostles' fearless words, "they took knowledge of them, that they had been with Jesus."

Of the disciples after the transfiguration of Christ it is written that at the close of that wonderful scene "they saw no man, save Jesus only." Matthew 17:8. "Jesus only"— in these words is contained the secret of the life and power that marked the history of the early church. When the disciples first heard the words of Christ, they felt their need of Him. They sought, they found, they followed Him. They were with Him in the temple, at the table, on the mountainside, in the field. They were as pupils with a teacher, daily receiving from Him lessons of eternal truth.

After the Saviour's ascension, the sense of the divine presence, full of love and light, was still with them. It was a personal presence. Jesus, the Saviour, who had walked and talked and prayed with them, who had spoken hope and comfort to their hearts, had, while the message of peace was upon His lips, been taken from them into heaven. As the chariot of angels received Him, His words had come to them, "Lo, I am with you alway, even unto the end." Matthew

28:20. He had ascended to heaven in the form of humanity. They knew that He was before the throne of God, their Friend and Saviour still; that His sympathies were unchanged; that He would forever be identified with suffering humanity. They knew that He was presenting before God the merit of His blood, showing His wounded hands and feet as a remembrance of the price He had paid for His redeemed ones; and this thought strengthened them to endure reproach for His sake. Their union with Him was stronger now than when He was with them in person. The light and love and power of an indwelling Christ shone out through them, so that men, beholding, marveled.

Christ placed His seal on the words that Peter spoke in His defense. Close beside the disciple, as a convincing witness, stood the man who had been so miraculously healed. The appearance of this man, a few hours before a helpless cripple, but now restored to soundness of health, added a weight of testimony to Peter's words. Priests and rulers were silent. They were unable to refute Peter's statement, but they were nonetheless determined to put a stop to the teaching of the disciples.

Christ's crowning miracle—the raising of Lazarus—had sealed the determination of the priests to rid the world of Jesus and His wonderful works, which were fast destroying their influence over the people. They had crucified Him; but here was a convincing proof that they had not put a stop to the working of miracles in His name, nor to the proclamation of the truth He taught. Already the healing of the cripple and the preaching of the apostles had filled Jerusalem with excitement.

In order to conceal their perplexity, the priests and rulers ordered the apostles to be taken away, that they might counsel among themselves. They all agreed that it would be useless to deny that the man had been healed. Gladly would they have covered up the miracle by falsehoods; but this was impossible, for it had been wrought in the full light of day, before a multitude of people, and had already come to the knowledge of thousands. They felt that the work of the disciples must be stopped or Jesus would gain many followers. Their own disgrace would follow, for they would be held guilty of the murder of the Son of God.

But notwithstanding their desire to destroy the disciples, the priests dared not do more than threaten them with the severest punishment if they continued to speak or to work in the name of Jesus. Calling them again before the Sanhedrin, they commanded them not to speak or teach in the name of Jesus. But Peter and John answered: "Whether it be right in the sight of God to hearken unto you more than unto God, judge ye. For we cannot but speak the things which we have seen and heard."

Gladly would the priests have punished these men for their unswerving fidelity to their sacred calling, but they feared the people; "for all men glorified God for that which was done." So, with repeated threats and injunctions, the apostles were set at liberty.

While Peter and John were prisoners, the other disciples, knowing the malignity of the Jews, had prayed unceasingly for their brethren, fearing that the cruelty shown to Christ might be repeated. As soon as the apostles were released, they sought the rest of the disciples and reported to them the result of the examination. Great was the joy of the believers. "They lifted up their voice to God with one accord, and said, Lord, Thou art God, which hast made heaven, and earth, and the sea, and all that in them is: who by the mouth of Thy servant David hast said, Why did the heathen rage, and the people imagine vain things? The kings of the earth stood up, and the rulers were gathered together against the Lord, and against His Christ. For of a truth against Thy Holy Child Jesus, whom Thou hast anointed, both Herod, and Pontius Pilate, with the Gentiles, and the people of Israel, were gathered together, for to do whatsoever Thy hand and Thy counsel determined before to be done.

"And now, Lord, behold their threatenings: and grant unto Thy servants, that with all boldness they may speak Thy word, by stretching forth Thine hand to heal; and that signs and wonders may be done by the name of Thy Holy Child Jesus."

The disciples prayed that greater strength might be imparted to them in the work of the ministry; for they saw that they would meet the same determined opposition that Christ had encountered when upon the earth. While their united prayers were ascending in faith to heaven, the answer came. The place where they were assembled was shaken, and they were endowed anew with the Holy Spirit. Their hearts filled with courage, they again went forth to proclaim the word of God in Jerusalem. "With great power gave the apostles witness of the resurrection of the Lord Jesus," and God marvelously blessed their efforts.

The principle for which the disciples stood so fearlessly when, in answer to the command not to speak any more in the name of Jesus, they declared, "Whether it be right in the sight of God to hearken unto you more than unto God, judge ye," is the same that the adherents of the gospel struggled to maintain in the days of the

Reformation. When in 1529 the German princes assembled at the Diet of Spires, there was presented the emperor's decree restricting religious liberty, and prohibiting all further dissemination of the reformed doctrines. It seemed that the hope of the world was about to be crushed out. Would the princes accept the decree? Should the light of the gospel be shut out from the multitudes still in darkness? Mighty issues for the world were at stake. Those who had accepted the reformed faith met together, and their unanimous decision was, "Let us reject this decree. In matters of conscience the majority has no power."—Merle d'Aubigne, *History of the Reformation, b. 13, ch. 5.*

This principle we in our day are firmly to maintain. The banner of truth and religious liberty held aloft by the founders of the gospel church and by God's witnesses during the centuries that have passed since then, has, in this last conflict, been committed to our hands. The responsibility for this great gift rests with those whom God has blessed with a knowledge of His word. We are to receive this word as supreme authority. We are to recognize human government as an ordinance of divine appointment, and teach obedience to it as a sacred duty, within its legitimate sphere. But when its claims conflict with the claims of God, we must obey God rather than men. God's word must be recognized as above all human legislation. A "Thus saith the Lord" is not to be set aside for a "Thus saith the church" or a "Thus saith the state." The crown of Christ is to be lifted above the diadems of earthly potentates.

We are not required to defy authorities. Our words, whether spoken or written, should be carefully considered, lest we place ourselves on record as uttering that which would make us appear antagonistic to law and order. We are not to say or do anything that would unnecessarily close up our way. We are to go forward in Christ's name, advocating the truths committed to us. If we are forbidden by men to do this work, then we may say, as did the apostles, "Whether it be right in the sight of God to hearken unto you more than unto God, judge ye. For we cannot but speak the things which we have seen and heard."

7

A Warning Against Hypocrisy

This chapter is based on Acts 4:32-5:11

As the disciples proclaimed the truths of the gospel in Jerusalem, God bore witness to their word, and a multitude believed. Many of these early believers were immediately cut off from family and friends by the zealous bigotry of the Jews, and it was necessary to provide them with food and shelter.

The record declares, "Neither was there any among them that lacked," and it tells how the need was filled. Those among the believers who had money and possessions cheerfully sacrificed them to meet the emergency. Selling their houses or their lands, they brought the money and laid it at the apostles' feet, "and distribution was made unto every man according as he had need."

This liberality on the part of the believers was the result of the outpouring of the Spirit. The converts to the gospel were "of one heart and of one soul." One common interest controlled them—the success of the mission entrusted to them; and covetousness had no place in their lives. Their love for their brethren and the cause they had espoused, was greater than their love of money and possessions. Their works testified that they accounted the souls of men of higher value than earthly wealth.

Thus it will ever be when the Spirit of God takes possession of the life. Those whose hearts are filled with the love of Christ, will follow the example of Him who for our sake became poor, that through His poverty we might be made rich. Money, time, influence—all the gifts they have received from God's hand, they will value only as a means of advancing the work of the gospel. Thus it was in the early church; and when in the church of today it is seen that by the power of the Spirit the members have taken their affections from the things of the world, and that they are willing to make sacrifices in order that their fellow men may hear the gospel, the truths proclaimed will have a powerful influence upon the hearers.

In sharp contrast to the example of benevolence shown by the believers, was the conduct of Ananias and Sapphira, whose experience, traced by the pen of Inspiration, has left a dark stain upon the history of the early church. With others, these professed disciples had shared the privilege of hearing the gospel preached by the apostles. They had been present with other believers when, after the apostles had prayed, "the place was shaken where they were assembled together; and they were all filled with the Holy Ghost." Acts 4:31. Deep conviction had rested upon all present, and under the direct influence of the Spirit of God, Ananias and Sapphira had made a pledge to give to the Lord the proceeds from the sale of certain property.

Afterward, Ananias and Sapphira grieved the Holy Spirit by yielding to feelings of covetousness. They began to regret their promise and soon lost the sweet influence of the blessing that had warmed their hearts with a desire to do large things in behalf of the cause of Christ. They thought they had been too hasty, that they ought to reconsider their decision. They talked the matter over, and decided not to fulfill their pledge. They saw, however, that those who parted with their possessions to supply the needs of their poorer brethren, were held in high esteem among the believers; and ashamed to have their brethren know that their selfish souls grudged that which they had solemnly dedicated to God, they deliberately decided to sell their property and pretend to give all the proceeds into the general fund, but really to keep a large share for themselves. Thus they would secure their living from the common store and at the same time gain the high esteem of their brethren.

But God hates hypocrisy and falsehood. Ananias and Sapphira practiced fraud in their dealing with God; they lied to the Holy Spirit, and their sin was visited with swift and terrible judgment. When Ananias came with his offering, Peter said: "Ananias, why hath Satan filled thine heart to lie to the Holy Ghost, and to keep back part of the price of the land? Whiles it remained, was it not thine own? and after it was sold, was it not in thine own power? why hast thou conceived this thing in thine heart? thou hast not lied unto men, but unto God."

"Ananias hearing these words fell down, and gave up the ghost: and great fear came on all them that heard these things."

"Whiles it remained, was it not thine own?" Peter asked. No undue influence had been brought to bear upon Ananias to compel him to sacrifice his possessions to the general good. He had acted from choice. But in attempting to deceive the disciples, he had lied to the Almighty.

"It was about the space of three hours after, when his wife, not knowing what was done, came in. And Peter answered unto her, Tell me whether ye sold the land for so much? And she said, Yea, for so much. Then Peter said unto her, How is it that ye have agreed together to tempt the Spirit of the Lord? Behold, the feet of them which have buried thy husband are at the door, and shall carry thee out. Then fell she down straightway at his feet, and yielded up the ghost: and the young men came in, and found her dead, and, carrying her forth, buried her by her husband. And great fear came upon all the church, and upon as many as heard these things."

Infinite Wisdom saw that this signal manifestation of the wrath of God was necessary to guard the young church from becoming demoralized. Their numbers were rapidly increasing. The church would have been endangered if, in the rapid increase of converts, men and women had been added who, while professing to serve God, were worshiping mammon. This judgment testified that men cannot deceive God, that He detects the hidden sin of the heart, and that He will not be mocked. It was designed as a warning to the church, to lead them to avoid pretense and hypocrisy, and to beware of robbing God.

Not to the early church only, but to all future generations, this example of God's hatred of covetousness, fraud, and hypocrisy, was given as a danger-signal. It was covetousness that Ananias and Sapphira had first cherished. The desire to retain for themselves a part of that which they had promised to the Lord, led them into fraud and hypocrisy.

God has made the proclamation of the gospel dependent upon the labors and the gifts of His people. Voluntary offerings and the tithe constitute the revenue of the Lord's work. Of the means entrusted to man, God claims a certain portion,—the tenth. He leaves all free to say whether or not they will give more than this. But when the heart is stirred by the influence of the Holy Spirit, and a vow is made to give a certain amount, the one who vows has no longer any right to the consecrated portion. Promises of this kind made to men would be looked upon as binding; are those not more binding that are made to God? Are promises tried in the court of conscience less binding than written agreements of men?

When divine light is shining into the heart with unusual clearness and power, habitual selfishness relaxes its grasp and there is a disposition to give to the cause of God. But none need think that they will be allowed to fulfill the promises then made, without a protest on the part of Satan. He is not pleased to see the Redeemer's kingdom on earth built up. He suggests that the pledge made was too much, that it may cripple them in their efforts to acquire property or gratify the desires of their families.

It is God who blesses men with property, and He does this that they may be able to give toward the advancement of His cause. He sends the sunshine and the rain. He causes vegetation to flourish. He gives health and the ability to acquire means. All our blessings come from His bountiful hand. In turn, He would have men and women show their gratitude by returning Him a portion in tithes and offerings—in thank offerings, in freewill offerings, in trespass offerings. Should means flow into the treasury in accordance with this divinely appointed plan,—a tenth of all the increase, and liberal offerings,—there would be an abundance for the advancement of the Lord's work.

But the hearts of men become hardened through selfishness, and, like Ananias and Sapphira, they are tempted to withhold part of the price, while pretending to fulfill God's requirements. Many spend money lavishly in self-gratification. Men and women consult their pleasure and gratify their taste, while they bring to God, almost unwillingly, a stinted offering. They forget that God will one day demand a strict account of how His goods have been used, and that He will no more accept the pittance they hand into the treasury than He accepted the offering of Ananias and Sapphira.

From the stern punishment meted out to those perjurers, God would have us learn also how deep is His hatred and contempt for all hypocrisy and deception. In pretending that they had given all, Ananias and Sapphira lied to the Holy Spirit, and, as a result, they lost this life and the life that is to come. The same God who punished them, today condemns all falsehood. Lying lips are an abomination to Him. He declares that into the Holy City "there shall in no wise enter . . . anything that defileth, neither whatsoever worketh abomination, or maketh a lie." Revelation 21:27. Let truth telling be held with no loose hand or uncertain grasp. Let it become a part of the life. Playing fast and loose with truth, and dissembling to suit one's own selfish plans, means shipwreck of faith. "Stand therefore, having your loins girt about with truth." Ephesians 6:14. He who utters untruths sells his soul in a cheap market. His falsehoods may seem to serve in emergencies; he may thus seem to make business advancement that he could not gain by fair dealing; but he finally reaches the place where he can trust no one. Himself a falsifier, he has no confidence in the word of others.

In the case of Ananias and Sapphira, the sin of fraud against God was speedily punished. The same sin was often repeated in the after history of the church and is committed by many in our time. But though it may not be attended by the visible manifestation of God's displeasure, it is no less heinous in His sight now than in the apostles' time. The warning has been given; God has clearly manifested His abhorrence of this sin; and all who give themselves up to hypocrisy and covetousness may be sure that they are destroying their own souls.

8

Before the Sanhedrin

It was the cross, that instrument of shame and torture, which brought hope and salvation to the world. The disciples were but humble men, without wealth, and with no weapon but the word of God; yet in Christ's strength they went forth to tell the wonderful story of the manger and the cross, and to triumph over all opposition. Without earthly honor or recognition, they were heroes of faith. From their lips came words of divine eloquence that shook the world.

In Jerusalem, where the deepest prejudice existed, and where the most confused ideas prevailed in regard to Him who had been crucified as a malefactor, the disciples continued to speak with boldness the words of life, setting before the Jews the work and mission of Christ, His crucifixion, resurrection, and ascension. Priests and rulers heard with amazement the clear, bold testimony of the apostles. The power of the risen Saviour had indeed fallen on the disciples, and their work was accompanied by signs and miracles that daily increased the number of believers. Along the streets where the disciples were to pass, the people laid their sick "on beds and couches, that at the least the shadow of Peter passing by might overshadow some of them." Here also were brought those vexed with unclean spirits. The crowds gathered round them, and those who were healed shouted the praises of God and glorified the name of the Redeemer.

The priests and rulers saw that Christ was extolled above them. As the Sadducees, who did not believe in a resurrection, heard the apostles declaring that Christ had risen from the dead, they were enraged, realizing that if the apostles were allowed to preach a risen Saviour, and to work miracles in His name, the doctrine that there would be no resurrection would be rejected by all, and the sect of the Sadducees would soon become extinct. The Pharisees were angry as they perceived that the tendency of the disciples' teaching was to undermine the Jewish ceremonies, and make the sacrificial offerings of no effect.

Hitherto all the efforts made to suppress this new teaching had been in vain; but now both Sadducees and Pharisees determined that the work of the disciples should be stopped, for it was proving them guilty of the death of Jesus. Filled with indignation, the priests laid violent hands on Peter and John, and put them in the common prison.

The leaders in the Jewish nation had signally failed of fulfilling God's purpose for His chosen people. Those whom the Lord had made the depositaries of truth had proved unfaithful to their trust, and God chose others to do His work. In their blindness these leaders now gave full sway to what they called righteous indignation against the ones who were setting aside their cherished doctrines. They would not admit even the possibility that they themselves did not rightly understand the word, or that they had misinterpreted or misapplied the Scriptures. They acted like men who had lost their reason. What right have these teachers, they said, some of them mere fishermen, to present ideas contrary to the doctrines that we have taught the people? Being determined to suppress the teaching of these ideas, they imprisoned those who were presenting them.

The disciples were not intimidated or cast down by this treatment. The Holy Spirit brought to their minds the words spoken by Christ: "The servant is not greater than his lord. If they have persecuted Me, they will also persecute you; if they have kept My saying, they will keep yours also. But all these things will they do unto you for My name's sake, because they know not Him that sent Me." "They shall put you out of the synagogues: yea, the time cometh, that whosoever killeth you will think that he doeth God service." "These things have I told you, that when the time shall come, ye may remember that I told you of them." John 15:20, 21; 16:2, 4.

The God of heaven, the mighty Ruler of the universe, took the matter of the imprisonment of the disciples into His own hands, for men were warring against His work. By night the angel of the Lord opened the prison doors and said to the disciples, "Go, stand and speak in the temple to the people all the words of this life." This command was directly contrary to the order given by the Jewish rulers; but did the apostles say, We cannot do this until we have consulted the magistrates and received permission from them? No; God had said, "Go," and they obeyed. "They entered into the temple early in the morning, and taught."

When Peter and John appeared among the believers and recounted how the angel had led them directly through the band of soldiers guarding the prison, bidding them resume the work that had been interrupted, the brethren were filled with amazement and joy.

In the meantime the high priest and those with him had "called the council together, and all the senate of the children of Israel." The priests and rulers had decided to fix upon the disciples the charge of insurrection, to accuse them of murdering Ananias and Sapphira, and of conspiring to deprive the priests of their authority. They hoped so to excite the mob that it would take the matter in hand and deal with the disciples as it had dealt with Jesus. They were aware that many who did not accept the teachings of Christ were weary of the arbitrary rule of the Jewish authorities and anxious for some change. The priests feared that if these dissatisfied ones were to accept the truths proclaimed by the apostles, and were to acknowledge Jesus as the Messiah, the anger of the entire people would be raised against the religious leaders, who would then be made to answer for the murder of Christ. They decided to take strong measures to prevent this.

When they sent for the prisoners to be brought before them, great was their amazement at the word brought back that the prison doors were found to be securely bolted and the guard stationed before them, but that the prisoners were nowhere to be found.

Soon the astonishing report came, "Behold, the men whom ye put in prison are standing in the temple, and teaching the people. Then went the captain with the officers, and brought them without violence: for they feared the people, lest they should have been stoned."

Although the apostles were miraculously delivered from prison, they were not safe from examination and punishment. Christ had said when He was with them, "Take heed to yourselves: for they shall deliver you up to councils." Mark 13:9. By sending an angel to deliver them, God had given them a token of His love and an assurance of His presence. It was now their part to suffer for the sake of the One whose gospel they were preaching.

In the history of prophets and apostles, are many noble examples of loyalty to God. Christ's witnesses have endured imprisonment, torture, and death itself, rather than break God's commands. The record left by Peter and John is as heroic as any in the gospel dispensation. As they stood for the second time before the men who seemed bent on their destruction, no fear or hesitation could be discerned in their words or attitude. And when the high priest said, "Did we not straitly command you that ye should not teach in this name? and, behold, ye have filled Jerusalem with your doctrine, and intend to bring this Man's blood upon us," Peter answered, "We ought to obey God rather than men." It was an angel from heaven who delivered them from prison and bade them teach in the temple. In following his directions they were obeying the divine command, and this they must continue to do at whatever cost to themselves.

Then the Spirit of Inspiration came upon the disciples; the accused became the accusers, charging the murder of Christ upon those who composed the council. "The God of our fathers raised up Jesus," Peter declared, "whom ye slew and hanged on a tree. Him hath God exalted with His right hand to be a Prince and a Saviour, for to give repentance to Israel, and forgiveness of sins. And we are His witnesses of these things; and so is also the Holy Ghost, whom God hath given to them that obey Him."

So enraged were the Jews at these words that they decided to take the law into their own hands and without further trial, or without authority from the Roman officers, to put the prisoners to death. Already guilty of the blood of Christ, they were no eager to stain their hands with the blood of His disciples.

But in the council there was one man who recognized the voice of God in the words spoken by the disciples. This was Gamaliel, a Pharisee of good reputation and a man of learning and high position. His clear intellect saw that the violent step contemplated by the priests would lead to terrible consequences. Before addressing those present, he requested that the prisoners be removed. He well knew the elements he had to deal with; he knew that the murderers of Christ would hesitate at nothing in order to carry out their purpose.

He then spoke with great deliberation and calmness, saying: "Ye men of Israel, take heed to yourselves what ye intend to do as touching these men. For before these days rose up Theudas, boasting himself to be somebody; to whom a number of men, about four hundred, joined themselves: who was slain; and all, as many as obeyed him, were scattered, and brought to nought. After this man rose up Judas of Galilee in the days of the taxing, and drew away much people after him: he also perished; and all, even as many as obeyed him, were dispersed. And now I say unto you, Refrain from these men, and let them alone: for if this counsel or this work be of men, it will come to nought: but if it be of God, ye cannot overthrow it; lest haply ye be found even to fight against God."

The priests saw the reasonableness of these views, and were obliged to agree with Gamaliel. Yet their prejudice and hatred could hardly be restrained. Very reluctantly, after beating the disciples and charging them again at the peril of their lives to preach no more in the name of Jesus, they released them. "And they departed from the presence of the council, rejoicing that they were counted worthy to suffer shame for His name. And daily in the temple, and in every house, they ceased not to teach and preach Jesus Christ."

Shortly before His crucifixion Christ had bequeathed to His disciples a legacy of peace. "Peace I leave with you," He said, "My peace I give unto you: not as the world giveth, give I unto you. Let not your heart be troubled, neither let it be afraid." John 14:27. This peace is not the peace that comes through conformity to the world. Christ never purchased peace by compromise with evil. The peace that Christ left His disciples is internal rather than external and was ever to remain with His witnesses through strife and contention.

Christ said of Himself, "Think not that I am come to send peace on earth: I came not to send peace, but a sword." Matthew 10:34. The Prince of Peace, He was yet the cause of division. He who came to proclaim glad tidings and to create hope and joy in the hearts of the children of men, opened a controversy that burns deep and arouses intense passion in the human heart. And He warns His followers, "In the world ye shall have tribulation." "They shall lay their hands on you, and persecute you, delivering you up to the synagogues, and into prisons, being brought before kings and rulers for My name's sake." "Ye shall be betrayed both by parents, and brethren, and kinsfolks, and friends; and some of you shall they cause to be put to death." John 16:33; Luke 21:12, 16.

This prophecy has been fulfilled in a marked manner. Every indignity, reproach, and cruelty that Satan could instigate human hearts to devise, has been visited upon the followers of Jesus. And it will be again fulfilled in a marked manner; for the carnal heart is still at enmity with the law of God, and will not be subject to its commands. The world is no more in harmony with the principles of Christ today than it was in the days of the apostles. The same hatred that prompted the cry, "Crucify Him! crucify Him!" the same hatred that led to the persecution of the disciples, still works in the children of disobedience. The same spirit which in the Dark Ages consigned men and women to prison, to exile, and to death, which conceived the exquisite torture of the Inquisition, which planned and executed the Massacre of St. Bartholomew, and which kindled the fires of Smithfield, is still at work with malignant energy in unregenerate hearts. The history of truth has ever been the record of a struggle between right and wrong. The proclamation of the gospel has ever been carried forward in this world in the face of opposition, peril, loss, and suffering.

What was the strength of those who in the past have suffered persecution for Christ's sake? It was union with God, union with the Holy Spirit, union with Christ. Reproach and persecution have separated many from earthly friends, but never from the love of Christ. Never is the tempest-tried soul more dearly loved by His Saviour than when he is suffering reproach for the truth's sake. "I will love him," Christ said, "and will manifest Myself to him." John 14:21. When for the truth's sake the believer stands at the bar of earthly tribunals, Christ stands by his side. When he is confined within prison walls, Christ manifests Himself to him and cheers his heart with His love. When he suffers death for Christ's sake, the Saviour says to him, They may kill the body, but they cannot hurt the soul. "Be of good cheer; I have overcome the world." "Fear thou not; for I am with thee: be not dismayed; for I am thy God: I will strengthen thee; yea, I will help thee; yea, I will uphold thee with the right hand of My righteousness." John 16:33; Isaiah 41:10.

"They that trust in the Lord shall be as Mount Zion, which cannot be removed, but abideth forever. As the mountains are round about Jerusalem, so the Lord is round about His people from henceforth even forever." "He shall redeem their soul from deceit and violence: and precious shall their blood be in His sight." Psalms 125:1-3; 72:14.

"The Lord of hosts shall defend them; . . . the Lord their God shall save them in that day as the flock of His people: for they shall be as the stones of a crown, lifted up as an ensign upon His land." Zechariah 9:15, 16.

9

The Seven Deacons

Based on Acts 6:1-7

In those days, when the number of the disciples was multiplied, there arose a murmuring of the Grecians against the Hebrews, because their widows were neglected in the daily ministration."

The early church was made up of many classes of people, of various nationalities. At the time of the outpouring of the Holy Spirit at Pentecost, "there were dwelling at Jerusalem Jews, devout men, out of every nation under heaven." Acts 2:5. Among those of the Hebrew faith who were gathered at Jerusalem were some commonly known as Grecians, between whom and the Jews of Palestine there had long existed distrust and even antagonism.

The hearts of those who had been converted under the labors of the apostles, were softened and united by Christian love. Despite former prejudices, all were in harmony with one another. Satan knew that so long as this union continued to exist, he would be powerless to check the progress of gospel truth; and he sought to take advantage of former habits of thought, in the hope that thereby he might be able to introduce into the church elements of disunion.

Thus it came to pass that as disciples were multiplied, the enemy succeeded in arousing the suspicions of some who had formerly been in the habit of looking with jealousy on their brethren in the faith and of finding fault with their spiritual leaders, and so "there arose a murmuring of the Grecians against the Hebrews." The cause of complaint was an alleged neglect of the Greek widows in the daily distribution of assistance. Any inequality would have been contrary to the spirit of the gospel, yet Satan had succeeded in arousing suspicion. Prompt measures must now be taken to remove all occasion for dissatisfaction, lest the enemy triumph in his effort to bring about a division among the believers.

The disciples of Jesus had reached a crisis in their experience. Under the wise leadership of the apostles, who labored unitedly in the power of the Holy Spirit, the work committed to the gospel messengers was developing rapidly. The church was continually enlarging, and this growth in membership brought increasingly heavy burdens upon those in charge. No one man, or even one set of men, could continue to bear these burdens alone, without imperiling the future prosperity of the church. There was necessity for a further distribution of the responsibilities which had been borne so faithfully by a few during the earlier days of the church. The apostles must now take an important step in the perfecting of gospel order in the church by laying upon others some of the burdens thus far borne by themselves.

Summoning a meeting of the believers, the apostles were led by the Holy Spirit to outline a plan for the better organization of all the working forces of the church. The time had come, the apostles stated, when the spiritual leaders having the oversight of the church should be relieved from the task of distributing to the poor and from similar burdens, so that they might be free to carry forward the work of preaching the gospel. "Wherefore, brethren," they said, "look ye out among you seven men of honest report, full of the Holy Ghost and wisdom, whom we may appoint over this business. But we will give ourselves continually to prayer, and to the ministry of the word." This advice was followed, and by prayer and the laying on of hands, seven chosen men were solemnly set apart for their duties as deacons.

The appointment of the seven to take the oversight of special lines of work, proved a great blessing to the church. These officers gave careful consideration to individual needs as well as to the general financial interests of the church, and by their prudent management and their godly example they were an important aid to their fellow officers in binding together the various interests of the church into a united whole.

That this step was in the order of God, is revealed in the immediate results for good that were seen. "The word of God increased; and the number of the disciples multiplied in Jerusalem greatly; and a great company of the priests were obedient to the faith." This ingathering of souls was due both to the greater freedom secured by the apostles and to the zeal and power shown by the seven deacons. The fact that these brethren had been ordained for the special work of looking after the needs of the poor, did not exclude them from teaching the faith. On the contrary, they were fully qualified to instruct others in the truth, and they engaged in the work with great earnestness and success.

To the early church had been entrusted a constantly enlarging work—that of establishing centers of light and blessing wherever there were honest souls willing to give themselves to the service of Christ. The proclamation of the gospel was to be world-wide in its extent, and the messengers of the cross could not hope to fulfill their important mission unless they should remain united in the bonds of Christian unity, and thus reveal to the world that they were one with Christ in God. Had not their divine Leader prayed to the Father, "Keep through Thine own name those whom Thou hast given Me, that they may be one, as We are"? And had He not declared of His disciples, "The world hath hated them, because they are not of the world"? Had He not pleaded with the Father that they might be "made perfect in one," "that the world may believe that Thou hast sent Me"? John 17:11, 14, 23, 21. Their spiritual life and power was dependent on a close connection with the One by whom they had been commissioned to preach the gospel.

Only as they were united with Christ could the disciples hope to have the accompanying power of the Holy Spirit and the co-operation of angels of heaven. With the help of these divine agencies they would present before the world a united front and would be victorious in the conflict they were compelled to wage unceasingly against the powers of darkness. As they should continue to labor unitedly, heavenly messengers would go before them, opening the way; hearts would be prepared for the reception of truth, and many would be won to Christ. So long as they remained united, the church would go forth "fair as the moon, clear as the sun, and terrible as an army with banners." Song of Solomon 6:10. Nothing could withstand her onward progress. The church would advance from victory to victory, gloriously fulfilling her divine mission of proclaiming the gospel to the world.

The organization of the church at Jerusalem was to serve as a model for the organization of churches in every other place where messengers of truth should win converts to the gospel. Those to whom was given the responsibility of the general oversight of the church were not to lord it over God's heritage, but, as wise shepherds, were to "feed the flock of God,. . . being ensamples to the flock" (1 Peter 5:2, 3); and the deacons were to be "men of honest report, full of the Holy Ghost and wisdom." These men were to take their position unitedly on the side of right and to maintain it with firmness and decision. Thus they would have a uniting influence upon the entire flock.

Later in the history of the early church, when in various parts of the world many groups of believers had been formed into churches, the organization of the church was further perfected, so that order and harmonious action might be maintained. Every member was exhorted to act well his part. Each was to make a wise use of the talents entrusted to him. Some were endowed by the Holy Spirit with special gifts —"first apostles, secondarily prophets, thirdly teachers, after that miracles, then gifts of healings, helps, governments, diversities of tongues." 1 Corinthians 12:28. But all these classes of workers were to labor in harmony.

"There are diversities of gifts, but the same Spirit. And there are differences of administrations, but the same Lord. And there are diversities of operations, but it is the same God which worketh all in all. But the manifestation of the Spirit is given to every man to profit withal. For to one is given by the Spirit the word of wisdom; to another the word of knowledge by the same Spirit; to another faith by the same Spirit; to another the gifts of healing by the same Spirit; to another the working of miracles; to another prophecy; to another discerning of spirits; to another divers kinds of tongues; to another the interpretation of tongues: but all these worketh that one and the selfsame Spirit, dividing to every man severally as He will. For as the body is one, and hath many members, and all the members of that one body, being many, are one body: so also is Christ." 1 Corinthians 12:4-12.

Solemn are the responsibilities resting upon those who are called to act as leaders in the church of God on earth. In the days of the theocracy, when Moses was endeavoring to carry alone burdens so heavy that he would soon have worn away under them, he was counseled by Jethro to plan for a wise distribution of responsibilities. "Be thou for the people to Godward," Jethro advised, "that thou mayest bring the causes unto God: and thou shalt teach them ordinances and laws, and shalt show them the way wherein they must walk, and the work that they must do." Jethro further advised that men be appointed to act as "rulers of thousands, and rulers of hundreds, rulers of fifties, and rulers of tens." These were to be "able men, such as fear God, men of truth, hating covetousness." They were to "judge the people at all seasons," thus relieving Moses of the wearing responsibility of giving considera- tion to many minor matters that could be dealt with wisely by consecrated helpers.

The time and strength of those who in the providence of God have been placed in leading positions of responsibility in the church, should be spent in dealing with the weightier matters demanding special wisdom and largeness of heart. It is not in the order of God that such men should be appealed to for the adjustment of minor matters that others are well qualified to handle. "Every great matter they shall bring unto thee," Jethro proposed to Moses, "but every small matter they shall judge: so shall it be easier for thyself, and they shall bear the burden with thee. If thou shalt do this thing, and God command thee so, then thou shalt be able to endure, and all this people shall also go to their place in peace."

In harmony with this plan, "Moses chose able men out of all Israel, and made them heads over the people, rulers of thousands, rulers of hundreds, rulers of fifties, and rulers of tens. And they judged the people at all seasons: the hard causes they brought unto Moses, but every small matter they judged themselves." Exodus 18:19-26.

Later, when choosing seventy elders to share with him the responsibilities of leadership, Moses was careful to select, as his helpers, men possessing dignity, sound judgment, and experience. In his charge to these elders at the time of their ordination, he outlined some of the qualifications that fit a man to be a wise ruler in the church. "Hear the causes between your brethren," said Moses, "and judge righteously between every man and his brother, and the stranger that is with him. Ye shall not respect persons in judgment; but ye shall hear the small as well as the great; ye shall not be afraid of the face of man; for the judgment is God's." Deuteronomy 1:16, 17.

King David, toward the close of his reign, delivered a solemn charge to those bearing the burden of the work of God in his day. Summoning to Jerusalem "all the princes of Israel, the princes of the tribes, and the captains of the companies that ministered to the king by course, and the captains over the thousands, and captains over the hundreds, and the stewards over all the substance and possession of the king, and of his sons, with the officers, and with the mighty men, and with all the valiant men," the aged king solemnly charged them, "in the sight of all Israel the congregation of the Lord, and in the audience of our God," to "keep and seek for all the commandments of the Lord your God." I Chronicles 28:1, 8.

To Solomon, as one called to occupy a position of leading responsibility, David gave a special charge: "Thou, Solomon my son, know thou the God of thy father, and serve Him with a perfect heart and with a willing mind: for the Lord searcheth all hearts, and understandeth all the imaginations of the thoughts: if thou seek Him, He will be found of thee; but if thou forsake Him, He will cast thee off forever. Take heed now; for the Lord hath chosen thee: . . . be strong." I Chronicles 28:9, 10.

The same principles of piety and justice that were to guide the rulers among God's people in the time of Moses and of David, were also to be followed by those given the oversight of the newly organized church of God in the gospel dispensation. In the work of setting things in order in all the churches, and ordaining suitable men to act as officers, the apostles held to the high standards of leadership outlined in the Old Testament Scriptures. They maintained that he who is called to stand in a position of leading responsibility in the church "must be blameless, as the steward of God; not self-willed, not soon angry, not given to wine, no striker, not given to filthy lucre; but a lover of hospitality, a lover of good men, sober, just, holy, temperate; holding fast the faithful word as he hath been taught, that he may be able by sound doctrine both to exhort and to convince the gainsayers." Titus 1:7-9.

The order that was maintained in the early Christian church made it possible for them to move forward solidly as a well-disciplined army clad with the armor of God. The companies of believers, though scattered over a large territory, were all members of one body; all moved in concert and in harmony with one another. When dissension arose in a local church, as later it did arise in Antioch and elsewhere, and the believers were unable to come to an agreement among themselves, such matters were not permitted to create a division in the church, but were referred to a general council of the entire body of believers, made up of appointed delegates from the various local churches, with the apostles and elders in positions of leading responsibility. Thus the efforts of Satan to attack the church in isolated places were met by concerted action on the part of all, and the plans of the enemy to disrupt and destroy were thwarted.

"God is not the author of confusion, but of peace, as in all churches of the saints." I Corinthians 14:33. He requires that order and system be observed in the conduct of church affairs today no less than in the days of old. He desires His work to be carried forward with thoroughness and exactness so that He may place upon it the seal of His approval. Christian is to be united with Christian, church with church, the human instrumentality co-operating with the divine, every agency subordinate to the Holy Spirit, and all combined in giving to the world the good tidings of the grace of God.

10

The First Christian Martyr

This chapter is based on Acts 6:5-15; 7

Stephen, the foremost of the seven deacons, was a man of deep piety and broad faith. Though a Jew by birth, he spoke the Greek language and was familiar with the customs and manners of the Greeks. He therefore found opportunity to preach the gospel in the synagogues of the Greek Jews. He was very active in the cause of Christ and boldly proclaimed his faith. Learned rabbis and doctors of the law engaged in public discussion with him, confidently expecting an easy victory. But "they were not able to resist the wisdom and the spirit by which he spake." Not only did he speak in the power of the Holy Spirit, but it was plain that he was a student of the prophecies and learned in all matters of the law. He ably defended the truths that he advocated and utterly defeated his opponents. To him was the promise fulfilled, "Settle it therefore in your hearts, not to meditate before what ye shall answer: for I will give you a mouth and wisdom, which all your adversaries shall not be able to gainsay nor resist." Luke 21:14, 15.

As the priests and rulers saw the power that attended the preaching of Stephen, they were filled with bitter hatred. Instead of yielding to the evidence that he presented, they determined to silence his voice by putting him to death. On several occasions they had bribed the Roman authorities to pass over without comment instances where the Jews had taken the law into their own hands and had tried, condemned, and executed prisoners in accordance with their national custom. The enemies of Stephen did not doubt that they could again pursue such a course without danger to themselves. They determined to risk the consequences and therefore seized Stephen and brought him before the Sanhedrin council for trial.

Learned Jews from the surrounding countries were summoned for the purpose of refuting the arguments of the prisoner. Saul of Tarsus was present and took a leading part against Stephen. He brought the weight of eloquence and the logic of the rabbis to bear upon the case, to convince the people that Stephen was preaching delusive and dangerous doctrines; but in Stephen he met one who had a full understanding of the purpose of God in the spreading of the gospel to other nations.

Because the priests and rulers could not prevail against the clear, calm wisdom of Stephen, they determined to make an example of him; and while thus satisfying their revengeful hatred, they would prevent others, through fear, from adopting his belief. Witnesses were hired to bear false testimony that they had heard him speak blasphemous words against the temple and the law. "We have heard him say," these witnesses declared, "that this Jesus of Nazareth shall destroy this place, and shall change the customs which Moses delivered us."

As Stephen stood face to face with his judges to answer to the charge of blasphemy, a holy radiance shone upon his countenance, and "all that sat in the council, looking steadfastly on him, saw his face as it had been the face of an angel." Many who beheld this light trembled and veiled their faces, but the stubborn unbelief and prejudice of the rulers did not waver.

When Stephen was questioned as to the truth of the charges against him, he began his defense in a clear, thrilling voice, which rang through the council hall. In words that held the assembly spellbound, he proceeded to rehearse the history of the chosen people of God. He showed a thorough knowledge of the Jewish economy and the spiritual interpretation of it now made manifest through Christ. He repeated the words of Moses that foretold of the Messiah: "A Prophet shall the Lord your God raise up unto you of your brethren, like unto me; Him shall ye hear." He made plain his own loyalty to God and to the Jewish faith, while he showed that the law in which the Jews trusted for salvation had not been able to save Israel from idolatry. He connected Jesus Christ with all the Jewish history. He referred to the building of the temple by Solomon, and to the words of both Solomon and Isaiah: "Howbeit the Most High dwelleth not in temples made with hands; as saith the prophet, Heaven is My throne, and earth is My footstool: what house will ye build Me? saith the Lord: or what is the place of My rest? Hath not My hand made all these things?"

When Stephen reached this point, there was a tumult among the people. When he connected Christ with the prophecies and spoke as he did of the temple, the priest, pretending to be horror-stricken, rent his robe. To Stephen this act was a signal that his voice would soon be silenced forever. He saw the resistance that met his words and knew that he was giving his last testimony. Although in the midst of his sermon, he abruptly concluded it.

Suddenly breaking away from the train of history that he was following, and turning upon his infuriated judges, he cried: "Ye stiff-necked and uncircumcised in heart and ears, ye do always resist the Holy Ghost: as your fathers did, so do ye. Which of the prophets have not your fathers persecuted? and they have slain them which showed before of the coming of the Just One; of whom ye have been now the betrayers and murderers: who have received the law by the disposition of angels, and have not kept it."

At this, priests and rulers were beside themselves with anger. Acting more like beasts of prey than human beings, they rushed upon Stephen, gnashing their teeth. In the cruel faces about him the prisoner read his fate; but he did not waver. For him the fear of death was gone. For him the enraged priests and the excited mob had no terror. The scene before him faded from his vision. To him the gates of heaven were ajar, and, looking in, he saw the glory of the courts of God, and Christ, as if just risen from His throne, standing ready to sustain His servant. In words of triumph Stephen exclaimed, "Behold, I see the heavens opened, and the Son of man standing on the right hand of God."

As he described the glorious scene upon which his eyes were gazing, it was more than his persecutors could endure. Stopping their ears, that they might not hear his words, and uttering loud cries, they ran furiously upon him with one accord "and cast him out of the city." "And they stoned Stephen, calling upon God, and saying, Lord Jesus, receive my spirit. And he kneeled down, and cried with a loud voice, Lord, lay not this sin to their charge. And when he had said this, he fell asleep."

No legal sentence had been passed upon Stephen, but the Roman authorities were bribed by large sums of money to make no investigation into the case.

The martyrdom of Stephen made a deep impression upon all who witnessed it. The memory of the signet of God upon his face; his words, which touched the very souls of those who heard them, remained in the minds of the beholders, and testified to the truth of that which he had proclaimed. His death was a sore trial to the church, but it resulted in the conviction of Saul, who could not efface from his memory the faith and constancy of the martyr, and the glory that had rested on his countenance.

At the scene of Stephen's trial and death, Saul had seemed to be imbued with a frenzied zeal. Afterward he was angered by his own secret conviction that Stephen had been honored by God at the very time when he was dishonored by men. Saul continued to persecute the church of God, hunting them down, seizing them in their houses, and delivering them up to the priests and rulers for imprisonment and death. His zeal in carrying forward this persecution brought terror to the Christians at Jerusalem. The Roman authorities made no special effort to stay the cruel work and secretly aided the Jews in order to conciliate them and to secure their favor.

After the death of Stephen, Saul was elected a member of the Sanhedrin council in consideration of the part he had acted on that occasion. For a time he was a mighty instrument in the hands of Satan to carry out his rebellion against the Son of God. But soon this relentless persecutor was to be employed in building up the church that he was now tearing down. A Mightier than Satan had chosen Saul to take the place of the martyred Stephen, to preach and suffer for His name, and to spread far and wide the tidings of salvation through His blood.

11

The Gospel in Samaria

This chapter is based on Acts 8

After the death of Stephen there arose against the believers in Jerusalem a persecution so relentless that "they were all scattered abroad throughout the regions of Judea and Samaria." Saul "made havoc of the church, entering into every house, and haling men and women committed them to prison." Of his zeal in this cruel work he said at a later date: "I verily thought with myself, that I ought to do many things contrary to the name of Jesus of Nazareth. Which thing I also did in Jerusalem: and many of the saints did I shut up in prison. . . . And I punished them oft in every synagogue, and compelled them to blaspheme; and being exceedingly mad against them, I persecuted them even unto strange cities." That Stephen was not the only one who suffered death may be seen from Saul's own words, "And when they were put to death, I gave my voice against them." Acts 26:9-11.

At this time of peril Nicodemus came forward in fearless avowal of his faith in the crucified Saviour. Nicodemus was a member of the Sanhedrin and with others had been stirred by the teaching of Jesus. As he had witnessed Christ's wonderful works, the conviction had fastened itself upon his mind that this was the Sent of God. Too proud openly to acknowledge himself in sympathy with the Galilean Teacher, he had sought a secret interview. In this interview Jesus had unfolded to him the plan of salvation and His mission to the world, yet still Nicodemus had hesitated. He hid the truth in his heart, and for three years there was little apparent fruit. But while Nicodemus had not publicly acknowledged Christ, he had in the Sanhedrin council repeatedly thwarted the schemes of the priests to destroy Him. When at last Christ had been lifted up on the cross, Nicodemus remembered the words that He had spoken to him in the night interview on the Mount of Olives, "As Moses lifted up the serpent in the wilderness, even so must the Son of man be lifted up" (John 3:14); and he saw in Jesus the world's Redeemer.

With Joseph of Arimathea, Nicodemus had borne the expense of the burial of Jesus. The disciples had been afraid to show themselves openly as Christ's followers, but Nicodemus and

Joseph had come boldly to their aid. The help of these rich and honored men was greatly needed in that hour of darkness. They had been able to do for their dead Master what it would have been impossible for the poor disciples to do; and their wealth and influence had protected them, in a great measure, from the malice of the priests and rulers.

Now, when the Jews were trying to destroy the infant church, Nicodemus came forward in its defense. No longer cautious and questioning, he encouraged the faith of the disciples and used his wealth in helping to sustain the church at Jerusalem and in advancing the work of the gospel. Those who in other days had paid him reverence, now scorned and persecuted him, and he became poor in this world's goods; yet he faltered not in the defense of his faith.

The persecution that came upon the church in Jerusalem resulted in giving a great impetus to the work of the gospel. Success had attended the ministry of the word in that place, and there was danger that the disciples would linger there too long, unmindful of the Saviour's commission to go to all the world. Forgetting that strength to resist evil is best gained by aggressive service, they began to think that they had no work so important as that of shielding the church in Jerusalem from the attacks of the enemy. Instead of educating the new converts to carry the gospel to those who had not heard it, they were in danger of taking a course that would lead all to be satisfied with what had been accomplished. To scatter His representatives abroad, where they could work for others, God permitted persecution to come upon them. Driven from Jerusalem, the believers "went everywhere preaching the word."

Among those to whom the Saviour had given the commission, "Go ye therefore, and teach all nations" (Matthew 28:19), were many from the humbler walks of life—men and women who had learned to love their Lord and who had determined to follow His example of unselfish service. To these lowly ones, as well as to the disciples who had been with the Saviour during His earthly ministry, had been given a precious trust. They were to carry to the world the glad tidings of salvation through Christ.

When they were scattered by persecution they went forth filled with missionary zeal. They realized the responsibility of their mission. They knew that they held in their hands the bread of life for a famishing world; and they were constrained by the love of Christ to break this bread to all who were in need. The Lord wrought through them. Wherever they went, the sick were healed and the poor had the gospel preached unto them.

Philip, one of the seven deacons, was among those driven from Jerusalem. He "went down to the city of Samaria, and preached Christ unto them. And the people with one accord gave heed unto those things which Philip spake, hearing and seeing the miracles which he did. For unclean spirits . . . came out of many that were possessed with them: and many taken with palsies, and that were lame, were healed. And there was great joy in that city."

Christ's message to the Samaritan woman with whom He had talked at Jacob's well had borne fruit. After listening to His words, the woman had gone to the men of the city, saying, "Come, see a man, which told me all things that ever I did: is not this the Christ? They went with her, heard Jesus, and believed on Him. Anxious to hear more, they begged Him to remain. For two days He stayed with them, "and many more believed because of His own word." John 4:29, 41.

And when His disciples were driven from Jerusalem, some found in Samaria a safe asylum. The Samaritans welcomed these messengers of the gospel, and the Jewish converts gathered a precious harvest from among those who had once been their bitterest enemies.

Philip's work in Samaria was marked with great success, and, thus encouraged, he sent to Jerusalem for help. The apostles now perceived more fully the meaning of the words of Christ, "Ye shall be witnesses unto Me both in Jerusalem, and in all Judea, and in Samaria, and unto the uttermost part of the earth." Acts 1:8.

While Philip was still in Samaria, he was directed by a heavenly messenger to "go toward the south unto the way that goeth down from Jerusalem unto Gaza. . . . And he arose and went." He did not question the call, nor did he hesitate to obey; for he had learned the lesson of conformity to God's will.

"And, behold, a man of Ethiopia, a eunuch of great authority under Candace queen of the Ethiopians, who had the charge of all her treasure, and had come to Jerusalem for to worship, was returning, and sitting in his chariot read Esaias the prophet." This Ethiopian was a man of good standing and of wide influence. God saw that when converted he would give others the light he had received and would exert a strong influence in favor of the gospel. Angels of God were attending this seeker for light, and he was being drawn to the Saviour. By the ministration of the Holy Spirit the Lord brought him into touch with one who could lead him to the light.

Philip was directed to go to the Ethiopian and explain to him the prophecy that he was reading. "Go near," the Spirit said, "and join thyself to this chariot." As Philip drew near, he asked the eunuch, "Understandest thou what thou readest? And he said, How can I, except some man should guide me? And he desired Philip that he would come up and sit with him." The scripture that he was reading was the prophecy of Isaiah relating to Christ: "He was led as a sheep to the slaughter; and like a lamb dumb before his shearer, so opened He not His mouth: in His humiliation His judgment was taken away: and who shall declare His generation? for His life is taken from the earth."

"Of whom speaketh the prophet this?" the eunuch asked, "of himself, or of some other man?" Then Philip opened to him the great truth of redemption. Beginning at the same scripture, he "preached unto him Jesus."

The man's heart thrilled with interest as the Scriptures were explained to him; and when the disciple had finished, he was ready to accept the light given. He did not make his high worldly position an excuse for refusing the gospel. "As they went on their way, they came unto a certain water: and the eunuch said, See, here is water; what doth hinder me to be baptized? And Philip said, If thou believest with all thine heart, thou mayest. And he answered and said, I believe that Jesus Christ is the Son of God. And he commanded the chariot to stand still: and they went down both into the water, both Philip and the eunuch; and he baptized him.

"And when they were come up out of the water, the Spirit of the Lord caught away Philip, that the eunuch saw him no more: and he went on his way rejoicing. But Philip was found at Azotus: and passing through he preached in all the cities, till he came to Caesarea."

This Ethiopian represented a large class who need to be taught by such missionaries as Philip—men who will hear the voice of God and go where He sends them. There are many who are reading the Scriptures who cannot understand their true import. All over the world men and women are looking wistfully to heaven. Prayers and tears and inquiries go up from souls longing for light, for grace, for the Holy Spirit. Many are on the verge of the kingdom, waiting only to be gathered in.

An angel guided Philip to the one who was seeking for light and who was ready to receive the gospel, and today angels will guide the footsteps of those workers who will allow the Holy Spirit to sanctify their tongues and refine and ennoble their hearts. The angel sent to Philip could himself have done the work for the Ethiopian, but this is not God's way of working. It is His plan that men are to work for their fellow men.

In the trust given to the first disciples, believers in every age have shared. Everyone who has received the gospel has been given sacred truth to impart to the world. God's faithful people have always been aggressive missionaries, consecrating their resources to the honor of His name and wisely using their talents in His service.

The unselfish labor of Christians in the past should be to us an object lesson and an inspiration. The members of God's church are to be zealous of good works, separating from worldly ambition and walking in the footsteps of Him who went about doing good. With hearts filled with sympathy and compassion, they are to minister to those in need of help, bringing to sinners a knowledge of the Saviour's love. Such work calls for laborious effort, but it brings a rich reward. Those who engage in it with sincerity of purpose will see souls won to the Saviour, for the influence that attends the practical carrying out of the divine commission is irresistible.

Not upon the ordained minister only rests the responsibility of going forth to fulfill this commission. Everyone who has received Christ is called to work for the salvation of his fellow men. "The Spirit and the bride say, Come. And let him that heareth say, Come." Revelation 22:17. The charge to give this invitation includes the entire church. Everyone who has heard the invitation is to echo the message from hill and valley, saying, "Come."

It is fatal mistake to suppose that the work of soul-saving depends alone upon the ministry. The humble, consecrated believer upon whom the Master of the vineyard places a burden for souls is to be given encouragement by the men upon whom the Lord has laid larger responsibilities. Those who stand as leaders in the church of God are to realize that the Saviour's commission is given to all who believe in His name. God will send forth into His vineyard many who have not been dedicated to the ministry by the laying on of hands.

Hundreds, yea, thousands, who have heard the message of salvation are still idlers in the market place, when they might be engaged in some line of active service. To these Christ is saying, "Why stand ye here all the day idle?" and He adds, "Go ye also into the vineyard." Matthew 20:6, 7. Why is it that many more do not respond to the call? Is it because they think themselves excused in that they do not stand in the pulpit? Let them understand that there is a large work to be done outside the pulpit by thousands of consecrated lay members.

Long has God waited for the spirit of service to take possession of the whole church so that everyone shall be working for Him according to his ability. When the members of the church of God do their appointed work in the needy fields at home and abroad, in fulfillment of the gospel commission, the whole world will soon be warned and the Lord Jesus will return to this earth with power and great glory. "This gospel of the kingdom shall be preached in all the world for a witness unto all nations; and then shall the end come." Matthew 24:14.

12

From Persecutor to Disciple

This chapter is based on Acts 9:1-18

Prominent among the Jewish leaders who became thoroughly aroused by the success attending the proclamation of the gospel, was Saul of Tarsus. A Roman citizen by birth, Saul was nevertheless a Jew by descent and had been educated in Jerusalem by the most eminent of the rabbis. "Of the stock of Israel, of the tribe of Benjamin," Saul was "a Hebrew of the Hebrews; as touching the law, a Pharisee; concerning zeal, persecuting the church; touching the righteousness which is in the law, blameless." Philippians 3:5, 6. He was regarded by the rabbis as a young man of great promise, and high hopes were cherished concerning him as an able and zealous defender of the ancient faith. His elevation to membership in the Sanhedrin council placed him in a position of power.

Saul had taken a prominent part in the trial and conviction of Stephen, and the striking evidences of God's presence with the martyr had led Saul to doubt the righteousness of the cause he had espoused against the followers of Jesus. His mind was deeply stirred. In his perplexity he appealed to those in whose wisdom and judgment he had full confidence. The arguments of the priests and rulers finally convinced him that Stephen was a blasphemer, that the Christ whom the martyred disciple had preached was an impostor, and that those ministering in holy office must be right.

Not without severe trial did Saul come to this conclusion. But in the end his education and prejudices, his respect for his former teachers, and his pride of popularity braced him to rebel against the voice of conscience and the grace of God. And having fully decided that the priests and scribes were right, Saul became very bitter in his opposition to the doctrines taught by the disciples of Jesus. His activity in causing holy men and women to be dragged before tribunals, where some were condemned to imprisonment and some even to death, solely because of their faith in Jesus, brought sadness and gloom to the newly organized church, and caused many to seek safety in flight.

Those who were driven from Jerusalem by this persecution

"went everywhere preaching the word." Acts 8:4. Among the cities to which they went was Damascus, where the new faith gained many converts.

The priests and rulers had hoped that by vigilant effort and stern persecution the heresy might be suppressed. Now they felt that they must carry forward in other places the decided measures taken in Jerusalem against the new teaching. For the special work that they desired to have done at Damascus, Saul offered his services. "Breathing out threatenings and slaughter against the disciples of the Lord," he "went unto the high priest, and desired of him letters to Damascus to the synagogues, that if he found any of this way, whether they were men or women, he might bring them bound unto Jerusalem." Thus "with authority and commission from the chief priests" (Acts 26:12), Saul of Tarsus, in the strength and vigor of manhood, and fired with mistaken zeal, set out on that memorable journey, the strange occurrences of which were to change the whole current of his life.

On the last day of the journey, "at midday," as the weary travelers neared Damascus, they came within full view of broad stretches of fertile lands, beautiful gardens, and fruitful orchards, watered by cool streams from the surrounding mountains. After the long journey over desolate wastes such scenes were refreshing indeed. While Saul, with his companions, gazed with admiration on the fruitful plain and the fair city below, "suddenly," as he afterward declared, there shone "round about me and them which journeyed with me" "a light from heaven, above the brightness of the sun" (Acts 26:13), too glorious for mortal eyes to bear. Blinded and bewildered, Saul fell prostrate to the ground.

While the light continued to shine round about them, Saul heard, "a voice speaking . . . in the Hebrew tongue" (Acts 26:14), "saying unto him, Saul, Saul, why persecutest thou Me? And he said, Who art Thou, Lord? And the Lord said, I am Jesus whom thou persecutest: it is hard for thee to kick against the pricks."

Filled with fear, and almost blinded by the intensity of the light, the companions of Saul heard a voice, but saw no man. But Saul understood the words that were spoken, and to him was clearly revealed the One who spoke—even the Son of God. In the glorious Being who stood before him he saw the Crucified One. Upon the soul of the stricken Jew the image of the Saviour's countenance was imprinted forever. The words spoken struck home to his heart with appalling force. Into the darkened chambers of his mind there poured a flood of light, revealing the ignorance and error of his former life and his present need of the enlightenment of the Holy Spirit.

Saul now saw that in persecuting the followers of Jesus he had in reality been doing the work of Satan. He saw that his convictions of right and of his own duty had been based largely on his implicit confidence in the priests and rulers. He had believed them when they told him that the story of the resurrection was an artful fabrication of the disciples. Now that Jesus Himself stood revealed, Saul was convinced of the truthfulness of the claims made by the disciples.

In that hour of heavenly illumination Saul's mind acted with remarkable rapidity. The prophetic records of Holy Writ were opened to his understanding. He saw that the rejection of Jesus by the Jews, His crucifixion, resurrection, and ascension, had been foretold by the prophets and proved Him to be the promised Messiah. Stephen's sermon at the time of his martyrdom was brought forcibly to Saul's mind, and he realized that the martyr had indeed beheld "the glory of God" when he said, "Behold, I see the heavens opened, and the Son of man standing on the right hand of God." Acts 7:55, 56. The priests had pronounced these words blasphemy, but Saul now knew them to be truth.

What a revelation was all this to the persecutor! Now Saul knew for a certainty that the promised Messiah had come to this earth as Jesus of Nazareth and that He had been rejected and crucified by those whom He came to save. He knew also that the Saviour had risen in triumph from the tomb and had ascended into the heavens. In that moment of divine revelation Saul remembered with terror that Stephen, who had borne witness of a crucified and risen Saviour, had been sacrificed by his consent, and that later, through his instrumentality, many other worthy followers of Jesus had met their death by cruel persecution.

The Saviour had spoken to Saul through Stephen, whose clear reasoning could not be controverted. The learned Jew had seen the face of the martyr reflecting the light of Christ's glory—appearing as if "it had been the face of an angel." Acts 6:15. He had witnessed Stephen's forbearance toward his enemies and his forgiveness of them. He had also witnessed the fortitude and cheerful resignation of many whom he had caused to be tormented and afflicted. He had seen some yield up even their lives with rejoicing for the sake of their faith.

All these things had appealed loudly to Saul and at times had thrust upon his mind an almost overwhelming conviction that Jesus was the promised Messiah. At such times he had struggled for entire nights against this conviction, and always he had ended the matter by avowing his belief that Jesus was not the Messiah and that His followers were deluded fanatics.

Now Christ had spoken to Saul with His own voice, saying, "Saul, Saul, why persecutest thou Me?" And the question, "Who art Thou, Lord?" was answered by the same voice, "I am Jesus whom thou persecutest." Christ here identifies Himself with His people. In persecuting the followers of Jesus, Saul had struck directly against the Lord of heaven. In falsely accusing and testifying against them, he had falsely accused and testified against the Saviour of the world.

No doubt entered the mind of Saul that the One who spoke to him was Jesus of Nazareth, the long-looked-for Messiah, the Consolation and Redeemer of Israel. "Trembling and astonished," he inquired, "Lord, what wilt Thou have me to do? And the Lord said unto him, Arise, and go into the city, and it shall be told thee what thou must do."

When the glory was withdrawn, and Saul arose from the ground, he found himself totally deprived of sight. The brightness of Christ's glory had been too intense for his mortal eyes; and when it was removed, the blackness of night settled upon his vision. He believed that this blindness was a punishment from God for his cruel persecution of the followers of Jesus. In terrible darkness he groped about, and his companions, in fear and amazement, "led him by the hand, and brought him into Damascus."

On the morning of that eventful day, Saul had neared Damascus with feelings of self-satisfaction because of the confidence that had been placed in him by the chief priest. To him had been entrusted grave responsibilities. He was commissioned to further the interests of the Jewish religion by checking, if possible, the spread of the new faith in Damascus. He had determined that his mission should be crowned with success and had looked forward with eager anticipation to the experiences that he expected were before him.

But how unlike his anticipations was his entrance into the city? Stricken with blindness, helpless, tortured by remorse, knowing not what further judgment might be in store for him, he sought out the home of the disciple Judas, where, in solitude, he had ample opportunity for reflection and prayer.

For three days Saul was "without sight, and neither did eat nor drink." These days of soul agony were to him as years. Again and again he recalled, with anguish of spirit, the part he had taken in the martyrdom of Stephen. With horror he thought of his guilt in allowing himself to be controlled by the malice and prejudice of the priests and rulers, even when the face of Stephen had been lighted up with the radiance of heaven. In sadness and brokenness of spirit he recounted the many times he had closed his eyes and ears against the most striking evidences and had relentlessly urged on the persecution of the believers in Jesus of Nazareth.

These days of close self-examination and of heart humiliation were spent in lonely seclusion. The believers, having been given warning of the purpose of Saul in coming to Damascus, feared that he might be acting a part, in order the more readily to deceive them; and they held themselves aloof, refusing him their sympathy. He had no desire to appeal to the unconverted Jews, with whom he had planned to unite in persecuting the believers; for he knew that they would not even listen to his story. Thus he seemed to be shut away from all human sympathy. His only hope of help was in a merciful God, and to Him he appealed in brokenness of heart.

During the long hours when Saul was shut in with God alone, he recalled many of the passages of Scripture referring to the first advent of Christ. Carefully he traced down the prophecies, with a memory sharpened by the conviction that had taken possession of his mind. As he reflected on the meaning of these prophecies he was astonished at his former blindness of understanding and at the blindness of the Jews in general, which had led to the rejection of Jesus as the promised Messiah. To his enlightened vision all now seemed plain. He knew that his former prejudice and unbelief had clouded his spiritual perception and had prevented him from discerning in Jesus of Nazareth the Messiah of prophecy.

As Saul yielded himself fully to the convicting power of the Holy Spirit, he saw the mistakes of his life and recognized the far-reaching claims of the law of God. He who had been a proud Pharisee, confident that he was justified by his good works, now bowed before God with the humility and simplicity of a little child, confessing his own unworthiness and pleading the merits of a crucified and risen Saviour. Saul longed to come into full harmony and communion with the Father and the Son; and in the intensity of his desire for pardon and acceptance he offered up fervent supplications to the throne of grace.

The prayers of the penitent Pharisee were not in vain. The inmost thoughts and emotions of his heart were transformed by divine grave; and his nobler faculties were brought into harmony with the eternal purposes of God. Christ and His righteousness became to Saul more than the whole world.

The conversion of Saul is a striking evidence of the miraculous power of the Holy Spirit to convict men of sin. He had verily believed that Jesus of Nazareth had disregarded the law of God and had taught His disciples that it was of no effect. But after his conversion, Saul recognized Jesus as the one who had come into the world for the express purpose of vindicating His Father's law. He was convinced that Jesus was the originator of the entire Jewish system of sacrifices. He saw that at the crucifixion type had met antitype, that Jesus had fulfilled the Old Testament prophecies concerning the Redeemer of Israel.

In the record of the conversion of Saul important principles are given us, which we should ever bear in mind. Saul was brought directly into the presence of Christ. He was one whom Christ intended for a most important work, one who was to be a "chosen vessel" unto Him; yet the Lord did not at once tell him of the work that had been assigned him. He arrested him in his course and convicted him of sin; but when Saul asked, "What wilt Thou have me to do?" the Saviour placed the inquiring Jew in connection with His church, there to obtain a knowledge of God's will concerning him.

The marvelous light that illumined the darkness of Saul was the work of the Lord; but there was also a work that was to be done for him by the disciples. Christ had performed the work of revelation and conviction; and now the penitent was in a condition to learn from those whom God had ordained to teach His truth.

While Saul in solitude at the house of Judas continued in prayer and supplication, the Lord appeared in vision to "a certain disciple at Damascus, named Ananias," telling him that Saul of Tarsus was praying and in need of help. "Arise, and go into the street which is called Straight," the heavenly messenger said, "and inquire in the house of Judas for one called Saul, of Tarsus: for, behold, he prayeth, and hath seen in a vision a man named Ananias coming in, and putting his hand on him, that he might receive his sight."

Ananias could scarcely credit the words of the angel; for the reports of Saul's bitter persecution of the saints at Jerusalem had spread far and wide. He presumed to expostulate: "Lord, I have heard by many of this man, how much evil he hath done to Thy saints at Jerusalem: and here he hath authority from the chief priests to bind all that call on Thy name." But the command was imperative: "Go thy way: for he is a chosen vessel unto Me, to bear My name before the Gentiles, and kings, and the children of Israel."

Obedient to the direction of the angel, Ananias sought out the man who had but recently breathed out threatenings against all who believed on the name of Jesus; and putting his hands on the head of the penitent sufferer, he said, "Brother Saul, the Lord, even Jesus, that appeared unto thee in the way as thou camest, hath sent me, that thou mightest receive thy sight, and be filled with the Holy Ghost.

"And immediately there fell from his eyes as it had been scales: and he received sight forthwith, and arose, and was baptized."

Thus Jesus gave sanction to the authority of His organized church and placed Saul in connection with His appointed agencies on earth. Christ had now a church as His representative on earth, and to it belonged the work of directing the repentant sinner in the way of life.

Many have an idea that they are responsible to Christ alone for their light and experience, independent of His recognized followers on earth. Jesus is the friend of sinners, and His heart is touched with their woe. He has all power, both in heaven and on earth; but He respects the means that He has ordained for the enlightenment and salvation of men; He directs sinners to the church, which He has made a channel of light to the world.

When, in the midst of his blind error and prejudice, Saul was given a revelation of the Christ whom he was persecuting, he was placed in direct communication with the church, which is the light of the world. In this case Ananias represents Christ, and also represents Christ's ministers upon the earth, who are appointed to act in His stead. In Christ's stead Ananias touches the eyes of Saul, that they may receive sight. In Christ's stead he places his hands upon him, and, as he prays in Christ's name, Saul receives the Holy Ghost. All is done in the name and by the authority of Christ. Christ is the fountain; the church is the channel of communication.

13

Days of Preparation

This chapter is based on Acts 9:19-30

After his baptism, Paul broke his fast and remained "certain days with the disciples which were at Damascus. And straightway he preached Christ in the synagogues, that He is the Son of God." Boldly he declared Jesus of Nazareth to be the long-looked-for Messiah, who "died for our sins according to the Scriptures; . . . was buried, and . . . rose again the third day," after which He was seen by the Twelve and by others. "And last of all," Paul added, "He was seen of me also, as of one born out of due time." I Corinthians 15:3, 4, 8. His arguments from prophecy were so conclusive, and his efforts were so manifestly attended by the power of God, that the Jews were confounded and unable to answer him.

The news of Paul's conversion had come to the Jews as a great surprise. He who had journeyed to Damascus "with authority and commission from the chief priests" (Acts 26:12) to apprehend and persecute the believers was now preaching the gospel of a crucified and risen Saviour, strengthening the hands of those who were already its disciples, and continually bringing in new converts to the faith he had once so bitterly opposed.

Paul had formerly been known as a zealous defender of the Jewish religion and an untiring persecutor of the followers of Jesus. Courageous, independent, persevering, his talents and training would have enabled him to serve in almost any capacity. He could reason with extraordinary clearness, and by his withering sarcasm could place an opponent in no enviable light. And now the Jews saw this young man of unusual promise united with those whom he formerly persecuted, and fearlessly preaching in the name of Jesus.

A general slain in battle is lost to his army, but his death gives no additional strength to the enemy. But when a man of prominence joins the opposing force, not only are his services lost, but those to whom he joins himself gain a decided advantage. Saul of Tarsus, on his way to Damascus, might easily have been struck dead by the Lord, and much strength would have been withdrawn from the persecuting power. But God in His providence not only spared Saul's life, but converted him, thus transferring a champion from the side of the enemy to the side of Christ. An eloquent speaker and a severe critic, Paul, with his stern purpose and undaunted courage, possessed the very qualifications needed in the early church.

As Paul preached Christ in Damascus, all who heard him were amazed and said, "Is not this he that destroyed them which called on this name in Jerusalem, and came hither for that intent, that he might bring them bound unto the chief priests?" Paul declared that his change of faith had not been prompted by impulse or fanaticism, but had been brought about by overwhelming evidence. In his presentation of the gospel he sought to make plain the prophecies relating to the first advent of Christ. He showed conclusively that these prophecies had been literally fulfilled in Jesus of Nazareth. The foundation of his faith was the sure word of prophecy.

As Paul continued to appeal to his astonished hearers to "repent and turn to God, and do works meet for repentance" (Acts 26:20), he "increased the more in strength, and confounded the Jews which dwelt at Damascus, proving that this is very Christ." But many hardened their hearts, refusing to respond to his message, and soon their astonishment at his conversion was changed into intense hatred like that which they had shown toward Jesus.

The opposition grew so fierce that Paul was not allowed to continue his labors at Damascus. A messenger from heaven bade him leave for a time, and he "went into Arabia" (Galatians 1:17), where he found a safe retreat.

Here, in the solitude of the desert, Paul had ample opportunity for quiet study and meditation. He calmly reviewed his past experience and made sure work of repentance. He sought God with all his heart, resting not until he knew for a certainty that his repentance was accepted and his sin pardoned. He longed for the assurance that Jesus would be with him in his coming ministry. He emptied his soul of the prejudices and traditions that had hitherto shaped his life, and received instruction from the Source of truth. Jesus communed with him and established him in the faith, bestowing upon him a rich measure of wisdom and grace.

When the mind of man is brought into communion with the mind of God, the finite with the Infinite, the effect on body and mind and soul is beyond estimate. In such communion is found the highest education. It is God's own method of development. "Acquaint now thyself with Him" (Job 22:21), is His message to mankind.

The solemn charge that had been given Paul on the occasion of his interview with Ananias, rested with increasing weight upon his heart. When, in response to the word, "Brother Saul, receive thy sight," Paul had for the first time looked upon the face of this devout man, Ananias under the inspiration of the Holy Spirit said to him: "The God of our fathers hath chosen thee, that thou shouldest know His will, and see that Just One, and shouldest hear the voice of His mouth. For thou shalt be His witness unto all men of what thou hast seen and heard. And now why tarriest thou? arise, and be baptized, and wash away thy sins, calling on the name of the Lord." Acts 22:13-16.

These words were in harmony with the words of Jesus Himself, who, when He arrested Saul on the journey to Damascus, declared: "I have appeared unto thee for this purpose, to make thee a minister and a witness both of these things which thou hast seen, and of those things in the which I will appear unto thee; delivering thee from the people, and from the Gentiles, unto whom now I send thee, to open their eyes, and to turn them from darkness to light, and from the power of Satan unto God, that they may receive forgiveness of sins, and inheritance among them which are sanctified by faith that is in Me." Acts 26:16-18.

As he pondered these things in his heart, Paul understood more and more clearly the meaning of his call "to be an apostle of Jesus Christ through the will of God." 1 Corinthians 1:1. His call had come, "not of men, neither by man, but by Jesus Christ, and God the Father." Galatians 1:1. The greatness of the work before him led him to give much study to the Holy Scriptures, in order that he might preach the gospel "not with wisdom of words, lest the cross of Christ should be made of none effect," "but in demonstration of the Spirit and of power," that the faith of all who heard "should not stand in the wisdom of men, but in the power of God." 1 Corinthians 1:17; 2:4, 5.

As Paul searched the Scriptures, he learned that throughout the ages "not many wise men after the flesh, not many mighty, not many noble, are called: but God hath chosen the foolish things of the world to confound the wise; and God hath chosen the weak things of the world to confound the things which are mighty; and base things of the world, and things which are despised, hath God chosen, yea, and things which are not, to bring to nought things that are: that no flesh should glory in His presence." 1 Corinthians 1:26-29. And so, viewing the wisdom of the world in the light of the cross, Paul "determined not to know anything, . . . save Jesus Christ, and Him crucified." 1 Corinthians 2:2.

Throughout his later ministry, Paul never lost sight of the Source of his wisdom and strength. Hear him, years afterward, still declaring, "For to me to live is Christ." Philippians 1:21. And again: "I count all things but loss for the excellency of the knowledge of Christ Jesus my Lord: for whom I have suffered the loss of all things, . . . that I may win Christ, and be found in Him, not having mine own righteousness, which is of the law, but that which is through the faith of Christ, the righteousness which is of God by faith: that I may know Him, and the power of His resurrection, and the fellowship of His sufferings." Philippians 3:8-10.

From Arabia Paul "returned again unto Damascus" (Galatians 1:17), and "preached boldly . . . in the name of Jesus." Unable to withstand the wisdom of his arguments, "the Jews took counsel to kill him." The gates of the city were diligently guarded day and night to cut off his escape. This crisis led the disciples to seek God earnestly, and finally they "took him by night, and let him down through the wall, lowering him in a basket." Acts 9:25, R.V.

After his escape from Damascus, Paul went to Jerusalem, about three years having passed since his conversion. His chief object in making this visit, as he himself declared afterward, was "to see Peter." Galatians 1:18. Upon arriving in the city where he had once been well known as "Saul the persecutor," "he assayed to join himself to the disciples: but they were all afraid of him, and believed not that he was a disciple." It was difficult for them to believe that so bigoted a Pharisee, and one who had done so much to destroy the church, could become a sincere follower of Jesus. "But Barnabas took him, and brought him to the apostles, and declared unto them how he had seen the Lord in the way, and that He had spoken to him, and how he had preached boldly at Damascus in the name of Jesus."

Upon hearing this, the disciples received him as one of their number. Soon they had abundant evidence as to the genuineness of his Christian experience. The future apostle to the Gentiles was now in the city where many of his former associates lived, and to these Jewish leaders he longed to make plain the prophecies concerning the Messiah, which had been fulfilled by the advent of the Saviour. Paul felt sure that these teachers in Israel, with whom he had once been so well acquainted, were as sincere and honest as he had been. But he had miscalculated the spirit of his Jewish brethren, and in the hope of their speedy conversion he was doomed to bitter disappointment. Although "he spake boldly in the name of the Lord Jesus, and disputed against the Grecians," those who stood at the head of the Jewish church refused to believe, but "went about to slay him." Sorrow filled his heart. He would willingly have yielded up his life if by that means he might bring some to a knowledge of the truth. With shame he thought of the active part he had taken in the martyrdom of Stephen, and now in his anxiety to wipe out the stain resting upon one so falsely accused, he sought to vindicate the truth for which Stephen had given his life.

Burdened in behalf of those who refused to believe, Paul was praying in the temple, as he himself afterward testified, when he fell into a trance; whereupon a heavenly messenger appeared before him and said, "Make haste, and get thee quickly out of Jerusalem: for they will not receive thy testimony concerning Me." Acts 22:18.

Paul was inclined to remain at Jerusalem, where he could face the opposition. To him it seemed an act of cowardice to flee, if by remaining he might be able to convince some of the obstinate Jews of the truth of the gospel message, even if to remain should cost him his life. And so he answered, "Lord, they know that I imprisoned and beat in every synagogue them that believed on Thee: and when the blood of Thy martyr Stephen was shed, I was also standing by, and consenting unto his death, and kept the raiment of them that slew him." But it was not in harmony with the purpose of God that His servant should needlessly expose his life; and the heavenly messenger replied, "Depart: for I will send thee far hence unto the Gentiles." Acts 22:19-21.

Upon learning of this vision, the brethren hastened Paul's secret escape from Jerusalem, for fear of his assassination. "They brought him down to Caesarea, and sent him forth to Tarsus." The departure of Paul suspended for a time the violent opposition of the Jews, and the church had a period of rest, in which many were added to the number of believers.

14

A Seeker for Truth

This chapter is based on Acts 9:19-30

In the course of his ministry the apostle Peter visited the believers at Lydda. Here he healed Aeneas, who for eight years had been confined to his bed with palsy. "Aeneas, Jesus Christ maketh thee whole," the apostle said; "arise, and make thy bed." "He arose immediately. And all that dwelt at Lydda and Saron saw him, and turned to the Lord."

At Joppa, which was near Lydda, there lived a woman named Dorcas, whose good deeds had made her greatly beloved. She was a worthy disciple of Jesus, and her life was filled with acts of kindness. She knew who needed comfortable clothing and who needed sympathy, and she freely ministered to the poor and the sorrowful. Her skillful fingers were more active than her tongue.

"And it came to pass in those days, that she was sick, and died." The church in Joppa realized their loss, and hearing that Peter was at Lydda, the believers sent messengers to him, "desiring him that he would not delay to come to them. Then Peter arose and went with them. When he was come, they brought him into the upper chamber: and all the widows stood by him weeping, and showing the coats and garments which Dorcas made, while she was with them." In view of the life of service that Dorcas had lived, it is little wonder that they mourned, that warm teardrops fell upon the inanimate clay.

The apostle's heart was touched with sympathy as he beheld their sorrow. Then, directing that the weeping friends be sent from the room, he kneeled down and prayed fervently to God to restore Dorcas to life and health. Turning to the body, he said, "Tabitha, arise. And she opened her eyes: and when she saw Peter, she sat up." Dorcas had been of great service to the church, and God saw fit to bring her back from the land of the enemy, that her skill and energy might still be a blessing to others, and also that by this manifestation of His power the cause of Christ might be strengthened.

It was while Peter was still at Joppa that he was called by God to take the gospel to Cornelius, in Caesarea.

Cornelius was a Roman centurion. He was a man of wealth and noble birth, and his position was one of trust and honor. A heathen by birth, training, and education, through contact with the Jews he had gained a knowledge of God, and he worshiped Him with a true heart, showing the sincerity of his faith by compassion to the poor. He was known far and near for his beneficence, and his righteous life made him of good repute among both Jews and Gentiles. His influence was a blessing to all with whom he came in contact. The inspired record describes him as "a devout man, and one that feared God with all his house, which gave much alms to the people, and prayed to God alway."

Believing in God as the Creator of heaven and earth, Cornelius revered Him, acknowledged His authority, and sought His counsel in all the affairs of life. He was faithful to Jehovah in his home life and in his official duties. He had erected the altar of God in his home, for he dared not attempt to carry out his plans or to bear his responsibilities without the help of God.

Though Cornelius believed the prophecies and was looking for the Messiah to come, he had not a knowledge of the gospel as revealed in the life and death of Christ. He was not a member of the Jewish church and would have been looked upon by the rabbis as a heathen and unclean. But the same Holy Watcher who said of Abraham, "I know him," knew Cornelius also, and sent a message direct from heaven to him.

The angel appeared to Cornelius while he was at prayer. As the centurion heard himself addressed by name, he was afraid, yet he knew that the messenger had come from God, and he said, "What is it, Lord?" The angel answered, "Thy prayers and thine alms are come up for a memorial before God. And now send men to Joppa, and call for one Simon, whose surname is Peter: he lodgeth with one Simon a tanner, whose house is by the seaside."

The explicitness of these directions, in which was named even the occupation of the man with whom Peter was staying, shows that Heaven is acquainted with the history and business of men in every station of life. God is familiar with the experience and work of the humble laborer, as well as with that of the king upon his throne.

"Send men to Joppa, and call for one Simon." Thus God gave evidence of His regard for the gospel ministry and for His organized church. The angel was not commissioned to tell Cornelius the story of the cross. A man subject, even as the centurion himself, to human frailties and temptations, was to be the one to tell him of the crucified and risen Saviour.

As His representatives among men, God does not choose angels who have never fallen, but human beings, men of like passions with those they seek to save. Christ took humanity that He might reach humanity. A divine-human Saviour was needed to bring salvation to the world. And to men and women has been committed the sacred trust of making known "the unsearchable riches of Christ." Ephesians 3:8.

In His wisdom the Lord brings those who are seeking for truth into touch with fellow beings who know the truth. It is the plan of Heaven that those who have received light shall impart it to those in darkness. Humanity, drawing its efficiency from the great Source of wisdom, is made the instrumentality, the working agency, through which the gospel exercises its transforming power on mind and heart.

Cornelius was gladly obedient to the vision. When the angel had gone, the centurion "called two of his household servants, and a devout soldier of them that waited on him continually; and when he had declared all these things unto them, he sent them to Joppa."

The angel, after his interview with Cornelius, went to Peter, in Joppa. At the time, Peter was praying upon the housetop of his lodging, and we read that he "became very hungry, and would have eaten: but while they made ready, he fell into a trance." It was not for physical food alone that Peter hungered. As from the housetop he viewed the city of Joppa and the surrounding country be hungered for the salvation of his countrymen. He had an intense desire to point out to them from the Scriptures the prophecies relating to the sufferings and death of Christ.

In the vision Peter "saw heaven opened, and a certain vessel descending unto them, as it had been a great sheet knit at the four corners, and let down to the earth: wherein were all manner of four-footed beasts of the earth, and wild beasts, and creeping things, and fowls of the air. And there came a voice to him, Rise, Peter; kill, and eat. But Peter said, Not so, Lord; for I have never eaten anything that is common or unclean. And the voice spake unto him again the second time, What God hath cleansed, that call not thou common. This was done thrice: and the vessel was received up again into heaven."

This vision conveyed to Peter both reproof and instruction. It revealed to him the purpose of God—that by the death of Christ the Gentiles should be made fellow heirs with the Jews to the blessings of salvation. As yet none of the disciples had preached the gospel to the Gentiles. In their minds the middle wall of partition, broken down by the death of Christ, still existed, and their labors had been confined to the Jews, for they had looked upon the Gentiles as excluded from the blessings of the gospel. Now the Lord was seeking to teach Peter the world-wide extent of the divine plan.

Many of the Gentiles had been interested listeners to the preaching of Peter and the other apostles, and many of the Greek Jews had become believers in Christ, but the conversion of Cornelius was to be the first of importance among the Gentiles.

The time had come for an entirely new phase of work to be entered upon by the church of Christ. The door that many of the Jewish converts had closed against the Gentiles was now to be thrown open. And the Gentiles who accepted the gospel were to be regarded as on an equality with the Jewish disciples, without the necessity of observing the rite of circumcision.

How carefully the Lord worked to overcome the prejudice against the Gentiles that had been so firmly fixed in Peter's mind by his Jewish training! By the vision of the sheet and its contents He sought to divest the apostle's mind of this prejudice and to teach the important truth that in heaven there is no respect of persons; that Jew and Gentile are alike precious in God's sight; that through Christ the heathen may be made partakers of the blessings and privileges of the gospel.

While Peter was meditating on the meaning of the vision, the men sent from Cornelius arrived in Joppa and stood before the gate of his lodginghouse. Then the Spirit said to him, "Behold, three men seek thee. Arise therefore, and get thee down, and go with them, doubting nothing: for I have sent them."

To Peter this was a trying command, and it was with reluctance at every step that he undertook the duty laid upon him; but he dared not disobey. He "went down to the men which were sent unto him from Cornelius; and said, Behold, I am he whom ye seek: what is the cause wherefore ye are come?" They told him of their singular errand, saying, "Cornelius the centurion, a just man, and one that feareth God, and of good report among all the nation of the Jews, was warned from God by a holy angel to send for thee into his house, and to hear words of thee."

In obedience to the directions just received from God, the apostle promised to go with them. On the following morning he set out for Caesarea, accompanied by six of his brethren. These were to be witnesses of all that he should say or do while visiting the Gentiles, for Peter knew that he would be called to account for so direct a violation of the Jewish teachings.

As Peter entered the house of the Gentile, Cornelius did not salute him as an ordinary visitor, but as one honored of Heaven and sent to him by God. It is an Eastern custom to bow before a prince or other high dignitary and for children to bow before their parents; but Cornelius, overwhelmed with reverence for the one sent by God to teach him, fell at the apostle's feet and worshiped him. Peter was horror-stricken, and he lifted the centurion up, saying, "Stand up; I myself also am a man."

While the messengers of Cornelius had been gone upon their errand, the centurion "had called together his kinsmen and near friends," that they as well as he might hear the preaching of the gospel. When Peter arrived, he found a large company eagerly waiting to listen to his words.

To those assembled, Peter spoke first of the custom of the Jews, saying that it was looked upon as unlawful for Jews to mingle socially with the Gentiles, that to do this involved ceremonial defilement. "Ye know," he said, "how that it is an unlawful thing for a man that is a Jew to keep company, or come unto one of another nation; but God hath showed me that I should not call any man common or unclean. Therefore came I unto you without gainsaying, as soon as I was sent for: I ask therefore for what intent ye have sent for me?"

Cornelius then related his experience and the words of the angel, saying in conclusion, "Immediately therefore I sent to thee; and thou hast well done that thou art come. Now therefore are we all here present before God, to hear all things that are commanded thee of God."

Peter said, "Of a truth I perceive that God is no respecter of persons: but in every nation he that feareth Him, and worketh righteousness, is accepted with Him."

Then to that company of attentive hearers the apostle preached Christ—His life, His miracles, His betrayal and crucifixion, His resurrection and ascension, and His work in heaven as man's representative and advocate. As Peter pointed those present to Jesus as the sinner's only hope, he himself understood more fully the meaning of the vision he had seen, and his heart glowed with the spirit of the truth that he was presenting.

Suddenly the discourse was interrupted by the descent of the Holy Spirit. "While Peter yet spake these words, the Holy Ghost fell on all them which heard the world. And they of the circumcision which believed were astonished, as many as came with Peter, because that on the Gentiles also was poured out the gift of the Holy Ghost. For they heard them speak with tongues, and magnify God.

"Then answered Peter, Can any man forbid water, that these should not be baptized, which have received the Holy Ghost as well as we? And he commanded them to be baptized in the name of the Lord."

Thus was the gospel brought to those who had been strangers and foreigners, making them fellow citizens with the saints, and members of the household of God. The conversion of Cornelius and his household was but the first fruits of a harvest to be gathered in. From this household a wide-spread work of grace was carried on in that heathen city.

Today God is seeking for souls among the high as well as the lowly. There are many like Cornelius, men whom the Lord desires to connect with His work in the world. Their sympathies are with the Lord's people, but the ties that bind them to the world hold them firmly. It requires moral courage for them to take their position for Christ. Special efforts should be made for these souls, who are in so great danger, because of their responsibilities and associations.

God calls for earnest, humble workers, who will carry the gospel to the higher class. There are miracles to be wrought in genuine conversions,—miracles that are not now discerned. The greatest men of this earth are not beyond the power of a wonder-working God. If those who are workers together with Him will be men of opportunity, doing their duty bravely and faithfully, God will convert men who occupy responsible positions, men of intellect and influence. Through the power of the Holy Spirit many will accept the divine principles. Converted to the truth, they will become agencies in the hand of God to communicate the light. They will have a special burden for other souls of this neglected class. Time and money will be consecrated to the work of the Lord, and new efficiency and power will be added to the church.

Because Cornelius was living in obedience to all the instruction he had received, God so ordered events that he was given more truth. A messenger from the courts of heaven was sent to the Roman officer and to Peter in order that Cornelius might be brought into touch with one who could lead him into greater light.

There are in our world many who are nearer the kingdom of God than we suppose. In this dark world of sin the Lord has many precious jewels, to whom He will guide His messengers. Everywhere there are those who will take their stand for Christ. Many will prize the wisdom of God above any earthly advantage, and will become faithful light bearers. Constrained by the love of Christ, they will constrain others to come to Him.

When the brethren in Judea heard that Peter had gone to the house of a Gentile and preached to those assembled, they were surprised and offended. They feared that such a course, which looked to them presumptuous, would have the effect of counteracting his own teaching. When they next saw Peter they met him with severe censure, saying, "Thou wentest in to men uncircumcised, and didst eat with them."

Peter laid the whole matter before them. He related his experience in regard to the vision and pleaded that it admonished him to observe no longer the ceremonial distinction of circumcision and uncircumcision, nor to look upon the Gentiles as unclean. He told them of the command given him to go to the Gentiles, of the coming of the messengers, of his journey to Caesarea, and of the meeting with Cornelius. He recounted the substance of his interview with the centurion, in which the latter had told him of the vision by which he had been directed to send for Peter.

"As I began to speak," he said, in relating his experience, "the Holy Ghost fell on them, as on us at the beginning. Then remembered I the word of the Lord, how that He said, John indeed baptized with water; but ye shall be baptized with the Holy Ghost. Forasmuch then as God gave them the like gift as He did unto us, who believed on the Lord Jesus Christ; what was I, that I could withstand God?"

On hearing this account, the brethren were silenced. Convinced that Peter's course was in direct fulfillment of the plan of God, and that their prejudices and exclusiveness were utterly contrary to the spirit of the gospel, they glorified God, saying, "Then hath God also to the Gentiles granted repentance unto life."

Thus, without controversy, prejudice was broken down, the exclusiveness established by the custom of ages was abandoned, and the way was opened for the gospel to be proclaimed to the Gentiles.

15

Delivered From Prison

This chapter is based on Acts 12:1-23

Now about that time Herod the king stretched forth his hands to vex certain of the church." The government of Judea was then in the hands of Herod Agrippa, subject to Claudius, the Roman emperor. Herod also held the position of tetrarch of Galilee. He was professedly a proselyte to the Jewish faith, and apparently very zealous in carrying out the ceremonies of the Jewish law. Desirous of obtaining the favor of the Jews, hoping thus to make secure his offices and honors, he proceeded to carry out their desires by persecuting the church of Christ, spoiling the houses and goods of the believers, and imprisoning the leading members of the church. He cast James, the brother of John, into prison, and sent an executioner to kill him with the sword, as another Herod had caused the prophet John to be beheaded. Seeing that the Jews were well pleased with these efforts, he imprisoned Peter also.

It was during the Passover that these cruelties were practiced. While the Jews were celebrating their deliverance from Egypt and pretending great zeal for the law of God, they were at the same time transgressing every principle of that law by persecuting and murdering the believers in Christ.

The death of James caused great grief and consternation among the believers. When Peter also was imprisoned, the entire church engaged in fasting and prayer.

Herod's act in putting James to death was applauded by the Jews, though some complained of the private manner in which it was accomplished, maintaining that a public execution would have more thoroughly intimidated the believers and those sympathizing with them. Herod therefore held Peter in custody, meaning still further to gratify the Jews by the public spectacle of his death. But it was suggested that it would not be safe to bring the veteran apostle out for execution before all the people then assembled in Jerusalem. It was feared that the sight of him being led out to die might excite the pity of the multitude.

The priests and elders also feared lest Peter might make one of those powerful appeals which had frequently aroused the people to study the life and character of Jesus—appeals which they, with all their arguments, had been unable to controvert. Peter's zeal in advocating the cause of Christ had led many to take their stand for the gospel, and the rulers feared that should he be given an opportunity to defend his faith in the presence of the multitude who had come to the city to worship, his release would be demanded at the hands of the king.

While, upon various pretexts, the execution of Peter was being delayed until after the Passover, the members of the church had time for deep searching of heart and earnest prayer. They prayed without ceasing for Peter, for they felt that he could not be spared from the cause. They realized that they had reached a place where, without the special help of God, the church of Christ would be destroyed.

Meanwhile worshipers from every nation sought the temple which had been dedicated to the worship of God. Glittering with gold and precious stones, it was a vision of beauty and grandeur. But Jehovah was no longer to be found in that palace of loveliness. Israel as a nation had divorced herself from God. When Christ, near the close of His earthly ministry, looked for the last time upon the interior of the temple, He said, "Behold, your house is left unto you desolate." Matthew 23:38. Hitherto He had called the temple His Father's house; but as the Son of God passed our from those walls, God's presence was withdrawn forever from the temple built to His glory.

The day of Peter's execution was at last appointed, but still the prayers of the believers ascended to heaven; and while all their energies and sympathies were called out in fervent appeals for help, angels of God were watching over the imprisoned apostle.

Remembering the former escape of the apostles from prison, Herod on this occasion had taken double precautions. To prevent all possibility of release, Peter had been put under the charge of sixteen soldiers, who, in different watches, guarded him day and night. In his cell he was placed between two soldiers and was bound by two chains, each chain being fastened to the wrist of one of the soldiers. He was unable to move without their knowledge. With the prison doors securely fastened, and a strong guard before them, all chance of rescue or escape through human means was cut off. But man's extremity is God's opportunity.

Peter was confined in a rock-hewn cell, the doors of which were strongly bolted and barred; and the soldiers on guard were made answerable for the safekeeping of the prisoner. But the bolts and bars and the Roman guard, which effectually cut off all possibility of human aid, were but to make more complete the triumph of God in the deliverance of Peter. Herod was lifting his hand against Omnipotence, and he was to be utterly defeated. By the putting forth of His might, God was about to save the precious life that the Jews were plotting to destroy.

It is the last night before the proposed execution. A mighty angel is sent from heaven to rescue Peter. The strong gates that shut in the saint of God open without the aid of human hands. The angel of the Most High passes through, and the gates close noiselessly behind him. He enters the cell, and there lies Peter, sleeping the peaceful sleep of perfect trust.

The light that surrounds the angel fills the cell, but does not rouse the apostle. Not until he feels the touch of the angel's hand and hears a voice saying, "Arise up quickly," does he awaken sufficiently to see his cell illuminated by the light of heaven, and an angel of great glory standing before him. Mechanically he obeys the word spoken to him, and as in rising he lifts his hands he is dimly conscious that the chains have fallen from his wrists.

Again the voice of the heavenly messenger bids him, "Gird thyself, and bind on thy sandals," and again Peter mechanically obeys, keeping his wondering gaze riveted upon his vistor and believing himself to be dreaming or in a vision. Once more the angel commands, "Cast thy garment about thee, and follow me." He moves toward the door, followed by the usually talkative Peter, now dumb from amazement. They step over the guard and reach the heavily bolted door, which of its own accord swings open and closes again immediately, while the guards within and without are motionless at their post.

The second door, also guarded within and without, is reached. It opens as did the first, with no creaking of hinges or rattling of iron bolts. They pass through, and it closes again as noiselessly. In the same way they pass through the third gateway and find themselves in the open street. No word is spoken; there is no sound of footsteps. The angel glides on in front, encircled by a light of dazzling brightness, and Peter, bewildered, and still believing himself to be in a dream, follows his deliverer. Thus they pass on through one street, and then, the mission of the angel being accomplished, he suddenly disappears.

The heavenly light faded away, and Peter felt himself to be in profound darkness; but as his eyes became accustomed to the darkness, it gradually seemed to lessen, and he found himself alone in the silent street, with the cool night air blowing upon his brow. He now realized that he was free, in a familiar part of the city; he recognized the place as one that he had often frequented and had expected to pass on the morrow for the last time.

He tried to recall the events of the past few moments. He remembered falling asleep, bound between two soldiers, with his sandals and outer garments removed. He examined his person and found himself fully dressed and girded. His wrists, swollen from wearing the cruel irons, were free from the manacles. He realized that his freedom was no delusion, no dream or vision, but a blessed reality. On the morrow he was to have been led forth to die; but, lo, an angel had delivered him from prison and from death. "And when Peter was come to himself, he said, Now I know of a surety, that the Lord hath sent His angel, and hath delivered me out of the hand of Herod, and from all the expectation of the people of the Jews."

The apostle made his way at once to the house where his brethren were assembled and where they were at that moment engaged in earnest prayer for him. "As Peter knocked at the door of the gate, a damsel came to hearken, named Rhoda. And when she knew Peter's voice, she opened not the gate for gladness, but ran in, and told how Peter stood before the gate. And they said unto her, Thou art mad. But she constantly affirmed that it was even so. Then said they, It is his angel."

"But Peter continued knocking: and when they had opened the door, and saw him, they were astonished. But he, beckoning unto them with the hand to hold their peace, declared unto them how the Lord had brought him out of the prison." And Peter "departed, and went into another place." Joy and praise filled the hearts of the believers, because God had heard and answered their prayers and had delivered Peter from the hands of Herod.

In the morning a large concourse of people gathered to witness the execution of the apostle. Herod sent officers to the prison for Peter, who was to be brought with a great display of arms and guards in order not only to ensure against his escape, but to intimidate all sympathizers and to show the power of the king.

When the keepers before the door found that Peter had escaped, they were seized with terror. It had been expressly stated that their lives would be required for the life of their charge, and because of this they had been especially vigilant. When the officers came for Peter, the soldiers were still at the door of the prison, the bolts and bars were still fast, the chains were still secured to the wrists of the two soldiers; but the prisoner was gone.

When the report of Peter's escape was brought to Herod, he was exasperated and enraged. Charging the prison guard with unfaithfulness, he ordered them to be put to death. Herod knew that no human power had rescued Peter, but he was determined not to acknowledge that a divine power had frustrated his design, and he set himself in bold defiance against God.

Not long after Peter's deliverance from prison, Herod went to Caesarea. While there he made a great festival designed to excite the admiration and gain the applause of the people. This festival was attended by pleasure lovers from all quarters, and there was much feasting and wine drinking. With great pomp and ceremony Herod appeared before the people and addressed them in an eloquent oration. Clad in a robe sparkling with silver and gold, which caught the rays of the sun in its glittering folds and dazzled the eyes of the beholders, he was a gorgeous figure. The majesty of his appearance and the force of his well-chosen language swayed the assembly with a mighty power. Their senses already perverted by feasting and wine drinking, they were dazzled by Herod's decorations and charmed by his deportment and oratory; and wild with enthusiasm they showered adulation upon him, declaring that no mortal could present such an appearance or command such startling eloquence. They further declared that while they had ever respected him as a ruler, henceforth they should worship him as a god.

Some of those whose voices were now heard glorifying a vile sinner had but a few years before raised the frenzied cry, Away with Jesus! Crucify Him, crucify Him! The Jews had refused to receive Christ, whose garments, coarse and often travel-stained, covered a heart of divine love. Their eyes could not discern, under the humble exterior, the Lord of life and glory, even though Christ's power was revealed before them in works that no mere man could do. But they were ready to worship as a god the haughty king whose splendid garments of silver and gold covered a corrupt, cruel heart.

Herod knew that he deserved none of the praise and homage offered him, yet he accepted the idolatry of the people as his due. His heart bounded with triumph, and a glow of gratified pride overspread his countenance as he heard the shout ascend, "It is the voice of a god, and not of a man."

But suddenly a terrible change came over him. His face became pallid as death and distorted with agony. Great drops of sweat started from his pores. He stood for a moment as if transfixed with pain and terror; then turning his blanched and livid face to his horror-stricken friends, he cried in hollow, despairing tones, He whom you have exalted as a god is stricken with death.

Suffering the most excruciating anguish, he was borne from the scene of revelry and display. A moment before he had been the proud recipient of the praise and worship of that vast throng; now he realized that he was in the hands of a Ruler mightier than himself. Remorse seized him; he remembered his relentless persecution of the followers of Christ; he remembered his cruel command to slay the innocent James, and his design to put to death the apostle Peter; he remembered how in his mortification and disappointed rage he had wreaked an unreasoning vengeance upon the prison guards. He felt that God was now dealing with him, the relentless persecutor. He found no relief from pain of body or anguish of mind, and he expected none.

Herod was acquainted with the law of God, which says, "Thou shalt have no other gods before Me" (Exodus 20:3); and he knew that in accepting the worship of the people he had filled up the measure of his iniquity and brought upon himself the just wrath of Jehovah.

The same angel who had come from the royal courts to rescue Peter, had been the messenger of wrath and judgment to Herod. The angel smote Peter to arouse him from slumber; it was with a different stroke that he smote the wicked king, laying low his pride and bringing upon him the punishment of the Almighty. Herod died in great agony of mind and body, under the retributive judgment of God.

This demonstration of divine justice had a powerful influence upon the people. The tidings that the apostle of Christ had been miraculously delivered from prison and death, while his persecutor had been stricken down by the curse of God, were borne to all lands and became the means of leading many to a belief in Christ.

The experience of Philip, directed by an angel from heaven to go to the place where he met one seeking for truth; of Cornelius, visited by an angel with a message from God; of Peter, in prison and condemned to death, led by an angel forth to safety—all show the closeness of the connection between heaven and earth.

To the worker for God the record of these angel visits should bring strength and courage. Today, as verily as in the days of the apostles, heavenly messengers are passing through the length and breadth of the land, seeking to comfort the sorrowing, to protect the impenitent, to win the hearts of men to Christ. We cannot see them personally; nevertheless they are with us, guiding, directing, protecting.

Heaven is brought near to earth by that mystic ladder, the base of which is firmly planted on the earth, while the topmost round reaches the throne of the Infinite. Angels are constantly ascending and descending this ladder of shining brightness, bearing the prayers of the needy and distressed to the Father above, and bringing blessing and hope, courage and help, to the children of men. These angels of light create a heavenly atmosphere about the soul, lifting us toward the unseen and the eternal. We cannot behold their forms with our natural sight; only by spiritual vision can we discern heavenly things. The spiritual ear alone can hear the harmony of heavenly voices.

"The angel of the Lord encampeth round about them that fear Him, and delivereth them." Psalm 34:7. God commissions His angels to save His chosen ones from calamity, to guard them from "the pestilence that walketh in darkness" and "the destruction that wasteth at noonday." Psalm 91:6. Again and again have angels talked with men as a man speaketh with a friend, and led them to places of security. Again and again have the encouraging words of angels renewed the drooping spirits of the faithful and, carrying their minds above the things of earth, caused them to behold by faith the white robes, the crowns, the palm branches of victory, which overcomers will receive when they surround the great white throne.

It is the work of the angels to come close to the tried, the suffering, the tempted. They labor untiringly in behalf of those for whom Christ died. When sinners are led to give themselves to the Saviour, angels bear the tidings heavenward, and there is great rejoicing among the heavenly host. "Joy shall be in heaven over one sinner that repenteth, more than over ninety and nine just persons, which need no repentance." Luke 15:7. A report is borne to heaven of every successful effort on our part to dispel the darkness and to spread abroad the knowledge of Christ. As the deed is recounted before the Father, joy thrills through all the heavenly host.

The principalities and powers of heaven are watching the warfare which, under apparently discouraging circumstances, God's servants are carrying on. New conquests are being achieved, new honors won, as the Christians, rallying round the banner of their Redeemer, go forth to fight the good fight of faith. All the heavenly angels are at the service of the humble, believing people of God;

and as the Lord's army of workers here below sing their songs of praise, the choir above join with them in ascribing praise to God and to His Son.

We need to understand better than we do the mission of the angels. It would be well to remember that every true child of God has the co-operation of heavenly beings. Invisible armies of light and power attend the meek and lowly ones who believe and claim the promises of God. Cherubim and seraphim, and angels that excel in strength, stand at God's right hand, "all ministering spirits, sent forth to minister for them who shall be heirs of salvation." Hebrews 1:14.

16

The Gospel Message in Antioch

This chapter is based on Acts 11:19-26; 13:1-3

After the disciples had been driven from Jerusalem by persecution, the gospel message spread rapidly through the regions lying beyond the limits of Palestine; and many small companies of believers were formed in important centers. Some of the disciples "traveled as far as Phenice, and Cyprus, and Antioch, preaching the word." Their labors were usually confined to the Hebrew and Greek Jews, large colonies of whom were at this time to be found in nearly all the cities of the world.

Among the places mentioned where the gospel was gladly received is Antioch, at that time the metropolis of Syria. The extensive commerce carried on from that populous center brought to the city many people of various nationalities. Besides, Antioch was favorably known as a resort for lovers of ease and pleasure, because of its healthful situation, its beautiful surroundings, and the wealth, culture, and refinement to be found there. In the days of the apostles it had become a city of luxury and vice.

The gospel was publicly taught in Antioch by certain disciples from Cyprus and Cyrene, who came "preaching the Lord Jesus." "The hand of the Lord was with them," and their earnest labors were productive of fruit. "A great number believed, and turned unto the Lord."

"Tidings of these things came unto the ears of the church which was in Jerusalem: and they sent forth Barnabas, that he should go as far as Antioch." Upon arrival in his new field of labor, Barnabas saw the work that had already been accomplished by divine grace, and he "was glad, and exhorted them all, that with purpose of heart they would cleave unto the Lord."

The labors of Barnabas in Antioch were richly blessed, and many were added to the number of believers there. As the work developed, Barnabas felt the need of suitable help in order to advance in the opening providences of God, and he went to Tarsus to seek for Paul, who, after his departure from Jerusalem some time before, had been laboring in "the regions of Syria and Cilicia," proclaiming "the faith which once he destroyed." Galatians 1:21,

23. Barnabas was successful in finding Paul and in persuading him to return with him as a companion in ministry.

In the populous city of Antioch, Paul found an excellent field of labor. His learning, wisdom, and zeal exerted a powerful influence over the inhabitants and frequenters of that city of culture; and he proved just the help that Barnabas needed. For a year the two disciples labored unitedly in faithful ministry, bringing to many a saving knowledge of Jesus of Nazareth, the world's Redeemer.

It was in Antioch that the disciples were first called Christians. The name was given them because Christ was the main theme of their preaching, their teaching, and their conversation. Continually they were recounting the incidents that had occurred during the days of His earthly ministry, when His disciples were blessed with His personal presence. Untiringly they dwelt upon His teachings and His miracles of healing. With quivering lips and tearful eyes they spoke of His agony in the garden, His betrayal, trial, and execution, the forbearance and humility with which He had endured the contumely and torture imposed upon Him by His enemies, and the Godlike pity with which He had prayed for those who persecuted Him. His resurrection and ascension, and His work in heaven as the Mediator for fallen man, were topics on which they rejoiced to dwell. Well might the heathen call them Christians, since they preached Christ and addressed their prayers to God through Him.

It was God who gave to them the name of Christian. This is a royal name, given to all who join themselves to Christ. It was of this name that James wrote later, "Do not rich men oppress you, and draw you before the judgment seats? Do not they blaspheme that worthy name by the which ye are called?" James 2:6, 7. And Peter declared, "If any man suffer as a Christian, let him not be ashamed; but let him glorify God on this behalf." "If ye be reproached for the name of Christ, happy are ye; for the spirit of glory and of God resteth upon you." 1 Peter 4:16, 14.

The believers at Antioch realized that God was willing to work in their lives "both to will and to do of His good pleasure." Philippians 2:13. Living, as they were, in the midst of a people who seemed to care but little for the things of eternal value, they sought to arrest the attention of the honest in heart, and to bear positive testimony concerning Him whom they loved and served. In their humble ministry they learned to depend upon the power of the Holy Spirit to make effective the word of life. And so, in the various walks of life, they daily bore testimony of their faith in Christ.

The example of the followers of Christ at Antioch should be an inspiration to every believer living in the great cities of the world today. While it is in the order of God that chosen workers of consecration and talent should be stationed in important centers of population to lead out in public efforts, it is also His purpose that the church members living in these cities shall use their God-given talents in working for souls. There are rich blessings in store for those who surrender fully to the call of God. As such workers endeavor to win souls to Jesus, they will find that many who never could have been reached in any other way are ready to respond to intelligent personal effort.

The cause of God in the earth today is in need of living representatives of Bible truth. The ordained ministers alone are not equal to the task of warning the great cities. God is calling not only upon ministers, but also upon physicians, nurses, colporteurs, Bible workers, and other consecrated laymen of varied talent who have a knowledge of the word of God and who know the power of His grace, to consider the needs of the unwarned cities. Time is rapidly passing, and there is much to be done. Every agency must be set in operation, that present opportunities may be wisely improved.

Paul's labors at Antioch, in association with Barnabas, strengthened him in his conviction that the Lord had called him to do a special work for the Gentile world. At the time of Paul's conversion, the Lord had declared that he was to be made a minister to the Gentiles, "to open their eyes, and to turn them from darkness to light, and from the power of Satan unto God, that they may receive forgiveness of sins, and inheritance among them which are sanctified by faith that is in Me." Acts 26:18. The angel that appeared to Ananias had said of Paul, "He is a chosen vessel unto Me, to bear My name before the Gentiles, and kings, and the children of Israel." Acts 9:15. And Paul himself, later in his Christian experience, while praying in the temple at Jerusalem, had been visited by an angel from heaven, who bade him, "Depart: for I will send thee far hence unto the Gentiles." Acts 22:21.

Thus the Lord had given Paul his commission to enter the broad missionary field of the Gentile world. To prepare him for this extensive and difficult work, God had brought him into close connection with Himself and had opened before his enraptured vision views of the beauty and glory of heaven. To him had been given the ministry of making known "the mystery" which had been "kept secret since the world began" (Romans 16:25),—"the mystery of His will" (Ephesians 1:9), "which in other ages was not made known unto the sons of men, as it is now revealed unto His holy apostles and prophets by the Spirit; that the Gentiles should be fellow heirs, and of the same body, and partakers of His promise in Christ by the gospel: whereof," declares Paul, "I was made a minister. . . . Unto me, who am less than the least of all saints, is this grace given, that I should preach among the Gentiles the unsearchable riches of Christ; and to make all men see what is the fellowship of the mystery, which from the beginning of the world hath been hid in God, who created all things by Jesus Christ: to the intent that now unto the principalities and powers in heavenly places might be known by the church the manifold wisdom of God, according to the eternal purpose which He purposed in Christ Jesus our Lord." Ephesians 3:5-11.

God had abundantly blessed the labors of Paul and Barnabas during the year they remained with the believers in Antioch. But neither of them had as yet been formally ordained to the gospel ministry. They had now reached a point in their Christian experience when God was about to entrust them with the carrying forward of a difficult missionary enterprise, in the prosecution of which they would need every advantage that could be obtained through the agency of the church.

"There were in the church that was at Antioch certain prophets and teachers; as Barnabas, and Simeon that was called Niger, and Lucius of Cyrene, and Manaen, . . . and Saul. As they ministered to the Lord, and fasted, the Holy Ghost said, Separate Me Barnabas and Saul for the work whereunto I have called them." Before being sent forth as missionaries to the heathen world, these apostles were solemnly dedicated to God by fasting and prayer and the laying on of hands. Thus they were authorized by the church, not only to teach the truth, but to perform the rite of baptism and to organize churches, being invested with full ecclesiastical authority.

The Christian church was at this time entering upon an important era. The work of proclaiming the gospel message among the Gentiles was now to be prosecuted with vigor; and as a result the church was to be strengthened by a great ingathering of souls. The apostles who had been appointed to lead out in this work would be exposed to suspicion, prejudice, and jealousy. Their teachings concerning the breaking down of "the middle wall of partition" (Ephesians 2:14) that had so long separated the Jewish and the Gentile world, would naturally subject them to the charge of heresy, and their authority as ministers of the gospel would be questioned by many zealous, believing Jews. God foresaw the difficulties that His servants would be called to meet, and, in order that their work should be above challenge, He instructed the church by revelation to set them apart publicly to the work of the ministry. Their ordination was a public recognition of their divine appointment to bear to the Gentiles the glad tidings of the gospel.

Both Paul and Barnabas had already received their commission from God Himself, and the ceremony of the laying on of hands added no new grace or virtual qualification. It was an acknowledged form of designation to an appointed office and a recognition of one's authority in that office. By it the seal of the church was set upon the work of God.

To the Jew this form was a significant one. When a Jewish father blessed his children, he laid his hands reverently upon their heads. When an animal was devoted to sacrifice, the hand of the one invested with priestly authority was laid upon the head of the victim. And when the ministers of the church of believers in Antioch laid their hands upon Paul and Barnabas, they, by that action, asked God to bestow His blessing upon the chosen apostles in their devotion to the specific work to which they had been appointed.

At a later date the rite of ordination by the laying on of hands was greatly abused; unwarrantable importance was attached to the act, as if a power came at once upon those who received such ordination, which immediately qualified them for any and all ministerial work. But in the setting apart of these two apostles, there is no record indicating that any virtue was imparted by the mere act of laying on of hands. There is only the simple record of their ordination and of the bearing that it had on their future work.

The circumstances connected with the separation of Paul and Barnabas by the Holy Spirit to a definite line of service show clearly that the Lord works through appointed agencies in His organized church. Years before, when the divine purpose concerning Paul was first revealed to him by the Saviour Himself, Paul was immediately afterward brought into contact with members of the newly organized church at Damascus. Furthermore, the church at that place was not long left in darkness as to the personal experience of the converted Pharisee. And now, when the divine commission given at that time was to be more fully carried out, the Holy Spirit, again bearing witness concerning Paul as a chosen vessel to bear the gospel to the Gentiles, laid upon the church the work of ordaining him and his fellow laborer. As the leaders of the church in Antioch "ministered to the Lord, and fasted, the Holy Ghost said, Separate Me Barnabas and Saul for the work whereunto I have called them."

God has made His church on the earth a channel of light, and through it He communicates His purposes and His will. He does not give to one of His servants an experience independent of and contrary to the experience of the church itself. Neither does He give one man a knowledge of His will for the entire church while the church—Christ's body —is left in darkness. In His providence He places His servants in close connection with His church in order that they may have less confidence in themselves and greater confidence in others whom He is leading out to advance His work.

There have ever been in the church those who are constantly inclined toward individual independence. They seem unable to realize that independence of spirit is liable to lead the human agent to have too much confidence in himself and to trust in his own judgment rather than to respect the counsel and highly esteem the judgment of his brethren, especially of those in the offices that God has appointed for the leadership of His people. God has invested His church with special authority and power which no one can be justified in disregarding and despising, for he who does this despises the voice of God.

Those who are inclined to regard their individual judgment as supreme are in grave peril. It is Satan's studied effort to separate such ones from those who are channels of light, through whom God has wrought to build up and extend His work in the earth. To neglect or despise those whom God has appointed to bear the responsibilities of leadership in connection with the advancement of the truth, is to reject the means that He has ordained for the help, encouragement, and strength of His people. For any worker in the Lord's cause to pass these by, and to think that his light must come through no other channel than directly from God, is to place himself in a position where he is liable to be deceived by the enemy and overthrown. The Lord in His wisdom has arranged that by means of the close relationship that should be maintained by all believers, Christian shall be united to Christian and church to church. Thus the human instrumentality will be enabled to co-operate with the divine. Every agency will be subordinate to the Holy Spirit, and all the believers will be united in an organized and well-directed effort to give to the world the glad tidings of the grace of God.

Paul regarded the occasion of his formal ordination as marking the beginning of a new and important epoch in his lifework. It was from this time that he afterward dated the beginning of his apostleship in the Christian church.

While the light of the gospel was shining brightly at Antioch, an important work was continued by the apostles who had remained in Jerusalem. Every year, at the time of the festivals, many Jews from all lands came to Jerusalem to worship at the temple. Some of these pilgrims were men of fervent piety and earnest students of the prophecies. They were looking and longing for the advent of the promised Messiah, the hope of Israel. While Jerusalem was filled with these strangers, the apostles preached Christ with unflinching courage, though they knew that in so doing they were placing their lives in constant jeopardy. The Spirit of God set its seal upon their labors; many converts to the faith were made; and these, returning to their homes in different parts of the world, scattered the seeds of truth through all nations and among all classes of society.

Prominent among the apostles who engaged in this work were Peter, James, and John, who felt confident that God had appointed them to preach Christ among their countrymen at home. Faithfully and wisely they labored, testifying of the things they had seen and heard, and appealing to "a more sure word of prophecy" (2 Peter 1:19), in an effort to persuade "the house of Israel. . . that God hath made that same Jesus, whom" the Jews "crucified, both Lord and Christ" (Acts 2:36).

17

Heralds of the Gospel

This chapter is based on Acts 13:4-52

S ent forth by the Holy Ghost," Paul and Barnabas, after their ordination by the brethren in Antioch, "departed unto Seleucia; and from thence they sailed to Cyprus." Thus the apostles began their first missionary journey.

Cyprus was one of the places to which the believers had fled from Jerusalem because of the persecution following the death of Stephen. It was from Cyprus that certain men had journeyed to Antioch, "preaching the Lord Jesus." Acts 11:20. Barnabas himself was "of the country of Cyprus" (Acts 4:36); and now he and Paul, accompanied by John Mark, a kinsman of Barnabas, visited this island field.

Mark's mother was a convert to the Christian religion, and her home at Jerusalem was an asylum for the disciples. There they were always sure of a welcome and a season of rest. It was during one of these visits of the apostles to his mother's home, that Mark proposed to Paul and Barnabas that he should accompany them on their missionary tour. He felt the favor of God in his heart and longed to devote himself entirely to the work of the gospel ministry.

Arriving at Salamis, the apostles "preached the word of God in the synagogues of the Jews. . . . And when they had gone through the isle unto Paphos, they found a certain sorcerer, a false prophet, a Jew, whose name was Bar-Jesus: which was with the deputy of the country, Sergius Paulus, a prudent man; who called for Barnabas and Saul, and desired to hear the word of God. But Elymas the sorcerer (for so is his name by interpretation) withstood them, seeking to turn away the deputy from the faith."

Not without a struggle does Satan allow the kingdom of God to be built up in the earth. The forces of evil are engaged in unceasing warfare against the agencies appointed for the spread of the gospel, and these powers of darkness are especially active when the truth is proclaimed before men of repute and sterling integrity. Thus it was when Sergius Paulus, the deputy of Cyprus, was listening to the gospel message. The deputy had sent for the apostles, that he might be instructed in the message they had come to bear, and now the forces of evil, working through the sorcerer Elymas, sought with their baleful suggestions to turn him from the faith and so thwart the purpose of God.

Thus the fallen foe ever works to keep in his ranks men of influence who, if converted, might render effective service in God's cause. But the faithful gospel worker need not fear defeat at the hand of the enemy; for it is his privilege to be endued with power from above to withstand every satanic influence.

Although sorely beset by Satan, Paul had the courage to rebuke the one through whom the enemy was working. "Filled with the Holy Ghost," the apostle "set his eyes on him, and said, O full of all subtlety and all mischief, thou child of the devil, thou enemy of all righteousness, wilt thou not cease to pervert the right ways of the Lord? And now, behold, the hand of the Lord is upon thee, and thou shalt be blind, not seeing the sun for a season. And immediately there fell on him a mist and a darkness; and he went about seeking some to lead him by the hand. Then the deputy, when he saw what was done, believed, being astonished at the doctrine of the Lord."

The sorcerer had closed his eyes to the evidences of gospel truth, and the Lord, in righteous anger, caused his natural eyes to be closed, shutting out from him the light of day. This blindness was not permanent, but only for a season, that he might be warned to repent and seek pardon of the God whom he had so grievously offended. The confusion into which he was thus brought made of no effect his subtle arts against the doctrine of Christ. The fact that he was obliged to grope about in blindness proved to all that the miracles which the apostles had performed, and which Elymas had denounced as sleight of hand, were wrought by the power of God. The deputy, convinced of the truth of the doctrine taught by the apostles, accepted the gospel.

Elymas was not a man of education, yet he was peculiarly fitted to do the work of Satan. Those who preach the truth of God will meet the wily foe in many different forms. Sometimes it will be in the person of learned, but more often of ignorant, men, whom Satan has trained to be successful instruments to deceive souls. It is the duty of the minister of Christ to stand faithful at his post, in the fear of God and in the power of His might. Thus he may put to confusion the hosts of Satan and may triumph in the name of the Lord.

Paul and his company continued their journey, going to Perga, in Pamphylia. Their way was toilsome; they encountered hardships and privations, and were beset with dangers on every side. In the towns and cities through which they passed, and along the lonely highways, they were surrounded by dangers seen and unseen. But Paul and Barnabas had learned to trust God's power to deliver. Their hearts were filled with fervent love for perishing souls. As faithful shepherds in search of the lost sheep, they gave no thought to their own ease and convenience. Forgetful of self, they faltered not when weary, hungry, and cold. They had in view but one object—the salvation of those who had wandered far from the fold.

It was here that Mark, overwhelmed with fear and discouragement, wavered for a time in his purpose to give himself wholeheartedly to the Lord's work. Unused to hardships, he was disheartened by the perils and privations of the way. He had labored with success under favorable circumstances; but now, amidst the opposition and perils that so often beset the pioneer worker, he failed to endure hardness as a good soldier of the cross. He had yet to learn to face danger and persecution and adversity with a brave heart. As the apostles advanced, and still greater difficulties were apprehended, Mark was intimidated and, losing all courage, refused to go farther and returned to Jerusalem.

This desertion caused Paul to judge Mark unfavorably, and even severely, for a time. Barnabas, on the other hand, was inclined to excuse him because of his inexperience. He felt anxious that Mark should not abandon the ministry, for he saw in him qualifications that would fit him to be a useful worker for Christ. In after years his solicitude in Mark's behalf was richly rewarded, for the young man gave himself unreservedly to the Lord and to the work of proclaiming the gospel message in difficult fields. Under the blessing of God, and the wise training of Barnabas, he developed into a valuable worker.

Paul was afterward reconciled to Mark and received him as a fellow laborer. He also recommended him to the Colossians as one who was a fellow worker "unto the kingdom of God," and "a comfort unto me." Colossians 4:11. Again, not long before his own death, he spoke of Mark as "profitable" to him "for the ministry." 2 Timothy 4:11.

After the departure of Mark, Paul and Barnabas visited Antioch in Pisidia and on the Sabbath day went into the Jewish synagogue and sat down. "After the reading of the law and the prophets the rulers of the synagogue sent unto them, saying, Ye men and brethren, if ye have any word of exhortation for the people, say on." Being thus invited to speak, "Paul stood up, and beckoning with his hand said, Men of Israel, and ye that fear God, give audience."

Then followed a wonderful discourse. He proceeded to give a history of the manner in which the Lord had dealt with the Jews from the time of their deliverance from Egyptian bondage, and how a Saviour had been promised, of the seed of David, and he boldly declared that "of this man's seed hath God according to His promise raised unto Israel a Saviour, Jesus: when John had first preached before His coming the baptism of repentance to all the people of Israel. And as John fulfilled his course, he said, Whom think ye that I am? I am not He. But, behold, there cometh One after me, whose shoes of His feet I am not worthy to loose." Thus with power he preached Jesus as the Saviour of men, the Messiah of prophecy.

Having made this declaration, Paul said, "Men and brethren, children of the stock of Abraham, and whosoever among you feareth God, to you is the word of this salvation sent. For they that dwell at Jerusalem, and their rulers, because they knew Him not, nor yet the voices of the prophets which are read every Sabbath day, they have fulfilled them in condemning Him."

Paul did not hesitate to speak the plain truth concerning the rejection of the Saviour by the Jewish leaders. "Though they found no cause of death in Him," the apostle declared, "yet desired they Pilate that He should be slain. And when they had fulfilled all that was written of Him, they took Him down from the tree, and laid Him in a sepulcher. But God raised Him from the dead: and He was seen many days of them which came up with Him from Galilee to Jerusalem, who are His witnesses unto the people."

"We declare unto you glad tidings," the apostle continued, "how that the promise which was made unto the fathers, God hath fulfilled the same unto us their children, in that He hath raised up Jesus again; as it is also written in the second psalm, Thou art My Son, this day have I begotten Thee. And as concerning that He raised Him up from the dead, now no more to return to corruption, He said on this wise, I will give you the sure mercies of David. Wherefore He saith also in another psalm, Thou shalt not suffer Thine Holy One to see corruption. For David, after he had served his own generation by the will of God, fell on sleep, and was laid unto his fathers, and saw corruption: but He, whom God raised again, saw no corruption."

And now, having spoken plainly of the fulfillment of familiar prophecies concerning the Messiah, Paul preached unto them repentance and the remission of sin through the merits of Jesus their Saviour. "Be it known unto you," he said, "that through this Man is preached unto you the forgiveness of sins: and by Him all that believe are justified from all things, from which ye could not be justified by the law of Moses."

The Spirit of God accompanied the words that were spoken, and hearts were touched. The apostle's appeal to Old Testament prophecies, and his declaration that these had been fulfilled in the ministry of Jesus of Nazareth, carried conviction to many a soul longing for the advent of the promised Messiah. And the speaker's words of assurance that the "glad tidings" of salvation were for Jew and Gentile alike, brought hope and joy to those who had not been numbered among the children of Abraham according to the flesh.

"When the Jews were gone out of the synagogue, the Gentiles besought that these words might be preached to them the next Sabbath." The congregation having finally broken up, "many of the Jews and religious proselytes," who had accepted the glad tidings borne to them that day, "followed Paul and Barnabas: who, speaking to them, persuaded them to continue in the grace of God."

The interest aroused in Antioch of Pisidia by Paul's discourse brought together on the next Sabbath day, "almost the whole city . . . to hear the word of God. But when the Jews saw the multitudes, they were filled with envy, and spake against those things which were spoken by Paul, contradicting and blaspheming.

"Then Paul and Barnabas waxed bold, and said, It was necessary that the word of God should first have been spoken to you: but seeing ye put it from you, and judge yourselves unworthy of everlasting life, lo, we turn to the Gentiles. For so hath the Lord commanded us, saying, I have set thee to be a light of the Gentiles, that thou shouldest be for salvation unto the ends of the earth."

"When the Gentiles heard this, they were glad, and glorified the word of the Lord: and as many as were ordained to eternal life believed." They rejoiced exceedingly that Christ recognized them as the children of God, and with grateful hearts they listened to the word preached. Those who believed were zealous in communicating the gospel message to others, and thus "the word of the Lord was published throughout all the region."

Centuries before, the pen of inspiration had traced this ingathering of the Gentiles; but those prophetic utterances had been but dimly understood. Hosea had said: "Yet the number of the children of Israel shall be as the sand of the sea, which cannot be measured nor numbered; and it shall come to pass, that in the place where it was said unto them, Ye are not My people, there it shall be said unto them, Ye are the sons of the living God." And again: I will sow her unto Me in the earth; and I will have mercy upon her that had not obtained mercy; and I will say to them which were not My people, Thou art My people; and they shall say, Thou art my God." Hosea 1:10; 2:23.   GENTILES

The Saviour Himself, during His earthly ministry, foretold the spread of the gospel among the Gentiles. In the parable of the vineyard He declared to the impenitent Jews, "The kingdom of God shall be taken from you, and given to a nation bringing forth the fruits thereof." Matthew 21:43. And after His resurrection He commissioned His disciples to go "into all the world" and "teach all nations." They were to leave none unwarned, but were to "preach the gospel to every creature." Matthew 28:19; Mark 16:15.

In turning to the Gentiles in Antioch of Pisidia, Paul and Barnabas did not cease laboring for the Jews elsewhere, wherever there was a favorable opportunity to gain a hearing. Later, in Thessalonica, in Corinth, in Ephesus, and in other important centers, Paul and his companions in labor preached the gospel to both Jews and Gentiles. But their chief energies were henceforth directed toward the building up of the kingdom of God in heathen territory, among peoples who had but little or no knowledge of the true God and of His Son.

The hearts of Paul and his associate workers were drawn out in behalf of those who were "without Christ, being aliens from the commonwealth of Israel, and strangers from the covenants of promise, having no hope, and without God in the world." Through the untiring ministrations of the apostles to the Gentiles, the "strangers and foreigners," who "sometimes were far off," learned that they had been "made nigh by the blood of Christ," and that through faith in His atoning sacrifice they might become "fellow citizens with the saints, and of the household of God." Ephesians 2:12, 13, 19.

Advancing in faith, Paul labored unceasingly for the upbuilding of God's kingdom among those who had been neglected by the teachers in Israel. Constantly he exalted Christ Jesus as "the King of kings, and Lord of lords" (1 Timothy 6:15), and exhorted the believers to be "rooted and built up in Him, and stablished in the faith." Colossians 2:7.

To those who believe, Christ is a sure foundation. Upon this living stone, Jews and Gentiles alike may build. It is broad enough for all and strong enough to sustain the weight and burden of the whole world. This is a fact plainly recognized by Paul himself. In the closing days of his ministry, when addressing a group of Gentile believers who had remained steadfast in their love of the gospel truth, the apostle wrote, "Ye . . .are built upon the foundation of the apostles and prophets, Jesus Christ Himself being the chief corner-stone." Ephesians 2:19, 20.

As the gospel message spread in Pisidia, the unbelieving Jews of Antioch in their blind prejudice "stirred up the devout and honorable women, and the chief men of the city, and raised perse-cution against Paul and Barnabas, and expelled them" from that district.

The apostles were not discouraged by this treatment; they remembered the words of their Master: "Blessed are ye, when men shall revile you, and persecute you, and shall say all manner of evil against you falsely, for My sake. Rejoice, and be exceeding glad: for great is your reward in heaven: for so persecuted they the prophets which were before you." Matthew 5:11, 12.

The gospel message was advancing, and the apostles had every reason for feeling encouraged. Their labors had been richly blessed among the Pisidians at Antioch, and the believers whom they left to carry forward the work alone for a time, "were filled with joy, and with the Holy Ghost."

18

Preaching Among the Heathen

This chapter is based on Acs 14:1-26

From Antioch in Pisidia, Paul and Barnabas went to Iconium. In this place, as at Antioch, they began their labors in the synagogue of their own people. They met with marked success; "a great multitude both of the Jews and also of the Greeks believed." But in Iconium, as in other places where the apostles labored, "the unbelieving Jews stirred up the Gentiles, and made their minds evil affected against the brethren."

The apostles, however, were not turned aside from their mission, for many were accepting the gospel of Christ. In the face of opposition, envy, and prejudice they went on with their work, "speaking boldly in the Lord," and God "gave testimony unto the word of His grace, and granted signs and wonders to be done by their hands." These evidences of divine approval had a powerful influence on those whose minds were open to conviction, and converts to the gospel multiplied.

The increasing popularity of the message borne by the apostles, filled the unbelieving Jews with envy and hatred, and they determined to stop the labors of Paul and Barnabas at once. By means of false and exaggerated reports they led the authorities to fear that the entire city was in danger of being incited to insurrection. They declared that large numbers were attaching themselves to the apostles and suggested that it was for secret and dangerous designs.

In consequence of these charges the disciples were repeatedly brought before the authorities; but their defense was so clear and sensible, and their statement of what they were teaching so calm and comprehensive, that a strong influence was exerted in their favor. Although the magistrates were prejudiced against them by the false statements they had heard, they dared not condemn them. They could but acknowledge that the teachings of Paul and Barnabas tended to make men virtuous, law-abiding citizens, and that the morals and order of the city would improve if the truths taught by the apostles were accepted.

Through the opposition that the disciples met, the message of truth gained great publicity; the Jews saw that their efforts to thwart the work of the new teachers resulted only in adding greater numbers to the new faith. "The multitude of the city was divided: and part held with the Jews, and part with the apostles."

So enraged were the leaders among the Jews by the turn that matters were taking, that they determined to gain their ends by violence. Arousing the worst passions of the ignorant, noisy mob, they succeeded in creating a tumult, which they attributed to the teaching of the disciples. By this false charge they hoped to gain the help of the magistrates in carrying out their purpose. They determined that the apostles should have no opportunity to vindicate themselves and that the mob should interfere by stoning Paul and Barnabas, thus putting an end to their labors.

Friends of the apostles, though unbelievers, warned them of the malicious designs of the Jews and urged them not to expose themselves needlessly to the fury of the mob, but to escape for their lives. Paul and Barnabas accordingly departed in secret from Iconium, leaving the believers to carry on the work alone for a time. But they by no means took final leave; they purposed to return after the excitement had abated, and complete the work begun.

In every age and in every land, God's messengers have been called upon to meet bitter opposition from those who deliberately chose to reject the light of heaven. Often, by misrepresentation and falsehood, the enemies of the gospel have seemingly triumphed, closing the doors by which God's messengers might gain access to the people. But these doors cannot remain forever closed, and often, as God's servants have returned after a time to resume their labors, the Lord has wrought mightily in their behalf, enabling them to establish memorials to the glory of His name.

Driven by persecution from Iconium, the apostles went to Lystra and Derbe, in Lycaonia. These towns were inhabited largely by a heathen, superstitious people, but among them were some who were willing to hear and accept the gospel message. In these places and in the surrounding country the apostles decided to labor, hoping to avoid Jewish prejudice and persecution.

In Lystra there was no Jewish synagogue, though a few Jews were living in the town. Many of the inhabitants of Lystra worshiped at a temple dedicated to Jupiter. When Paul and Barnabas appeared in the town and, gathering the Lystrians about them, explained the simple truths of the gospel, many sought to connect these doctrines with their own superstitious belief in the worship of Jupiter.

The apostles endeavored to impart to these idolaters a knowledge of God the Creator and of His Son, the Saviour of the human race. They first directed attention to the wonderful works of God— the sun, the moon, and the stars, the beautiful order of the recurring seasons, the mighty snow-capped mountains, the lofty trees, and other varied wonders of nature, which showed a skill beyond human comprehension. Through these works of the Almighty, the apostles led the minds of the heathen to a contemplation of the great Ruler of the universe.

Having made plain these fundamental truths concerning the Creator, the apostles told the Lystrians of the Son of God, who came from heaven to our world because He loved the children of men. They spoke of His life and ministry, His rejection by those He came to save, His trial and crucifixion, His resurrection, and His ascension to heaven, there to act as man's advocate. Thus, in the Spirit and power of God, Paul and Barnabas preached the gospel in Lystra.

At one time, while Paul was telling the people of Christ's work as a healer of the sick and afflicted, he saw among his hearers a cripple whose eyes were fastened on him and who received and believed his words. Paul's heart went out in sympathy toward the afflicted man, in whom he discerned one who "had faith to be healed." In the presence of the idolatrous assembly Paul commanded the cripple to stand upright on his feet. Heretofore the sufferer had been able to take a sitting posture only, but now he instantly obeyed Paul's command and for the first time in his life stood on his feet. Strength came with this effort of faith, and he who had been a cripple "leaped and walked."

"When the people saw what Paul had done, they lifted up their voices, saying in the speech of Lycaonia, The gods are come down to us in the likeness of men." This statement was in harmony with a tradition of theirs that the gods occasionally visited the earth. Barnabas they called Jupiter, the father of gods, because of his venerable appearance, his dignified bearing, and the mildness and benevolence expressed in his countenance. Paul they believe to be Mercury, "because he was the chief speaker," earnest and active, and eloquent with words of warning and exhortation.

The Lystrians, eager to show their gratitude, prevailed upon the priest of Jupiter to do the apostles honor, and he "brought oxen and garlands unto the gates, and would have done sacrifice with the people." Paul and Barnabas, who had sought retirement and rest, were not aware of these preparations. Soon, however, their attention was attracted by the sound of music and the enthusiastic shouting of a large crowd who had come to the house where they were staying.

When the apostles ascertained the cause of this visit and its attendant excitement, "they rent their clothes, and ran in among the people" in the hope of preventing further proceedings. In a loud, ringing voice, which rose above the shouting of the people, Paul demanded their attention; and as the tumult suddenly ceased, he said: "Sirs, why do ye these things? We also are men of like passions with you, and preach unto you that ye should turn from these vanities unto the living God, which made heaven, and earth, and the sea, and all things that are therein: who in times past suffered all nations to walk in their own ways. Nevertheless He left not Himself without witness, in that He did good, and gave us rain from heaven, and fruitful seasons, filling our hearts with food and gladness."

Notwithstanding the positive denial of the apostles that they were divine, and notwithstanding Paul's endeavors to direct the minds of the people to the true God as the only object worthy of adoration, it was almost impossible to turn the heathen from their intention to offer sacrifice. So firm had been their belief that these men were indeed gods, and so great their enthusiasm, that they were loath to acknowledge their error. The record says that they were "scarce restrained."

The Lystrians reasoned that they had beheld with their own eyes the miraculous power exercised by the apostles. They had seen a cripple who had never before been able to walk, made to rejoice in perfect health and strength. It was only after much persuasion on the part of Paul, and careful explanation regarding the mission of himself and Barnabas as representatives of the God of heaven and of His Son, the great Healer, that the people were persuaded to give up their purpose.

The labors of Paul and Barnabas at Lystra were suddenly checked by the malice of "certain Jews from Antioch and Iconium," who, upon learning of the success of the apostles' work among the Lycaonians, had determined to follow them and persecute them. On arriving at Lystra, these Jews soon succeeded in inspiring the people with the same bitterness of spirit that actuated their own minds. By words of misrepresentation and calumny those who had recently regarded Paul and Barnabas as divine beings were persuaded that in reality the apostles were worse than murderers and were deserving of death.

The disappointment that the Lystrians had suffered in being

refused the privilege of offering sacrifice to the apostles, prepared them to turn against Paul and Barnabas with an enthusiasm approaching that with which they had hailed them as gods. Incited by the Jews, they planned to attack the apostles by force. The Jews charged them not to allow Paul an opportunity to speak, alleging that if they were to grant him this privilege, he would bewitch the people.

Soon the murderous designs of the enemies of the gospel were carried out. Yielding to the influence of evil, the Lystrians became possessed with a satanic fury and, seizing Paul, mercilessly stoned him. The apostle thought that his end had come. The martyrdom of Stephen, and the cruel part that he himself had acted upon that occasion, came vividly to his mind. Covered with bruises and faint with pain, he fell to the ground, and the infuriated mob "drew him out of the city, supposing he had been dead."

In this dark and trying hour the company of Lystrian believers, who through the ministry of Paul and Barnabas had been converted to the faith of Jesus, remained loyal and true. The unreasoning opposition and cruel persecution by their enemies served only to confirm the faith of these devoted brethren; and now, in the face of danger and scorn, they showed their loyalty by gathering sorrowfully about the form of him whom they believed to be dead.

What was their surprise when in the midst of their lamentations the apostle suddenly lifted up his head and rose to his feet with the praise of God upon his lips. To the believers this unexpected restoration of God's servant was regarded as a miracle of divine power and seemed to set the signet of Heaven upon their change of belief. They rejoiced with inexpressible gladness and praised God with renewed faith.

Among those who had been converted at Lystra, and who were eyewitnesses of the sufferings of Paul, was one who was afterward to become a prominent worker for Christ and who was to share with the apostle the trials and the joys of pioneer service in difficult fields. This was a young man named Timothy. When Paul was dragged out of the city, this youthful disciple was among the number who took their stand beside his apparently lifeless body and who saw him arise, bruised and covered with blood, but with praises upon his lips because he had been permitted to suffer for the sake of Christ.

The day following the stoning of Paul, the apostles departed for Derbe, where their labors were blessed, and many souls were led to receive Christ as the Saviour. But "when they had preached the gospel to that city, and had taught many," neither Paul nor Barnabas was content to take up work elsewhere without confirming the faith of the converts whom they had been compelled to leave alone for a time in the places where they had recently labored. And so, undaunted by danger, "they returned again to Lystra, and to Iconium, and Antioch, confirming the souls of the disciples, and exhorting them to continue in the faith." Many had accepted the glad tidings of the gospel and had thus exposed themselves to reproach and opposition. These the apostles sought to establish in the faith in order that the work done might abide.

As an important factor in the spiritual growth of the new converts the apostles were careful to surround them with the safeguards of gospel order. Churches were duly organized in all places in Lycaonia and Pisidia where there were believers. Officers were appointed in each church, and proper order and system were established for the conduct of all the affairs pertaining to the spiritual welfare of the believers.

This was in harmony with the gospel plan of uniting in one body all believers in Christ, and this plan Paul was careful to follow throughout his ministry. Those who in any place were by his labor led to accept Christ as the Saviour were at the proper time organized into a church. Even when the believers were but few in number, this was done. The Christians were thus taught to help one another, remembering the promise, "Where two or three are gathered together in My name, there am I in the midst of them." Matthew 18:20.

And Paul did not forget the churches thus established. The care of these churches rested on his mind as an ever-increasing burden. However small a company might be, it was nevertheless the object of his constant solicitude. He watched over the smaller churches tenderly, realizing that they were in need of special care in order that the members might be thoroughly established in the truth and taught to put forth earnest, unselfish efforts for those around them.

In all their missionary endeavors Paul and Barnabas sought to follow Christ's example of willing sacrifice and faithful, earnest labor for souls. Wide-awake, zealous, untiring, they did not consult inclination or personal ease, but with prayerful anxiety and unceasing activity they sowed the seed of truth. And with the sowing of the seed, the apostles were careful to give to all who took their stand for the gospel, practical instruction that was of untold value. This spirit of earnestness and godly fear made upon the minds of the new disciples a lasting impression regarding the importance of the gospel message.

When men of promise and ability were converted, as in the case of Timothy, Paul and Barnabas sought earnestly to show them the necessity of laboring in the vineyard. And when the apostles left for another place, the faith of these men did not fail, but rather increased. They had been faithfully instructed in the way of the Lord, and had been taught how to labor unselfishly, earnestly, perseveringly, for the salvation of their fellow men. This careful training of new converts was an important factor in the remarkable success that attended Paul and Barnabas as they preached the gospel in heathen lands.

The first missionary journey was fast drawing to a close. Commending the newly organized churches to the Lord, the apostles went to Pamphylia, "and when they had preached the word in Perga, they went down into Attalia, and thence sailed to Antioch."

19

Jew and Gentile

This chapter is based on Acts 15:1-35

On reaching Antioch in Syria, from which place they had been sent forth on their mission, Paul and Barnabas took advantage of an early opportunity to assemble the believers and rehearse "all that God had done with them, and how He had opened the door of faith unto the Gentiles." Acts 14:27. The church at Antioch was a large and growing one. A center of missionary activity, it was one of the most important of the groups of Christian believers. Its membership was made up of many classes of people from among both Jews and Gentiles.

While the apostles united with the ministers and lay members at Antioch in an earnest effort to win many souls to Christ, certain Jewish believers from Judea "of the sect of the Pharisees" succeeded in introducing a question that soon led to wide-spread controversy in the church and brought consternation to the believing Gentiles. With great assurance these Judaizing teachers asserted that in order to be saved, one must be circumcised and must keep the entire ceremonial law.

Paul and Barnabas met this false doctrine with promptness and opposed the introduction of the subject to the Gentiles. On the other hand, many of the believing Jews of Antioch favored the position of the brethren recently come from Judea.

The Jewish converts generally were not inclined to move as rapidly as the providence of God opened the way. From the result of the apostles' labors among the Gentiles it was evident that the converts among the latter people would far exceed the Jewish converts in number. The Jews feared that if the restrictions and ceremonies of their law were not made obligatory upon the Gentiles as a condition of church fellowship, the national peculiarities of the Jews, which had hitherto kept them distinct from all other people, would finally disappear from among those who received the gospel message.

The Jews had always prided themselves upon their divinely appointed services, and many of those who had been converted to the faith of Christ still felt that since God had once clearly outlined the Hebrew manner of worship, it was improbable that He would ever authorize a change in any of its specifications. They insisted that the Jewish laws and ceremonies should be incorporated into the rites of the Christian religion. They were slow to discern that all the sacrificial offerings had but prefigured the death of the Son of God, in which type met antitype, and after which the rites and ceremonies of the Mosaic dispensation were no longer binding.

Before his conversion Paul had regarded himself as blameless "touching the righteousness which is in the law." Philippians 3:6. But since his change of heart he had gained a clear conception of the mission of the Saviour as the Redeemer of the entire race, Gentile as well as Jew, and had learned the difference between a living faith and a dead formalism. In the light of the gospel the ancient rites and ceremonies committed to Israel had gained a new and deeper significance. That which they shadowed forth had come to pass, and those who were living under the gospel dispensation had been freed from their observance. God's unchangeable law of Ten Commandments, however, Paul still kept in spirit as well as in letter.

In the church at Antioch the consideration of the question of circumcision resulted in much discussion and contention. Finally, the members of the church, fearing that a division among them would be the outcome of continued discussion, decided to send Paul and Barnabas, with some responsible men from the church, to Jerusalem to lay the matter before the apostles and elders. There they were to meet delegates from the different churches and those who had come to Jerusalem to attend the approaching festivals. Meanwhile all controversy was to cease until a final decision should be given in general council. This decision was then to be universally accepted by the different churches throughout the country.

On the way to Jerusalem the apostles visited the believers in the cities through which they passed, and encouraged them by relating their experience in the work of God and the conversion of the Gentiles.

At Jerusalem the delegates from Antioch met the brethren of the various churches, who had gathered for a general meeting, and to them they related the success that had attended their ministry among the Gentiles. They then gave a clear outline of the confusion that had resulted because certain converted Pharisees had gone to Antioch declaring that, in order to be saved, the Gentile converts must be circumcised and keep the law of Moses.

This question was warmly discussed in the assembly. Intimately connected with the question of circumcision were several others demanding careful study. One was the problem as to what attitude should be taken toward the use of meats offered to idols. Many of the Gentile converts were living among ignorant and superstitious people who made frequent sacrifices and offerings to idols. The priests of this heathen worship carried on an extensive merchandise with the offerings brought to them, and the Jews feared that the Gentile converts would bring Christianity into disrepute by purchasing that which had been offered to idols, thereby sanctioning, in some measure, idolatrous customs.

Again, the Gentiles were accustomed to eat the flesh of animals that has been strangled, while the Jews had been divinely instructed that when beasts were killed for food, particular care was to be taken that the blood should flow from the body; otherwise the meat would not be regarded as wholesome. God had given these injunctions to the Jews for the purpose of preserving their health. The Jews regarded it as sinful to use blood as an article of diet. They held that the blood was the life, and that the shedding of blood was in consequence of sin.

The Gentiles, on the contrary, practiced catching the blood that flowed from the sacrificial victim and using it in the preparation of food. The Jews could not believe that they ought to change the customs they had adopted under the special direction of God. Therefore, as things then stood, if Jew and Gentile should attempt to eat at the same table, the former would be shocked and outraged by the latter.

The Gentiles, and especially the Greeks, were extremely licentious, and there was danger that some, unconverted in heart, would make a profession of faith without renouncing their evil practices. The Jewish Christians could not tolerate the immorality that was not even regarded as criminal by the heathen. The Jews therefore held it as highly proper that circumcision and the observance of the ceremonial law should be enjoined on the Gentile converts as a test of their sincerity and devotion. This, they believed, would prevent the addition to the church of those who, adopting the faith without true conversion of heart, might afterward bring reproach upon the cause by immorality and excess.

The various points involved in the settlement of the main question at issue seemed to present before the council insurmountable difficulties. But the Holy Spirit had, in reality, already settled this question, upon the decision of which seemed to depend the prosperity, if not the very existence, of the Christian church.

"When there had been much disputing, Peter rose up, and said unto them, Men and brethren, ye know how that a good while ago

God made choice among us, that the Gentiles by my mouth should hear the word of the gospel, and believe." He reasoned that the Holy Spirit had decided the matter under dispute by descending with equal power upon the uncircumcised Gentiles and the circumcised Jews. He recounted his vision, in which God had presented before him a sheet filled with all manner of four-footed beasts and had bidden him kill and eat. When he refused, affirming that he had never eaten that which was common or unclean, the answer had been, "What God hath cleansed, that call not thou common." Acts 10:15.

Peter related the plain interpretation of these words, which was given him almost immediately in his summons to go to the centurion and instruct him in the faith of Christ. This message showed that God was no respecter of persons, but accepted and acknowledged all who feared Him. Peter told of his astonishment when, in speaking the words of truth to those assembled at the home of Cornelius, he witnessed the Holy Spirit taking possession of his hearers, Gentiles as well as Jews. The same light and glory that was reflected upon the circumcised Jews shone also upon the faces of the uncircumcised Gentiles. This was God's warning that Peter was not to regard one as inferior to the other, for the blood of Christ could cleanse from all uncleanness.

Once before, Peter had reasoned with his brethren concerning the conversion of Cornelius and his friends, and his fellowship with them. As he on that occasion related how the Holy Spirit fell on the Gentiles he declared, "Forasmuch then as God gave them the like gift as He did unto us, who believed on the Lord Jesus Christ; what was I, that I could withstand God?" Acts 11:17. Now, with equal fervor and force, he said: "God, which knoweth the hearts, bare them witness, giving them the Holy Ghost, even as He did unto us; and put no difference between us and them, purifying their hearts by faith. Now therefore why tempt ye God, to put a yoke upon the neck of the disciples, which neither our fathers nor we were able to bear?" This yoke was not the law of Ten Commandments, as some who oppose the binding claims of the law assert; Peter here referred to the law of ceremonies, which was made null and void by the crucifixion of Christ.

Peter's address brought the assembly to a point where they could listen with patience to Paul and Barnabas, who related their experience in working for the Gentiles. "All the multitude kept silence, and gave audience to Barnabas and Paul, declaring what miracles and wonders God had wrought among the Gentiles by them."

James also bore his testimony with decision, declaring that it was God's purpose to bestow upon the Gentiles the same privileges and blessings that had been granted to the Jews.

The Holy Spirit saw good not to impose the ceremonial law on the Gentile converts, and the mind of the apostles regarding this matter was as the mind of the Spirit of God. James presided at the council, and his final decision was, "Wherefore my sentence is, that we trouble not them, which from among the Gentiles are turned to God."

This ended the discussion. In this instance we have a refutation of the doctrine held by the Roman Catholic Church that Peter was the head of the church. Those who, as popes, have claimed to be his successors, have no Scriptural foundation for their pretensions. Nothing in the life of Peter gives sanction to the claim that he was elevated above his brethren as the vicegerent of the Most High. If those who are declared to be the successors of Peter had followed his example, they would always have been content to remain on an equality with their brethren.

In this instance James seems to have been chosen as the one to announce the decision arrived at by the council. It was his sentence that the ceremonial law, and especially the ordinance of circumcision, should not be urged upon the Gentiles, or even recommended to them. James sought to impress the minds of his brethren with the fact that, in turning to God, the Gentiles had made a great change in their lives and that much caution should be used not to trouble them with perplexing and doubtful questions of minor importance, lest they be discouraged in following Christ.

The Gentile converts, however, were to give up the customs that were inconsistent with the principles of Christianity. The apostles and elders therefore agreed to instruct the Gentiles by letter to abstain from meats offered to idols, from fornication, from things strangled, and from blood. They were to be urged to keep the commandments and to lead holy lives. They were also to be assured that the men who had declared circumcision to be binding were not authorized to do so by the apostles.

Paul and Barnabas were recommended to them as men who had hazarded their lives for the Lord. Judas and Silas were sent with these apostles to declare to the Gentiles by word of mouth the decision of the council: "It seemed good to the Holy Ghost, and to us, to lay upon you no greater burden than these necessary things; that ye abstain from meats offered to idols, and from blood, and from things strangled, and from fornication: from which if ye keep yourselves, ye shall do well." The four servants of God were sent to Antioch with the epistle and message that was to put an end to all controversy; for it was the voice of the highest authority upon the earth.

The council which decided this case was composed of apostles and teachers who had been prominent in raising up the Jewish and Gentile Christian churches, with chosen delegates from various places. Elders from Jerusalem and deputies from Antioch were present, and the most influential churches were represented. The council moved in accordance with the dictates of enlightened judgment, and with the dignity of a church established by the divine will. As a result of their deliberations they all saw that God Himself had answered the question at issue by bestowing upon the Gentiles the Holy Ghost; and they realized that it was their part to follow the guidance of the Spirit.

The entire body of Christians was not called to vote upon the question. The "apostles and elders," men of influence and judgment, framed and issued the decree, which was thereupon generally accepted by the Christian churches. Not all, however, were pleased with the decision; there was a faction of ambitious and self-confident brethren who disagreed with it. These men assumed to engage in the work on their own responsibility. They indulged in much murmuring and faultfinding, proposing new plans and seeking to pull down the work of the men whom God had ordained to teach the gospel message. From the first the church has had such obstacles to meet and ever will have till the close of time.

Jerusalem was the metropolis of the Jews, and it was there that the greatest exclusiveness and bigotry were found. The Jewish Christians living within sight of the temple naturally allowed their minds to revert to the peculiar privileges of the Jews as a nation. When they saw the Christian church departing from the ceremonies and traditions of Judaism, and perceived that the peculiar sacredness with which the Jewish customs had been invested would soon be lost sight of in the light of the new faith, many grew indignant with Paul as the one who had, in a large measure, caused this change. Even the disciples were not all prepared to accept willingly the decision of the council. Some were zealous for the ceremonial law, and they regarded Paul with disfavor because they thought that his principles in regard to the obligations of the Jewish law were lax.

The broad and far-reaching decisions of the general council brought confidence into the ranks of the Gentile believers, and the cause of God prospered. In Antioch the church was favored with the presence of Judas and Silas, the special messengers who had returned with the apostles from the meeting in Jerusalem. "Being prophets also themselves," Judas and Silas, "exhorted the brethren with many words, and confirmed them." These godly men tarried in Antioch for a time. "Paul also and Barnabas continued in Antioch, teaching and preaching the word of the Lord, with many others also."

When Peter, at a later date, visited Antioch, he won the confidence of many by his prudent conduct toward the Gentile converts. For a time he acted in accordance with the light given from heaven. He so far overcame his natural prejudice as to sit at table with the Gentile converts. But when certain Jews who were zealous for the ceremonial law, came from Jerusalem, Peter injudiciously changed his deportment toward the converts from paganism. A number of the Jews "dissembled likewise with him; insomuch that Barnabas also was carried away with their dissimulation." This revelation of weakness on the part of those who had been respected and loved as leaders, left a most painful impression on the minds of the Gentile believers. The church was threatened with division. But Paul, who saw the subverting influence of the wrong done to the church through the double part acted by Peter, openly rebuked him for thus disguising his true sentiments. In the presence of the church, Paul inquired of Peter, "If thou, being a Jew, livest after the manner of Gentiles, and not as do the Jews, why compellest thou the Gentiles to live as do the Jews?" Galatians 2:13, 14.

Peter saw the error into which he had fallen, and immediately set about repairing the evil that had been wrought, so far as was in his power. God, who knows the end from the beginning, permitted Peter to reveal this weakness of character in order that the tried apostle might see that there was nothing in himself whereof he might boast. Even the best of men, if left to themselves, will err in judgment. God also saw that in time to come some would be so deluded as to claim for Peter and his pretended successors the exalted prerogatives that belong to God alone. And this record of the apostle's weakness was to remain as a proof of his fallibility and of the fact that he stood in no way above the level of the other apostles.

The history of this departure from right principles stands as a solemn warning to men in positions of trust in the cause of God, that they may not fail in integrity, but firmly adhere to principle. The greater the responsibilities placed upon the human agent, and the larger his opportunities to dictate and control, the more harm

WE MAY FALL ANY TIME
EVEN SPIRITS OF PROPHETS ARE SUBJECT
TO THE PROPHETS

he is sure to do if he does not carefully follow the way of the Lord and labor in harmony with the decisions arrived at by the general body of believers in united council.

After all Peter's failures; after his fall and restoration, his long course of service, his intimate acquaintance with Christ, his knowledge of the Saviour's straightforward practice of right principles; after all the instruction he had received, all the gifts and knowledge and influence he had gained by preaching and teaching the word—is it not strange that he should dissemble and evade the principles of the gospel through fear of man, or in order to gain esteem? Is it not strange that he should waver in his adherence to right? May God give every man a realization of his helplessness, his inability to steer his own vessel straight and safe into the harbor.

In his ministry, Paul was often compelled to stand alone. He was specially taught of God and dared make no concessions that would involve principle. At times the burden was heavy, but Paul stood firm for the right. He realized that the church must never be brought under the control of human power. The traditions and maxims of men must not take the place of revealed truth. The advance of the gospel message must not be hindered by the prejudices and preferences of men, whatever might be their position in the church.

Paul had dedicated himself and all his powers to the service of God. He had received the truths of the gospel direct from heaven, and throughout his ministry he maintained a vital connection with heavenly agencies. He had been taught by God regarding the binding of unnecessary burdens upon the Gentile Christians; thus when the Judaizing believers introduced into the Antioch church the question of circumcision, Paul knew the mind of the Spirit of God concerning such teaching and took a firm and unyielding position which brought to the churches freedom from Jewish rites and ceremonies.

Notwithstanding the fact that Paul was personally taught by God, he had no strained ideas of individual responsibility. While looking to God for direct guidance, he was ever ready to recognize the authority vested in the body of believers united in church fellowship. He felt the need of counsel, and when matters of importance arose, he was glad to lay these before the church and to unite with his brethren in seeking God for wisdom to make right decisions. Even "the spirits of the prophets," he declared, "are subject to the prophets. For God is not the author of confusion, but of peace, as in all churches of the saints." 1 Corinthians 14:32, 33. With Peter, he taught that all united in church capacity should be "subject one to another." 1 Peter 5:5.

20

Exalting the Cross

This chapter is based on Acts 15:36-41; 16:1-6

After spending some time in ministry at Antioch, Paul proposed to his fellow worker that they set forth on another missionary journey. "Let us go again," he said to Barnabas, "and visit our brethren in every city where we have preached the word of the Lord, and see how they do."

Both Paul and Barnabas had a tender regard for those who had recently accepted the gospel message under their ministry, and they longed to see them once more. This solicitude Paul never lost. Even when in distant mission fields, far from the scene of his earlier labors, he continued to bear upon his heart the burden of urging these converts to remain faithful, "perfecting holiness in the fear of God." 2 Corinthians 7:1. Constantly he tried to help them to become self-reliant, growing Christians, strong in faith, ardent in zeal, and wholehearted in their consecration to God and to the work of advancing His kingdom.

Barnabas was ready to go with Paul, but wished to take with them Mark, who had again decided to devote himself to the ministry. To this Paul objected. He "thought not good to take . . . with them" one who during their first missionary journey had left them in a time of need. He was not inclined to excuse Mark's weakness in deserting the work for the safety and comforts of home. He urged that one with so little stamina was unfitted for a work requiring patience, self-denial, bravery, devotion, faith, and a willingness to sacrifice, if need be, even life itself. So sharp was the contention that Paul and Barnabas separated, the latter following out his convictions and taking Mark with him. "So Barnabas took Mark, and sailed unto Cyprus; and Paul chose Silas, and departed, being recommended by the brethren unto the grace of God."

Journeying through Syria and Cilicia, where they strengthened the church, Paul and Silas at length reached Derbe and Lystra in the province of Lycaonia. It was at Lystra that Paul had been stoned, yet we find him again on the scene of his former danger. He was anxious to see how those who through his labors had accepted the gospel were enduring the test of trial. He was not disappointed, for he found that the Lystrian believers had remained firm in the face of violent opposition.

Here Paul again met Timothy, who had witnessed his sufferings at the close of his first visit to Lystra and upon whose mind the impression then made had deepened with the passing of time until he was convinced that it was his duty to give himself fully to the work of the ministry. His heart was knit with the heart of Paul, and he longed to share the apostle's labors by assisting as the way might open.

Silas, Paul's companion in labor, was a tried worker, gifted with the spirit of prophecy; but the work to be done was so great that there was need of training more laborers for active service. In Timothy Paul saw one who appreciated the sacredness of the work of a minister; who was not appalled at the prospect of suffering and persecution; and who was willing to be taught. Yet the apostle did not venture to take the responsibility of giving Timothy, an untried youth, a training in the gospel ministry, without first fully satisfying himself in regard to his character and his past life.

Timothy's father was a Greek and his mother a Jewess. From a child he had known the Scriptures. The piety that he saw in his home life was sound and sensible. The faith of his mother and his grandmother in the sacred oracles was to him a constant reminder of the blessing in doing God's will. The word of God was the rule by which these two godly women had guided Timothy. The spiritual power of the lessons that he had received from them kept him pure in speech and unsullied by the evil influences with which he was surrounded. Thus his home instructors had co-operated with God in preparing him to bear burdens.

Paul saw that Timothy was faithful, steadfast, and true, and he chose him as a companion in labor and travel. Those who had taught Timothy in his childhood were rewarded by seeing the son of their care linked in close fellowship with the great apostle. Timothy was a mere youth when he was chosen by God to be a teacher, but his principles had been so established by his early education that he was fitted to take his place as Paul's helper. And though young, he bore his responsibilities with Christian meekness.

As a precautionary measure, Paul wisely advised Timothy to be circumcised—not that God required it, but in order to remove from the minds of the Jews that which might be an objection to Timothy's ministration. In his work Paul was to journey from city to city, in many lands, and often he would have opportunity to preach Christ in Jewish synagogues, as well as in other places of assembly. If it

should be known that one of his companions in labor was uncircumcised, his work might be greatly hindered by the prejudice and
bigotry of the Jews. Everywhere the apostle met determined opposition and severe persecution. He desired to bring to his Jewish
brethren, as well as to the Gentiles, a knowledge of the gospel, and
therefore he sought, so far as was consistent with the faith, to
remove every pretext for opposition. Yet while he conceded this
much to Jewish prejudice, he believed and taught circumcision or
uncircumcision to be nothing and the gospel of Christ everything.

Paul loved Timothy, his "own son in the faith." 1 Timothy 1:2.
The great apostle often drew the younger disciple out, questioning
him in regard to Scripture history, and as they traveled from place
to place, he carefully taught him how to do successful work. Both
Paul and Silas, in all their association with Timothy, sought to
deepen the impression that had already been made upon his mind,
of the sacred, serious nature of the work of the gospel minister.

In his work, Timothy constantly sought Paul's advice and
instruction. He did not move from impulse, but exercised consideration and calm thought, inquiring at every step, Is this the way of
the Lord? The Holy Spirit found in him one who could be molded
and fashioned as a temple for the indwelling of the divine Presence.

As the lessons of the Bible are wrought into the daily life, they
have a deep and lasting influence upon the character. These lessons
Timothy learned and practiced. He had no specially brilliant talents,
but his work was valuable because he used his God-given abilities
in the Master's service. His knowledge of experimental piety
distinguished him from other believers and gave him influence.

Those who labor for souls must attain to a deeper, fuller, clearer
knowledge of God than can be gained by ordinary effort. They must
throw all their energies into the work of the Master. They are
engaged in a high and holy calling, and if they gain souls for their
hire they must lay firm hold upon God, daily receiving grace and
power from the Source of all blessing. "For the grace of God that
bringeth salvation hath appeared to all men, teaching us that,
denying ungodliness and worldly lusts, we should live soberly,
righteously, and godly, in this present world; looking for that
blessed hope, and the glorious appearing of the great God and our
Saviour Jesus Christ; who gave Himself for us, that He might
redeem us from all iniquity, and purify unto Himself a peculiar
people, zealous of good works." Titus 2:11-14.

Before pressing forward into new territory, Paul and his companions visited the churches that had been established in Pisidia

TRUTH THAT IS NOT LIVED, LOOSES ITS LIFE-GIVING POWER - ITS HEALING VIRTUE.

and the regions round about. "As they went through the cities, they delivered them the decrees for to keep, that were ordained of the apostles and elders which were at Jerusalem. And so were the churches established in the faith, and increased in number daily."

The apostle Paul felt a deep responsibility for those converted under his labors. Above all things, he longed that they should be faithful, "that I may rejoice in the day of Christ," he said, "that I have not run in vain, neither labored in vain." Philippians 2:16. He trembled for the result of his ministry. He felt that even his own salvation might be imperiled if he should fail of fulfilling his duty and the church should fail of co-operating with him in the work of saving souls. He knew that preaching alone would not suffice to educate the believers to hold forth the word of life. He knew that line upon line, precept upon precept, here a little and there a little, they must be taught to advance in the work of Christ.

It is a universal principle that whenever one refuses to use his God-given powers, these powers decay and perish. Truth that is not lived, that is not imparted, loses its life-giving power, its healing virtue. Hence the apostle's fear that he might fail of presenting every man perfect in Christ. Paul's hope of heaven grew dim when he contemplated any failure on his part that would result in giving the church the mold of the human instead of the divine. His knowledge, his eloquence, his miracles, his view of eternal scenes when caught up to the third heaven—all would be unavailing if through unfaithfulness in his work those for whom he labored should fail of the grace of God. And so, by word of mouth and by letter, he pleaded with those who had accepted Christ, to pursue a course that would enable them to be "blameless and harmless, the sons of God, without rebuke, in the midst of a crooked and perverse nation, . . . as lights in the world, holding forth the word of life." Philippians 2:15, 16.

Every true minister feels a heavy responsibility for the spiritual advancement of the believers entrusted to his care, a longing desire that they shall be laborers together with God. He realizes that upon the faithful performance of his God-given work depends in a large degree the well-being of the church. Earnestly and untiringly he seeks to inspire the believers with a desire to win souls for Christ, remembering that every addition to the church should be one more agency for the carrying out of the plan of redemption.

Having visited the churches in Pisidia and the neighboring region, Paul and Silas, with Timothy, pressed on into "Phrygia and the region of Galatia," where with mighty power they proclaimed the glad tidings of salvation. The Galatians were given up to the worship of idols; but, as the apostles preached to them, they rejoiced in the message that promised freedom from the thralldom of sin. Paul and his fellow workers proclaimed the doctrine of righteousness by faith in the atoning sacrifice of Christ. They presented Christ as the one who, seeing the helpless condition of the fallen race, came to redeem men and women by living a life of obedience to God's law and by paying the penalty of disobedience. And in the light of the cross many who had never before known of the true God, began to comprehend the greatness of the Father's love.

Thus the Galatians were taught the fundamental truths concerning "God the Father" and "our Lord Jesus Christ, who gave Himself for our sins, that He might deliver us from this present evil world, according to the will of God and our Father." "By the hearing of faith" they received the Spirit of God and became "the children of God by faith in Christ." Galatians 1:3, 4; 3:2, 26.

Paul's manner of life while among the Galatians was such that he could afterward say, "I beseech you, be as I am." Galatians 4:12. His lips had been touched with a live coal from off the altar, and he was enabled to rise above bodily infirmities and to present Jesus as the sinner's only hope. Those who heard him knew that he had been with Jesus. Endued with power from on high, he was able to compare spiritual things with spiritual and to tear down the strongholds of Satan. Hearts were broken by his presentation of the love of God, as revealed in the sacrifice of His only-begotten Son, and many were led to inquire, What must I do to be saved?

This method of presenting the gospel characterized the labors of the apostle throughout his ministry among the Gentiles. Always he kept before them the cross of Calvary. "We preach not ourselves," he declared in the later years of his experience, "but Christ Jesus the Lord; and ourselves your servants for Jesus' sake. For God, who commanded the light to shine out of darkness, hath shined in our hearts, to give the light of the knowledge of the glory of God in the face of Jesus Christ." 2 Corinthians 4:5, 6.

The consecrated messengers who in the early days of Christianity carried to a perishing world the glad tidings of salvation, allowed no thought of self-exaltation to mar their presentation of Christ and Him crucified. They coveted neither authority nor pre-eminence. Hiding self in the Saviour, they exalted the great plan of salvation, and the life of Christ, the Author and Finisher of this plan. Christ, the same yesterday, today, and forever, was the burden of their teaching.

If those who today are teaching the word of God, would uplift the cross of Christ higher and still higher, their ministry would be far more successful. If sinners can be led to give one earnest look at the cross, if they can obtain a full view of the crucified Saviour, they will realize the depth of God's compassion and the sinfulness of sin.

Christ's death proves God's great love for man. It is our pledge of salvation. To remove the cross from the Christian would be like blotting the sun from the sky. The cross brings us near to God, reconciling us to Him. With the relenting compassion of a father's love, Jehovah looks upon the suffering that His Son endured in order to save the race from eternal death, and accepts us in the Beloved.

Without the cross, man could have no union with the Father. On it depends our every hope. From it shines the light of the Saviour's love, and when at the foot of the cross the sinner looks up to the One who died to save him, he may rejoice with fullness of joy, for his sins are pardoned. Kneeling in faith at the cross, he has reached the highest place to which man can attain.

Through the cross we learn that the heavenly Father loves us with a love that is infinite. Can we wonder that Paul exclaimed, "God forbid that I should glory, save in the cross of our Lord Jesus Christ"? Galatians 6:14. It is our privilege also to glory in the cross, our privilege to give ourselves wholly to Him who gave Himself for us. Then, with the light that streams from Calvary shining in our faces, we may go forth to reveal this light to those in darkness.

21

In the Regions Beyond

This chapter is based on Acts 16:7-40

The time had come for the gospel to be proclaimed beyond the confines of Asia Minor. The way was preparing for Paul and his fellow workers to cross over into Europe. At Troas, on the borders of the Mediterranean Sea, "a vision appeared to Paul in the night: There stood a man of Macedonia, and prayed him, saying, Come over into Macedonia, and help us."

The call was imperative, admitting of no delay. "After he had seen the vision," declares Luke, who accompanied Paul and Silas and Timothy on the journey across to Europe, "immediately we endeavored to go into Macedonia, assuredly gathering that the Lord had called us for to preach the gospel unto them. Therefore loosing from Troas, we came with a straight course to Samothracia, and the next day to Neapolis; and from thence to Philippi, which is the chief city of that part of Macedonia, and a colony."

"On the Sabbath," Lukes continues, "we went out of the city by a riverside, where prayer was wont to be made; and we sat down, and spake unto the women which resorted thither. And a certain woman named Lydia, a seller of purple, of the city of Thyatira, which worshiped God, heard us: whose heart the Lord opened." Lydia received the truth gladly. She and her household were converted and baptized, and she entreated the apostles to make her house their home.

As the messengers of the cross went about their work of teaching, a woman possessed of a spirit of divination followed them, crying, "These men are the servants of the most high God, which show unto us the way of salvation. And this did she many days."

This woman was a special agent of Satan and had brought to her masters much gain by soothsaying. Her influence had helped to strengthen idolatry. Satan knew that his kingdom was being invaded, and he resorted to this means of opposing the work of God, hoping to mingle his sophistry with the truths taught by those who were proclaiming the gospel message. The words of recommendation uttered by this woman were an injury to the cause of truth, distracting the minds of the people from the teachings of the apostles and bringing disrepute upon the gospel, and by them many were led to believe that the men who spoke with the Spirit and power of God were actuated by the same spirit as this emissary of Satan.

For some time the apostles endured this opposition; then under the inspiration of the Holy Ghost Paul commanded the evil spirit to leave the woman. Her immediate silence testified that the apostles were the servants of God and that the demon had acknowledged them to be such and had obeyed their command.

Dispossessed of the evil spirit and restored to her right mind, the woman chose to become a follower of Christ. Then her masters were alarmed for their craft. They saw that all hope of receiving money from her divinations and soothsayings was at an end and that their source of income would soon be entirely cut off if the apostles were allowed to continue the work of the gospel.

Many others in the city were interested in gaining money through satanic delusions, and these, fearing the influence of a power that could so effectually stop their work, raised a mighty cry against the servants of God. They brought the apostles before the magistrates with the charge: "These men, being Jews, do exceedingly trouble our city, and teach customs, which are not lawful for us to receive, neither to observe, being Romans."

Stirred by a frenzy of excitement, the multitude rose against the disciples. A mob spirit prevailed and was sanctioned by the authorities, who tore the outer garments from the apostles and commanded that they should be scourged. "And when they had laid many stripes upon them, they cast them into prison, charging the jailer to keep them safely: who, having received such a charge, thrust them into the inner prison, and made their feet fast in the stocks."

The apostles suffered extreme torture because of the painful position in which they were left, but they did not murmur. Instead, in the utter darkness and desolation of the dungeon, they encouraged each other by words of prayer and sang praises to God because they were found worthy to suffer shame for His sake. Their hearts were cheered by a deep and earnest love for the cause of their Redeemer. Paul thought of the persecution he had been instrumental in bringing upon the disciples of Christ, and he rejoiced that his eyes had been opened to see, and his heart to feel, the power of the glorious truths which once he despised.

With astonishment the other prisoners heard the sound of prayer and singing issuing from the inner prison. They had been accustomed to hear shrieks and moans, cursing and swearing, breaking the silence of the night; but never before had they heard words of prayer and praise ascending from that gloomy cell. Guards and prisoners marveled and asked themselves who these men could be, who, cold, hungry, and tortured, could yet rejoice.

Meanwhile the magistrates returned to their homes, congratulating themselves that by prompt and decisive measures they had quelled a tumult. But on the way they heard further particulars concerning the character and work of the men they had sentenced to scourging and imprisonment. They saw the woman who had been freed from satanic influence and were struck by the change in her countenance and demeanor. In the past she had caused the city much trouble; now she was quiet and peaceable. As they realized that in all probability they had visited upon two innocent men the rigorous penalty of the Roman law they were indignant with themselves and decided that in the morning they would command that the apostles be privately released and escorted from the city, beyond the danger of violence from the mob.

But while men were cruel and vindictive, or criminally negligent of the solemn responsibilities devolving upon them, God had not forgotten to be gracious to His servants. All heaven was interested in the men who were suffering for Christ's sake, and angels were sent to visit the prison. At their tread the earth trembled. The heavily bolted prison doors were thrown open; the chains and fetters fell from the hands and feet of the prisoners; and a bright light flooded the prison.

The keeper of the jail had heard with amazement the prayers and songs of the imprisoned apostles. When they were led in, he had seen their swollen and bleeding wounds, and had himself caused their feet to be fastened in the stocks. He had expected to hear from them bitter groans and imprecations, but he heard instead songs of joy and praise. With these sounds in his ears the jailer had fallen into a sleep from which he was awakened by the earthquake and the shaking of the prison walls.

Starting up in alarm, he saw with dismay that all the prison doors were open, and the fear flashed upon him that the prisoners had escaped. He remembered with what explicit charge Paul and Silas had been entrusted to his care the night before, and he was certain that death would be the penalty of his apparent unfaithfulness. In the bitterness of his spirit he felt that it was better for him to die by his own hand than to submit to a disgraceful execution. Drawing his sword, he was about to kill himself, when Paul's voice was heard in the words of cheer, "Do thyself no harm: for we are all here." Every man was in his place, restrained by the power of God exerted through one fellow prisoner.

The severity with which the jailer had treated the apostles had not aroused their resentment. Paul and Silas had the spirit of Christ, not the spirit of revenge. Their hearts, filled with the love of the Saviour, had no room for malice against their persecutors.

The jailer dropped his sword and, calling for lights, hastened into the inner dungeon. He would see what manner of men these were who repaid with kindness the cruelty with which they had been treated. Reaching the place where the apostles were, and casting himself before them, he asked their forgiveness. Then, bringing them out into the open court, he inquired, "Sirs, what must I do to be saved?"

The jailer had trembled as he beheld the wrath of God manifested in the earthquake; when he thought that the prisoners had escaped he had been ready to die by his own hand; but now all these things seemed of little consequence compared with the new, strange dread that agitated his mind, and his desire to possess the tranquillity and cheerfulness shown by the apostles under suffering and abuse. He saw in their countenances the light of heaven; he knew that God had interposed in a miraculous manner to save their lives; and with peculiar force the words of the spirit-possessed woman came to his mind: "These men are the servants of the most high God, which show unto us the way of salvation.

With deep humility he asked the apostles to show him the way of life. "Believe on the Lord Jesus Christ, and thou shalt be saved, and thy house," they answered; and "they spake unto him the word of the Lord, and to all that were in his house." The jailer then washed the wounds of the apostles and ministered to them, after which he was baptized by them, with all his household. A sanctifying influence diffused itself among the inmates of the prison, and the minds of all were opened to listen to the truths spoken by the apostles. They were convinced that the God whom these men served had miraculously released them from bondage.

The citizens of Philippi had been greatly terrified by the earthquake, and when in the morning the officers of the prison told the magistrates of what had occurred during the night, they were alarmed and sent the sergeants to liberate the apostles. But Paul declared, "They have beaten us openly uncondemned, being Romans, and have cast us into prison; and now do they thrust us out privily? nay verily; but let them come themselves and fetch us out."

The apostles were Roman citizens, and it was unlawful to

scourge a Roman, save for the most flagrant crime, or to deprive him of his liberty without a fair trial. Paul and Silas had been publicly imprisoned, and they now refused to be privately released without the proper explanation on the part of the magistrates.

When this word was brought to the authorities, they were alarmed for fear that the apostles would complain to the emperor, and going at once to the prison, they apologized to Paul and Silas for the injustice and cruelty done them and personally conducted them out of the prison, entreating them to depart from the city. The magistrates feared the apostles' influence over the people, and they also feared the Power that had interposed in behalf of these innocent men.

Acting upon the instruction given by Christ, the apostles would not urge their presence where it was not desired. "They went out of the prison, and entered into the house of Lydia: and when they had seen the brethren, they comforted them, and departed."

The apostles did not regard as in vain their labors in Philippi. They had met much opposition and persecution; but the intervention of Providence in their behalf, and the conversion of the jailer and his household, more than atoned for the disgrace and suffering they had endured. The news of their unjust imprisonment and miraculous deliverance became known through all that region, and this brought the work of the apostles to the notice of a large number who otherwise would not have been reached.

Paul's labors at Philippi resulted in the establishment of a church whose membership steadily increased. His zeal and devotion, and, above all, his willingness to suffer for Christ's sake, exerted a deep and lasting influence upon the converts. They prized the precious truths for which the apostles had sacrificed so much, and gave themselves with wholehearted devotion to the cause of their Redeemer.

That this church did not escape persecution is shown by an expression in Paul's letter to them. He says, "Unto you it is given in the behalf of Christ, not only to believe on Him, but also to suffer for His sake; having the same conflict which ye saw in me." Yet such was their steadfastness in the faith that he declares, "I thank my God upon every remembrance of you, always in every prayer of mine for you all making request with joy, for your fellowship in the gospel from the first day until now." Philippians 1:29, 30, 3-5.

Terrible is the struggle that takes place between the forces of good and of evil in important centers where the messengers of truth are called upon to labor. "We wrestle not against flesh and blood," declares Paul, "but against principalities, against powers, against the rulers of the darkness of this world." Ephesians 6:12. Till the close of time there will be a conflict between the church of God and those who are under the control of evil angels.

The early Christians were often called to meet the powers of darkness face to face. By sophistry and by persecution the enemy endeavored to turn them from the true faith. At the present time, when the end of all things earthly is rapidly approaching, Satan is putting forth desperate efforts to ensnare the world. He is devising many plans to occupy minds and to divert attention from the truths essential to salvation. In every city his agencies are busily organizing into parties those who are opposed to the law of God. The archdeceiver is at work to introduce elements of confusion and rebellion, and men are being fired with a zeal that is not according to knowledge.

Wickedness is reaching a height never before attained, and yet many ministers of the gospel are crying, "Peace and safety." But God's faithful messengers are to go steadily forward with their work. Clothed with the panoply of heaven, they are to advance fearlessly and victoriously, never ceasing their warfare until every soul within their reach shall have received the message of truth for this time.

22

Thessalonica

This chapter is based on Acts 17:1-10

After leaving Philippi, Paul and Silas made their way to Thessalonica. Here they were given the privilege of addressing large congregations in the Jewish synagogue. Their appearance bore evidence of the shameful treatment they had recently received, and necessitated an explanation of what had taken place. This they made without exalting themselves, but magnified the One who had wrought their deliverance.

In preaching to the Thessalonians, Paul appealed to the Old Testament prophecies concerning the Messiah. Christ in His ministry had opened the minds of His disciples to these prophecies; "beginning at Moses and all the prophets, He expounded unto them in all the Scriptures the things concerning Himself." Luke 24:27. Peter in preaching Christ had produced his evidence from the Old Testament. Stephen had pursued the same course. And Paul also in his ministry appealed to the scriptures foretelling the birth, sufferings, death, resurrection, and ascension of Christ. By the inspired testimony of Moses and the prophets he clearly proved the identity of Jesus of Nazareth with the Messiah and showed that from the days of Adam it was the voice of Christ which had been speaking through patriarchs and prophets.

Plain and specific prophecies had been given regarding the appearance of the Promised One. To Adam was given an assurance of the coming of the Redeemer. The sentence pronounced on Satan, "I will put enmity between thee and the woman, and between thy seed and her seed; it shall bruise thy head, and thou shalt bruise his heel" (Genesis 3:15), was to our first parents a promise of the redemption to be wrought out through Christ.

To Abraham was given the promise that of his line of Saviour of the world should come: "In thy seed shall all the nations of the earth be blessed." "He saith not, And to seeds, as of many; but as of one, And to thy seed, which is Christ." Genesis 22:18; Galatians 3:16.

Moses, near the close of his work as a leader and teacher of Israel, plainly prophesied of the Messiah to come. "The Lord thy

God," he declared to the assembled hosts of Israel, "will raise up unto thee a Prophet from the midst of thee, of thy brethren, like unto me; unto Him ye shall hearken." And Moses assured the Israelites that God Himself had revealed this to him while in Mount Horeb, saying, "I will raise them up a Prophet from among their brethren, like unto thee, and will put My words in His mouth; and He shall speak unto them all that I shall command Him." Deuteronomy 18:15, 18.

The Messiah was to be of the royal line, for in the prophecy uttered by Jacob the Lord said, "The scepter shall not depart from Judah, nor a lawgiver from between his feet, until Shiloh come; and unto Him shall the gathering of the people be." Genesis 49:10.

Isaiah prophesied: "There shall come forth a rod out of the stem of Jesse, and a Branch shall grow out of his roots." "Incline your ear, and come unto Me: hear, and your soul shall live; and I will make an everlasting covenant with you, even the sure mercies of David. Behold, I have given Him for a witness to the people, a leader and commander to the people. Behold, thou shalt call a nation that thou knowest not, and nations that knew not thee shall run unto thee because of the Lord thy God, and for the Holy One of Israel; for He hath glorified thee." Isaiah 11:1; 55:3-5.

Jeremiah also bore witness of the coming Redeemer as a Prince of the house of David: "Behold, the days come, saith the Lord, that I will raise unto David a righteous Branch, and a King shall reign and prosper, and shall execute judgment and justice in the earth. In His days Judah shall be saved, and Israel shall dwell safely: and this is His name whereby He shall be called, The Lord Our Righteousness." And again: "Thus saith the Lord: David shall never want a man to sit upon the throne of the house of Israel; neither shall the priests the Levites want a man before Me to offer burnt offerings, and to kindle meat offerings, and to do sacrifice continually." Jeremiah 23:5, 6; 33:17, 18.

Even the birthplace of the Messiah was foretold: "Thou, Bethlehem Ephratah, though thou be little among the thousands of Judah, yet out of thee shall He come forth unto Me that is to be Ruler in Israel; whose goings forth have been from of old, from everlasting." Micah 5:2.

The work that the Saviour was to do on the earth had been fully outlined: "The Spirit of the Lord shall rest upon Him, the spirit of wisdom and understanding, the spirit of counsel and might, the spirit of knowledge and of the fear of the Lord; and shall make Him of quick understanding in the fear of the Lord." The One thus anointed was "to preach good tidings unto the meek; . . . to bind up the brokenhearted, to proclaim liberty to the captives, and the opening of the prison to them that are bound; to proclaim the acceptable year of the Lord, and the day of vengeance of our God; to comfort all that mourn; to appoint unto them that mourn in Zion, to give unto them beauty for ashes, the oil of joy for mourning, the garment of praise for the spirit of heaviness; that they might be called trees of righteousness, the planting of the Lord, that He might be glorified." Isaiah 11:2, 3; 61:1-3.

"Behold My servant, whom I uphold; Mine elect, in whom My soul delighteth; I have put My Spirit upon Him: He shall bring forth judgment to the Gentiles. He shall not cry, nor lift up, nor cause His voice to be heard in the street. A bruised reed shall He not break, and the smoking flax shall He not quench: He shall bring forth judgment unto truth. He shall not fail nor be discouraged, till He have set judgment in the earth: and the isles shall wait for His law." Isaiah 42:1-4.

With convincing power Paul reasoned from the Old Testament Scriptures that "Christ must needs have suffered, and risen again from the dead." Had not Micah prophesied, "They shall smite the Judge of Israel with a rod upon the cheek"? Micah 5:1. And had not the Promised One, through Isaiah, prophesied of Himself, "I gave My back to the smiters, and My cheeks to them that plucked off the hair: I hid not My face from shame and spitting"? Isaiah 50:6. Through the psalmist Christ had foretold the treatment that He should receive from men: "I am . . . a reproach of men, and despised of the people. All they that see Me laugh Me to scorn: they shoot out the lip, they shake the head, saying, He trusted on the Lord that He would deliver Him: let Him deliver Him, seeing He delighted in Him." "I may tell all My bones: they look and stare upon Me. They part My garments among them, and cast lots upon My vesture." "I am become a stranger unto My brethren, and an alien unto My mother's children. For the zeal of Thine house hath eaten Me up; and the reproaches of them that reproached Thee are fallen upon Me." "Reproach hath broken My heart; and I am full of heaviness: and I looked for some to take pity, but there was none; and for comforters, but I found none." Psalms 22:6-8, 17, 18; 69:8, 9, 20.

How unmistakably plain were Isaiah's prophecies of Christ's sufferings and death! "Who hath believed our report? "the prophet inquires, "and to whom is the arm of the Lord revealed? For He shall grow up before Him as a tender plant, and as a root out of a dry ground: He hath no form nor comeliness; and when we shall see Him, there is no beauty that we should desire Him. He is despised and rejected of men; a man of sorrows, and acquainted with grief: and we hid as it were our faces from Him; He was despised, and we esteemed Him not.

"Surely He hath borne our griefs, and carried our sorrows: yet we did esteem Him stricken, smitten of God, and afflicted. But He was wounded for our transgressions, He was bruised for our iniquities: the chastisement of our peace was upon Him; and with His stripes we are healed.

"All we like sheep have gone astray; we have turned everyone to his own way; and the Lord hath laid on Him the iniquity of us all. He was oppressed, and he was afflicted, yet He opened not His mouth: He is brought as a lamb to the slaughter, and as a sheep before her shearers is dumb, so He openeth not His mouth. He was taken from prison and from judgment: and who shall declare His generation? for He was cut off out of the land of the living: for the transgression of my people was He stricken." Isaiah 53:1-8.

Even the manner of His death had been shadowed forth. As the brazen serpent had been uplifted in the wilderness, so was the coming Redeemer to be lifted up, "that whosoever believeth in Him should not perish, but have everlasting life." John 3:16.

"One shall say unto Him, What are these wounds in Thine hands? Then He shall answer, Those with which I was wounded in the house of My friends." Zechariah 13:6.

"He made His grave with the wicked, and with the rich in His death; because He had done no violence, neither was any deceit in His mouth. Yet it pleased the Lord to bruise Him; He hath put Him to grief." Isaiah 53:9, 10.

But He who was to suffer death at the hands of evil men was to rise again as a conqueror over sin and the grave. Under the inspiration of the Almighty the Sweet Singer of Israel had testified of the glories of the resurrection morn. "My flesh also," he joyously proclaimed, "shall rest in hope. For Thou wilt not leave My soul in hell [the grave]; neither wilt Thou suffer Thine Holy One to see corruption." Psalm 16:9, 10.

Paul showed how closely God had linked the sacrificial service with the prophecies relating to the One who was to be "brought as a lamb to the slaughter." The Messiah was to give His life as "an offering for sin." Looking down through the centuries to the scenes of the Saviour's atonement, the prophet Isaiah had testified that the Lamb of God "poured out His soul unto death: and He was numbered with the transgressors; and He bare the sin of many, and made intercession for the transgressors." Isaiah 53:7, 10, 12.

The Saviour of prophecy was to come, not as a temporal king, to deliver the Jewish nation from earthly oppressors, but as a man among men, to live a life of poverty and humility, and at last to be despised, rejected, and slain. The Saviour foretold in the Old Testament Scriptures was to offer Himself as a sacrifice in behalf of the fallen race, thus fulfilling every requirement of the broken law. In Him the sacrificial types were to meet their antitype, and His death on the cross was to lend significance to the entire Jewish economy.

Paul told the Thessalonian Jews of his former zeal for the ceremonial law and of his wonderful experience at the gate of Damascus. Before his conversion he had been confident in a hereditary piety, a false hope. His faith had not been anchored in Christ; he had trusted instead in forms and ceremonies. His zeal for the law had been disconnected from faith in Christ and was of no avail. While boasting that he was blameless in the performance of the deeds of the law, he had refused the One who made the law of value.

But at the time of his conversion all had been changed. Jesus of Nazareth, whom he had been persecuting in the person of His saints, appeared before him as the promised Messiah. The persecutor saw Him as the Son of God, the one who had come to the earth in fulfillment of the prophecies and who in His life had met every specification of the Sacred Writings.

As with holy boldness Paul proclaimed the gospel in the synagogue at Thessalonica, a flood of light was thrown upon the true meaning of the rites and ceremonies connected with the tabernacle service. He carried the minds of his hearers beyond the earthly service and the ministry of Christ in the heavenly sanctuary, to the time when, having completed His mediatorial work, Christ would come again in power and great glory, and establish His kingdom on the earth. Paul was a believer in the second coming of Christ; so clearly and forcibly did he present the truths concerning this event, that upon the minds of many who heard there was made an impression which never wore away.

For three successive Sabbaths Paul preached to the Thessalonians, reasoning with them from the Scriptures regarding the life, death, resurrection, office work, and future glory of Christ, the "Lamb slain from the foundation of the world." Revelation 13:8. He exalted Christ, the proper understanding of whose ministry is the key that unlocks the Old Testament Scriptures, giving access to their rich treasures.

As the truths of the gospel were thus proclaimed in Thessalonica with mighty power, the attention of large congregations was arrested. "Some of them believed, and consorted with Paul and Silas; and of the devout Greeks a great multitude, and of the chief women not a few."

As in the places formerly entered, the apostles met with determined opposition. "The Jews which believed not" were "moved with envy." These Jews were not then in favor with the Roman power, because, not long before, they had raised an insurrection in Rome. They were looked upon with suspicion, and their liberty was in a measure restricted. They now saw an opportunity to take advantage of circumstances to re-establish themselves in favor and at the same time to throw reproach upon the apostles and the converts to Christianity.

This they set about doing by uniting with "certain lewd fellows of the baser sort," by which means they succeeded in setting "all the city on an uproar." In the hope of finding the apostles, they "assaulted the house of Jason;" but they could find neither Paul nor Silas. And "when they found them not," the mob in their mad disappointment "drew Jason and certain brethren unto the rulers of the city, crying, These that have turned the world upside down are come hither also; whom Jason hath received: and these all do contrary to the decrees of Caesar, saying that there is another king, one Jesus."

As Paul and Silas were not to be found, the magistrates put the accused believers under bonds to keep the peace. Fearing further violence, "the brethren immediately sent away Paul and Silas by night unto Berea."

Those who today teach unpopular truths need not be discouraged if at times they meet with no more favorable reception, even from those who claim to be Christians, than did Paul and his fellow workers from the people among whom they labored. The messengers of the cross must arm themselves with watchfulness and prayer, and move forward with faith and courage, working always in the name of Jesus. They must exalt Christ as man's mediator in the heavenly sanctuary, the One in whom all the sacrifices of the Old Testament dispensation centered, and through whose atoning sacrifice the transgressors of God's law may find peace and pardon.

23

Berea and Athens

This chapter is based on Acts 17:11-34

At Berea Paul found Jews who were willing to investigate the truths he taught. Luke's record declares of them: "These were more noble than those in Thessalonica, in that they received the word with all readiness of mind, and searched the Scriptures daily, whether those things were so. Therefore many of them believed; also of honorable women which were Greeks, and of men, not a few."

The minds of the Bereans were not narrowed by prejudice. They were willing to investigate the truthfulness of the doctrines preached by the apostles. They studied the Bible, not from curiosity, but in order that they might learn what had been written concerning the promised Messiah. Daily they searched the inspired records, and as they compared scripture with scripture, heavenly angels were beside them, enlightening their minds and impressing their hearts.

Wherever the truths of the gospel are proclaimed, those who honestly desire to do right are led to a diligent searching of the Scriptures. If, in the closing scenes of this earth's history, those to whom testing truths are proclaimed would follow the example of the Bereans, searching the Scriptures daily, and comparing with God's word the messages brought them, there would today be a large number loyal to the precepts of God's law, where now there are comparatively few. But when unpopular Bible truths are presented, many refuse to make this investigation. Though unable to controvert the plain teachings of Scripture, they yet manifest the utmost reluctance to study the evidences offered. Some assume that even if these doctrines are indeed true, it matters little whether or not they accept the new light, and they cling to pleasing fables which the enemy uses to lead souls astray. Thus their minds are blinded by error, and they become separated from heaven.

All will be judged according to the light that has been given. The Lord sends forth His ambassadors with a message of salvation, and those who hear He will hold responsible for the way in which they treat the words of His servants. Those who are sincerely seeking for truth will make a careful investigation, in the light of God's word, of the doctrines presented to them.

The unbelieving Jews of Thessalonica, filled with jealousy and hatred of the apostles, and not content with having driven them from their own city, followed them to Berea and aroused against them the excitable passions of the lower class. Fearing that violence would be done to Paul if he remained there, the brethren sent him to Athens, accompanied by some of the Bereans who had newly accepted the faith.

Thus persecution followed the teachers of truth from city to city. The enemies of Christ could not prevent the advancement of the gospel, but they succeeded in making the work of the apostles exceedingly hard. Yet in the face of opposition and conflict, Paul pressed steadily forward, determined to carry out the purpose of God as revealed to him in the vision at Jerusalem: "I will send thee far hence unto the Gentiles." Acts 22:21.

Paul's hasty departure from Berea deprived him of the opportunity he had anticipated of visiting the brethren at Thessalonica.

On arriving at Athens, the apostle sent the Berean brethren back with a message to Silas and Timothy to join him immediately. Timothy had come to Berea prior to Paul's departure, and with Silas had remained to carry on the work so well begun there, and to instruct the new converts in the principles of the faith.

The city of Athens was the metropolis of heathendom. Here Paul did not meet with an ignorant, credulous populace, as at Lystra, but with a people famous for their intelligence and culture. Everywhere statues of their gods and of the deified heroes of history and poetry met the eye, while magnificent architecture and paintings represented the national glory and the popular worship of heathen deities. The senses of the people were entranced by the beauty and splendor of art. On every hand sanctuaries and temples, involving untold expense, reared their massive forms. Victories of arms and deeds of celebrated men were commemorated by sculpture, shrines, and tablets. All these made Athens a vast gallery of art.

As Paul looked upon the beauty and grandeur surrounding him, and saw the city wholly given to idolatry, his spirit was stirred with jealousy for God, whom he saw dishonored on every side, and his heart was drawn out in pity for the people of Athens, who, notwithstanding their intellectual culture, were ignorant of the true God.

The apostle was not deceived by that which he saw in this center of learning. His spiritual nature was so alive to the attraction of heavenly things that the joy and glory of the riches which will never perish made valueless in his eyes the pomp and splendor with which he was surrounded. As he saw the magnificence of Athens he realized its seductive power over lovers of art and science, and his mind was deeply impressed with the importance of the work before him.

In this great city, where God was not worshiped, Paul was oppressed by a feeling of solitude, and he longed for the sympathy and aid of his fellow laborers. So far as human friendship was concerned, he felt himself to be utterly alone. In his epistle to the Thessalonians he expresses his feelings in the words, "Left at the Athens alone." 1 Thessalonians 3:1. Obstacles that were apparently insurmountable presented themselves before him, making it seem almost hopeless for him to attempt to reach the hearts of the people.

While waiting for Silas and Timothy, Paul was not idle. He "disputed . . . in the synagogue with the Jews, and with the devout persons, and in the market daily with them that met with him." But his principal work in Athens was to bear the tidings of salvation to those who had no intelligent conception of God and of His purpose in behalf of the fallen race. The apostle was soon to meet paganism in its most subtle, alluring form.

The great men of Athens were not long in learning of the presence in their city of a singular teacher who was setting before the people doctrines new and strange. Some of these men sought Paul out and entered into conversation with him. Soon a crowd of listeners gathered about them. Some were prepared to ridicule the apostle as one who was far beneath them both socially and intellectually, and these said jeeringly among themselves, "What will this babbler say?" Others, "because he preached unto them Jesus, and the resurrection," said, "He seemeth to be a setter forth of strange gods."

Among those who encountered Paul in the market place were "certain philosophers of the Epicureans, and of the Stoics;" but they, and all others who came in contact with him, soon saw that he had a store of knowledge even greater than their own. His intellectual power commanded the respect of the learned; while his earnest, logical reasoning and the power of his oratory held the attention of all in the audience. His hearers recognized the fact that he was no novice, but was able to meet all classes with convincing arguments in support of the doctrines he taught. Thus the apostle stood undaunted, meeting his opposers on their own ground, matching logic with logic, philosophy with philosophy, eloquence with eloquence.

His heathen opponents called his attention to the fate of Socrates, who, because he was a setter forth of strange gods, had been condemned to death, and they counseled Paul not to endanger his life in the same way. But the apostle's discourses riveted the attention of the people, and his unaffected wisdom commanded their respect and admiration. He was not silenced by the science or the irony of the philosophers, and satisfying themselves that he was determined to accomplish his errand among them, and, at all hazards, to tell his story, they decided to give him a fair hearing.

They accordingly conducted him to Mars' Hill. This was one of the most sacred spots in all Athens, and its recollections and associations were such as to cause it to be regarded with a superstitious reverence that in the minds of some amounted to dread. It was in this place that matters connected with religion were often carefully considered by men who acted as final judges on all the more important moral as well as civil questions.

Here, away from the noise and bustle of crowded thoroughfares, and the tumult of promiscuous discussion, the apostle could be heard without interruption. Around him gathered poets, artists, and philosophers—the scholars and sages of Athens, who thus addressed him: "May we know what this new doctrine, whereof thou speakest, is? for thou bringest certain strange things to our ears: we would know thereof what these things mean."

In that hour of solemn responsibility, the apostle was calm and self-possessed. His heart was burdened with an important message, and the words that fell from his lips convinced his hearers that he was no idle babbler. "Ye men of Athens," he said, "I perceive that in all things ye are too superstitious. For as I passed by, and beheld your devotions, I found an altar with this inscription, To the Unknown God. Whom therefore ye ignorantly worship, Him declare I unto you." With all their intelligence and general knowledge, they were ignorant of the God who created the universe. Yet there were some who were longing for greater light. They were reaching out toward the Infinite.

With hand outstretched toward the temple crowded with idols, Paul poured out the burden of his soul, and exposed the fallacies of the religion of the Athenians. The wisest of his hearers were astonished as they listened to his reasoning. He showed himself familiar with their works of art, their literature, and their religion. Pointing to their statuary and idols, he declared that God could not be likened to forms of man's devising. These graven images could not, in the faintest sense, represent the glory of Jehovah. He reminded them that these images had no life, but were controlled by human power, moving only when the hands of men moved them;

and therefore those who worshiped them were in every way superior to that which they worshiped.

Paul drew the minds of his idolatrous hearers beyond the limits of their false religion to a true view of the Deity, whom they had styled the "Unknown God." This Being, whom he now declared unto them, was independent of man, needing nothing from human hands to add to His power and glory.

The people were carried away with admiration for Paul's earnest and logical presentation of the attributes of the true God—of His creative power and the existence of His overruling providence. With earnest and fervid eloquence the apostle declared, "God that made the world and all things therein, seeing that He is Lord of heaven and earth, dwelleth not in temples made with hands; neither is worshiped with men's hands, as though He needed anything, seeing He giveth to all life, and breath, and all things." The heavens were not large enough to contain God, how much less were the temples made by human hands!

In that age of caste, when the rights of men were often unrecognized, Paul set forth the great truth of human brotherhood, declaring that God "hath made of one blood all nations of men for to dwell on all the face of the earth." In the sight of God all are on an equality, and to the Creator every human being owes supreme allegiance. Then the apostle showed how, through all God's dealings with man, His purpose of grace and mercy runs like a thread of gold. He "hath determined the times before appointed, and the bounds of their habitation; that they should seek the Lord, if haply they might feel after Him, and find Him, though He be not far from every one of us."

Pointing to the noble specimens of manhood about him, with words borrowed from a poet of their own he pictured the infinite God as a Father, whose children they were. "In Him we live, and move, and have our being," he declared; "as certain also of your own poets have said, For we are also His offspring. Forasmuch then as we are the offspring of God, we ought not to think that the Godhead is like unto gold, or silver, or stone, graven by art and man's device.

"And the times of this ignorance God winked at; but now commandeth all men everywhere to repent." In the ages of darkness that had preceded the advent of Christ, the divine Ruler had passed lightly over the idolatry of the heathen; but now, through His Son, He had sent men the light of truth; and He expected from all repentance unto salvation, not only from the poor and humble, but from the proud philosopher and the princes of the earth. "Because

He hath appointed a day, in the which He will judge the world in righteousness by that Man whom He hath ordained; whereof He hath given assurance unto all men, in that He hath raised Him from the dead." As Paul spoke of the resurrection from the dead, "some mocked: and others said, We will hear thee again of this matter."

Thus closed the labors of the apostle at Athens, the center of heathen learning, for the Athenians, clinging persistently to their idolatry, turned from the light of the true religion. When a people are wholly satisfied with their own attainments, little more need be expected of them. Though boasting of learning and refinement, the Athenians were constantly becoming more corrupt and more content with the vague mysteries of idolatry.

Among those who listened to the words of Paul were some to whose minds the truths presented brought conviction, but they would not humble themselves to acknowledge God and to accept the plan of salvation. No eloquence of words, no force of argument, can convert the sinner. The power of God alone can apply the truth to the heart. He who persistently turns from this power cannot be reached. The Greeks sought after wisdom, yet the message of the cross was to them foolishness because they valued their own wisdom more highly than the wisdom that comes from above.

In their pride of intellect and human wisdom may be found the reason why the gospel message met with comparatively little success among the Athenians. The worldly-wise men who come to Christ as poor lost sinners, will become wise unto salvation; but those who come as distinguished men, extolling their own wisdom, will fail of receiving the light and knowledge that He alone can give.

Thus Paul met the paganism of his day. His labors in Athens were not wholly in vain. Dionysius, one of the most prominent citizens, and some others, accepted the gospel message and united themselves fully with the believers.

Inspiration has given us this glance into the life of the Athenians, who, with all their knowledge, refinement, and art, were yet sunken in vice, that it might be seen how God, through His servant, rebuked idolatry and the sins of a proud, self-sufficient people. The words of the apostle, and the description of his attitude and surroundings, as traced by the pen of inspiration, were to be handed down to all coming generations, bearing witness of his unshaken confidence, his courage in loneliness and adversity, and the victory he gained for Christianity in the very heart of paganism.

Paul's words contain a treasure of knowledge for the church.

He was in a position where he might easily have said that which would have irritated his proud listeners and brought himself into difficulty. Had his oration been a direct attack upon their gods and the great men of the city, he would have been in danger of meeting the fate of Socrates. But with a tact born of divine love, he carefully drew their minds away from heathen deities, by revealing to them the true God, who was to them unknown.

Today the truths of Scripture are to be brought before the great men of the world in order that they may choose between obedience to God's law and allegiance to the prince of evil. God sets everlasting truth before them—truth that will make them wise unto salvation, but He does not force them to accept it. If they turn from it, He leaves them to themselves, to be filled with the fruit of their own doings.

"The preaching of the cross is to them that perish foolishness; but unto us which are saved it is the power of God. For it is written, I will destroy the wisdom of the wise, and will bring to nothing the understanding of the prudent." "God hath chosen the foolish things of the world to confound the wise; and God hath chosen the weak things of the world to confound the things which are mighty; and base things of the world, and things which are despised, hath God chosen, yea, and things which are not, to bring to nought things that are." 1 Corinthians 1:18, 19, 27, 28. Many of the greatest scholars and statesmen, the world's most eminent men, will in these last days turn from the light because the world by wisdom knows not God. Yet God's servants are to improve every opportunity to communicate the truth to these men. Some will acknowledge their ignorance of the things of God and will take their place as humble learners at the feet of Jesus, the Master Teacher.

In every effort to reach the higher classes, the worker for God needs strong faith. Appearances may seem forbidding, but in the darkest hour there is light above. The strength of those who love and serve God will be renewed day by day. The understanding of the Infinite is placed at their service, that in carrying out His purposes they may not err. Let these workers hold the beginning of their confidence firm unto the end, remembering that the light of God's truth is to shine amid the darkness that enshrouds our world. There is to be no despondency in connection with God's service. The faith of the consecrated worker is to stand every test brought to bear upon it. God is able and willing to bestow upon His servants all the strength they need and to give them the wisdom that their varied necessities demand. He will more than fulfill the highest expectations of those who put their trust in Him.

24

Corinth

This chapter is based on Acts 18:1-18

During the first century of the Christian Era, Corinth was one of the leading cities, not only of Greece, but of the world. Greeks, Jews, and Romans, with travelers from every land, thronged its streets, eagerly intent on business and pleasure. A great commercial center, situated within easy access of all parts of the Roman Empire, it was an important place in which to establish memorials for God and His truth.

Among the Jews who had taken up their residence in Corinth were Aquila and Priscilla, who afterward became distinguished as earnest workers for Christ. Becoming acquainted with the character of these persons, Paul "abode with them."

At the very beginning of his labors in this thoroughfare of travel, Paul saw on every hand serious obstacles to the progress of his work. The city was almost wholly given up to idolatry. Venus was the favorite goddess, and with the worship of Venus were connected many demoralizing rites and ceremonies. The Corinthians had become conspicuous, even among the heathen, for their gross immorality. They seemed to have little thought or care beyond the pleasures and gaieties of the hour.

In preaching the gospel in Corinth, the apostle followed a course different from that which had marked his labors at Athens. While in the latter place, he had sought to adapt his style to the character of his audience; he had met logic with logic, science with science, philosophy with philosophy. As he thought of the time thus spent, and realized that his teaching in Athens had been productive of but little fruit, he decided to follow another plan of labor in Corinth in his efforts to arrest the attention of the careless and the indifferent. He determined to avoid elaborate arguments and discussions, and "not to know anything" among the Corinthians "save Jesus Christ, and Him crucified." He would preach to them "not with enticing words of man's wisdom, but in demonstration of the Spirit and of power." 1 Corinthians 2:2, 4.

Jesus, whom Paul was about to present before the Greeks in Corinth as the Christ, was a Jew of lowly origin, reared in a town proverbial for its wickedness. He had been rejected by His own nation and at last crucified as a malefactor. The Greeks believed that there was need of elevating the human race, but they regarded the study of philosophy and science as the only means of attaining to true elevation and honor. Could Paul lead them to believe that faith in the power of this obscure Jew would uplift and ennoble every power of the being?

To the minds of multitudes living at the present time, the cross of Calvary is surrounded by sacred memories. Hallowed associations are connected with the scenes of the crucifixion. But in Paul's day the cross was regarded with feelings of repulsion and horror. To uphold as the Saviour of mankind one who had met death on the cross, would naturally call forth ridicule and opposition.

Paul well knew how his message would be regarded by both the Jews and the Greeks of Corinth. "We preach Christ crucified," he admitted, "unto the Jews a stumbling block, and unto the Greeks foolishness." 1 Corinthians 1:23. Among his Jewish hearers there were many who would be angered by the message he was about to proclaim. In the estimation of the Greeks his words would be absurd folly. He would be looked upon as weak-minded for attempting to show how the cross could have any connection with the elevation of the race or the salvation of mankind.

But to Paul the cross was the one object of supreme interest. Ever since he had been arrested in his career of persecution against the followers of the crucified Nazarene he had never ceased to glory in the cross. At that time there had been given him a revelation of the infinite love of God, as revealed in the death of Christ; and a marvelous transformation had been wrought in his life, bringing all his plans and purposes into harmony with heaven. From that hour he had been a new man in Christ. He knew by personal experience that when a sinner once beholds the love of the Father, as seen in the sacrifice of His Son, and yields to the divine influence, a change of heart takes place, and henceforth Christ is all and in all.

At the time of his conversion, Paul was inspired with a longing desire to help his fellow men to behold Jesus of Nazareth as the Son of the living God, mighty to transform and to save. Henceforth his life was wholly devoted to an effort to portray the love and power of the Crucified One. His great heart of sympathy took in all classes. "I am debtor," he declared, "both to the Greeks, and to the barbarians; both to the wise, and to the unwise." Romans 1:14. Love for the Lord of glory, whom he had so relentlessly persecuted in the person of His saints, was the actuating principle of his conduct, his motive power. If ever his ardor in the path of duty flagged, one glance at the cross and the amazing love there revealed, was enough to cause him to gird up the loins of his mind and press forward in the path of self-denial.

Behold the apostle preaching in the synagogue at Corinth, reasoning from the writings of Moses and the prophets, and bringing his hearers down to the advent of the promised Messiah. Listen as he makes plain the work of the Redeemer as the great high priest of mankind—the One who through the sacrifice of His own life was to make atonement for sin once for all, and was then to take up His ministry in the heavenly sanctuary. Paul's hearers were made to understand that the Messiah for whose advent they had been longing, had already come; that His death was the antitype of all the sacrificial offerings, and that His ministry in the sanctuary in heaven was the great object that cast its shadow backward and made clear the ministry of the Jewish priesthood.

Paul "testified to the Jews that Jesus was Christ." From the Old Testament Scriptures he showed that according to the prophecies and the universal expectation of the Jews, the Messiah would be of the lineage of Abraham and of David; then he traced the descent of Jesus from the patriarch Abraham through the royal psalmist. He read the testimony of the prophets regarding the character and work of the promised Messiah, and His reception and treatment on the earth; then he showed that all these predictions had been fulfilled in the life, ministry, and death of Jesus of Nazareth.

Paul showed that Christ had come to offer salvation first of all to the nation that was looking for the Messiah's coming as the consummation and glory of their national existence. But that nation had rejected Him who would have given them life, and had chosen another leader, whose reign would end in death. He endeavored to bring home to his hearers the fact that repentance alone could save the Jewish nation from impending ruin. He revealed their ignorance concerning the meaning of those Scriptures which it was their chief boast and glory that they fully understood. He rebuked their worldliness, their love of station, titles, and display, and their inordinate selfishness.

In the power of the Spirit, Paul related the story of his own miraculous conversion and of his confidence in the Old Testament Scriptures, which had been so completely fulfilled in Jesus of Nazareth. His words were spoken with solemn earnestness, and his hearers could not but discern that he loved with all his heart the crucified and risen Saviour. They saw that his mind was centered in Christ, that his whole life was bound up with his Lord. So impressive were his words, that only those who were filled with the bitterest hatred against the Christian religion could stand unmoved by them.

But the Jews of Corinth closed their eyes to the evidence so clearly presented by the apostle, and refused to listen to his appeals. The same spirit that had led them to reject Christ, filled them with wrath and fury against His servant; and had not God especially protected him, that he might continue to bear the gospel message to the Gentiles, they would have put an end to his life.

"And when they opposed themselves, and blasphemed, he shook his raiment, and said unto them, Your blood be upon your own heads; I am clean: from henceforth I will go unto the Gentiles. And he departed thence, and entered into a certain man's house, named Justus, one that worshiped God, whose house joined hard to the synagogue."

Silas and Timothy had "come from Macedonia" to help Paul, and together they labored for the Gentiles. To the heathen, as well as to the Jews, Paul and his companions preached Christ as the Saviour of the fallen race. Avoiding complicated, far-fetched reasoning, the messengers of the cross dwelt upon the attributes of the Creator of the world, the Supreme Ruler of the universe. Their hearts aglow with the love of God and of His Son, they appealed to the heathen to behold the infinite sacrifice made in man's behalf. They knew that if those who had long been groping in the darkness of heathenism could but see the light streaming from Calvary's cross, they would be drawn to the Redeemer. "I, if I be lifted up," the Saviour had declared, "will draw all men unto Me." John 12:32.

The gospel workers in Corinth realized the terrible dangers threatening the souls of those for whom they were laboring; and it was with a sense of the responsibility resting on them that they presented the truth as it is in Jesus. Clear, plain, and decided was their message—a savor of life unto life, or of death unto death. And not only in their words, but in the daily life, was the gospel revealed. Angels co-operated with them, and the grace and power of God was shown in the conversion of many. "Crispus, the chief ruler of the synagogue, believed on the Lord with all his house; and many of the Corinthians hearing believed, and were baptized."

The hatred with which the Jews had always regarded the apostles was now intensified. The conversion and baptism of Crispus had the effect of exasperating instead of convincing these stubborn opposers. They could not bring arguments to disprove Paul's preaching, and for lack of such evidence they resorted to deception and malignant attack. They blasphemed the gospel and the name of Jesus. In their blind anger no words were too bitter, no device too low, for them to use. They could not deny that Christ had worked miracles; but they declared that He had performed them through the power of Satan; and they boldly affirmed that the wonderful works wrought by Paul were accomplished through the same agency.

Though Paul had a measure of success in Corinth, yet the wickedness that he saw and heard in that corrupt city almost disheartened him. The depravity that he witnessed among the Gentiles, and the contempt and insult that he received from the Jews, caused him great anguish of spirit. He doubted the wisdom of trying to build up a church from the material that he found there.

As he was planning to leave the city for a more promising field, and seeking earnestly to understand his duty, the Lord appeared to him in a vision and said, "Be not afraid, but speak, and hold not thy peace: for I am with thee, and no man shall set on thee to hurt thee: for I have much people in this city." Paul understood this to be a command to remain in Corinth and a guarantee that the Lord would give increase to the seed sown. Strengthened and encouraged, he continued to labor there with zeal and perseverance.

The apostle's efforts were not confined to public speaking; there were many who could not have been reached in that way. He spent much time in house-to-house labor, thus availing himself of the familiar intercourse of the home circle. He visited the sick and the sorrowing, comforted the afflicted, and lifted up the oppressed. And in all that he said and did he magnified the name of Jesus. Thus he labored, "in weakness, and in fear, and in much trembling." 1 Corinthians 2:3. He trembled lest his teaching should reveal the impress of the human rather than the divine.

"We speak wisdom among them that are perfect," Paul afterward declared; "yet not the wisdom of this world, nor of the princes of this world, that come to nought: but we speak the wisdom of God in a mystery, even the hidden wisdom, which God ordained before the world unto our glory: which none of the princes of this world knew: for had they known it, they would not have crucified the Lord of glory. But as it is written, Eye hath not seen, nor ear heard, neither have entered into the heart of man, the things which God hath prepared for them that love Him. But God hath revealed them unto us by His Spirit: for the Spirit searcheth all things, yea, the deep things of God. For what man knoweth the things of a man, save the spirit of man which is in him? even so the things of God knoweth no man, but the Spirit of God.

"Now we have received, not the spirit of the world, but the spirit which is of God; that we might know the things that are freely given to us of God. Which things also we speak, not in the words which man's wisdom teacheth, but which the Holy Ghost teacheth; comparing spiritual things with spiritual." 1 Corinthians 2:6-13.

Paul realized that his sufficiency was not in himself, but in the presence of the Holy Spirit, whose gracious influence filled his heart, bringing every thought into subjection to Christ. He spoke of himself as "always bearing about in the body the dying of the Lord Jesus, that the life also of Jesus might be made manifest in our body." 2 Corinthians 4:10. In the apostle's teachings Christ was the central figure. "I live," he declared, "yet not I, but Christ liveth in me." Galatians 2:20. Self was hidden; Christ was revealed and exalted.

Paul was an eloquent speaker. Before his conversion he had often sought to impress his hearers by flights of oratory. But now he set all this aside. Instead of indulging in poetic descriptions and fanciful representations, which might please the senses and feed the imagination, but which would not touch the daily experience, Paul sought by the use of simple language to bring home to the heart the truths that are of vital importance. Fanciful representations of truth may cause an ecstasy of feeling, but all too often truths presented in this way do not supply the food necessary to strengthen and fortify the believer for the battles of life. The immediate needs, the present trials, of struggling souls—these must be met with sound, practical instruction in the fundamental principles of Christianity.

Paul's efforts in Corinth were not without fruit. Many turned from the worship of idols to serve the living God, and a large church was enrolled under the banner of Christ. Some were rescued from among the most dissipated of the Gentiles and became monuments of the mercy of God and the efficacy of the blood of Christ to cleanse from sin.

The increased success that Paul had in presenting Christ, roused the unbelieving Jews to more determined opposition. They rose in a body and "made insurrection with one accord against Paul, and brought him to the judgment seat" of Gallio, who was then proconsul of Achaia. They expected that the authorities, as on former occasions, would side with them; and with loud, angry voices they uttered their complaints against the apostle, saying, "This fellow persuadeth men to worship God contrary to the law."

The Jewish religion was under the protection of the Roman power, and the accusers of Paul thought that if they could fasten upon him the charge of violating the laws of their religion, he would probably be delivered to them for trial and sentence. They hoped thus to compass his death. But Gallio was a man of integrity, and he refused to become the dupe of the jealous, intriguing Jews. Disgusted with their bigotry and self-righteousness, he would take no notice of the charge. As Paul prepared to speak in self-defense, Gallio told him that it was not necessary. Then turning to the angry accusers, he said, "If it were a matter of wrong or wicked lewdness, O ye Jews, reason would that I should bear with you: but if it be a question of words and names, and of your law, look ye to it; for I will be no judge of such matters. And he drave them from the judgment seat."

Both Jews and Greeks had waited eagerly for Gallio's decision; and his immediate dismissal of the case, as one that had no bearing upon the public interest, was the signal for the Jews to retire, baffled and angry. The proconsul's decided course opened the eyes of the clamorous crowd who had been abetting the Jews. For the first time during Paul's labors in Europe, the mob turned to his side; under the very eye of the proconsul, and without interference from him, they violently beset the most prominent accusers of the apostle. "All the Greeks took Sosthenes, the chief ruler of the synagogue, and beat him before the judgment seat. And Gallio cared for none of those things." Thus Christianity obtained a signal victory.

"Paul after this tarried there yet a good while." If the apostle had at this time been compelled to leave Corinth, the converts to the faith of Jesus would have been placed in a perilous position. The Jews would have endeavored to follow up the advantage gained, even to the extermination of Christianity in that region.

25

The Thessalonian Letters

This chapter is based on the Epistles to the Thessalonians

The arrival of Silas and Timothy from Macedonia, during Paul's sojourn in Corinth, had greatly cheered the apostle. They brought him "good tidings" of the "faith and charity" of those who had accepted the truth during the first visit of the gospel messengers to Thessalonica. Paul's heart went out in tender sympathy toward these believers, who, in the midst of trial and adversity, had remained true to God. He longed to visit them in person, but as this was not then possible, he wrote to them.

In this letter to the church at Thessalonica the apostle expresses his gratitude to God for the joyful news of their increase of faith. "Brethren," he wrote, "we were comforted over you in all our affliction and distress by your faith: for now we live, if ye stand fast in the Lord. For what thanks can we render to God again for you, for all the joy wherewith we joy for your sakes before our God; night and day praying exceedingly that we might see your face, and might perfect that which is lacking in your faith?"

"We give thanks to God always for you all, making mention of you in our prayers; remembering without ceasing your work of faith, and labor of love, and patience of hope in our Lord Jesus Christ, in the sight of God and our Father."

Many of the believers in Thessalonica had "turned . . . from idols to serve the living and true God." They had "received the word in much affliction;" and their hearts were filled with "joy of the Holy Ghost." The apostle declared that in their faithfulness in following the Lord they were "ensamples to all that believe in Macedonia and Achaia." These words of commendation were not unmerited; "for from you," he wrote, "sounded out the word of the Lord not only in Macedonia and Achaia, but also in every place your faith to Godward is spread abroad."

The Thessalonian believers were true missionaries. Their hearts burned with zeal for their Saviour, who had delivered them from fear of "the wrath to come." Through the grace of Christ a marvelous transformation had taken place in their lives, and the word of the Lord, as spoken through them, was accompanied with power.

Hearts were won by the truths presented, and souls were added to the number of believers.

In this first epistle, Paul referred to his manner of labor among the Thessalonians. He declared that he had not sought to win converts through deception or guile. "As we were allowed of God to be put in trust with the gospel, even so we speak; not as pleasing men, but God, which trieth our hearts. For neither at any time used we flattering words, as ye know, nor a cloak of covetousness; God is witness: nor of men sought we glory, neither of you, nor yet of others, when we might have been burdensome, as the apostles of Christ. But we were gentle among you, even as a nurse cherisheth her children: so being affectionately desirous of you, we were willing to have imparted unto you, not the gospel of God only, but also our own souls, because ye were dear unto us."

"Ye are witnesses, and God also," the apostle continued, "how holily and justly and unblamably we behaved ourselves among you that believe: as ye know how we exhorted and comforted and charged every one of you, as a father doth his children, that ye would walk worthy of God, who hath called you unto His kingdom and glory.

"For this cause also thank we God without ceasing, because, when ye receive the word of God which ye heard of us, ye received it not as the word of men, but as it is in truth, the word of God, which effectually worketh also in you that believe." "What is our hope, or joy, or crown of rejoicing? Are not even ye in the presence of our Lord Jesus Christ at His coming? For ye are our glory and joy."

In his first epistle to the Thessalonian believers, Paul endeavored to instruct them regarding the true state of the dead. He spoke of those who die as being asleep—in a state of unconsciousness: "I would not have you to be ignorant, brethren, concerning them which are asleep, that ye sorrow not, even as others which have no hope. For if we believe that Jesus died and rose again, even so them also which sleep in Jesus will God bring with Him. . . . For the Lord Himself shall descend from heaven with a shout, with the voice of the Archangel, and with the trump of God: and the dead in Christ shall rise first: then we which are alive and remain shall be caught up together with them in the clouds, to meet the Lord in the air: and so shall we ever be with the Lord."

The Thessalonians had eagerly grasped the idea that Christ was coming to change the faithful who were alive, and to take them to Himself. They had carefully guarded the lives of their friends, lest they should die and lose the blessing which they looked forward to receiving at the coming of their Lord. But one after another their loved ones had been taken from them, and with anguish the Thessalonians had looked for the last time upon the faces of their dead, hardly daring to hope to meet them in a future life.

As Paul's epistle was opened and read, great joy and consolation was brought to the church by the words revealing the true state of the dead. Paul showed that those living when Christ should come would not go to meet their Lord in advance of those who had fallen asleep in Jesus. The voice of the Archangel and the trump of God would reach the sleeping ones, and the dead in Christ should rise first, before the touch of immortality should be given to the living. "Then we which are alive and remain shall be caught up together with them in the clouds, to meet the Lord in the air: and so shall we ever be with the Lord. Wherefore comfort one another with these words."

The hope and joy that this assurance brought to the young church at Thessalonica can scarcely be appreciated by us. They believed and cherished the letter sent to them by their father in the gospel, and their hearts went out in love to him. He had told them these things before; but at that time their minds were striving to grasp doctrines that seemed new and strange, and it is not surprising that the force of some points had not been vividly impressed on their minds. But they were hungering for truth, and Paul's epistle gave them new hope and strength, and a firmer faith in, and a deeper affection for, the One who through His death had brought life and immortality to light.

Now they rejoiced in the knowledge that their believing friends would be raised from the grave to live forever in the kingdom of God. The darkness that had enshrouded the resting place of the dead was dispelled. A new splendor crowned the Christian faith, and they saw a new glory in the life, death, and resurrection of Christ.

"Even so them also which sleep in Jesus will God bring with Him," Paul wrote. Many interpret this passage to mean that the sleeping ones will be brought with Christ from heaven; but Paul meant that as Christ was raised from the dead, so God will call the sleeping saints from their graves and take them with Him to heaven. Precious consolation! glorious hope! not only to the church of Thessalonica, but to all Christians wherever they may be.

While laboring at Thessalonica, Paul had so fully covered the subject of the signs of the times, showing what events would occur prior to the revelation of the Son of man in the clouds of heaven, that he did not think it necessary to write at length regarding this subject. He, however, pointedly referred to his former teachings. "Of the times and the seasons," he said, "ye have no need that I write unto you. For yourselves know perfectly that the day of the Lord so cometh as a thief in the night. For when they shall say, Peace and safety; then sudden destruction cometh upon them."

There are in the world today many who close their eyes to the evidences that Christ has given to warn men of His coming. They seek to quiet all apprehension, while at the same time the signs of the end are rapidly fulfilling, and the world is hastening to the time when the Son of man shall be revealed in the clouds of heaven. Paul teaches that it is sinful to be indifferent to the signs which are to precede the second coming of Christ. Those guilty of this neglect he calls children of the night and of darkness. He encourages the vigilant and watchful with these words: "But ye, brethren, are not in darkness, that that day should overtake you as a thief. Ye are all the children of light, and the children of the day: we are not of the night, nor of darkness. Therefore let us not sleep, as do others; but let us watch and be sober."

Especially important to the church in our time are the teachings of the apostle upon this point. To those living so near the great consummation, the words of Paul should come with telling force: "Let us, who are of the day, be sober, putting on the breastplate of faith and love; and for a helmet, the hope of salvation. For God hath not appointed us to wrath, but to obtain salvation by our Lord Jesus Christ, who died for us, that, whether we wake or sleep, we should live together with Him."

The watchful Christian is a working Christian, seeking zealously to do all in his power for the advancement of the gospel. As love for his Redeemer increases, so also does love for his fellow men. He has severe trials, as had his Master; but he does not allow affliction to sour his temper or destroy his peace of mind. He knows that trial, if well borne, will refine and purify him, and bring him into closer fellowship with Christ. Those who are partakers of Christ's sufferings will also be partakers of His consolation and at last sharers of His glory.

"We beseech you, brethren," Paul continued in his letter to the Thessalonians, "to know them which labor among you, and are over you in the Lord, and admonish you; and to esteem them very highly in love for their work's sake. And be at peace among yourselves."

The Thessalonian believers were greatly annoyed by men coming among them with fanatical ideas and doctrines. Some were "disorderly, working not at all, but . . . busy-bodies." The church had been properly organized, and officers had been appointed to act as ministers and deacons. But there were some, self-willed and impetuous, who refused to be subordinate to those who held positions of authority in the church. They claimed not only the right of private judgment, but that of publicly urging their views upon the church. In view of this, Paul called the attention of the Thessalonians to the respect and deference due to those who had been chosen to occupy positions of authority in the church.

In his anxiety that the believers at Thessalonica should walk in the fear of God, the apostle pleaded with them to reveal practical godliness in the daily life. "We beseech you, brethren," he wrote, "and exhort you by the Lord Jesus, that as ye have received of us how ye ought to walk and to please God, so ye would abound more and more. For ye know what commandments we gave you by the Lord Jesus. For this is the will of God, even your sanctification, that ye should abstain from fornication." "For God hath not called us unto uncleanness, but unto holiness."

The apostle felt that he was to a large extent responsible for the spiritual welfare of those converted under his labors. His desire for them was that they might increase in a knowledge of the only true God, and Jesus Christ, whom He had sent. Often in his ministry he would meet with little companies of men and women who loved Jesus, and bow with them in prayer, asking God to teach them how to maintain a living connection with Him. Often he took counsel with them as to the best methods of giving to others the light of gospel truth. And often, when separated from those for whom he had thus labored, he pleaded with God to keep them from evil and help them to be earnest, active missionaries.

One of the strongest evidences of true conversion is love to God and man. Those who accept Jesus as their Redeemer have a deep, sincere love for others of like precious faith. Thus it was with the believers at Thessalonica. "As touching brotherly love," the apostle wrote, "ye need not that I write unto you: for ye yourselves are taught of God to love one another. And indeed ye do it toward all the brethren which are in all Macedonia: but we beseech you, brethren, that ye increase more and more; and that ye study to be quiet, and to do your own business, and to work with your own hands, as we commanded you; that ye may walk honestly toward them that are without, and that ye may have lack of nothing."

"The Lord make you to increase and abound in love one toward another, and toward all men, even as we do toward you: to the end

He may stablish your hearts unblamable in holiness before God, even our Father, at the coming of our Lord Jesus Christ with all His saints."

"Now we exhort you, brethren, warn them that are unruly, comfort the feeble-minded, support the weak, be patient toward all men. See that none render evil for evil unto any man; but ever follow that which is good, both among yourselves, and to all men. Rejoice evermore. Pray without ceasing. In everything give thanks: for this is the will of God in Christ Jesus concerning you."

The apostle cautioned the Thessalonians not to despise the gift of prophecy, and in the words, "Quench not the Spirit; despise not prophesyings; prove all things; hold fast that which is good," he enjoined a careful discrimination in distinguishing the false from the true. He besought them to "abstain from all appearance of evil;" and closed his letter with the prayer that God would sanctify them wholly, that in "Spirit and soul and body" they might "be preserved blameless unto the coming of our Lord Jesus Christ. Faithful is He that calleth you," he added, "who also will do it."

The instruction that Paul sent the Thessalonians in his first epistle regarding the second coming of Christ, was in perfect harmony with his former teaching. Yet his words were misapprehended by some of the Thessalonian brethren. They understood him to express the hope that he himself would live to witness the Saviour's advent. This belief served to increase their enthusiasm and excitement. Those who had previously neglected their responsibilities and duties, now became more persistent in urging their erroneous views.

In his second letter Paul sought to correct their misunderstanding of his teaching and to set before them his true position. He again expressed his confidence in their integrity, and his gratitude that their faith was strong, and that their love abounded for one another and for the cause of their Master. He told them that he presented them to other churches as an example of the patient, persevering faith that bravely withstands persecution and tribulation, and he carried their minds forward to the time of the second coming of Christ, when the people of God shall rest from all their cares and perplexities.

"We ourselves," he wrote, "glory in you in the churches of God for your patience and faith in all your persecutions and tribulations that ye endure: . . . and to you who are troubled rest with us, when the Lord Jesus shall be revealed from heaven with His mighty angels, in flaming fire taking vengeance on them that know not

God, and that obey not the gospel of our Lord Jesus Christ: who shall be punished with everlasting destruction from the presence of the Lord, and from the glory of His power. . . . Wherefore also we pray always for you, that our God would count you worthy of this calling, and fulfill all the good pleasure of His goodness, and the work of faith with power: that the name of our Lord Jesus Christ may be glorified in you, and ye in Him, according to the grace of our God and the Lord Jesus Christ."

But before the coming of Christ, important developments in the religious world, foretold in prophecy, were to take place. The apostle declared: "Be not soon shaken in mind, or be troubled, neither by spirit, nor by word, nor by letter as from us, as that the day of Christ is at hand. Let no man deceive you by any means: for that day shall not come, except there come a falling away first, and that man of sin be revealed, the son of perdition; who opposeth and exalteth himself above all that is called God, or that is worshiped; so that he as God sitteth in the temple of God, showing himself that he is God."

Paul's words were not to be misinterpreted. It was not to be taught that he, by special revelation, had warned the Thessalonians of the immediate coming of Christ. Such a position would cause confusion of faith; for disappointment often leads to unbelief. The apostle therefore cautioned the brethren to receive no such message as coming from him, and he proceeded to emphasize the fact that the papal power, so clearly described by the prophet Daniel, was yet to rise and wage war against God's people. Until this power should have performed its deadly and blasphemous work, it would be in vain for the church to look for the coming of their Lord. "Remember ye not," Paul inquired, "that, when I was yet with you, I told you these things?"

Terrible were the trials that were to beset the true church. Even at the time when the apostle was writing, the "mystery of iniquity" had already begun to work. The developments that were to take place in the future were to be "after the working of Satan with all power and signs and lying wonders, and with all deceivableness of unrighteousness in them that perish."

Especially solemn is the apostle's statement regarding those who should refuse to receive "the love of the truth." "For this cause," he declared of all who should deliberately reject the messages of truth, "God shall send them strong delusion, that they should believe a lie: that they all might be damned who believed not the truth, but had pleasure in unrighteousness." Men cannot with impunity reject the warnings that God in mercy sends them. From those who persist in turning from these warnings, God withdraws His Spirit, leaving them to the deceptions that they love.

Thus Paul outlined the baleful work of that power of evil which was to continue through long centuries of darkness and persecution before the second coming of Christ. The Thessalonian believers had hoped for immediate deliverance; now they were admonished to take up bravely and in the fear of God the work before them. The apostle charged them not to neglect their duties or resign themselves to idle waiting. After their glowing anticipations of immediate deliverance the round of daily life and the opposition that they must meet would appear doubly forbidding. He therefore exhorted them to steadfastness in the faith:

"Stand fast, and hold the traditions which ye have been taught, whether by word, or our epistle. Now our Lord Jesus Christ Himself, and God, even our Father, which hath loved us, and hath given us everlasting consolation and good hope through grace, comfort your hearts, and stablish you in every good word and work." "The Lord is faithful, who shall stablish you, and keep you from evil. And we have confidence in the Lord touching you, that ye both do and will do the things which we command you. And the Lord direct your hearts into the love of God, and into the patient waiting for Christ."

The work of the believers had been given them by God. By their faithful adherence to the truth they were to give to others the light which they had received. The apostle bade them not to become weary in well-doing, and pointed them to his own example of diligence in temporal matters while laboring with untiring zeal in the cause of Christ. He reproved those who had given themselves up to sloth and aimless excitement, and directed that "with quietness they work, and eat their own bread." He also enjoined upon the church to separate from their fellowship anyone who should persist in disregarding the instruction given by God's ministers. "Yet," he added, "count him not as an enemy, but admonish him as a brother."

This epistle also Paul concluded with a prayer that amidst life's toils and trials the peace of God and the grace of the Lord Jesus Christ might be their consolation and support.

26

Apollos at Corinth

This chapter is based on Acts 18:18-28

After leaving Corinth, Paul's next scene of labor was Ephesus. He was on his way to Jerusalem to attend an approaching festival, and his stay at Ephesus was necessarily brief. He reasoned with the Jews in the synagogue, and so favorable was the impression made upon them that they entreated him to continue his labors among them. His plan to visit Jerusalem prevented him from tarrying then, but he promised to return to them, "if God will." Aquila and Priscilla had accompanied him to Ephesus, and he left them there to carry on the work that he had begun.

It was at this time that "a certain Jew named Apollos, born at Alexandria, an eloquent man, and mighty in the Scriptures, came to Ephesus." He had heard the preaching of John the Baptist, had received the baptism of repentance, and was a living witness that the work of the prophet had not been in vain. The Scripture record of Apollos is that he "was instructed in the way of the Lord; and being fervent in the spirit, he spake and taught diligently the things of the Lord, knowing only the baptism of John."

While in Ephesus, Apollos "began to speak boldly in the synagogue." Among his hearers were Aquila and Priscilla, who, perceiving that he had not yet received the full light of the gospel, "took him unto them, and expounded unto him the way of God more perfectly." Through their teaching he obtained a clearer understanding of the Scriptures and became one of the ablest advocates of the Christian faith.

Apollos was desirous of going on into Achaia, and the brethren at Ephesus "wrote, exhorting the disciples to receive him" as a teacher in full harmony with the church of Christ. He went to Corinth, where, in public labor and from house to house, "he mightily convinced the Jews, . . . showing by the Scriptures that Jesus was Christ." Paul had planted the seed of truth; Apollos now watered it. The success that attended Apollos in preaching the gospel led some of the believers to exalt his labors above those of Paul. This comparison of man with man brought into the church a party spirit that threatened to hinder greatly the progress of the gospel.

During the year and a half that Paul had spent in Corinth, he had purposely presented the gospel in its simplicity. "Not with excellency of speech or of wisdom" had he come to the Corinthians; but with fear and trembling, and "in demonstration of the Spirit and of power," had he declared "the testimony of God," that their "faith should not stand in the wisdom of men, but in the power of God." 1 Corinthians 2:1, 4, 5.

Paul had necessarily adapted his manner to teaching to the condition of the church. "I, brethren could not speak unto you as unto spiritual," he afterward explained to them, "but as unto carnal, even as unto babes in Christ. I have fed you with milk, and not with meat: for hitherto ye were not able to bear it, neither yet now are ye able." 1 Corinthians 3:1, 2. Many of the Corinthian believers had been slow to learn the lessons that he was endeavoring to teach them. Their advancement in spiritual knowledge had not been proportionate to their privileges and opportunities. When they should have been far advanced in Christian experience, and able to comprehend and to practice the deeper truths of the word, they were standing where the disciples stood when Christ said to them, "I have yet many things to say unto you, but ye cannot bear them now." John 16:12. Jealousy, evil surmising, and accusation had closed the hearts of many of the Corinthian believers against the full working of the Holy Spirit, which "searcheth all things, yea, the deep things of God." 1 Corinthians 2:10. However wise they might be in worldly knowledge, they were but babes in the knowledge of Christ.

It had been Paul's work to instruct the Corinthian converts in the rudiments, the very alphabet, of the Christian faith. He had been obliged to instruct them as those who were ignorant of the operations of divine power upon the heart. At that time they were unable to comprehend the mysteries of salvation; for "the natural man receiveth not the things of the Spirit of God: for they are foolishness unto him: neither can he know them, because they are spiritually discerned." 1 Corinthians 2:14. Paul had endeavored to sow the seed, which others must water. Those who followed him must carry forward the work from the point where he had left it, giving spiritual light and knowledge in due season, as the church was able to bear it.

When the apostle took up his work in Corinth, he realized that he must introduce most carefully the great truths he wished to teach. He knew that among his hearers would be proud believers in human theories, and exponents of false systems of worship, who were groping with blinds eyes, hoping to find in the book of nature theories that would contradict the reality of the spiritual and immortal life as revealed in the Scriptures. He also knew that critics would endeavor to controvert the Christian interpretation of the revealed word, and that skeptics would treat the gospel of Christ with scoffing and derision.

As he endeavored to lead souls to the foot of the cross, Paul did not venture to rebuke, directly, those who were licentious, or to show how heinous was their sin in the sight of a holy God. Rather he set before them the true object of life and tried to impress upon their minds the lessons of the divine Teacher, which, if received, would lift them from worldliness and sin to purity and righteousness. He dwelt especially upon practical godliness and the holiness to which those must attain who shall be accounted worthy of a place in God's kingdom. He longed to see the light of the gospel of Christ piercing the darkness of their minds, that they might see how offensive in the sight of God were their immoral practices. Therefore the burden of his teaching among them was Christ and Him crucified. He sought to show them that their most earnest study and their greatest joy must be the wonderful truth of salvation through repentance toward God and faith in the Lord Jesus Christ.

The philosopher turns aside from the light of salvation, because it puts his proud theories to shame; the worldling refuses to receive it, because it would separate him from his earthly idols. Paul saw that the character of Christ must be understood before men could love Him or view the cross with the eye of faith. Here must begin that study which shall be the science and the song of the redeemed through all eternity. In the light of the cross alone can the true value of the human soul be estimated.

The refining influence of the grace of God changes the natural disposition of man. Heaven would not be desirable to the carnal-minded; their natural, unsanctified hearts would feel no attraction toward that pure and holy place, and if it were possible for them to enter, they would find there nothing congenial. The propensities that control the natural heart must be subdued by the grace of Christ before fallen man is fitted to enter heaven and enjoy the society of the pure, holy angels. When man dies to sin and is quickened to new life in Christ, divine love fills his heart; his understanding is sanctified; he drinks from an inexhaustible fountain of joy and knowledge, and the light of an eternal day shines upon his path, for with him continually is the Light of life.

Paul had sought to impress upon the minds of his Corinthian brethren the fact that he and the ministers associated with him were but men commissioned by God to teach the truth, that they were all engaged in the same work, and that they were alike dependent upon God for success in their labors. The discussion that had arisen in the church regarding the relative merits of different ministers was not in the order of God, but was the result of cherishing the attributes of the natural heart. "While one saith, I am of Paul; and another, I am of Apollos; are ye not carnal? Who then is Paul, and who is Apollos, but ministers by whom ye believed, even as the Lord gave to every man? I have planted, Apollos watered; but God gave the increase. So then neither is he that planteth anything, neither he that watereth; but God that giveth the increase." 1 Corinthians 3:4-7.

It was Paul who had first preached the gospel in Corinth, and who had organized the church there. This was the work that the Lord had assigned him. Later, by God's direction, other workers were brought in, to stand in their lot and place. The seed sown must be watered, and this Apollos was to do. He followed Paul in his work, to give further instruction, and to help the seed sown to develop. He won his way to the hearts of the people, but it was God who gave the increase. It is not human, but divine power, that works transformation of character. Those who plant and those who water do not cause the growth of the seed; they work under God, as His appointed agencies, co-operating with Him in His work. To the Master Worker belongs the honor and glory that comes with success.

God's servants do not all possess the same gifts, but they are all His workmen. Each is to learn of the Great Teacher, and is then to communicate what he has learned. God has given to each of His messengers an individual work. There is a diversity of gifts, but all the workers are to blend in harmony, controlled by the sanctifying influence of the Holy Spirit. As they make known the gospel of salvation, many will be convicted and converted by the power of God. The human instrumentality is hid with Christ in God, and Christ appears as the chiefest among ten thousand, the One altogether lovely.

"Now he that planteth and he that watereth are one: and every man shall receive his own reward according to his own labor. For we are laborers together with God: ye are God's husbandry, ye are God's building." 2 Corinthians 3:8, 9. In this scripture the apostle compares the church to a cultivated field, in which the husbandmen labor, caring for the vines of the Lord's planting; and also to a building, which is to grow into a holy temple for the Lord. God is the Master Worker, and He has appointed to each man his work. All are to labor under His supervision, letting Him work for and through His workmen. He gives them tact and skill, and if they heed His instruction, crowns their efforts with success.

God's servants are to work together, blending in kindly, courteous order, "in honor preferring one another." Romans 12:10. There is to be no unkind criticism, no pulling to pieces of another's work; and there are to be no separate parties. Every man to whom the Lord has entrusted a message has his specific work. Each one has an individuality of his own, which he is not to sink in that of any other man. Yet each is to work in harmony with his brethren. In their service God's workers are to be essentially one. No one is to set himself up as a criterion, speaking disrespectfully of his fellow workers or treating them as inferior. Under God each is to do his appointed work, respected, loved, and encouraged by the other laborers. Together they are to carry the work forward to completion.

These principles are dwelt upon at length in Paul's first letter to the Corinthian church. The apostle refers to "the ministers of Christ" as "stewards of the mysteries of God," and of their work he declares: "It is required in stewards, that a man be found faithful. But with me it is a very small thing that I should be judged of you, or of man's judgment: yea, I judge not mine own self. For I know nothing by myself; yet I am not hereby justified: but He that judgeth me is the Lord. Therefore judge nothing before the time, until the Lord come, who both will bring to light the hidden things of darkness, and will make manifest the counsels of the hearts: and then shall every man have praise of God." 1 Corinthians 4:1-5.

It is not given to any human being to judge between the different servants of God. The Lord alone is the judge of man's work, and He will give to each his just reward.

The apostle, continuing, referred directly to the comparisons that had been made between his labors and those of Apollos: "These things, brethren, I have in a figure transferred to myself and to Apollos for your sakes; that ye might learn in us not to think of men above that which is written, that no one of you be puffed up for one against another. For who maketh thee to differ from another? and what hast thou that thou didst not receive? now if thou didst receive it, why dost thou glory, as if thou hadst not received it?" 1 Corinthians 4:6, 7.

Paul plainly set before the church the perils and the hardships that he and his associates had patiently endured in their service for Christ. "Even unto this present hour," he declared, "we both hunger, and thirst, and are naked, and are buffeted, and have no certain dwelling place; and labor, working with our own hands: being reviled, we bless; being persecuted, we suffer it: being defamed, we entreat: we are made as the filth of the world, and are the offscouring of all things unto this day. I write not these things to shame you, but as my beloved sons I warn you. For though ye have ten thousand instructors in Christ, yet have ye not many fathers: for in Christ Jesus I have begotten you through the gospel." 1 Corinthians 4:11-15.

He who sends forth gospel workers as His ambassadors is dishonored when there is manifested among the hearers so strong an attachment to some favorite minister that there is an unwillingness to accept the labors of some other teacher. The Lord sends help to His people, not always as they may choose, but as they need; for men are shortsighted and cannot discern what is for their highest good. It is seldom that one minister has all the qualifications necessary to perfect a church in all the requirements of Christianity; therefore God often sends to them other ministers, each possessing some qualifications in which the others were deficient.

The church should gratefully accept these servants of Christ, even as they would accept the Master Himself. They should seek to derive all the benefit possible from the instruction which each minister may give them from the word of God. The truths that the servants of God bring are to be accepted and appreciated in the meekness of humility, but no minister is to be idolized.

Through the grace of Christ, God's ministers are made messengers of light and blessing. As by earnest, persevering prayer they obtain the endowment of the Holy Spirit and go forth weighted with the burden of soulsaving, their hearts filled with zeal to extend the triumphs of the cross, they will see fruit of their labors. Resolutely refusing to display human wisdom or to exalt self, they will accomplish a work that will withstand the assaults of Satan. Many souls will be turned from darkness to light, and many churches will be established. Men will be converted, not to the human instrumentality, but to Christ. Self will be kept in the background; Jesus only, the Man of Calvary, will appear.

Those who are working for Christ today may reveal the same distinguishing excellencies revealed by those who in the apostolic age proclaimed the gospel. God is just as ready to give power to

His servants today as He was to give power to Paul and Apollos, to Silas and Timothy, to Peter, James, and John.

In the apostles' day there were some misguided souls who claimed to believe in Christ, yet refused to show respect to His ambassadors. They declared that they followed no human teacher, but were taught directly by Christ without the aid of the ministers of the gospel. They were independent in spirit and unwilling to submit to the voice of the church. Such men were in grave danger of being deceived.

God has placed in the church, as His appointed helpers, men of varied talents, that through the combined wisdom of many the mind of the Spirit may be met. Men who move in accordance with their own strong traits of character, refusing to yoke up with others who have had a long experience in the work of God, will become blinded by self-confidence, unable to discern between the false and the true. It is not safe for such ones to be chosen as leaders in the church; for they would follow their own judgment and plans, regardless of the judgment of their brethren. It is easy for the enemy to work through those who, themselves needing counsel at every step, undertake the guardianship of souls in their own strength, without having learned the lowliness of Christ.

Impressions alone are not a safe guide to duty. The enemy often persuades men to believe that it is God who is guiding them, when in reality they are following only human impulse. But if we watch carefully, and take counsel with our brethren, we shall be given an understanding of the Lord's will; for the promise is, "The meek will He guide in judgment: and the meek will He teach His way." Psalm 25:9.

In the early Christian church there were some who refused to recognize either Paul or Apollos, but held that Peter was their leader. They affirmed that Peter had been most intimate with Christ when the Master was upon the earth, while Paul had been a persecutor of the believers. Their views and feelings were bound about by prejudice. They did not show the liberality, the generosity, the tenderness, which reveals that Christ is abiding in the heart.

There was danger that this party spirit would result in great evil to the Christian church, and Paul was instructed by the Lord to utter words of earnest admonition and solemn protest. Of those who were saying, "I am of Paul; and I of Apollos; and I of Cephas; and I of Christ," the apostle inquired, "Is Christ divided? was Paul crucified for you? or were ye baptized in the name of Paul?" "Let no man glory in men," he pleaded. "For all things are yours; whether Paul, or Apollos, or Cephas, or the world, or life, or death, or things present, or things to come; all are yours; and ye are Christ's; and Christ is God's." 1 Corinthians 1:12, 13; 3:21-23.

Paul and Apollos were in perfect harmony. The latter was disappointed and grieved because of the dissension in the church at Corinth; he took no advantage of the preference shown to himself, nor did he encourage it, but hastily left the field of strife. When Paul afterward urged him to revisit Corinth, he declined and did not again labor there until long afterward when the church had reached a better spiritual state.

27

Ephesus

This chapter is based on Acts 19:1-20

While Apollos was preaching at Corinth, Paul fulfilled his promise to return to Ephesus. He had made a brief visit to Jerusalem and had spent some time at Antioch, the scene of his early labors. Thence he traveled through Asia Minor, "over all the country of Galatia and Phrygia" (Acts 18:23), visiting the churches which he himself had established, and strengthening the faith of the believers.

In the time of the apostles the western portion of Asia Minor was known as the Roman province of Asia. Ephesus, the capital, was a great commercial center. Its harbor was crowded with shipping, and its streets were thronged with people from every country. Like Corinth, it presented a promising field for missionary effort.

The Jews, now widely dispersed in all civilized lands, were generally expecting the advent of the Messiah. When John the Baptist was preaching, many, in their visits to Jerusalem at the annual feasts, had gone out to the banks of the Jordan to listen to him. There they had heard Jesus proclaimed as the Promised One, and they had carried the tidings to all parts of the world. Thus had Providence prepared the way for the labors of the apostles.

On his arrival at Ephesus, Paul found twelve brethren, who, like Apollos, had been disciples of John the Baptist, and like him had gained some knowledge of the mission of Christ. They had not the ability of Apollos, but with the same sincerity and faith they were seeking to spread abroad the knowledge they had received.

These brethren knew nothing of the mission of the Holy Spirit. When asked by Paul if they had received the Holy Ghost, they answered, "We have not so much as heard whether there be any Holy Ghost." "Unto what then were ye baptized?" Paul inquired, and they said, "Unto John's baptism."

Then the apostle set before them the great truths that are the foundation of the Christian's hope. He told them of Christ's life on this earth and of His cruel death of shame. He told them how the Lord of life had broken the barriers of the tomb and risen triumphant over death. He repeated the Saviour's commission to His disciples:

"All power is given unto Me in heaven and in earth. Go ye therefore, and teach all nations, baptizing them in the name of the Father, and of the Son, and of the Holy Ghost." Matthew 28:18, 19. He told them also of Christ's promise to send the Comforter, through whose power mighty signs and wonders would be wrought, and he described how gloriously this promise had been fulfilled on the Day of Pentecost.

With deep interest and grateful, wondering joy the brethren listened to Paul's words. By faith they grasped the wonderful truth of Christ's atoning sacrifice and received Him as their Redeemer. They were then baptized in the name of Jesus, and as Paul "laid his hands upon them," they received also the baptism of the Holy Spirit, by which they were enabled to speak the languages of other nations and to prophesy. Thus they were qualified to labor as missionaries in Ephesus and its vicinity and also to go forth to proclaim the gospel in Asia Minor.

It was by cherishing a humble, teachable spirit that these men gained the experience that enabled them to go out as workers into the harvest field. Their example presents to Christians a lesson of great value. There are many who make but little progress in the divine life because they are too self-sufficient to occupy the position of learners. They are content with a superficial knowledge of God's word. They do not wish to change their faith or practice and hence make no effort to obtain greater light.

If the followers of Christ were but earnest seekers after wisdom, they would be led into rich fields of truth as yet wholly unknown to them. He who will give himself fully to God will be guided by the divine hand. He may be lowly and apparently ungifted; yet if with a loving, trusting heart he obeys every intimation of God's will, his powers will be purified, ennobled, energized, and his capabilities will be increased. As he treasures the lessons of divine wisdom, a sacred commission will be entrusted to him; he will be enabled to make his life an honor to God and a blessing to the world. "The entrance of Thy words giveth light; it giveth understanding unto the simple." Psalm 119:130.

There are today many as ignorant of the Holy Spirit's work upon the heart as were those believers in Ephesus; yet no truth is more clearly taught in the word of God. Prophets and apostles have dwelt upon this theme. Christ Himself calls our attention to the growth of the vegetable world as an illustration of the agency of His Spirit in sustaining spiritual life. The sap of the vine, ascending from the root, is diffused to the branches, sustaining growth and producing blossoms and fruit. So the life-giving power of the Holy Spirit, proceeding from the Saviour, pervades the soul, renews the motives and affections, and brings even the thoughts into obedience to the will of God, enabling the receiver to bear the precious fruit of holy deeds.

The Author of this spiritual life is unseen, and the exact method by which that life is imparted and sustained, it is beyond the power of human philosophy to explain. Yet the operations of the Spirit are always in harmony with the written word. As in the natural, so in the spiritual world. The natural life is preserved moment by moment by divine power; yet it is not sustained by a direct miracle, but through the use of blessings placed within our reach. So the spiritual life is sustained by the use of those means that Providence has supplied. If the follower of Christ would grow up "unto a perfect man, unto the measure of the stature of the fullness of Christ" (Ephesians 4:13), he must eat of the bread of life and drink of the water of salvation. He must watch and pray and work, in all things giving heed to the instructions of God in His word.

There is still another lesson for us in the experience of those Jewish converts. When they received baptism at the hand of John they did not fully comprehend the mission of Jesus as the Sin Bearer. They were holding serious errors. But with clearer light, they gladly accepted Christ as their Redeemer, and with this step of advance came a change in their obligations. As they received a purer faith, there was a corresponding change in their life. In token of this change, and as an acknowledgment of their faith in Christ, they were rebaptized in the name of Jesus.

As was his custom, Paul had begun his work at Ephesus by preaching in the synagogue of the Jews. He continued to labor there for three months, "disputing and persuading the things concerning the kingdom of God." At first he met with a favorable reception; but as in other fields, he was soon violently opposed. "Divers were hardened, and believed not, but spake evil of that way before the multitude." As they persisted in their rejection of the gospel, the apostle ceased to preach in the synagogue.

The Spirit of God had wrought with and through Paul in his labors for his countrymen. Sufficient evidence had been presented to convince all who honestly desired to know the truth. But many permitted themselves to be controlled by prejudice and unbelief, and refused to yield to the most conclusive evidence. Fearing that the faith of the believers would be endangered by continued association with these opposers of the truth, Paul separated from them and gathered the disciples into a distinct body, continuing his public instructions in the school of Tyrannus, a teacher of some note.

Paul saw that "a great door and effectual" was opening before him, although there were "many adversaries." 1 Corinthians 16:9. Ephesus was not only the most magnificent, but the most corrupt, of the cities of Asia. Superstition and sensual pleasure held sway over her teeming population. Under the shadow of her temples, criminals of every grade found shelter, and the most degrading vices flourished.

Ephesus was a popular center for the worship of Diana. The fame of the magnificent temple of "Diana of the Ephesians" extended throughout all Asia and the world. Its surpassing splendor made it the pride, not only of the city, but of the nation. The idol within the temple was declared by tradition to have fallen from the sky. Upon it were inscribed symbolic characters, which were believed to possess great power. Books had been written by the Ephesians to explain the meaning and use of these symbols.

Among those who gave close study to these costly books were many magicians, who wielded a powerful influence over the minds of the superstitious worshipers of the image within the temple.

The apostle Paul, in his labors at Ephesus, was given special tokens of divine favor. The power of God accompanied his efforts, and many were healed of physical maladies. "God wrought special miracles by the hands of Paul: so that from his body were brought unto the sick handkerchiefs or aprons, and the diseases departed from them, and the evil spirits went out of them." These manifestations of supernatural power were far more potent than had ever before been witnessed in Ephesus, and were of such a character that they could not be imitated by the skill of the juggler or the enchantments of the sorcerer. As these miracles were wrought in the name of Jesus of Nazareth, the people had opportunity to see that the God of heaven was more powerful than the magicians who were worshipers of the goddess Diana. Thus the Lord exalted His servant, even before the idolaters themselves, immeasurably above the most powerful and favored of the magicians.

But the One to whom all the spirits of evil are subject and who had given His servants authority over them, was about to bring still greater shame and defeat upon those who despised and profaned His holy name. Sorcery had been prohibited by the Mosaic law, on pain of death, yet from time to time it had been secretly practiced by apostate Jews. At the time of Paul's visit to Ephesus there were in the city "certain of the vagabond Jews, exorcists," who, seeing the wonders wrought by him, "took upon them to call over them which had evil spirits the name of the Lord Jesus." An attempt was made by "seven sons of one Sceva, a Jew, and chief of the priests." Finding a man possessed with a demon, they addressed him, "We adjure you by Jesus whom Paul preacheth." But "the evil spirit answered and said, Jesus I know, and Paul I know; but who are ye? And the man in whom the evil spirit was leaped on them, and overcame them, and prevailed against them, so that they fled out of that house naked and wounded."

Thus unmistakable proof was given of the sacredness of the name of Christ, and the peril which they incurred who should invoke it without faith in the divinity of the Saviour's mission. "Fear fell on them all, and the name of the Lord Jesus was magnified."

Facts which had previously been concealed were now brought to light. In accepting Christianity, some of the believers had not fully renounced their superstitions. To some extent they still continued the practice of magic. Now, convinced of their error, "many that believed came, and confessed, and showed their deeds." Even to some of the sorcerers themselves the good work extended; and "many of them also which used curious arts brought their books together, and burned them before all men: and they counted the price of them, and found it fifty thousand pieces of silver. So mightily grew the word of God and prevailed."

By burning their books on magic, the Ephesian converts showed that the things in which they had once delighted they now abhorred. It was by and through magic that they had especially offended God and imperiled their souls; and it was against magic that they showed such indignation. Thus they gave evidence of true conversion.

These treatises on divination contained rules and forms of communication with evil spirits. They were the regulations of the worship of Satan—directions for soliciting his help and obtaining information from him. By retaining these books the disciples would have exposed themselves to temptation; by selling them they would have placed temptation in the way of others. They had renounced the kingdom of darkness, and to destroy its power they did not hesitate at any sacrifice. Thus truth triumphed over men's prejudices and their love of money.

By this manifestation of the power of Christ, a mighty victory for Christianity was gained in the very stronghold of superstition. The influence of what had taken place was more widespread than even Paul realized. From Ephesus the news was widely circulated, and a strong impetus was given to the cause of Christ. Long after the apostle himself had finished his course, these scenes lived in the memory of men and were the means of winning converts to the gospel.

It is fondly supposed that heathen superstitions have disappeared before the civilization of the twentieth century. But the word of God and the stern testimony of facts declare that sorcery is practiced in this age as verily as in the days of the old-time magicians. The ancient system of magic is, in reality, the same as what is now known as modern spiritualism. Satan is finding access to thousands of minds by presenting himself under the guise of departed friends. The Scriptures declare that "the dead know not anything." Ecclesiastes 9:5. Their thoughts, their love, their hatred, have perished. The dead do not hold communion with the living. But true to his early cunning, Satan employs this device in order to gain control of minds.

Through spiritualism many of the sick, the bereaved, the curious, are communicating with evil spirits. All who venture to do this are on dangerous ground. The word of truth declares how God regards them. In ancient times He pronounced a stern judgment on a king who had sent for counsel to a heathen oracle: "Is it not because there is not a God in Israel, that ye go to inquire of Baal-zebub the god of Ekron? Now therefore thus saith the Lord, Thou shalt not come down from that bed on which thou art gone up, but shalt surely die." 2 Kings 1:3, 4.

The magicians of heathen times have their counterpart in the spiritualistic mediums, the clairvoyants, and the fortune-tellers of today. The mystic voices that spoke at Endor and at Ephesus are still by their lying words misleading the children of men. Could the veil be lifted from before our eyes, we should see evil angels employing all their arts to deceive and to destroy. Wherever an influence is exerted to cause men to forget God, there Satan is exercising his bewitching power. When men yield to his influence, ere they are aware the mind is bewildered and the soul polluted. The apostle's admonition to the Ephesian church should be heeded by the people of God today: "Have no fellowship with the unfruitful works of darkness, but rather reprove them." Ephesians 5:11.

28

Days of Toil and Trial

This chapter is based on Acts 19:21-41; 20:1

For over three years Ephesus was the center of Paul's work. A flourishing church was raised up here, and from this city the gospel spread throughout the province of Asia, among both Jews and Gentiles.

The apostle had now for some time had been contemplating another missionary journey. He "purposed in the spirit, when he had passed through Macedonia and Achaia, to go to Jerusalem, saying, After I have been there, I must also see Rome." In harmony with this plan "he sent into Macedonia two of them that ministered unto him, Timotheus and Erastus;" but feeling that the cause in Ephesus still demanded his presence, he decided to remain until after Pentecost. An event soon occurred, however, which hastened his departure.

Once a year, special ceremonies were held at Ephesus in honor of the goddess Diana. These attracted great numbers of people from all parts of the province. Throughout this period, festivities were conducted with the utmost pomp and splendor.

This gala season was a trying time for those who had newly come to the faith. The company of believers who met in the school of Tyrannus were an inharmonious note in the festive chorus, and ridicule, reproach, and insult were freely heaped upon them. Paul's labors had given the heathen worship a telling blow, in consequence of which there was a perceptible falling off in the attendance at the national festival and in the enthusiasm of the worshipers. The influence of his teachings extended far beyond the actual converts to the faith. Many who had not openly accepted the new doctrines became so far enlightened as to lose all confidence in their heathen gods.

There existed also another cause of dissatisfaction. An extensive and profitable business had grown up at Ephesus from the manufacture and sale of small shrines and images, modeled after the temple and the image of Diana. Those interested in this industry found their gains diminishing, and all united in attributing the unwelcome change to Paul's labors.

Demetrius, a manufacturer of silver shrines, calling together the workmen of his craft, said: "Sirs, ye know that by this craft we have our wealth. Moreover ye see and hear, that not alone at Ephesus, but almost throughout all Asia, this Paul hath persuaded and turned away much people, saying that they be no gods, which are made with hands: so that not only this our craft is in danger to be set at nought; but also that the temple of the great goddess Diana should be despised, and her magnificence should be destroyed, whom all Asia and the world worshipeth." These words roused the excitable passions of the people. "They were full of wrath, and cried out, saying, Great is Diana of the Ephesians."

A report of this speech was rapidly circulated. "The whole city was filled with confusion." Search was made for Paul, but the apostle was not to be found. His brethren, receiving an intimation of the danger, had hurried him from the place. Angels of God had been sent to guard the apostle; his time to die a martyr's death had not yet come.

Failing to find the object of their wrath, the mob seized "Gaius and Aristarchus, men of Macedonia, Paul's companions in travel," and with these "they rushed with one accord into the theater."

Paul's place of concealment was not far distant, and he soon learned of the peril of his beloved brethren. Forgetful of his own safety, he desired to go at once to the theater to address the rioters. But "the disciples suffered him not." Gaius and Aristarchus were not the prey the people sought; no serious harm to them was apprehended. But should the apostle's pale, care-worn face be seen, it would arouse at once the worst passions of the mob and there would not be the least human possibility of saving his life.

Paul was still eager to defend the truth before the multitude, but he was at last deterred by a message of warning from the theater. "Certain of the chief of Asia, which were his friends, sent unto him, desiring him that he would not adventure himself into the theater."

The tumult in the theater was continually increasing. "Some . . . cried one thing, and some another: for the assembly was confused; and the more part knew not wherefore they were come together." The fact that Paul and some of his companions were of Hebrew extraction made the Jews anxious to show plainly that they were not sympathizers with him and his work. They therefore brought forward one of their own number to set the matter before the people. The speaker chosen was Alexander, one of the craftsmen, a coppersmith, to whom Paul afterward referred as having done him much evil. 2 Timothy 4:14. Alexander was a man of considerable ability, and he bent all his energies to direct the wrath of the people exclusively against Paul and his companions. But the crowd, seeing that Alexander was a Jew, thrust him aside, and "all with one voice about the space of two hours cried out, Great is Diana of the Ephesians."

At last, from sheer exhaustion, they ceased, and there was a momentary silence. Then the recorder of the city arrested the attention of the crowd, and by virtue of his office obtained a hearing. He met the people on their own ground and showed that there was no cause for the present tumult. He appealed to their reason. "Ye men of Ephesus," he said, "what man is there that knoweth not how that the city of the Ephesians is a worshiper of the great goddess Diana, and of the image which fell down from Jupiter? Seeing then that these things cannot be spoken against, ye ought to be quiet, and to do nothing rashly. For ye have brought hither these men, which are neither robbers of churches, nor yet blasphemers of your goddess. Wherefore if Demetrius, and the craftsmen which are with him, have a matter against any man, the law is open, and there are deputies: let them implead one another. But if ye inquire anything concerning other matters, it shall be determined in a lawful assembly. For we are in danger to be called in question for this day's uproar, there being no cause whereby we may give an account of this concourse. And when he had thus spoken, he dismissed the assembly."

In his speech Demetrius had said, "This our craft is in danger." These words reveal the real cause of the tumult at Ephesus, and also the cause of much of the persecution which followed the apostles in their work. Demetrius and his fellow craftsmen saw that by the teaching and spread of the gospel the business of image making was endangered. The income of pagan priests and artisans was at stake, and for this reason they aroused against Paul the most bitter opposition.

The decision of the recorder and of others holding honorable offices in the city had set Paul before the people as one innocent of any unlawful act. This was another triumph of Christianity over error and superstition. God had raised up a great magistrate to vindicate His apostle and hold the tumultuous mob in check. Paul's heart was filled with gratitude to God that his life had been preserved and that Christianity had not been brought into disrepute by the tumult at Ephesus.

"After the uproar was ceased, Paul called unto him the disciples, and embraced them, and departed for to go into Macedonia." On this journey he was accompanied by two faithful Ephesian brethren, Tychicus and Trophimus.

Paul's labors in Ephesus were concluded. His ministry there had been a season of incessant labor, of many trials, and of deep anguish. He had taught the people in public and from house to house, with many tears instructing and warning them. Continually he had been opposed by the Jews, who lost no opportunity to stir up the popular feeling against him.

And while thus battling against opposition, pushing forward with untiring zeal the gospel work, and guarding the interests of a church yet young in the faith, Paul was bearing upon his soul a heavy burden for all the churches.

News of apostasy in some of the churches of his planting caused him deep sorrow. He feared that his efforts in their behalf might prove to be in vain. Many a sleepless night was spent in prayer and earnest thought as he learned of the methods employed to counteract his work. As he had opportunity and as their condition demanded, he wrote to the churches, giving reproof, counsel, admonition, and encouragement. In these letters the apostle does not dwell on his own trials, yet there are occasional glimpses of his labors and sufferings in the cause of Christ. Stripes and imprisonment, cold and hunger and thirst, perils by land and by sea, in the city and in the wilderness, from his own countrymen, from the heathen, and from false brethren— all this he endured for the sake of the gospel. He was "defamed," "reviled," made "the offscouring of all things," "perplexed," "persecuted," "troubled on every side," "in jeopardy every hour," "alway delivered unto death for Jesus' sake."

Amidst the constant storm of opposition, the clamor of enemies, and the desertion of friends the intrepid apostle almost lost heart. But he looked back to Calvary and with new ardor pressed on to spread the knowledge of the Crucified. He was but treading the blood-stained path that Christ had trodden before him. He sought no discharge from the warfare till he should lay off his armor at the feet of his Redeemer.

29

A Message of Warning and Entreaty

This chapter is based on the First Epistle to the Corinthians

The first epistle to the Corinthian church was written by the apostle Paul during the latter part of his stay at Ephesus. For no others had he felt a deeper interest or put forth more untiring effort than for the believers in Corinth. For a year and a half he had labored among them, pointing them to a crucified and risen Saviour as the only means of salvation, and urging them to rely implicitly on the transforming power of His grace. Before accepting into church fellowship those who made a profession of Christianity, he had been careful to give them special instruction as to the privileges and duties of the Christian believer, and he had earnestly endeavored to help them to be faithful to their baptismal vows.

Paul had a keen sense of the conflict which every soul must wage with the agencies of evil that are continually seeking to deceive and ensnare, and he had worked untiringly to strengthen and confirm those who were young in the faith. He had entreated them to make an entire surrender to God; for he knew that when the soul fails to make this surrender, then sin is not forsaken, the appetites and passions still strive for the mastery, and temptations confuse the conscience.

The surrender must be complete. Every weak, doubting, struggling soul who yields fully to the Lord is placed in direct touch with agencies that enable him to overcome. Heaven is near to him, and he has the support and help of angels of mercy in every time of trial and need.

The members of the church at Corinth were surrounded by idolatry and sensuality of the most alluring form. While the apostle was with them, these influences had but little power over them. Paul's firm faith, his fervent prayers and earnest words of instruction, and, above all, his godly life had helped them to deny self for Christ's sake rather than to enjoy the pleasures of sin.

After the departure of Paul, however, unfavorable conditions arose; tares that had been sown by the enemy appeared among the wheat, and erelong these began to bring forth their evil fruit. This was a time of severe trial to the Corinthian church. The apostle was no longer with them to quicken their zeal and aid them in their endeavors to live in harmony with God, and little by little many became careless and indifferent, and allowed natural tastes and inclinations to control them. He who had so often urged them to high ideals of purity and uprightness was no longer with them, and not a few who, at the time of their conversion, had put away their evil habits, returned to the debasing sins of heathenism.

Paul had written briefly to the church, admonishing them "not to company" with members who should persist in profligacy; but many of the believers perverted the apostle's meaning, quibbled over his words, and excused themselves for disregarding his instruction.

A letter was sent to Paul by the church, asking for counsel concerning various matters, but saying nothing of the grievous sins existing among them. The apostle was, however, forcibly impressed by the Holy Spirit that the true state of the church had been concealed and that this letter was an attempt to draw from him statements which the writers could construe to serve their own purposes.

About this time there came to Ephesus members of the household of Chloe, a Christian family of high repute in Corinth. Paul asked them regarding the condition of things, and they told him that the church was rent by divisions. The dissensions that had prevailed at the time of Apollos's visit had greatly increased. False teachers were leading the members to despise the instructions of Paul. The doctrines and ordinances of the gospel had been perverted. Pride, idolatry, and sensualism, were steadily increasing among those who had once been zealous in the Christian life.

As this picture was presented before him, Paul saw that his worst fears were more than realized. But he did not because of this give way to the thought that his work had been a failure. With "anguish of heart" and with "many tears" he sought counsel from God. Gladly would he have visited Corinth at once, had this been the wisest course to pursue. But he knew that in their present condition the believers would not profit by his labors, and therefore he sent Titus to prepare the way for a visit from himself later on. Then, putting aside all personal feelings over the course of those whose conduct revealed such strange perverseness, and keeping his soul stayed upon God, the apostle wrote to the church at Corinth one of the richest, most instructive, most powerful of all his letters.

With remarkable clearness he proceeded to answer the various questions brought forward by the church, and to lay down general principles, which, if heeded, would lead them to a higher spiritual plane. They were in peril, and he could not bear the thought of failing at this critical time to reach their hearts. Faithfully he warned them of their dangers and reproved them for their sins. He pointed them again to Christ and sought to kindle anew the fervor of their early devotion.

The apostle's great love for the Corinthian believers was revealed in his tender greeting to the church. He referred to their experience in turning from idolatry to the worship and service of the true God. He reminded them of the gifts of the Holy Spirit which they had received, and showed that it was their privilege to make continual advancement in the Christian life until they should attain to the purity and holiness of Christ. "In everything ye are enriched by Him," he wrote, "in all utterance, and in all knowledge; even as the testimony of Christ was confirmed in you: so that ye come behind in no gift; waiting for the coming of our Lord Jesus Christ: who shall also confirm you unto the end, that ye may be blameless in the day of our Lord Jesus Christ."

Paul spoke plainly of the dissensions that had arisen in the Corinthian church, and exhorted the members to cease from strife. "I beseech you, brethren," he wrote, "by the name of our Lord Jesus Christ, that ye all speak the same thing, and that there be no divisions among you; but that ye be perfectly joined together in the same mind and in the same judgment."

The apostle felt at liberty to mention how and by whom he had been informed of the divisions in the church. "It hath been declared unto me of you, my brethren, by them which are of the house of Chloe, that there are contentions among you."

Paul was an inspired apostle. The truths he taught to others he had received "by revelation;" yet the Lord did not directly reveal to him at all times just the condition of His people. In this instance those who were interested in the prosperity of the church at Corinth, and who had seen evils creeping in, had presented the matter before the apostle, and from divine revelations which he had formerly received he was prepared to judge of the character of these developments. Notwithstanding the fact that the Lord did not give him a new revelation for that special time, those who were really seeking for light accepted his message as expressing the mind of Christ. The Lord had shown him the difficulties and dangers which would arise in the churches, and, as these evils developed, the apostle recognized their significance. He had been set for the defense of the church. He was to watch for souls as one who must render account to God, and was it not consistent and right for him to take notice of the reports concerning the anarchy and divisions among them? Most assuredly; and the reproof he sent them was as certainly written under the inspiration of the Spirit of God as were any of his other epistles.

The apostle made no mention of the false teachers who were seeking to destroy the fruit of his labor. Because of the darkness and division in the church, he wisely forbore to irritate them by such references, for fear of turning some entirely from the truth. He called attention to his own work among them as that of "a wise master builder," who had laid the foundation upon which others had built. But he did not thereby exalt himself; for he declared, "We are laborers together with God." He claimed no wisdom of his own, but acknowledged that divine power alone had enabled him to present the truth in a manner pleasing to God. United with Christ, the greatest of all teachers, Paul had been enabled to communicate lessons of divine wisdom, which met the necessities of all classes, and which were to apply at all times, in all places, and under all conditions.

Among the more serious of the evils that had developed among the Corinthian believers, was that of a return to many of the debasing customs of heathenism. One former convert had so far backslidden that his licentious course was a violation of even the low standard of morality held by the Gentile world. The apostle pleaded with the church to put away from among them "that wicked person." "Know ye not," he admonished them, "that a little leaven leaveneth the whole lump? Purge out therefore the old leaven, that ye may be a new lump, as ye are unleavened."

Another grave evil that had arisen in the church was that of brethren going to law against one another. Abundant provision had been made for the settlement of difficulties among believers. Christ Himself had given plain instruction as to how such matters were to be adjusted. "If thy brother shall trespass against thee," the Saviour had counseled, "go and tell him his fault between thee and him alone: if he shall hear thee, thou hast gained thy brother. But if he will not hear thee, then take with thee one or two more, that in the mouth of two or three witnesses every word may be established. And if he shall neglect to hear them, tell it unto the church: but if he neglect to hear the church, let him be unto thee as a heathen man and a publican. Verily I say unto you, Whatsoever ye shall bind on earth shall be bound in heaven: and whatsoever ye shall loose on earth shall be loosed in heaven." Matthew 18:15-18.

To the Corinthian believers who had lost sight of this plain counsel, Paul wrote in no uncertain terms of admonition and rebuke. "Dare any of you," he asked, "having a matter against another, go to law before the unjust, and not before the saints? Do ye not know that the saints shall judge the world? and if the world shall be judged by you, are ye unworthy to judge the smallest matters? Know ye not that we shall judge angels? how much more things that pertain to this life? If then ye have judgments of things pertaining to this life, set them to judge who are least esteemed in the church. I speak to your shame. Is it so, that there is not a wise man among you? no, not one that shall be able to judge between his brethren? But brother goeth to law with brother, and that before the unbelievers. Now therefore there is utterly a fault among you, because ye go to law one with another. Why do ye not rather take wrong? . . . Nay, ye do wrong, and defraud, and that your brethren. Know ye not that the unrighteous shall not inherit the kingdom of God?"

Satan is constantly seeking to introduce distrust, alienation, and malice among God's people. We shall often be tempted to feel that our rights are invaded, even when there is no real cause for such feelings. Those whose love for self is stronger than their love for Christ and His cause will place their own interests first and will resort to almost any expedient to guard and maintain them. Even many who appear to be conscientious Christians are hindered by pride and self-esteem from going privately to those whom they think in error, that they may talk with them in the spirit of Christ and pray together for one another. When they think themselves injured by their brethren, some will even go to law instead of following the Saviour's rule.

Christians should not appeal to civil tribunals to settle differences that may arise among church members. Such differences should be settled among themselves, or by the church, in harmony with Christ's instruction. Even though injustice may have been done, the follower of the meek and lowly Jesus will suffer himself "to be defrauded" rather than open before the world the sins of his brethren in the church.

Lawsuits between brethren are a reproach to the cause of truth. Christians who go to law with one another expose the church to the ridicule of her enemies and cause the powers of darkness to triumph. They are wounding Christ afresh and putting Him to open shame. By ignoring the authority of the church, they show contempt for God, who gave to the church its authority.

In this letter to the Corinthians Paul endeavored to show them Christ's power to keep them from evil. He knew that if they would comply with the conditions laid down, they would be strong in the strength of the Mighty One. As a means of helping them to break away from the thralldom of sin and to perfect holiness in the fear of the Lord, Paul urged upon them the claims of Him to whom they had dedicated their lives at the time of their conversion. "Ye are Christ's," he declared. "Ye are not your own. . . . Ye are bought with a price: therefore glorify God in your body, and in your spirit, which are God's."

The apostle plainly outlined the result of turning from a life of purity and holiness to the corrupt practices of heathenism. "Be not deceived," he wrote; "neither fornicators, nor idolaters, nor adulterers, . . . nor thieves, nor covetous, nor drunkards, nor revilers, nor extortioners, shall inherit the kingdom of God." He begged them to control the lower passions and appetites. "Know ye not," he asked, "that your body is the temple of the Holy Ghost which is in you, which ye have of God?"

While Paul possessed high intellectual endowments, his life revealed the power of a rarer wisdom, which gave him quickness of insight and sympathy of heart, and brought him into close touch with others, enabling him to arouse their better nature and inspire them to strive for a higher life. His heart was filled with an earnest love for the Corinthian believers. He longed to see them revealing an inward piety that would fortify them against temptation. He knew that at every step in the Christian pathway they would be opposed by the synagogue of Satan and that they would have to engage in conflicts daily. They would have to guard against the stealthy approach of the enemy, forcing back old habits and natural inclinations, and ever watching unto prayer. Paul knew that the higher Christian attainments can be reached only through much prayer and constant watchfulness, and this he tried to instill into their minds. But he knew also that in Christ crucified they were offered power sufficient to convert the soul and divinely adapted to enable them to resist all temptations to evil. With faith in God as their armor, and with His word as their weapon of warfare, they would be supplied with an inner power that would enable them to turn aside the attacks of the enemy.

The Corinthian believers needed a deeper experience in the things of God. They did not know fully what it meant to behold His glory and to be changed from character to character. They had seen but the first rays of the early dawn of that glory. Paul's desire for them was that they might be filled with all the fullness of God, following on to know Him whose going forth is prepared as the morning, and continuing to learn of Him until they should come into the full noontide of a perfect gospel faith.

30

Called to Reach a Higher Standard

This chapter is based on the First Epistle to the Corinthians

In the hope of impressing vividly upon the minds of the Corinthian believers the importance of firm self-control, strict temperance, and unflagging zeal in the service of Christ, Paul in his letter to them made a striking comparison between the Christian warfare and the celebrated foot races held at stated intervals near Corinth. Of all the games instituted among the Greeks and the Romans, the foot races were the most ancient and the most highly esteemed. They were witnessed by kings, nobles, and statesmen. Young men of rank and wealth took part in them and shrank from no effort or discipline necessary to obtain the prize.

The contests were governed by strict regulations, from which there was no appeal. Those who desired their names entered as competitors for the prize had first to undergo a severe preparatory training. Harmful indulgence of appetite, or any other gratification that would lower mental or physical vigor, was strictly forbidden. For one to have any hope of success in these trials of strength and speed, the muscles must be strong and supple, and the nerves well under control. Every movement must be certain, every step swift and unswerving; the physical powers must reach the highest mark.

As the contestants in the race made their appearance before the waiting multitude, their names were heralded, and the rules of the race were distinctly stated. Then they all started together, the fixed attention of the spectators inspiring them with a determination to win. The judges were seated near the goal, that they might watch the race from its beginning to its close and give the prize to the true victor. If a man reached the goal first by taking an unlawful advantage, he was not awarded the prize.

In these contests great risks were run. Some never recovered from the terrible physical strain. It was not unusual for men to fall on the course, bleeding at the mouth and nose, and sometimes a contestant would drop dead when about to seize the prize. But the possibility of lifelong injury or of death was not looked upon as too great a risk to run for the sake of the honor awarded the successful contestant.

As the winner reached the goal, the applause of the vast multitude of onlookers rent the air and awoke the echoes of the surrounding hills and mountains. In full view of the spectators, the judge presented him with the emblems of victory—a laurel crown and a palm branch to carry in his right hand. His praise was sung throughout the land; his parents received their share of honor; and even the city in which he lived was held in high esteem for having produced so great an athlete.

In referring to these races as a figure of the Christian warfare, Paul emphasized the preparation necessary to the success of the contestants in the race—the preliminary discipline, the abstemious diet, the necessity for temperance. "Every man that striveth for the mastery," he declared, "is temperate in all things." The runners put aside every indulgence that would tend to weaken the physical powers, and by severe and continuous discipline trained their muscles to strength and endurance, that when the day of the contest should arrive, they might put the heaviest tax upon their powers. How much more important that the Christian, whose eternal interests are at stake, bring appetite and passion under subjection to reason and the will of God! Never must he allow his attention to be diverted by amusements, luxuries, or ease. All his habits and passions must be brought under the strictest discipline. Reason, enlightened by the teachings of God's word and guided by His Spirit, must hold the reins of control.

And after this has been done, the Christian must put forth the utmost exertion in order to gain the victory. In the Corinthian games the last few strides of the contestants in the race were made with agonizing effort to keep up undiminished speed. So the Christian, as he nears the goal, will press onward with even more zeal and determination than at the first of his course.

Paul presents the contrast between the chaplet of fading laurel received by the victor in the foot races, and the crown of immortal glory that will be given to him who runs with triumph the Christian race. "They do it," he declares, "to obtain a corruptible crown; but we an incorruptible." To win a perishable prize, the Grecian runners spared themselves no toil or discipline. We are striving for a prize infinitely more valuable, even the crown of everlasting life. How much more careful should be our striving, how much more willing our sacrifice and self-denial!

In the epistle to the Hebrews is pointed out the single-hearted purpose that should characterize the Christian's race for eternal life: "Let us lay aside every weight, and the sin which doth so easily beset us, and let us run with patience the race that is set before us, looking unto Jesus the author and finisher of our faith." Hebrews 12:1, 2. Envy, malice, evil thinking, evilspeaking, covetousness— these are weights that the Christian must lay aside if he would run successfully the race for immortality. Every habit or practice that leads into sin and brings dishonor upon Christ must be put away, whatever the sacrifice. The blessing of heaven cannot attend any man in violating the eternal principles of right. One sin cherished is sufficient to work degradation of character and to mislead others.

"If thy hand cause thee to stumble," the Saviour said, "Cut it off: it is good for thee to enter into life maimed, rather than having thy two hands to go into hell, into the unquenchable fire. And if thy foot cause thee to stumble, cut it off: it is good for thee to enter into life halt, rather than having thy two feet to be cast into hell." Mark 9:43-45, R.V. If to save the body from death, the foot or the hand should be cut off, or even the eye plucked out, how much more earnest should the Christian be to put away sin, which brings death to the soul!

The competitors in the ancient games, after they had submitted to self-denial and rigid discipline, were not even then sure of the victory. "Know ye not," Paul asked, "that they which run in a race run all, but one receiveth the prize?" However eagerly and earnestly the runners might strive, the prize could be awarded to but one. One hand only could grasp the coveted garland. Some might put forth the utmost effort to obtain the prize, but as they reached forth the hand to secure it, another, an instant before them, might grasp the coveted treasure.

Such is not the case in the Christian warfare. Not one who complies with the conditions will be disappointed at the end of the race. Not one who is earnest and persevering will fail of success. The race is not to the swift, nor the battle to the strong. The weakest saint, as well as the strongest, may wear the crown of immortal glory. All may win who, through the power of divine grace, bring their lives into conformity to the will of Christ. The practice, in the details of life, of the principles laid down in God's word, is too often looked upon as unimportant—a matter too trivial to demand attention. But in view of the issue at stake, nothing is small that will help or hinder. Every act casts its weight into the scale that deter-mines life's victory or defeat. And the reward given to those who win will be in proportion to the energy and earnestness with which they have striven.

The apostle compared himself to a man running in a race,

straining every nerve to win the prize. "I therefore so run," he says, "not as uncertainly; so fight I, not as one that beateth the air: but I keep under my body, and bring it into subjection: lest that by any means, when I have preached to others, I myself should be a castaway." That he might not run uncertainly or at random in the Christian race, Paul subjected himself to severe training. The words, "I keep under my body," literally mean to beat back by severe discipline the desires, impulses, and passions. WE DON'T?

Paul feared lest, having preached to others, he himself should be a castaway. He realized that if he did not carry out in his life the principles he believed and preached, his labors in behalf of others would avail him nothing. His conversation, his influence, his refusal to yield to self-gratification, must show that his religion was not a profession merely, but a daily, living connection with God. One goal he kept ever before him, and strove earnestly to reach— "the righteousness which is of God by faith." Philippians 3:9.

Paul knew that his warfare against evil would not end so long as life should last. Ever he realized the need of putting a strict guard upon himself, that earthly desires might not overcome spiritual zeal. With all his power he continued to strive against natural inclinations. Ever he kept before him the ideal to be attained, and this ideal he strove to reach by willing obedience to the law of God. His words, his practices, his passions—all were brought under the control of the Spirit of God.

It was this singlehearted purpose to win the race for eternal life that Paul longed to see revealed in the lives of the Corinthian believers. He knew that in order to reach Christ's ideal for them, they had before them a life struggle from which there would be no release. He entreated them to strive lawfully, day by day seeking for piety and moral excellence. He pleaded with them to lay aside every weight and to press forward to the goal of perfection in Christ.

Paul pointed the Corinthians to the experience of ancient Israel, to the blessings that rewarded their obedience, and to the judgments that followed their transgressions. He reminded them of the miraculous way in which the Hebrews were led from Egypt under the protection of the cloud by day and the pillar of fire by night. Thus they were safely conducted through the Red Sea, while the Egyptians, essaying to cross in like manner, were all drowned. By these acts God had acknowledged Israel as His church. They "did all eat the same spiritual meat; and did all drink the same spiritual drink: for they drank of that spiritual Rock that followed them: and that Rock was Christ." The Hebrews, in all their travels, had Christ as a leader. The smitten rock typified Christ, who was to be wounded for men's transgressions, that the stream of salvation might flow to all.

Notwithstanding the favor that God showed to the Hebrews, yet because of their lust for the luxuries left behind in Egypt, and because of their sin and rebellion, the judgments of God came upon them. The apostle enjoined the Corinthian believers to heed the lesson contained in Israel's experience. "Now these things were our examples," he declared, "to the intent we should not lust after evil things, as they also lusted." He showed how love of ease and pleasure had prepared the way for sins that called forth the signal vengeance of God. It was when the children of Israel sat down to eat and drink, and rose up to play, that they threw off the fear of God, which they had felt as they listened to the giving of the law; and, making a golden calf to represent God, they worshiped it. And it was after enjoying a luxurious feast connected with the worship of Baalpeor, that many of the Hebrews fell through licentiousness. The anger of God was aroused, and at His command "three and twenty thousand" were slain by the plague in one day.

The apostle adjured the Corinthians, "Let him that thinketh he standeth take heed lest he fall." Should they become boastful and self-confident, neglecting to watch and pray, they would fall into grievous sin, calling down upon themselves the wrath of God. Yet Paul would not have them yield to despondency or discouragement. He gave them the assurance: "God is faithful, who will not suffer you to be tempted above that ye are able; but will with the temptation also make a way of escape, that ye may be able to bear it."

Paul urged his brethren to ask themselves what influence their words and deeds would have upon others and to do nothing, however innocent in itself, that would seem to sanction idolatry or offend the scruples of those who might be weak in the faith. "Whether therefore ye eat, or drink, or whatsoever ye do, do all to the glory of God. Give none offense, neither to the Jews, nor to the Gentiles, nor to the church of God."

The apostle's words of warning to the Corinthian church are applicable to all time and are especially adapted to our day. By idolatry he meant not only the worship of idols, but self-serving, love of ease, the gratification of appetite and passion. A mere profession of faith in Christ, a boastful knowledge of the truth, does not make a man a Christian. A religion that seeks only to gratify the eye, the ear, and the taste, or that sanctions self-indulgence, is not the religion of Christ.

By a comparison of the church with the human body, the apostle aptly illustrated the close and harmonious relationship that should exist among all members of the church of Christ. "By one Spirit," he wrote, "are well all baptized into one body, whether we be Jews or Gentiles, whether we be bond or free; and have been all made to drink into one Spirit. For the body is not one member, but many. If the foot shall say, Because I am not the hand, I am not of the body; is it therefore not of the body? And if the ear shall say, Because I am not the eye, I am not of the body; is it therefore not of the body? If the whole body were an eye, where were the hearing? If the whole were hearing, where were the smelling? But now hath God set the members every one of them in the body, as it hath pleased Him. And if they were all one member, where were the body? But now are they many members, yet but one body. And the eye cannot say unto the hand, I have no need of thee: nor again the head to the feet, I have no need of you. . . . God hath tempered the body together, having given more abundant honor to that part which lacked: that there should be no schism in the body; but that the members should have the same care one for another. And whether one member suffer, all the members suffer with it; or one member be honored, all the members rejoice with it. Now ye are the body of Christ, and members in particular."

And then, in words which from that day to this have been to men and women a source of inspiration and encouragement, Paul set forth the importance of that love which should be cherished by the followers of Christ: "Though I speak with the tongues of men and of angels, and have not charity, I am become as sounding brass, or a tinkling cymbal. And though I have the gift of prophecy, and understand all mysteries, and all knowledge; and though I have all faith, so that I could remove mountains, and have not charity, I am nothing. And though I bestow all my goods to feed the poor, and though I give my body to be burned, and have not charity, it profiteth me nothing." 1 Corinthians 13:1-3.

No matter how high the profession, he whose heart is not filled with love for God and his fellow men is not a true disciple of Christ. Though he should possess great faith and have power even to work miracles, yet without love his faith would be worthless. He might display great liberality; but should he, from some other motive than genuine love, bestow all his goods to feed the poor, the act would not commend him to the favor of God. In his zeal he might even meet a martyr's death, yet if not actuated by love, he would be regarded by God as a deluded enthusiast or an ambitious hypocrite.

"Charity suffereth long, and is kind; charity envieth not; charity vaunteth not itself, is not puffed up." The purest joy springs from the deepest humiliation. The strongest and noblest characters are built on the foundation of patience, love, and submission to God's will.

Charity "doth not behave itself unseemly, seeketh not her own, is not easily provoked, thinketh no evil." Christ-like love places the most favorable construction on the motives and acts of others. It does not needlessly expose their faults; it does not listen eagerly to unfavorable reports, but seeks rather to bring to mind the good qualities of others.

Love "rejoiceth not in iniquity, but rejoiceth in the truth; beareth all things, believeth all things, hopeth all things, endureth all things." This love "never faileth." It can never lose its value; it is a heavenly attribute. As a precious treasure, it will be carried by its possessor through the portals of the city of God.

"And now abideth faith, hope, charity, these three; but the greatest of these is charity."

In the lowering of the moral standard among the Corinthian believers, there were those who had given up some of the fundamental features of their faith. Some had gone so far as to deny the doctrine of the resurrection. Paul met this heresy with a very plain testimony regarding the unmistakable evidence of the resurrection of Christ. He declared that Christ, after His death, "rose again the third day according to the Scriptures," after which "He was seen of Cephas, then of the Twelve: after that, He was seen of above five hundred brethren at once; of whom the greater part remain unto this present, but some are fallen asleep. After that, He was seen of James; then of all the apostles. And last of all He was seen of me also."

With convincing power the apostle set forth the great truth of the resurrection. "If there be no resurrection of the dead," he argued, "then is Christ not risen: and if Christ be not risen, then is our preaching vain, and your faith is also vain. Yea, and we are found false witnesses of God; because we have testified of God that He raised up Christ: whom He raised not up, if so be that the dead rise not. For if the dead rise not, then is not Christ raised: and if Christ be not raised, your faith is vain; ye are yet in your sins. Then they also which are fallen asleep in Christ are perished. If in this life only we have hope in Christ, we are of all men most miserable. But now is Christ risen from the dead, and become the first fruits of them that slept."

The apostle carried the minds of the Corinthian brethren forward to the triumphs of the resurrection morn, when all the sleeping saints are to be raised, henceforth to live forever with their Lord. "Behold," the apostle declared, "I show you a mystery: We shall not all sleep, but we shall all be changed, in a moment, in the twinkling of an eye, at the last trump: for the trumpet shall sound, and the dead shall be raised incorruptible, and we shall be changed. For this corruptible must put on incorruption, and this mortal must put on immortality. So when this corruptible shall have put on incorruption, and this mortal shall have put on immortality, then shall be brought to pass the saying that is written, Death is swallowed up in victory. O death, where is thy sting? O grave, where is thy victory? . . . Thanks be to God, which giveth us the victory through our Lord Jesus Christ." 1 Corinthians 15:51-55, 57.

Glorious is the triumph awaiting the faithful. The apostle, realizing the possibilities before the Corinthian believers, sought to set before them that which uplifts from the selfish and the sensual, and glorifies life with the hope of immortality. Earnestly he exhorted them to be true to their high calling in Christ. "My beloved brethren," he pleaded, "be ye steadfast, unmovable, always abounding in the work of the Lord, forasmuch as ye know that your labor is not in vain in the Lord."

Thus the apostle, in the most decided and impressive manner, endeavored to correct the false and dangerous ideas and practices that were prevailing in the Corinthian church. He spoke plainly, yet in love for their souls. In his warnings and reproofs, light from the throne of God was shining upon them, to reveal the hidden sins that were defiling their lives. How would it be received?

After the letter had been dispatched, Paul feared lest that which he had written might wound too deeply those whom he desired to benefit. He keenly dreaded a further alienation and sometimes longed to recall his words. Those who, like the apostle, have felt a responsibility for beloved churches or institutions, can best appreciate his depression of spirit and self-accusing. The servants of God who bear the burden of His work for this time know something of the same experience of labor, conflict, and anxious care that fell to the lot of the great apostle. Burdened by divisions in the church, meeting with ingratitude and betrayal from some to whom he looked for sympathy and support, realizing the peril of the churches that harbored iniquity, compelled to bear a close, searching testimony in reproof of sin, he was at the same time weighed down with fear that he might have dealt with too great severity. With trembling anxiety he waited to receive some tidings as to the reception of his message.

31

The Message Heeded

This chapter is based on the Second Epistle to the Corinthians

From Ephesus Paul set forth on another missionary tour, during which he hoped to visit once more the scenes of his former labors in Europe. Tarrying for a time at Troas, "to preach Christ's gospel," he found some who were ready to listen to his message. "A door was opened unto me of the Lord," he afterward declared of his labors in this place. But successful as were his efforts at Troas, he could not remain there long. "The care of all the churches," and particularly of the church at Corinth, rested heavily on his heart. He had hoped to meet Titus at Troas and to learn from him how the words of counsel and reproof sent to the Corinthian brethren had been received, but in this he was disappointed. "I had no rest in my spirit," he wrote concerning this experience, "because I found not Titus my brother." He therefore left Troas and crossed over to Macedonia, where, at Philippi he met Timothy.

During this time of anxiety concerning the church at Corinth, Paul hoped for the best; yet at times feelings of deep sadness would sweep over his soul, lest his counsels and admonitions might be misunderstood. "Our flesh had no rest," he afterward wrote, "but we were troubled on every side; without were fightings, within were fears. Nevertheless God, that comforteth those that are cast down, comforted us by the coming of Titus."

This faithful messenger brought the cheering news that a wonderful change had taken place among the Corinthian believers. Many had accepted the instruction contained in Paul's letter and had repented of their sins. Their lives were no longer a reproach to Christianity, but exerted a powerful influence in favor of practical godliness.

Filled with joy, the apostle sent another letter to the Corinthian believers, expressing his gladness of heart because of the good work wrought in them: "Though I made you sorry with a letter, I do not repent, though I did repent." When tortured by the fear that his words would be despised, he had sometimes regretted that he had written so decidedly and severely. "Now I rejoice," he continued, "not that ye were made sorry, but that ye sorrowed to repentance: for ye were made sorry after a godly manner, that ye might receive damage by us in nothing. For godly sorrow worketh repentance to salvation not to be repented of." That repentance which is produced by the influence of divine grace upon the heart will lead to confession and forsaking of sin. Such were the fruits which the apostle declared had been seen in the lives of the Corinthian believers. "What carefulness it wrought in you, yea, what clearing of yourselves, yea, what indignation, yea, what fear, yea, what vehement desire, yea, what zeal."

For some time Paul had been carrying a burden of soul for the churches—a burden so heavy that he could scarcely endure it. False teachers had sought to destroy his influence among the believers and to urge their own doctrines in the place of gospel truth. The perplexities and discouragements with which Paul was surrounded are revealed in the words, "We were pressed out of measure, above strength, insomuch that we despaired even of life."

But now one cause of anxiety was removed. At the tidings of the acceptance of his letter to the Corinthians, Paul broke forth into words of rejoicing: "Blessed be God, even the Father of our Lord Jesus Christ, the Father of mercies, and the God of all comfort; who comforteth us in all our tribulation, that we may be able to comfort them which are in any trouble, by the comfort wherewith we ourselves are comforted of God. For as the sufferings of Christ abound in us, so our consolation also aboundeth by Christ. And whether we be afflicted, it is for your consolation and salvation, which is effectual in the enduring of the same sufferings which we also suffer: or whether we be comforted, it is for your consolation and salvation. And our hope of you is steadfast, knowing, that as ye are partakers of the sufferings, so shall ye be also of the consolation."

In expressing his joy over their reconversion and their growth in grace, Paul ascribed to God all the praise for this transformation of heart and life. "Thanks be unto God," he exclaimed, "which always causeth us to triumph in Christ, and maketh manifest the savor of His knowledge by us in every place. For we are unto God a sweet savor of Christ, in them that are saved, and in them that perish." It was the custom of the day for a general victorious in warfare to bring with him on his return a train of captives. On such occasions incense bearers were appointed, and as the army marched triumphantly home, the fragrant odor was to the captives appointed to die, a savor of death, showing that they were nearing the time of their execution; but to those of the prisoners who had found favor with their captors, and whose lives were to be spared, it was a savor of life, in that it showed them that their freedom was near.

Paul was now full of faith and hope. He felt that Satan was not to triumph over the work of God in Corinth, and in words of praise he poured forth the gratitude of his heart. He and his fellow laborers would celebrate their victory over the enemies of Christ and the truth, by going forth with new zeal to extend the knowledge of the Saviour. Like incense the fragrance of the gospel was to be diffused throughout the world. To those who should accept Christ, the message would be a savor of life unto life; but to those who should persist in unbelief, a savor of death unto death.

Realizing the overwhelming magnitude of the work, Paul exclaimed, "Who is sufficient for these things?" Who is able to preach Christ in such a way that His enemies shall have no just cause to despise the messenger or the message that he bears? Paul desired to impress upon believers the solemn responsibility of the gospel ministry. Faithfulness in preaching the word, united with a pure, consistent life, can alone make the efforts of ministers acceptable to God and profitable to souls. Ministers of our day, burdened with a sense of the greatness of the work, may well exclaim with the apostle, "Who is sufficient for these things?"

There were those who had charged Paul with self-commendation in writing his former letter. The apostle now referred to this by asking the members of the church if they thus judged his motives. "Do we begin again to commend ourselves?" he inquired; "or need we, as some others, epistles of commendation to you, or letters of commendation from you?" Believers moving to a new place often carried with them letters of commendation from the church with which they had formerly been united; but the leading workers, the founders of these churches, had no need of such commendation. The Corinthian believers, who had been led from the worship of idols to the faith of the gospel, were themselves all the recommendation that Paul needed. Their reception of the truth, and the reformation wrought in their lives, bore eloquent testimony to the faithfulness of his labors and to his authority to counsel, reprove, and exhort as a minister of Christ.

Paul regarded the Corinthian brethren as his testimonial. "Ye are our epistle," he said, "written in our hearts, known and read of all men: forasmuch as ye are manifestly declared to be the epistle of Christ ministered by us, written not with ink, but with the Spirit of the living God; not in tables of stone, but in fleshy tables of the heart."

The conversion of sinners and their sanctification through the truth is the strongest proof a minister can have that God has called him to the ministry. The evidence of his apostleship is written upon the hearts of those converted, and is witnessed to by their renewed lives. Christ is formed within, the hope of glory. A minister is greatly strengthened by these seals of his ministry.

Today the ministers of Christ should have the same witness as that which the Corinthian church bore to Paul's labors. But though in this age there are many preachers, there is a great scarcity of able, holy ministers—men filled with the love that dwelt in the heart of Christ. Pride, self-confidence, love of the world, faultfinding, bitterness, envy, are the fruit borne by many who profess the religion of Christ. Their lives, in sharp contrast to the life of the Saviour, often bear sad testimony to the character of the ministerial labor under which they were converted.

A man can have no greater honor than to be accepted by God as an able minister of the gospel. But those whom the Lord blesses with power and success in His work do not boast. They acknowledge their entire dependence on Him, realizing that of themselves they have no power. With Paul they say, "Not that we are sufficient of ourselves to think anything as of ourselves; but our sufficiency is of God; who also hath made us able ministers of the new testament."

A true minister does the work of the Master. He feels the importance of his work, realizing that he sustains to the church and to the world a relation similar to that which Christ sustained. He works untiringly to lead sinners to a nobler, higher life, that they may obtain the reward of the overcomer. His lips are touched with a live coal from the altar, and he uplifts Jesus as the sinner's only hope. Those who hear him know that he has drawn near to God in fervent, effectual prayer. The Holy Spirit has rested upon him, his soul has felt the vital, heavenly fire, and he is able to compare spiritual things with spiritual. Power is given him to tear down the strongholds of Satan. Hearts are broken by his presentation of the love of God, and many are led to inquire, "What must I do to be saved?"

"Therefore seeing we have this ministry, as we have received mercy, we faint not; but have renounced the hidden things of dishonesty, not walking in craftiness, nor handling the word of God deceitfully; but by manifestation of the truth commending ourselves to every man's conscience in the sight of God. But if our gospel be hid, it is hid to them that are lost: in whom the god of this world hath blinded the minds of them which believe not, lest the light of the glorious gospel of Christ, who is the image of God, should shine unto them. For we preach not ourselves, but Christ Jesus the Lord; and ourselves your servants for Jesus' sake. For God, who commanded the light to shine out of darkness, hath shined in our hearts, to give the light of the knowledge of the glory of God in the face of Jesus Christ."

Thus the apostle magnified the grace and mercy of God, shown in the sacred trust committed to him as a minister of Christ. By God's abundant mercy he and his brethren had been sustained in difficulty, affliction, and danger. They had not modeled their faith and teaching to suit the desires of their hearers, nor kept back truths essential to salvation in order to make their teaching more attractive. They had presented the truth with simplicity and clearness, praying for the conviction and conversion of souls. And they had endeavored to bring their conduct into harmony with their teaching, that the truth presented might commend itself to every man's conscience.

"We have this treasure," the apostle continued, "in earthen vessels, that the excellency of the power may be of God, and not of us." God could have proclaimed His truth through sinless angels, but this is not His plan. He chooses human beings, men compassed with infirmity, as instruments in the working out of His designs. The priceless treasure is placed in earthen vessels. Through men His blessings are to be conveyed to the world. Through them His glory is to shine forth into the darkness of sin. In loving ministry they are to meet the sinful and the needy, and lead them to the cross. And in all their work they are to ascribe glory, honor, and praise to Him who is above all and over all.

Referring to his own experience, Paul showed that in choosing the service of Christ he had not been prompted by selfish motives, for his pathway had been beset by trial and temptation. "We are troubled on every side," he wrote, "yet not distressed; we are perplexed, but not in despair; persecuted, but not forsaken; cast down, but not destroyed; always bearing about in the body the dying of the Lord Jesus, that the life also of Jesus might be made manifest in our body."

Paul reminded his brethren that as Christ's messengers he and his fellow laborers were continually in peril. The hardships they endured were wearing away their strength. "We which live," he wrote, "are alway delivered unto death for Jesus' sake, that the life also of Jesus might be made manifest in our mortal flesh. So then death worketh in us, but life in you." Suffering physically through privation and toil, these ministers of Christ were conforming to His death. But that which was working death in them was bringing spiritual life and health to the Corinthians, who by a belief in the truth were being made partakers of life eternal. In view of this, the followers of Jesus were to be careful not to increase, by neglect and disaffection, the burdens and trials of the laborers.

"We having the same spirit of faith," Paul continued, "according as it is written, I believed, and therefore have I spoken; we also believe, and therefore speak." Fully convinced of the reality of the truth entrusted to him, nothing could induce Paul to handle the word of God deceitfully or to conceal the convictions of his soul. He would not purchase wealth, honor, or pleasure by conformity to the opinions of the world. Though in constant danger of martyrdom for the faith that he had preached to the Corinthians, he was not intimidated, for he knew that He who had died and risen again would raise him from the grave and present him to the Father.

"All things are for your sakes," he said, "that the abundant grace might through the thanksgiving of many redound to the glory of God." Not for self-aggrandizement did the apostles preach the gospel. It was the hope of saving souls that led them to devote their lives to this work. And it was this hope that kept them from ceasing their efforts because of threatened danger or actual suffering.

"For which cause," Paul declared, "we faint not; but though our outward man perish, yet the inward man is renewed day by day." Paul felt the power of the enemy; but though his physical strength was declining, yet faithfully and unflinchingly he declared the gospel of Christ. Clad in the whole armor of God, this hero of the cross pressed forward in the conflict. His voice of cheer proclaimed him triumphant in the combat. Fixing his gaze on the reward of the faithful, he exclaimed in tones of victory, "Our light affliction, which is but for a moment, worketh for us a far more exceeding and eternal weight of glory; while we look not at the things which are seen, but at the things which are not seen: for the things which are seen are temporal; but the things which are not seen are eternal."

Very earnest and touching is the apostle's appeal that his Corinthian brethren consider anew the matchless love of their Redeemer. "Ye know the grace of our Lord Jesus Christ," he wrote, "that, though He was rich, yet for your sakes He became poor, that ye through His poverty might be rich." You know the height from which He stooped, the depth of humiliation to which He descended. Having once entered upon the path of self-denial and sacrifice, he turned not aside until He had given His life. There was no rest for Him between the throne and the cross.

Point after point Paul lingered over, in order that those who should read his epistle might fully comprehend the wonderful condescension of the Saviour in their behalf. Presenting Christ as He was when equal with God and with Him receiving the homage of the angels, the apostle traced His course until He had reached the lowest depths of humiliation. Paul was convinced that if they could be brought to comprehend the amazing sacrifice made by the Majesty of heaven, all selfishness would be banished from their lives. He showed how the Son of God had laid aside His glory, voluntarily subjecting Himself to the conditions of human nature, and then had humbled Himself as a servant, becoming obedient unto death, "even the death of the cross" (Philippians 2:8), that He might lift fallen man from degradation to hope and joy and heaven.

When we study the divine character in the light of the cross we see mercy, tenderness, and forgiveness blended with equity and justice. We see in the midst of the throne One bearing in hands and feet and side the marks of the suffering endured to reconcile man to God. We see a Father, infinite, dwelling in light unapproachable, yet receiving us to Himself through the merits of His Son. The cloud of vengeance that threatened only misery and despair, in the light reflected from the cross reveals the writing of God: Live, sinner, live! ye penitent, believing souls, live! I have paid a ransom.

In the contemplation of Christ we linger on the shore of a love that is measureless. We endeavor to tell of this love, and language fails us. We consider His life on earth, His sacrifice for us, His work in heaven as our advocate, and the mansions He is preparing for those who love Him, and we can only exclaim, O the height and depth of the love of Christ! "Herein is love, not that we loved God, but that He loved us, and sent His Son to be the propitiation for our sins." "Behold, what manner of love the Father hath bestowed upon us, that we should be called the sons of God." 1 John 4:10; 3:1.

In every true disciple this love, like sacred fire, burns on the altar of the heart. It was on the earth that the love of God was revealed through Christ. It is on the earth that His children are to reflect this love through blameless lives. Thus sinners will be led to the cross to behold the Lamb of God.

32

A Liberal Church

In his first letter to the church at Corinth, Paul gave the believers instruction regarding the general principles underlying the support of God's work in the earth. Writing of his apostolic labors in their behalf, he inquired:

"Who goeth a warfare any time at his own charges? who planteth a vineyard, and eateth not of the fruit thereof? or who feedeth a flock, and eateth not of the milk of the flock? Say I these things as a man? or saith not the law the same also? For it is written in the law of Moses, Thou shalt not muzzle the mouth of the ox that treadeth out the corn. Doth God take care for oxen? or saith He it altogether for our sakes? For our sakes, no doubt, this is written: that he that ploweth should plow in hope; and that he that thresheth in hope should be partaker of his hope.

"If we have sown unto you spiritual things," the apostle further inquired, "is it a great thing if we shall reap your carnal things? If others be partakers of this power over you, are not we rather? Nevertheless we have not used this power; but suffer all things, lest we should hinder the gospel of Christ. Do ye not know that they which minister about holy things live of the things of the temple? and they which wait at the altar are partakers with the altar? Even so hath the Lord ordained that they which preach the gospel should live of the gospel." 1 Corinthians 9:7-14.

The apostle here referred to the Lord's plan for the maintenance of the priests who ministered in the temple. Those who were set apart to this holy office were supported by their brethren, to whom they ministered spiritual blessings. "Verily they that are of the sons of Levi, who receive the office of the priesthood, have a commandment to take tithes of the people according to the law." Hebrews 7:5. The tribe of Levi was chosen by the Lord for the sacred offices pertaining to the temple and the priesthood. Of the priest it was said, "The Lord thy God hath chosen him . . . to stand to minister in the name of the Lord." (Deuteronomy 18:5.) One tenth of all the increase was claimed by the Lord as His own, and to withhold the tithe was regarded by Him as robbery.

It was to this plan for the support of the ministry that Paul referred when he said, "Even so hath the Lord ordained that they which preach the gospel should live of the gospel." And later, in writing to Timothy, the apostle said, "The laborer is worthy of his reward." 1 Timothy 5:18.

The payment of the tithe was but a part of God's plan for the support of His service. Numerous gifts and offerings were divinely specified. Under the Jewish system the people were taught to cherish a spirit of liberality both in sustaining the cause of God and in supplying the wants of the needy. For special occasions there were freewill offerings. At the harvest and the vintage, the first fruits of the field—corn, wine, and oil—were consecrated as an offering to the Lord. The gleanings and the corners of the field were reserved for the poor. The first fruits of the wool when the sheep were shorn, of the grain when the wheat was threshed, were set apart for God. So also were the first-born of all animals, and a redemption price was paid for the first-born son. The first fruits were to be presented before the Lord at the sanctuary and were then devoted to the use of the priests.

By this system of benevolence the Lord sought to teach Israel that in everything He must be first. Thus they were reminded that God was the proprietor of their fields, their flocks, and their herds; that it was He who sent them the sunshine and the rain that developed and ripened the harvest. Everything that they possessed was His; they were but the stewards of His goods.

It is not God's purpose that Christians, whose privileges far exceed those of the Jewish nation, shall give less freely than they gave. "Unto whomsoever much is given," the Saviour declared, "of him shall be much required." Luke 12:48. The liberality required of the Hebrews was largely to benefit their own nation; today the work of God extends over all the earth. In the hands of His followers, Christ has placed the treasures of the gospel, and upon them He has laid the responsibility of giving the glad tidings of salvation to the world. Surely our obligations are much greater than were those of ancient Israel.

As God's work extends, calls for help will come more and more frequently. That these calls may be answered, Christians should heed the command, "Bring ye all the tithes into the storehouse, that there may be meat in Mine house." Malachi 3:10. If professing Christians would faithfully bring to God their tithes and offerings, His treasury would be full. There would then be no occasion to resort to fairs, lotteries, or parties of pleasure to secure funds for the support of the gospel.

Men are tempted to use their means in self-indulgence, in the gratification of appetite, in personal adornment, or in the embellishment of their homes. For these objects many church members do not hesitate to spend freely and even extravagantly. But when asked to give to the Lord's treasury, to carry forward His work in the earth, they demur. Perhaps, feeling that they cannot well do otherwise, they dole out a sum far smaller than they often spend for needless indulgence. They manifest no real love for Christ's service, no earnest interest in the salvation of souls. What marvel that the Christian life of such ones is but a dwarfed, sickly existence!

He whose heart is aglow with the love of Christ will regard it as not only a duty, but a pleasure, to aid in the advancement of the highest, holiest work committed to man—the work of presenting to the world the riches of goodness, mercy, and truth.

It is the spirit of covetousness which leads men to keep for gratification of self means that rightfully belong to God, and this spirit is as abhorrent to Him now as when through His prophet He sternly rebuked His people, saying, "Will a man rob God? Yet ye have robbed Me. But ye say, Wherein have we robbed Thee? In tithes and offerings. Ye are cursed with a curse: for ye have robbed Me, even this whole nation." Malachi 3:8, 9.

The spirit of liberality is the spirit of heaven. This spirit finds its highest manifestation in Christ's sacrifice on the cross. In our behalf the Father gave His only-begotten Son; and Christ, having given up all that He had, then gave Himself, that man might be saved. The cross of Calvary should appeal to the benevolence of every follower of the Saviour. The principle there illustrated is to give, give. "He that saith he abideth in Him ought himself also so to walk, even as He walked." 1 John 2:6.

On the other hand, the spirit of selfishness is the spirit of Satan. The principle illustrated in the lives of worldlings is to get, get. Thus they hope to secure happiness and ease, but the fruit of their sowing is misery and death.

Not until God ceases to bless His children will they cease to be under bonds to return to Him the portion that He claims. Not only should they render the Lord the portion that belongs to Him, but they should bring also to His treasury, as a gratitude offering, a liberal tribute. With joyful hearts they should dedicate to the Creator the first fruits of their bounties—their choicest possessions, their best and holiest service. Thus they will gain rich blessings. God Himself will make their souls like a watered garden whose waters fail not. And when the last great harvest is gathered in, the sheaves that they are enabled to bring to the Master will be the recompense of their unselfish use of the talents lent them.

God's chosen messengers, who are engaged in aggressive labor, should never be compelled to go a warfare at their own charges, unaided by the sympathetic and hearty support of their brethren. It is the part of church members to deal liberally with those who lay aside their secular employment that they may give themselves to the ministry. When God's ministers are encouraged, His cause is greatly advanced. But when, through the selfishness of men, their rightful support is withheld, their hands are weakened, and often their usefulness is seriously crippled.

The displeasure of God is kindled against those who claim to be His followers, yet allow consecrated workers to suffer for the necessities of life while engaged in active ministry. These selfish ones will be called to render an account, not only for the misuse of their Lord's money, but for the depression and heartache which their course has brought upon His faithful servants. Those who are called to the work of the ministry, and at the call of duty give up all to engage in God's service, should receive for their self-sacrificing efforts wages sufficient to support themselves and their families.

In the various departments of secular labor, mental and physical, faithful workmen can earn good wages. Is not the work of disseminating truth, and leading souls to Christ, of more importance than any ordinary business? And are not those who faithfully engage in this work justly entitled to ample remuneration? By our estimate of the relative value of labor for moral and for physical good, we show our appreciation of the heavenly in contrast with the earthly.

That there may be funds in the treasury for the support of the ministry, and to meet the calls for assistance in missionary enterprises, it is necessary that the people of God give cheerfully and liberally. A solemn responsibility rests upon ministers to keep before the churches the needs of the cause of God and to educate them to be liberal. When this is neglected, and the churches fail to give for the necessities of others, not only does the work of the Lord suffer, but the blessing that should come to believers is withheld.

Even the very poor should bring their offerings to God. They are to be sharers of the grace of Christ by denying self to help those whose need is more pressing than their own. The poor man's gift, the fruit of self-denial, comes up before God as fragrant incense. And every act of self-sacrifice strengthens the spirit of beneficence in the giver's heart, allying him more closely to the One who was rich, yet for our sakes became poor, that we through His poverty might be rich.

The act of the widow who cast two mites—all that she had—into the treasury, is placed on record for the encouragement of those who, struggling with poverty, still desire by their gifts to aid the cause of God. Christ called the attention of the disciples to this woman, who had given "all her living." Mark 12:44. He esteemed her gift of more value than the large offerings of those whose alms did not call for self-denial. From their abundance they had given a small portion. To make her offering, the widow had deprived herself of even the necessities of life, trusting God to supply her needs for the morrow. Of her the Saviour declared, "Verily I say unto you, That this poor widow hath cast more in, than all they which have cast into the treasury." Verse 43. Thus He taught that the value of the gift is estimated not by the amount, but by the proportion that is given and the motive that actuates the giver.

The apostle Paul in his ministry among the churches was untiring in his efforts to inspire in the hearts of the new converts a desire to do large things for the cause of God. Often he exhorted them to the exercise of liberality. In speaking to the elders of Ephesus of his former labors among them, he said, "I have showed you all things, how that so laboring ye ought to support the weak, and to remember the words of the Lord Jesus, how He said, It is more blessed to give than to receive." "He which soweth sparingly," he wrote to the Corinthians, "shall reap also sparingly; and he which soweth bountifully shall reap also bountifully. Every man according as he purposeth in his heart, so let him give; not grudgingly, or of necessity: for God loveth a cheerful giver." Acts 20:35; 2 Corinthians 9:6, 7.

Nearly all the Macedonian believers were poor in this world's goods, but their hearts were overflowing with love for God and His truth, and they gladly gave for the support of the gospel. When general collections were taken up in the Gentile churches for the relief of the Jewish believers, the liberality of the converts in Macedonia was held up as an example to other churches. Writing to the Corinthian believers, the apostle called their attention to "the grace of God bestowed on the churches of Macedonia; how that in a great trial of affliction the abundance of their joy and their deep poverty abounded unto the riches of their liberality. For to their power, . . . yea, and beyond their power they were willing of themselves; praying us with much entreaty that we would receive the gift, and take upon us the fellowship of the ministering to the saints." 2 Corinthians 8:1-4.

The willingness to sacrifice on the part of the Macedonian

believers came as a result of wholehearted consecration. Moved by the Spirit of God, they "first gave their own selves to the Lord" (2 Corinthians 8:5), then they were willing to give freely of their means for the support of the gospel. It was not necessary to urge them to give; rather, they rejoiced in the privilege of denying themselves even of necessary things in order to supply the needs of others. When the apostle would have restrained them, they importuned him to accept their offering. In their simplicity and integrity, and in their love for the brethren, they gladly denied self, and thus abounded in the fruit of benevolence.

When Paul sent Titus to Corinth to strengthen the believers there, he instructed him to build up that church in the grace of giving, and in a personal letter to the believers he also added his own appeal. "As ye abound in everything," he pleaded, "in faith, and utterance, and knowledge, and in all diligence, and in your love to us, see that ye abound in this grace also," "Now therefore perform the doing of it; that as there was a readiness to will, so there may be a performance also out of that which ye have. For if there be first a willing mind, it is accepted according to that a man hath, and not according to that he hath not." "And God is able to make all grace abound toward you; that ye, always having all sufficiency in all things, may abound to every good work: . . . . being enriched in everything to all bountifulness, which causeth through us thanksgiving to God." 2 Corinthians 8:7, 11, 12; 9:8-11.

Unselfish liberality threw the early church into a transport of joy; for the believers knew that their efforts were helping to send the gospel message to those in darkness. Their benevolence testified that they had not received the grace of God in vain. What could produce such liberality but the sanctification of the Spirit? In the eyes of believers and unbelievers it was a miracle of grace.

Spiritual prosperity is closely bound up with Christian liberality. The followers of Christ should rejoice in the privilege of revealing in their lives the beneficence of their Redeemer. As they give to the Lord they have the assurance that their treasure is going before them to the heavenly courts. Would men make their property secure? Let them place it in the hands that bear the marks of the crucifixion. Would they enjoy their substance? Let them use it to bless the needy and suffering. Would they increase their possessions? Let them heed the divine injunction, "Honor the Lord with thy substance, and with the first fruits of all thine increase: so shall thy barns be filled with plenty, and thy presses shall burst out with new wine." Proverbs 3:9, 10. Let them seek to retain their possessions for selfish purposes, and it will be to their eternal loss. But let their treasure be given to God, and from that moment it bears His inscription. It is sealed with His immutability.

God declares, "Blessed are ye that sow beside all waters." Isaiah 32:20. A continual imparting of God's gifts wherever the cause of God or the needs of humanity demand our aid, does not tend to poverty. "There is that scattereth, and yet increaseth; and there is that withholdeth more than is meet, but it tendeth to poverty." Proverbs 11:24. The sower multiplies his seed by casting it away. So it is with those who are faithful in distributing God's gifts. By imparting they increase their blessings. "Give, and it shall be given unto you," God has promised; "good measure, pressed down, and shaken together, and running over, shall men give into your bosom." Luke 6:38.

33

Laboring Under Difficulties

While Paul was careful to set before his converts the plain teaching of Scripture regarding the proper support of the work of God, and while he claimed for himself as a minister of the gospel the "power to forbear working" (1 Corinthians 9:6) at secular employment as a means of self-support, yet at various times during his ministry in the great centers of civilization he wrought at a handicraft for his own maintenance.

Among the Jews physical toil was not thought strange or degrading. Through Moses the Hebrews had been instructed to train their children to industrious habits, and it was regarded as a sin to allow the youth to grow up in ignorance of physical labor. Even though a child was to be educated for holy office, a knowledge of practical life was thought essential. Every youth, whether his parents were rich or poor, was taught some trade. Those parents who neglected to provide such a training for their children were looked upon as departing from the instruction of the Lord. In accordance with this custom, Paul had early learned the trade of tentmaking.

Before he became a disciple of Christ, Paul had occupied a high position and was not dependent upon manual labor for support. But afterward, when he had used all his means in furthering the cause of Christ, he resorted at times to his trade to gain a livelihood. Especially was this the case when he labored in places where his motives might have been misunderstood.

It is at Thessalonica that we first read of Paul's working with his hands in self-supporting labor while preaching the word. Writing to the church of believers there, he reminded them that he "might have been burdensome" to them, and added: "Ye remember, brethren, our labor and travail: for laboring night and day, because we would not be chargeable unto any of you, we preached unto you the gospel of God." 1 Thessalonians 2:6, 9. And again, in his second epistle to them, he declared that he and his fellow laborer while with them had not eaten "any man's bread for nought." Night and day we worked, he wrote, "that we might not be chargeable to any of you: not because we have not power, but to make ourselves an ensample unto you to follow us." 2 Thessalonians 3:8, 9.

At Thessalonica Paul had met those who refused to work with

their hands. It was of this class that he afterward wrote: "There are some which walk among you disorderly, working not at all, but are busybodies. Now them that are such we command and exhort by our Lord Jesus Christ, that with quietness they work, and eat their own bread." While laboring in Thessalonica, Paul had been careful to set before such ones a right example. "Even when we were with you," he wrote, "this we commanded you, that if any would not work, neither should he eat." 2 Thessalonians 3:11, 12, 10.

In every age Satan has sought to impair the efforts of God's servants by introducing into the church a spirit of fanaticism. Thus it was in Paul's day, and thus it was in later centuries during the time of the Reformation. Wycliffe, Luther, and many others who blessed the world by their influence and their faith, encountered the wiles by which the enemy seeks to lead into fanaticism overzealous, unbalanced, and unsanctified minds. Misguided souls have taught that the attainment of true holiness carries the mind above all earthly thoughts and leads men to refrain wholly from labor. Others, taking extreme views of certain texts of Scripture, have taught that it is a sin to work—that Christians should take no thought concerning the temporal welfare of themselves or their families, but should devote their lives wholly to spiritual things. The teaching and example of the apostle Paul are a rebuke to such extreme views.

Paul was not wholly dependent upon the labor of his hands for support while at Thessalonica. Referring later to his experiences in that city, he wrote to the Philippian believers in acknowledgment of the gifts he had received from them while there, saying, "Even in Thessalonica ye sent once and again unto my necessity." Philippians 4:16. Notwithstanding the fact that he received this help he was careful to set before the Thessalonians an example of diligence, so that none could rightfully accuse him of covetousness, and also that those who held fanatical views regarding manual labor might be given a practical rebuke.

When Paul first visited Corinth, he found himself among a people who were suspicious of the motives of strangers. The Greeks on the seacoast were keen traders. So long had they trained themselves in sharp business practices, that they had come to believe that gain was godliness, and that to make money, whether by fair means or foul, was commendable. Paul was acquainted with their characteristics, and he would give them no occasion for saying that he preached the gospel in order to enrich himself. He might justly have claimed support from his Corinthian hearers; but this right he was willing to forgo, lest his usefulness and success as a minister should be injured by the unjust suspicion that he was preaching the gospel for gain. He would seek to remove all occasion for misrepresentation, that the force of his message might not be lost.

Soon after his arrival at Corinth, Paul found "a certain Jew named Aquila, born in Pontus, lately come from Italy, with his wife Priscilla." These were "of the same craft" with himself. Banished by the decree of Claudius, which commanded all Jews to leave Rome, Aquila and Priscilla had come to Corinth, where they established a business as manufacturers of tents. Paul made inquiry concerning them, and learning that they feared God and were seeking to avoid the contaminating influences with which they were surrounded, "he abode with them, and wrought. . . . And he reasoned in the synagogue every Sabbath, and persuaded the Jews and the Greeks." Acts 18:2-4.

Later, Silas and Timothy joined Paul at Corinth. These brethren brought with them funds from the churches in Macedonia, for the support of the work.

In his second letter to the believers in Corinth, written after he had raised up a strong church there, Paul reviewed his manner of life among them. "Have I committed an offense," he asked, "in abasing myself that ye might be exalted, because I have preached to you the gospel of God freely? I robbed other churches, taking wages of them, to do you service. And when I was present with you, and wanted, I was chargeable to no man: for that which was lacking to me the brethren which came from Macedonia supplied: and in all things I have kept myself from being burdensome unto you, and so will I keep myself. As the truth of Christ is in me, no man shall stop me of this boasting in the regions of Achaia." 2 Corinthians 11:7-10.

Paul tells why he had followed this course in Corinth. It was that he might give no cause for reproach to "them which desire occasion." 2 Corinthians 11:12. While he had worked at tentmaking he had also labored faithfully in the proclamation of the gospel. He himself declares of his labors, "Truly the signs of an apostle were wrought among you in all patience, in signs, and wonders, and mighty deeds." And he adds, "For what is it wherein ye were inferior to other churches, except it be that I myself was not burdensome to you? Forgive me this wrong. Behold, the third time I am ready to come to you; and I will not be burdensome to you: for I seek not yours, but you. . . . And I will very gladly spend and be spent for you." 2 Corinthians 12:12-15.

During the long period of his ministry in Ephesus, where for three years he carried forward an aggressive evangelistic effort throughout that region, Paul again worked at his trade. In Ephesus, as in Corinth, the apostle was cheered by the presence of Aquila and Priscilla, who had accompanied him on his return to Asia at the close of his second missionary journey.

There were some who objected to Paul's toiling with his hands, declaring that it was inconsistent with the work of a gospel minister. Why should Paul, a minister of the highest rank, thus connect mechanical work with the preaching of the word? Was not the laborer worthy of his hire? Why should he spend in making tents time that to all appearance could be put to better account?

But Paul did not regard as lost the time thus spent. As he worked with Aquila he kept in touch with the Great Teacher, losing no opportunity of witnessing for the Saviour, and of helping those who needed help. His mind was ever reaching out for spiritual knowledge. He gave his fellow workers instruction in spiritual things, and he also set an example of industry and thoroughness. He was a quick, skillful worker, diligent in business, "fervent in spirit, serving the Lord." Romans 12:11. As he worked at his trade, the apostle had access to a class of people that he could not otherwise have reached. He showed his associates that skill in the common arts is a gift from God, who provides both the gift and the wisdom to use it aright. He taught that even in everyday toil God is to be honored. His toil-hardened hands detracted nothing from the force of his pathetic appeals as a Christian minister.

Paul sometimes worked night and day, not only for his own support, but that he might assist his fellow laborers. He shared his earnings with Luke, and he helped Timothy. He even suffered hunger at times, that he might relieve the necessities of others. His was an unselfish life. Toward the close of his ministry, on the occasion of his farewell talk to the elders of Ephesus, at Miletus, he could lift up before them his toilworn hands, and say, "I have coveted no man's silver, or gold, or apparel. Yea, ye yourselves know, that these hands have ministered unto my necessities, and to them that were with me. I have showed you all things, how that so laboring ye ought to support the weak, and to remember the words of the Lord Jesus, how He said, It is more blessed to give than to receive." Acts 20:33-35.

If ministers feel that they are suffering hardship and privation in the cause of Christ, let them in imagination visit the workshop where Paul labored. Let them bear in mind that while this chosen man of God is fashioning the canvas, he is working for bread which he has justly earned by his labors as an apostle.

Work is a blessing, not a curse. A spirit of indolence destroys godliness and grieves the Spirit of God. A stagnant pool is offensive, but a pure, flowing stream spreads health and gladness over the land. Paul knew that those who neglect physical work soon become enfeebled. He desired to teach young ministers that by working with their hands, by bringing into exercise their muscles and sinews, they would become strong to endure the toils and privations that awaited them in the gospel field. And he realized that his own teachings would lack vitality and force if he did not keep all parts of the system properly exercised.

The indolent forfeit the invaluable experience gained by a faithful performance of the common duties of life. Not a few, but thousands of human beings exist only to consume the benefits which God in His mercy bestows upon them. They forget to bring to the Lord gratitude offerings for the riches He has entrusted to them. They forget that by trading wisely on the talents lent them they are to be producers as well as consumers. If they comprehended the work that the Lord desires them to do as His helping hand they would not shun responsibility.

The usefulness of young men who feel that they are called by God to preach, depends much upon the manner in which they enter upon their labors. Those who are chosen of God for the work of the ministry will give proof of their high calling and by every possible means will seek to develop into able workmen. They will endeavor to gain an experience that will fit them to plan, organize, and execute. Appreciating the sacredness of their calling, they will, by self-discipline, become more and still more like their Master, revealing His goodness, love, and truth. And as they manifest earnestness in improving the talents entrusted to them, the church should help them judiciously.

Not all who feel that they have been called to preach, should be encouraged to throw themselves and their families at once upon the church for continuous financial support. There is danger that some of limited experience may be spoiled by flattery, and by unwise encouragement to expect full support independent of any serious effort on their part. The means dedicated to the extension of the work of God should not be consumed by men who desire to preach only that they may receive support and thus gratify a selfish ambition for an easy life.

Young men who desire to exercise their gifts in the work of the ministry, will find a helpful lesson in the example of Paul at Thessalonica, Corinth, Ephesus, and other places. Although an eloquent speaker, and chosen by God to do a special work, he was never above labor, nor did he ever weary of sacrificing for the cause he loved. "Even unto this present hour," he wrote to the Corinthians, "we both hunger, and thirst, and are naked, and are buffeted, and have no certain dwelling place; and labor, working with our own hands: being reviled, we bless; being persecuted, we suffer it." 1 Corinthians 4:11, 12.

One of the greatest of human teachers, Paul cheerfully performed the lowliest as well as the highest duties. When in his service for the Master circumstances seemed to require it, he willingly labored at his trade. Nevertheless, he ever held himself ready to lay aside his secular work, in order to meet the opposition of the enemies of the gospel, or to improve a special opportunity to win souls to Jesus. His zeal and industry are a rebuke to indolence and desire for ease.

Paul set an example against the sentiment, then gaining influence in the church, that the gospel could be proclaimed successfully only by those who were wholly freed from the necessity of physical toil. He illustrated in a practical way what might be done by consecrated laymen in many places where the people were unacquainted with the truths of the gospel. His course inspired many humble toilers with a desire to do what they could to advance the cause of God, while at the same time they supported themselves in daily labor. Aquila and Priscilla were not called to give their whole time to the ministry of the gospel, yet these humble laborers were used by God to show Apollos the way of truth more perfectly. The Lord employs various instrumentalities for the accomplishment of His purpose, and while some with special talents are chosen to devote all their energies to the work of teaching and preaching the gospel, many others, upon whom human hands have never been laid in ordination, are called to act an important part in soulsaving.

There is a large field open before the self-supporting gospel worker. Many may gain valuable experiences in ministry while toiling a portion of the time at some form of manual labor, and by this method strong workers may be developed for important service in needy fields.

The self-sacrificing servant of God who labors untiringly in word and doctrine, carries on his heart a heavy burden. He does not measure his work by hours. His wages do not influence him in his labor, nor is he turned from his duty because of unfavorable conditions. From heaven he received his commission, and to heaven he looks for his recompense when the work entrusted to him is done.

It is God's design that such workers shall be freed from unnecessary anxiety, that they may have full opportunity to obey the injunction of Paul to Timothy, "Meditate upon these things; give thyself wholly to them." 1 Timothy 4:15. While they should be careful to exercise sufficiently to keep mind and body vigorous, yet it is not God's plan that they should be compelled to spend a large part of their time at secular employment.

These faithful workers, though willing to spend and be spent for the gospel, are not exempt from temptation. When hampered and burdened with anxiety because of a failure on the part of the church to give them proper financial support, some are fiercely beset by the tempter. When they see their labors so lightly prized, they become depressed. True, they look forward to the time of the judgment for their just award, and this buoys them up; but meanwhile their families must have food and clothing. If they could feel that they were released from their divine commission they would willingly labor with their hands. But they realize that their time belongs to God, notwithstanding the short-sightedness of those who should provide them with sufficient funds. They rise above the temptation to enter into pursuits by which they could soon place themselves beyond the reach of want, and they continue to labor for the advancement of the cause that is dearer to them than life itself. In order to do this, they may, however, be forced to follow the example of Paul and engage for a time in manual labor while continuing to carry forward their ministerial work. This they do to advance not their own interests, but the interests of God's cause in the earth.

There are times when it seems to the servant of God impossible to do the work necessary to be done, because of the lack of means to carry on a strong, solid work. Some are fearful that with the facilities at their command they cannot do all that they feel it their duty to do. But if they advance in faith, the salvation of God will be revealed, and prosperity will attend their efforts. He who has bidden His followers go into all parts of the world will sustain every laborer who in obedience to His command seeks to proclaim His message.

In the upbuilding of His work the Lord does not always make everything plain before His servants. He sometimes tries the confidence of His people by bringing about circumstances which compel them to move forward in faith. Often He brings them into strait and trying places, and bids them advance when their feet seem to be touching the waters of Jordan. It is at such times, when the prayers of His servants ascend to Him in earnest faith, that God opens the way before them and brings them out into a large place.

When God's messengers recognize their responsibilities toward the needy portions of the Lord's vineyard, and in the spirit of the Master Worker labor untiringly for the conversion of souls, the angels of God will prepare the way before them, and the means necessary for the carrying forward of the work will be provided. Those who are enlightened will give freely to support the work done in their behalf. They will respond liberally to every call for help, and the Spirit of God will move upon their hearts to sustain the Lord's cause not only in the home fields, but in the regions beyond. Thus strength will come to the working forces in other places, and the work of the Lord will advance in His own appointed way.

34

A Consecrated Ministry

In His life and lessons Christ has given a perfect exemplification of the unselfish ministry which has its origin in God. God does not live for Himself. By creating the world, and by upholding all things, He is constantly ministering to others. "He maketh His sun to rise on the evil and on the good, and sendeth rain on the just and on the unjust." Matthew 5:45. This ideal of ministry the Father committed to His Son. Jesus was given to stand at the head of humanity, by His example to teach what it means to minister. His whole life was under a law of service. He served all, ministered to all.

Again and again Jesus tried to establish his principle among His disciples. When James and John made their request for pre-eminence, He said, "Whosoever will be great among you, let him be your minister; and whosoever will be chief among you, let him be your servant: even as the Son of man came not to be ministered unto, but to minister, and to give His life a ransom for many." Matthew 20:26-28.

Since His ascension Christ has carried forward His work on the earth by chosen ambassadors, through whom He speaks to the children of men and ministers to their needs. The great Head of the church superintends His work through the instrumentality of men ordained by God to act as His representatives.

The position of those who have been called of God to labor in word and doctrine for the upbuilding of His church, is one of grave responsibility. In Christ's stead they are to beseech men and women to be reconciled to God, and they can fulfill their mission only as they receive wisdom and power from above.

Christ's ministers are the spiritual guardians of the people entrusted to their care. Their work has been likened to that of watchmen. In ancient times sentinels were often stationed on the walls of cities, where, from points of vantage, they could overlook important posts to be guarded, and give warning of the approach of an enemy. Upon their faithfulness depended the safety of all within. At stated intervals they were required to call to one another, to make sure that all were awake and that no harm had befallen any. The cry of good cheer or of warning was borne from one to another, each repeating the call till it echoed round the city.

To every minister the Lord declares: "O son of man, I have set thee a watchman unto the house of Israel; therefore thou shalt hear the word at My mouth, and warn them from Me. When I say unto the wicked, O wicked man, thou shalt surely die; if thou dost not speak to warn the wicked from his way, that wicked man shall die in his iniquity; but his blood will I require at thine hand. Nevertheless, if thou warn the wicked of his way to turn from it, . . . thou hast delivered thy soul." Ezekiel 33:7-9.

The words of the prophet declare the solemn responsibility of those who are appointed as guardians of the church of God, stewards of the mysteries of God. They are to stand as watchmen on the walls of Zion, to sound the note of alarm at the approach of the enemy. Souls are in danger of falling under temptation, and they will perish unless God's ministers are faithful to their trust. If for any reason their spiritual senses become so benumbed that they are unable to discern danger, and through their failure to give warning the people perish, God will require at their hands the blood of those who are lost.

It is the privilege of the watchmen on the walls of Zion to live so near to God, and to be susceptible to the impressions of His Spirit, that He can work through them to tell men and women of their peril and point them to the place of safety. Faithfully are they to warn them of the sure result of transgression, and faithfully are they to safeguard the interests of the church. At no time may they relax their vigilance. Theirs is a work requiring the exercise of every faculty of the being. In trumpet tones their voices are to be lifted, and never are they to sound one wavering, uncertain note. Not for wages are they to labor, but because they cannot do otherwise, because they realize that there is a woe upon them if they fail to preach the gospel. Chosen of God, sealed with the blood of consecration, they are to rescue men and women from impending destruction.

The minister who is a co-worker with Christ will have a deep sense of the sacredness of his work and of the toil and sacrifice required to perform it successfully. He does not study his own ease or convenience. He is forgetful of self. In his search for the lost sheep he does not realize that he himself is weary, cold, and hungry. He has but one object in view—the saving of the lost.

He who serves under the bloodstained banner of Immanuel will have that to do which will call for heroic effort and patient endurance. But the soldier of the cross stands unshrinkingly in the forefront of the battle. As the enemy presses the attack against him, he turns to the stronghold for aid, and as he brings to the Lord the promises of the word, he is strengthened for the duties of the hour. He realizes his need of strength from above. The victories that he gains do not lead to self exaltation, but cause him to lean more and more heavily on the Mighty One. Relying upon that Power, he is enabled to present the message of salvation so forcibly that it vibrates in other minds.

He who teaches the word must himself live in conscious, hourly communion with God through prayer and a study of His word, for here is the source of strength. Communion with God will impart to the minister's efforts a power greater than the influence of his preaching. Of this power he must not allow himself to be deprived. With an earnestness that cannot be denied, he must plead with God to strengthen and fortify him for duty and trial, and to touch his lips with living fire. All too slight is the hold that Christ's ambassadors often have upon eternal realities. If men will walk with God, He will hide them in the cleft of the Rock. Thus hidden, they can see God, even as Moses saw Him. By the power and light that He imparts they can comprehend more and accomplish more than their finite judgment had seemed possible.

Satan's craft is most successfully used against those who are depressed. When discouragement threatens to overwhelm the minister, let him spread out before God his necessities. It was when the heavens were as brass over Paul that he trusted most fully in God. More than most men, he knew the meaning of affliction; but listen to his triumphant cry as, beset by temptation and conflict, his feet press heavenward: "Our light affliction, which is but for a moment, worketh for us a far more exceeding and eternal weight of glory; while we look not at the things which are seen, but at the things which are not seen." 2 Corinthians 4:17, 18. Paul's eyes were ever fastened on the unseen and eternal. Realizing that he was fighting against supernatural powers, he placed this dependence on God, and in this lay his strength. It is by seeing Him who is invisible that strength and vigor of soul are gained and the power of earth over mind and character is broken.

A pastor should mingle freely with the people for whom he labors, that by becoming acquainted with them he may know how to adapt his teaching to their needs. When a minister has preached a sermon, his work has but just begun. There is personal work for him to do. He should visit the people in their homes, talking and praying with them in earnestness and humility. There are families who will never be reached by the truths of God's word unless the stewards of His grace enter their homes and point them to the higher way. But the hearts of those who do this work must throb in unison with the heart of Christ.

Much is comprehended in the command, "Go out into the highways and hedges, and compel them to come in, that My house may be filled." Luke 14:23. Let ministers teach the truth in families, drawing close to those for whom they labor, and as they thus co-operate with God, He will clothe them with spiritual power. Christ will guide them in their work, giving them words to speak that will sink deep into the hearts of the listeners. It is the privilege of every minister to be able to say with Paul, "I have not shunned to declare unto you all the counsel of God." "I kept back nothing that was profitable unto you, but have showed you, and have taught you publicly, and from house to house,... repentance toward God, and faith toward our Lord Jesus Christ." Acts 20:27, 20, 21.

The Saviour went from house to house, healing the sick, comforting the mourners, soothing the afflicted, speaking peace to the disconsolate. He took the little children in His arms and blessed them, and spoke words of hope and comfort to the weary mothers. With unfailing tenderness and gentleness He met every form of human woe and affliction. Not for Himself but for others did He labor. He was the servant of all. It was His meat and drink to bring hope and strength to all with whom He came in contact. And as men and women listened to the truths that fell from His lips, so different from the traditions and dogmas taught by the rabbis, hope sprang up in their hearts. In His teaching there was an earnestness that sent His words home with convicting power.

God's ministers are to learn Christ's method of laboring, that they may bring from the storehouse of His word that which will supply the spiritual needs of those for whom they labor. Thus only can they fulfill their trust. The same Spirit that dwelt in Christ as He imparted the instruction He was constantly receiving, is to be the source of their knowledge and the secret of their power in carrying on the Saviour's work in the world.

Some who have labored in the ministry have failed of attaining success because they have not given their undivided interest to the Lord's work. Ministers should have no engrossing interests aside from the great work of leading souls to the Saviour. The fishermen whom Christ called, straightway left their nets and followed Him. Ministers cannot do acceptable work for God and at the same time carry the burden of large personal business enterprises. Such a division of interest dims their spiritual perception. The mind and heart are occupied with earthly things, and the service of Christ takes a second place. They seek to shape their work for God by their circumstances, instead of shaping circumstances to meet the demands of God.

The energies of the minister are all needed for his high calling. His best powers belong to God. He should not engage in speculation or in any other business that would turn him aside from his great work. "No man that warreth," Paul declared, "entangleth himself with the affairs of this life; that he may please him who hath chosen him to be a soldier." 2 Timothy 2:4. Thus the apostle emphasized the minister's need of unreserved consecration to the Master's service. The minister who is wholly consecrated to God refuses to engage in business that would hinder him from giving himself fully to his sacred calling. He is not striving for earthly honor or riches; his one purpose is to tell others of the Saviour, who gave Himself to bring to human beings the riches of eternal life. His highest desire is not to lay up treasure in this world, but to bring to the attention of the indifferent and the disloyal the realities of eternity. He may be asked to engage in enterprises which promise large worldly gain, but to such temptations he returns the answer, "What shall it profit a man, if he shall gain the whole world, and lose his own soul?" Mark 8:36.

Satan presented this inducement to Christ, knowing that if He accepted it, the world would never be ransomed. And under different guises he presents the same temptation to God's ministers today, knowing that those who are beguiled by it will be false to their trust.

It is not God's will that His ministers should seek to be rich. Regarding this, Paul wrote to Timothy: "The love of money is the root of all evil: which while some coveted after, they have erred from the faith, and pierced themselves through with many sorrows. But thou, O man of God, flee these things; and follow after righteousness, godliness, faith, love, patience, meekness." By example as well as by precept, the ambassador for Christ is to "charge them that are rich in this world, that they be not high-minded, nor trust in uncertain riches, but in the living God, who giveth us richly all things to enjoy; that they do good, that they be rich in good works, ready to distribute, willing to communicate; laying up in store for themselves a good foundation against the time to come, that they may lay hold on eternal life." 1 Timothy 6:10, 11, 17-19.

The experiences of the apostle Paul and his instruction regarding the sacredness of the minister's work are a source of help and inspiration to those engaged in the gospel ministry. Paul's heart burned with a love for sinners, and he put all his energies into the work of soul winning. There never lived a more self-denying, persevering worker. The blessings he received he prized as so many advantages to be used in blessing others. He lost no opportunity of speaking of the Saviour or of helping those in trouble. From place to place he went, preaching the gospel of Christ and establishing churches. Wherever he could find a hearing, he sought to counteract wrong, and to turn the feet of men and women into the path of righteousness.

Paul did not forget the churches that he had established. After making a missionary tour, he and Barnabas retraced their steps and visited the churches they had raised up, choosing from them men whom they could train to unite in proclaiming the gospel.

This feature of Paul's work contains an important lesson for ministers today. The apostle made it a part of his work to educate young men for the office of the ministry. He took them with him on his missionary journeys, and thus they gained an experience that later enabled them to fill positions of responsibility. When separated from them, he still kept in touch with their work, and his letters to Timothy and to Titus are evidences of how deep was his desire for their success.

Experienced workers today do a noble work when, instead of trying to carry all the burdens themselves, they train younger workers and place burdens on their shoulders.

Paul never forgot the responsibility resting on him as a minister of Christ, or that if souls were lost through unfaithfulness on his part, God would hold him accountable. "Whereof I am made a minister," he declared of the gospel, "according to the dispensation of God which is given to me for you, to fulfill the word of God; even the mystery which hath been hid from ages and from generations, but now is made manifest to His saints: to whom God would make known what is the riches of the glory of this mystery among the Gentiles; which is Christ in you, the hope of glory: whom we preach, warning every man, and teaching every man in all wisdom; that we may present every man perfect in Christ Jesus: whereunto I also labor, striving according to His working, which worketh in me mightily." Colossians 1:25-29.

These words present before the worker for Christ a high attainment, yet this attainment all can reach who, putting themselves under the control of the Great Teacher, learn daily in the school of Christ. The power at God's command is limitless, and the minister who in his great need shuts himself in with the Lord may be assured that he will receive that which will be to his hearers a savor of life unto life.

Paul's writings show that the gospel minister should be an example of the truths that he teaches, "giving no offense in anything, that the ministry be not blamed." Of his own work he has left us a picture in his letter to the Corinthian believers: "In all things approving ourselves as the ministers of God, in much patience, in afflictions, in necessities, in distresses, in stripes, in imprisonments, in tumults, in labors, in watchings, in fastings; but pureness, by knowledge, by long suffering, by kindness, by the Holy Ghost, by love unfeigned, by the word of truth, by the power of God, by the armor of righteousness on the right hand and on the left, by honor and dishonor, by evil report and good report: as deceivers, and yet true; as unknown, and yet well known; as dying, and, behold, we live; as chastened, and not killed; as sorrowful, yet alway rejoicing; as poor, yet making many rich." 2 Corinthians 6:3, 4-10.

To Titus he wrote: "Young men likewise exhort to be soberminded. In all things showing thyself a pattern of good works: in doctrine showing uncorruptness, gravity, sincerity, sound speech, that cannot be condemned; that he that is of the contrary part may be ashamed, having no evil thing to say of you." Titus 2:6-8.

There is nothing more precious in the sight of God than His ministers, who go forth into the waste places of the earth to sow the seeds of truth, looking forward to the harvest. None but Christ can measure the solicitude of His servants as they seek for the lost. He imparts His Spirit to them, and by their efforts souls are led to turn from sin to righteousness.

God is calling for men who are willing to leave their farms, their business, if need be their families, to become missionaries for Him. And the call will be answered. In the past there have been men who, stirred by the love of Christ and the needs of the lost, have left the comforts of home and the society of friends, even that of wife and children, to go into foreign lands, among idolaters and savages, to proclaim the message of mercy. Many in the attempt have lost their lives, but others have been raised up to carry on the work. Thus step by step the cause of Christ has progressed, and the seed sown in sorrow has yielded a bountiful harvest. The knowledge of God has been widely extended and the banner of the cross planted in heathen lands.

For the conversion of one sinner the minister should tax his resources to the utmost. The soul that God has created and Christ has redeemed is of great value because of the possibilities before it, the spiritual advantages that have been granted it, the capabilities that it may possess if vitalized by the word of God, and the immortality it may gain through the hope presented in the gospel. And if Christ left the ninety and nine that He might seek and save one lost sheep, can we be justified in doing less? Is not a neglect to work as Christ worked, to sacrifice as He sacrificed, a betrayal of sacred trusts, an insult to God?

The heart of the true minister is filled with an intense longing to save souls. Time and strength are spent, toilsome effort is not shunned; for others must hear the truths that brought to his own soul such gladness and peace and joy. The Spirit of Christ rests upon him. He watches for souls as one that must give an account. With his eyes fixed on the cross of Calvary, beholding the uplifted Saviour, relying on His grace, believing that He will be with him until the end, as his shield, his strength, his efficiency, he works for God. With invitations and pleadings, mingled with the assurances of God's love, he seeks to win souls to Jesus, and in heaven he is numbered among those who are "called, and chosen, and faithful." Revelation 17:14.

35

Salvation to the Jews

This chapter is based on the Epistle to the Romans

After many unavoidable delays, Paul at last reached Corinth, the scene of so much anxious labor in the past, and for a time the object of deep solicitude. He found that many of the early believers still regarded him with affection as the one who had first borne to them the light of the gospel. As he greeted these disciples and saw the evidences of their fidelity and zeal he rejoiced that his work in Corinth had not been in vain.

The Corinthian believers, once so prone to lose sight of their high calling in Christ, had developed strength of Christian character. Their words and acts revealed the transforming power of the grace of God, and they were now a strong force for good in that center of heathenism and superstition. In the society of his beloved companions and these faithful converts the apostle's worn and troubled spirit found rest.

During his sojourn at Corinth, Paul found time to look forward to new and wider fields of service. His contemplated journey to Rome especially occupied his thoughts. To see the Christian faith firmly established at the great center of the known world was one of his dearest hopes and most cherished plans. A church had already been established in Rome, and the apostle desired to secure the co-operation of the believers there in the work to be accomplished in Italy and in other countries. To prepare the way for his labors among these brethren, many of whom were as yet strangers to him, he sent them a letter announcing his purpose of visiting Rome and his hope of planting the standard of the cross in Spain.

In his epistle to the Romans, Paul set forth the great principles of the gospel. He stated his position on the questions which were agitating the Jewish and the Gentile churches, and showed that the hopes and promises which had once belonged especially to the Jews were now offered to the Gentiles also.

With great clearness and power the apostle presented the doctrine of justification by faith in Christ. He hoped that other churches also might be helped by the instruction sent to the Christians at Rome; but how dimly could he foresee the far-reaching influence of his words! Through all the ages the great truth of justification by faith has stood as a mighty beacon to guide repentant sinners into the way of life. It was this light that scattered the darkness which enveloped Luther's mind and revealed to him the power of the blood of Christ to cleanse from sin. The same light has guided thousands of sin-burdened souls to the true Source of pardon and peace. For the epistle to the church at Rome, every Christian has reason to thank God.

In this letter Paul gave free expression to his burden in behalf of the Jews. Ever since his conversion, he had longed to help his Jewish brethren to gain a clear understanding of the gospel message. "My heart's desire and prayer to God for Israel is," he declared, "that they might be saved."

It was no ordinary desire that the apostle felt. Constantly he was petitioning God to work in behalf of the Israelites who had failed to recognize Jesus of Nazareth as the promised Messiah. "I say the truth in Christ," he assured the believers at Rome, "my conscience also bearing me witness in the Holy Ghost, that I have great heaviness and continual sorrow in my heart. For I could wish that myself were accursed from Christ for my brethren, my kinsmen according to the flesh: who are Israelites, to whom pertaineth the adoption, and the glory, and the covenants, and the giving of the law, and the service of God, and the promises; whose are the fathers, and of whom as concerning the flesh Christ came, who is over all, God blessed forever."

The Jews were God's chosen people, through whom He had purposed to bless the entire race. From among them God had raised up many prophets. These had foretold the advent of a Redeemer who was to be rejected and slain by those who should have been the first to recognize Him as the Promised One.

The prophet Isaiah, looking down through the centuries and witnessing the rejection of prophet after prophet and finally of the Son of God, was inspired to write concerning the acceptance of the Redeemer by those who had never before been numbered among the children of Israel. Referring to this prophecy, Paul declares: "Esaias is very bold, and saith, I was found of them that sought Me not; I was made manifest unto them that asked not after Me. But to Israel He saith, All day long I have stretched forth My hands unto a disobedient and gainsaying people."

Even though Israel rejected His Son, God did not reject them. Listen to Paul as he continues the argument: "I say then, Hath God cast away His people? God forbid. For I also am an Israelite, of the seed of Abraham, of the tribe of Benjamin. God hath not cast away His people which He foreknew. Wot ye not what the Scripture saith of Elias? how he maketh intercession to God against Israel, saying, Lord, they have killed Thy prophets, and digged down Thine altars; and I am left alone, and they seek my life. But what saith the answer of God unto him? I have reserved to Myself seven thousand men, who have not bowed the knee to the image of Baal. Even so then at this present time also there is a remnant according to the election of grace."

Israel had stumbled and fallen, but this did not make it impossible for them to rise again. In answer to the question, "Have they stumbled that they should fall?" the apostle replies: "God forbid: but rather through their fall salvation is come unto the Gentiles, for to provoke them to jealousy. Now if the fall of them be the riches of the world, and the diminishing of them the riches of the Gentiles; how much more their fullness? For I speak to you Gentiles, inasmuch as I am the apostle of the Gentiles, I magnify mine office: if by any means I may provoke to emulation them which are my flesh, and might save some of them. For if the casting away of them be the reconciling of the world, what shall the receiving of them be, but life from the dead?"

It was God's purpose that His grace should be revealed among the Gentiles as well as among the Israelites. This had been plainly outlined in Old Testament prophecies. The apostle uses some of these prophecies in his argument. "Hath not the potter power over the clay," he inquires, "of the same lump to make one vessel unto honor, and another unto dishonor? What if God, willing to show His wrath, and to make His power known, endured with much long-suffering the vessels of wrath fitted to destruction: and that He might make known the riches of His glory on the vessels of mercy, which He had afore prepared unto glory, even us, whom He hath called, not of the Jews only, but also of the Gentiles? As He saith also in Osee, I will call them My people, which were not My people; and her beloved, which was not beloved. And it shall come to pass, that in the place where it was said unto them, Ye are not My people; there shall they be called the children of the living God." See Hosea 1:10.

Notwithstanding Israel's failure as a nation, there remained among them a goodly remnant of such as should be saved. At the time of the Saviour's advent there were faithful men and women who had received with gladness the message of John the Baptist, and had thus been led to study anew the prophecies concerning the Messiah. When the early Christian church was founded, it was composed of these faithful Jews who recognized Jesus of Nazareth as the one for whose advent they had been longing. It is to this remnant that Paul refers when he writes, "If the first fruit be holy, the lump is also holy: and if the root be holy, so are the branches."

Paul likens the remnant in Israel to a noble olive tree, some of whose branches have been broken off. He compares the Gentiles to branches from a wild olive tree, grafted into the parent stock. "If some of the branches be broken off," he writes to the Gentile believers, "and thou, being a wild olive tree, wert grafted in among them, and with them partakest of the root and fatness of the olive tree; boast not against the branches. But if thou boast, thou barest not the root, but the root thee. Thou wilt say then, The branches were broken off, that I might be grafted in. Well; because of unbelief they were broken off, and thou standest by faith. Be not high-minded, but fear: for if God spared not the natural branches, take heed lest He also spare not thee. Behold therefore the goodness and severity of God: on them which fell, severity; but toward thee, goodness, if thou continue in His goodness: otherwise thou also shalt be cut off."

Through unbelief and the rejection of Heaven's purpose for her, Israel as a nation had lost her connection with God. But the branches that had been separated from the parent stock God was able to reunite with the true stock of Israel —the remnant who had remained true to the God of their fathers. "They also," the apostle declares of these broken branches, "if they abide not still in unbelief, shall be grafted in: for God is able to graft them in again." "If thou," he writes to the Gentiles, "wert cut out of the olive tree which is wild by nature, and wert grafted contrary to nature into a good olive tree: how much more shall these, which be the natural branches, be grafted into their own olive tree? For I would not, brethren, that ye should be ignorant of this mystery, lest ye should be wise in your own conceits; that blindness in part is happened to Israel, until the fullness of the Gentiles be come in.

"And so all Israel shall be saved: as it is written, There shall come out of Sion the Deliverer, and shall turn away ungodliness from Jacob: for this is My covenant unto them, when I shall take away their sins. As concerning the gospel, they are enemies for your sakes: but as touching the election, they are beloved for the father's sakes. For the gifts and calling of God are without repentance. For as ye in times past have not believed God, yet have now obtained mercy through their unbelief: even so have these also now not believed, that through your mercy they also may obtain mercy. For

God had concluded them all in unbelief, that He might have mercy upon all.

"O the depth of the riches both of the wisdom and knowledge of God! how unsearchable are His judgments, and His ways past finding out! For who hath known the mind of the Lord? or who hath been His counselor? or who hath first given to Him, and it shall be recompensed unto him again? For of Him, and through Him, and to Him, are all things: to whom be glory forever."

Thus Paul shows that God is abundantly able to transform the hearts of Jew and Gentile alike, and to grant to every believer in Christ the blessings promised to Israel. He repeats Isaiah's declaration concerning God's people: "Though the number of children of Israel be as the sand of the sea, a remnant shall be saved: for He will finish the work, and cut it short in righteousness: because a short work will the Lord make upon the earth. And as Esaias said before, Except the Lord of Sabaoth had left us a seed, we had been as Sodoma and been made like unto Gomorrah."

At the time when Jerusalem was destroyed and the temple laid in ruins, many thousands of the Jews were sold to serve as bondmen in heathen lands. Like wrecks on a desert shore they were scattered among the nations. For eighteen hundred years the Jews have wandered from land to land throughout the world, and in no place have they been given the privilege of regaining their ancient prestige as a nation. Maligned, hated, persecuted, from century to century theirs has been a heritage of suffering.

Notwithstanding the awful doom pronounced upon the Jews as a nation at the time of their rejection of Jesus of Nazareth, there have lived from age to age many noble, God-fearing Jewish men and women who have suffered in silence. God has comforted their hearts in affliction and has beheld with pity their terrible situation. He has heard the agonizing prayers of those who have sought Him with all the heart for a right understanding of His word. Some have learned to see in the lowly Nazarene whom their forefathers rejected and crucified, the true Messiah of Israel. As their minds have grasped the significance of the familiar prophecies so long obscured by tradition and misinterpretation, their hearts have been filled with gratitude to God for the unspeakable gift He bestows upon every human being who chooses to accept Christ as a personal Saviour.

It is to this class that Isaiah referred in his prophecy, "A remnant shall be saved." From Paul's day to the present time, God by His Holy Spirit has been calling after the Jew as well as the Gentile. "There is no respect of persons with God," declared Paul. The apostle regarded himself as "debtor both to the Greeks, and to the barbarians," as well as to the Jews; but he never lost sight of the decided advantages possessed by the Jews over others, "chiefly, because that unto them were committed the oracles of God." "The gospel," he declared, "is the power of God unto salvation to everyone that believeth; to the Jew first, and also to the Greek. For therein is the righteousness of God revealed from faith to faith: as it is written, The just shall live by faith." It is of this gospel of Christ, equally efficacious for Jew and Gentile, that Paul in his epistle to the Romans declared he was not ashamed.

When this gospel shall be presented in its fullness to the Jews, many will accept Christ as the Messiah. Among Christian ministers there are only a few who feel called upon to labor for the Jewish people; but to those who have been often passed by, as well as to all others, the message of mercy and hope in Christ is to come.

In the closing proclamation of the gospel, when special work is to be done for classes of people hitherto neglected, God expects His messengers to take particular interest in the Jewish people whom they find in all parts of the earth. As the Old Testament Scriptures are blended with the New in an explanation of Jehovah's eternal purpose, this will be to many of the Jews as the dawn of a new creation, the resurrection of the soul. As they see the Christ of the gospel dispensation portrayed in the pages of the Old Testament Scriptures, and perceive how clearly the New Testament explains the Old, their slumbering faculties will be aroused, and they will recognize Christ as the Saviour of the world. Many will by faith receive Christ as their Redeemer. To them will be fulfilled the words, "As many as received Him, to them gave He power to become the sons of God, even to them that believe on His name." John 1:12.

Among the Jews are some who, like Saul of Tarsus, are mighty in the Scriptures, and these will proclaim with wonderful power the immutability of the law of God. The God of Israel will bring this to pass in our day. His arm is not shortened that it cannot save. As His servants labor in faith for those who have long been neglected and despised, His salvation will be revealed.

"Thus saith the Lord, who redeemed Abraham, concerning the house of Jacob, Jacob shall not now be ashamed, neither shall his face now wax pale. But when he seeth his children, the work of Mine hands, in the midst of him, they shall sanctify My name, and sanctify the Holy One of Jacob, and shall fear the God of Israel. They also that erred in spirit shall come to understanding, and they that murmured shall learn doctrine." Isaiah 29:22-24.

36

Apostasy in Galatia

This chapter is based on the Epistle to the Galatians

While tarrying at Corinth, Paul had cause for serious apprehension concerning some of the churches already established. Through the influence of false teachers who had arisen among the believers in Jerusalem, division, heresy, and sensualism were rapidly gaining ground among the believers in Galatia. These false teachers were mingling Jewish traditions with the truths of the gospel. Ignoring the decision of the general council at Jerusalem, they urged upon the Gentile converts the observance of the ceremonial law.

The situation was critical. The evils that had been introduced threatened speedily to destroy the Galatian churches.

Paul was cut to the heart, and his soul was stirred by this open apostasy on the part of those to whom he had faithfully taught the principles of the gospel. He immediately wrote to the deluded believers, exposing the false theories that they had accepted and with great severity rebuking those who were departing from the faith. After saluting the Galatians in the words, "Grace be to you and peace from God the Father, and from our Lord Jesus Christ," he addressed to them these words of sharp reproof:

"I marvel that ye are so soon removed from Him that called you into the grace of Christ unto another gospel: which is not another; but there be some that trouble you, and would pervert the gospel of Christ. But though we, or an angel from heaven, preach any other gospel unto you than that which we have preached unto you, let him be accursed." Paul's teachings had been in harmony with the Scriptures, and the Holy Spirit had witnessed to his labors; therefore he warned his brethren not to listen to anything that contradicted the truths he had taught them.

The apostle bade the Galatian believers consider carefully their first experience in the Christian life. "O foolish Galatians," he exclaimed, "who hath bewitched you, that ye should not obey the truth, before whose eyes Jesus Christ hath been evidently set forth, crucified among you? This only would I learn of you, Received ye the Spirit by the works of the law, or by the hearing of faith? Are ye so foolish? having begun in the Spirit, are ye now made perfect by the flesh? Have ye suffered so many things in vain? if it be yet in vain. He therefore that ministereth to you the Spirit, and worketh miracles among you, doeth he it by the works of the law, or by the hearing of faith?"

Thus Paul arraigned the believers in Galatia before the tribunal of their own conscience and sought to arrest them in their course. Relying on the power of God to save, and refusing to recognize the doctrines of the apostate teachers, the apostle endeavored to lead the converts to see that they had been grossly deceived, but that by returning to their former faith in the gospel they might yet defeat the purpose of Satan. He took his position firmly on the side of truth and righteousness; and his supreme faith and confidence in the message he bore, helped many whose faith had failed, to return to their allegiance to the Saviour.

How different from Paul's manner of writing to the Corinthian church was the course he pursued toward the Galatians! The former he rebuked with caution and tenderness, the latter with words of unsparing reproof. The Corinthians had been overcome by temptation. Deceived by the ingenious sophistry of teachers who presented errors under the guise of truth, they had become confused and bewildered. To teach them to distinguish the false from the true, called for caution and patience. Harshness or injudicious haste on Paul's part would have destroyed his influence over many of those whom he longed to help.

In the Galatian churches, open, unmasked error was supplanting the gospel message. Christ, the true foundation of the faith, was virtually renounced for the obsolete ceremonies of Judaism. The apostle saw that if the believers in Galatia were saved from the dangerous influences which threatened them, the most decisive measures must be taken, the sharpest warnings given.

An important lesson for every minister of Christ to learn is that of adapting his labors to the condition of those whom he seeks to benefit. Tenderness, patience, decision, and firmness are alike needful; but these are to be exercised with proper discrimination. To deal wisely with different classes of minds, under varied circumstances and conditions, is a work requiring wisdom and judgment enlightened and sanctified by the Spirit of God.

In his letter to the Galatian believers Paul briefly reviewed the leading incidents connected with his own conversion and early Christian experience. By this means he sought to show that it was through a special manifestation of divine power that he had been led to see and grasp the great truths of the gospel. It was through instruction received from God Himself that Paul was led to warn and admonish the Galatians in so solemn and positive a manner. He wrote, not in hesitancy and doubt, but with the assurance of settled conviction and absolute knowledge. He clearly outlined the difference between being taught by man and receiving instruction direct from Christ.

The apostle urged the Galatians to leave the false guides by whom they had been misled, and to return to the faith that had been accompanied by unmistakable evidences of divine approval. The men who had attempted to lead them from their belief in the gospel were hypocrites, unholy in heart and corrupt in life. Their religion was made up of a round of ceremonies, through the performance of which they expected to gain the favor of God. They had no desire for a gospel that called for obedience to the word, "Except a man be born again, he cannot see the kingdom of God." John 3:3. They felt that a religion based on such a doctrine, required too great a sacrifice, and they clung to their errors, deceiving themselves and others.

To substitute external forms of religion for holiness of heart and life is still as pleasing to the unrenewed nature as it was in the days of these Jewish teachers. Today, as then, there are false spiritual guides, to whose doctrines many listen eagerly. It is Satan's studied effort to divert minds from the hope of salvation through faith in Christ and obedience to the law of God. In every age the archenemy adapts his temptations to the prejudices or inclinations of those whom he is seeking to deceive. In apostolic times he led the Jews to exalt the ceremonial law and reject Christ; at the present time he induces many professing Christians, under pretense of honoring Christ, to cast contempt on the moral law and to teach that its precepts may be trangressed with impunity. It is the duty of every servant of God to withstand firmly and decidedly these perverters of the faith and by the word of truth fearlessly to expose their errors.

In his effort to regain the confidence of his brethren in Galatia, Paul ably vindicated his position as an apostle of Christ. He declared himself to be an apostle, "not of men, neither by man, but by Jesus Christ, and God the Father, who raised Him from the dead." Not from men, but from the highest Authority in heaven, had he received his commission. And his position had been acknowledged by a general council at Jerusalem, with the decisions of which Paul had complied in all his labors among the Gentiles.

It was not to exalt self, but to magnify the grace of God, that

Paul thus presented to those who were denying his apostleship, proof that he was "not a whit behind the very chiefest apostles." 2 Corinthians 11:5. Those who sought to belittle his calling and his work were fighting against Christ, whose grace and power were manifested through Paul. The apostle was forced, by the opposition of his enemies, to take a decided stand in maintaining his position and authority.

Paul pleaded with those who had once known in their lives the power of God, to return to their first love of gospel truth. With unanswerable arguments he set before them their privilege of becoming free men and women in Christ, through whose atoning grace all who make full surrender are clothed with the robe of His righteousness. He took the position that every soul who would be saved must have a genuine, personal experience in the things of God.

The apostle's earnest words of entreaty were not fruitless. The Holy Spirit wrought with mighty power, and many whose feet had wandered into strange paths, returned to their former faith in the gospel. Henceforth they were steadfast in the liberty wherewith Christ had made them free. In their lives were revealed the fruits of the Spirit—"love, joy, peace, long-suffering, gentleness, goodness, faith, meekness, temperance." The name of God was glorified, and many were added to the number of believers throughout that region.

37

Paul's Last Journey to Jerusalem

This chapter is based on Acts 20:4 to 21:16

Paul greatly desired to reach Jerusalem before the Passover as he would thus have an opportunity to meet those who should come from all parts of the world to attend the feast. Ever he cherished the hope that in some way he might be instrumental in removing the prejudice of his unbelieving countrymen, so that they might be led to accept the precious light of the gospel. He also desired to meet the church at Jerusalem and bear to them the gifts sent by the Gentile churches to the poor brethren in Judea. And by this visit he hoped to bring about a firmer union between the Jewish and the Gentile converts to the faith.

Having completed his work at Corinth, he determined to sail directly for one of the ports on the coast of Palestine. All the arrangements had been made, and he was about to step on board the ship, when he was told of a plot laid by the Jews to take his life. In the past these opposers of the faith had been foiled in all their efforts to put an end to the apostle's work.

The success attending the preaching of the gospel aroused the anger of the Jews anew. From every quarter were coming accounts of the spread of the new doctrine by which Jews were released from the observance of the rites of the ceremonial law and Gentiles were admitted to equal privileges with the Jews as children of Abraham. Paul, in his preaching at Corinth, presented the same arguments which he urged so forcibly in his epistles. His emphatic statement, "There is neither Greek nor Jew, circumcision nor uncircumcision" (Colossians 3:11), was regarded by his enemies as daring blasphemy, and they determined that his voice should be silenced.

Upon receiving warning of the plot, Paul decided to go around by way of Macedonia. His plan to reach Jerusalem in time for the Passover services had to be given up, but he hoped to be there at Pentecost.

Accompanying Paul and Luke were "Sopater of Berea; and of the Thessalonians, Aristarchus and Secundus; and Gaius of Derbe, and Timotheus; and of Asia, Tychicus and Trophimus." Paul had with him a large sum of money from the Gentile churches, which he purposed to place in the hands of the brethren in charge of the work in Judea; and because of this he made arrangements for these representative brethren from various contributing churches, to accompany him to Jerusalem.

At Philippi Paul tarried to keep the Passover. Only Luke remained with him, the other members of the company passing on to Troas to await him there. The Philippians were the most loving and truehearted of the apostle's converts, and during the eight days of the feast he enjoyed peaceful and happy communion with them.

Sailing from Philippi, Paul and Luke reached their companions at Troas five days later, and remained for seven days with the believers in that place.

Upon the last evening of his stay the brethren "came together to break bread." The fact that their beloved teacher was about to depart, had called together a larger company than usual. They assembled in an "upper chamber" on the third story. There, in the fervency of his love and solicitude for them, the apostle preached until midnight.

In one of the open windows sat a youth named Eutychus. In this perilous position he went to sleep and fell to the court below. At once all was alarm and confusion. The youth was taken up dead, and many gathered about him with cries and mourning. But Paul, passing through the frightened company, embraced him and offered up an earnest prayer that God would restore the dead to life. His petition was granted. Above the sound of mourning and lamentation the apostle's voice was heard, saying, "Trouble not yourselves; for his life is in him." With rejoicing the believers again assembled in the upper chamber. They partook of the Communion, and then Paul "talked a long while, even till break of day."

The ship on which Paul and his companions were to continue their journey, was about to sail, and the brethren hastened on board. The apostle himself, however, chose to take the nearer route by land between Troas and Assos, meeting his companions at the latter city. This gave him a short season for meditation and prayer. The difficulties and dangers connected with his coming visit to Jerusalem, the attitude of the church there toward him and his work, as well as the condition of the churches and the interests of the gospel work in other fields, were subjects of earnest, anxious thought, and he took advantage of this special opportunity to seek God for strength and guidance.

As the travelers sailed southward from Assos, they passed the city of Ephesus, so long the scene of the apostle's labors. Paul had greatly desired to visit the church there, for he had important instruction and counsel to give them. But upon consideration he determined to hasten on, for he desired, "if it were possible for him, to be at Jerusalem the Day of Pentecost." On arriving at Miletus, however, about thirty miles from Ephesus, he learned that it might be possible to communicate with the church before the ship should sail. He therefore immediately sent a message to the elders, urging them to hasten to Miletus, that he might see them before continuing his journey.

In answer to his call they came, and he spoke to them strong, touching words of admonition and farewell. "Ye know," he said, "from the first day that I came into Asia, after what manner I have been with you at all seasons, serving the Lord with all humility of mind, and with many tears, and temptations, which befell me by the lying in wait of the Jews: and how I kept back nothing that was profitable unto you, but have showed you, and have taught you publicly, and from house to house, testifying both to the Jews, and also to the Greeks, repentance toward God, and faith toward our Lord Jesus Christ."

Paul had ever exalted the divine law. He had shown that in the law there is no power to save men from the penalty of disobedience. Wrongdoers must repent of their sins and humble themselves before God, whose just wrath they have incurred by breaking His law, and they must also exercise faith in the blood of Christ as their only means of pardon. The Son of God had died as their sacrifice and had ascended to heaven to stand before the Father as their advocate. By repentance and faith they might be freed from the condemnation of sin and through the grace of Christ be enabled henceforth to render obedience to the low of God.

"And now, behold," Paul continued, "I go bound in the spirit unto Jerusalem, not knowing the things that shall befall me there: save that the Holy Ghost witnesseth in every city, saying that bonds and afflictions abide me. But none of these things move me, neither count I my life dear unto myself, so that I might finish my course with joy, and the ministry, which I have received of the Lord Jesus, to testify the gospel of the grace of God. And now, behold, I know that ye all, among whom I have gone preaching the kingdom of God, shall see my face no more."

Paul had no designed to bear this testimony; but, while he was speaking, the Spirit of Inspiration came upon him, confirming his fears that this would be his last meeting with his Ephesian brethren.

"Wherefore I take you to record this day, that I am pure from the blood of all men. For I have not shunned to declare unto you all the counsel of God." No fear of giving offense, no desire for friendship or applause, could lead Paul to withhold the words that God had given him for their instruction, warning, or correction. From His servants today God requires fearlessness in preaching the word and in carrying out its precepts. The minister of Christ is not to present to the people only those truths that are the most pleasing, while he withholds others that might cause them pain. He should watch with deep solicitude the development of character. If he sees that any of his flock are cherishing sin he must as a faithful shepherd give them from God's word the instruction that is applicable to their case. Should he permit them in their self-confidence to go on unwarned, he would be held responsible for their souls. The pastor who fulfills his high commission must give his people faithful instruction on every point of the Christian faith, showing them what they must be and do in order to stand perfect in the day of God. He only who is a faithful teacher of the truth will at the close of his work be able to say with Paul, "I am pure from the blood of all men."

"Take heed therefore unto yourselves," the apostle admonished his brethren, "and to all the flock, over the which the Holy Ghost hath made you overseers, to feed the church of God, which He hath purchased with His own blood." If ministers of the gospel were to bear constantly in mind the fact that they are dealing with the purchase of the blood of Christ, they would have a deeper sense of the importance of their work. They are to take heed to themselves and to their flock. Their own example is to illustrate and enforce their instructions. As teachers of the way of life they should give no occasion for the truth to be evil spoken of. As representatives of Christ they are to maintain the honor of His name. By their devotion, their purity of life, their godly conversation, they are to prove themselves worthy of their high calling.

The dangers that would assail the church at Ephesus were revealed to the apostle. "I know this," he said, "that after my departing shall grievous wolves enter in among you, not sparing the flock. Also of your own selves shall men arise, speaking perverse things, to draw away disciples after them." Paul trembled for the church as, looking into the future, he saw the attacks which she must suffer from both external and internal foes. With solemn earnestness he bade his brethren guard vigilantly their sacred trusts. For an example he pointed them to his own unwearied labors among them: "Therefore watch, and remember, that by the space of three years I ceased not to warn everyone night and day with tears.

"And now, brethren," he continued, "I commend you to God, and to the word of His grace, which is able to build you up, and to give you an inheritance among all them which are sanctified. I have coveted no man's silver, or gold, or apparel." Some of the Ephesian brethren were wealthy, but Paul had never sought personal benefit from them. It was no part of his message to call attention to his own wants. "These hands," he declared, "have ministered unto my necessities, and to them that were with me." Amidst his arduous labors and extensive journeys for the cause of Christ, he was able, not only to supply his own wants, but to spare something for the support of his fellow laborers and the relief of the worthy poor. This he accomplished only by unremitting diligence and the closest economy. Well might he point to his own example as he said, "I have showed you all things, how that so laboring ye ought to support the weak, and to remember the words of the Lord Jesus, how He said, It is more blessed to give than to receive.

"And when he had thus spoken, he kneeled down, and prayed with them all. And they all wept sore, and fell on Paul's neck, and kissed him, sorrowing most of all for the words which he spake, that they should see his face no more. And they accompanied him unto the ship."

From Miletus the travelers sailed in "a straight course unto Coos, and the day following unto Rhodes, and from thence unto Patara," on the southwest shore of Asia Minor, where, "finding a ship sailing over unto Phoenicia," they "went aboard, and set forth." At Tyre, where the ship was unloaded, they found a few disciples, with whom they were permitted to tarry seven days. Through the Holy Spirit these disciples were warned of the perils awaiting Paul at Jerusalem, and they urged him "that he should not go up to Jerusalem." But the apostle allowed not the fear of affliction and imprisonment to turn him from his purpose.

At the close of the week spent in Tyre, all the brethren, with their wives and children, went with Paul to the ship, and before he stepped on board, they knelt upon the shore and prayed, he for them, and they for him.

Pursuing their journey southward, the travelers arrived at Caesarea and "entered into the house of Philip the evangelist, which was one of the seven; and abode with him." Here Paul spent a few peaceful, happy days—the last of perfect freedom that he was to enjoy for a long time.

While Paul tarried at Caesarea, "there came down from Judea a certain prophet, named Agabus. And when he was come unto us," Luke says, "he took Paul's girdle, and bound his own hands and feet, and said, Thus saith the Holy Ghost, So shall the Jews at Jerusalem bind the man that owneth this girdle, and shall deliver him into the hands of the Gentiles."

"When we heard these things," Luke continues, "both we, and they of that place, besought him not to go up to Jerusalem." But Paul would not swerve from the path of duty. He would follow Christ if need be to prison and to death. "What mean ye to weep and to break mine heart?" he exclaimed; "for I am ready not to be bound only, but also to die at Jerusalem for the name of the Lord Jesus." Seeing that they caused him pain without changing his purpose, the brethren ceased their importunity, saying only, "The will of the Lord be done."

The time soon came for the brief stay at Caesarea to end, and, accompanied by some of the brethren, Paul and his company set out for Jerusalem, their hearts deeply shadowed by the presentiment of coming evil.

Never before had the apostle approached Jerusalem with so sad a heart. He knew that he would find few friends and many enemies. He was nearing the city which had rejected and slain the Son of God and over which now hung the threatenings of divine wrath. Remembering how bitter had been his own prejudice against the followers of Christ, he felt the deepest pity for his deluded countrymen. And yet how little could he hope that he would be able to help them! The same blind wrath which had once burned in his own heart, was now with untold power kindling the hearts of a whole nation against him.

And he could not count upon the sympathy and support of even his own brethren in the faith. The unconverted Jews who had followed so closely upon his track, had not been slow to circulate the most unfavorable reports at Jerusalem, both personally and by letter, concerning him and his work; and some, even of the apostles and elders, had received these reports as truth, making no attempt to contradict them, and manifesting no desire to harmonize with him.

Yet in the midst of discouragements the apostle was not in despair. He trusted that the Voice which had spoken to his own heart would yet speak to the hearts of his countrymen, and that the Master whom his fellow disciples loved and served would yet unite their hearts with his in the work of the gospel.

38

Paul a Prisoner

This chapter is based on Acts 21:17 to 23:35

When we were come to Jerusalem, the brethren received us gladly. And the day following Paul went in with us unto James; and all the elders were present."

On this occasion, Paul and his companions formally presented to the leaders of the work at Jerusalem the contributions forwarded by the Gentile churches for the support of the poor among their Jewish brethren. The gathering of these contributions had cost the apostle and his fellow workers much time, anxious thought, and wearisome labor. The sum, which far exceeded the expectations of the elders at Jerusalem, represented many sacrifices and even severe privations on the part of the Gentile believers.

These freewill offerings betokened the loyalty of the Gentile converts to the organized work of God throughout the world and should have been received by all with grateful acknowledgment, yet it was apparent to Paul and his companions that even among those before whom they now stood were some who were unable to appreciate the spirit of brotherly love that had prompted the gifts.

In the earlier years of the gospel work among the Gentiles some of the leading brethren at Jerusalem, clinging to former prejudices and habits of thought, had not co-operated heartily with Paul and his associates. In their anxiety to preserve a few meaningless forms and ceremonies, they had lost sight of the blessing that would come to them and to the cause they loved, through an effort to unite in one all parts of the Lord's work. Although desirous of safeguarding the best interests of the Christian church, they had failed to keep step with the advancing providences of God, and in their human wisdom attempted to throw about workers many unnecessary restrictions. Thus there arose a group of men who were unacquainted personally with the changing circumstances and peculiar needs met by laborers in distant fields, yet who insisted that they had the authority to direct their brethren in these fields to follow certain specified methods of labor. They felt as if the work of preaching the gospel should be carried forward in harmony with their opinions.

Several years had passed since the brethren in Jerusalem, with representatives from other leading churches, gave careful consideration to the perplexing questions that had arisen over methods followed by those who were laboring for the Gentiles. As a result of this council, the brethren had united in making definite recommendations to the churches concerning certain rites and customs, including circumcision. It was at this general council that the brethren had also united in commending to the Christian churches Barnabas and Paul as laborers worthy of the full confidence of every believer.

Among those present at this meeting, were some who had severely criticized the methods of labor followed by the apostles upon whom rested the chief burden of carrying the gospel to the Gentile world. But during the council their views of God's purpose had broadened, and they had united with their brethren in making wise decisions which made possible the unification of the entire body of believers.

Afterward, when it became apparent that the converts among the Gentiles were increasing rapidly, there were a few of the leading brethren at Jerusalem who began to cherish anew their former prejudices against the methods of Paul and his associates. These prejudices strengthened with the passing of the years, until some of the leaders determined that the work of preaching the gospel must henceforth be conducted in accordance with their own ideas. If Paul would conform his methods to certain policies which they advocated they would acknowledge and sustain his work; otherwise they could no longer look upon it with favor or grant it their support.

These men had lost sight of the fact that God is the teacher of His people; that every worker in His cause is to obtain an individual experience in following the divine Leader, not looking to man for direct guidance; that His workers are to be molded and fashioned, not after man's ideas, but after the similitude of the divine.

In his ministry the apostle Paul had taught the people "not with enticing words of man's wisdom, but in demonstration of the Spirit and of power." The truths that he proclaimed had been revealed to him by the Holy Spirit, "for the Spirit searcheth all things, yea, the deep things of God. For what man knoweth the things of a man, save the spirit of man which is in him? even so the things of God knoweth no man, but the Spirit of God. . . . Which things," declared Paul, "we speak, not in the words which man's wisdom teacheth, but which the Holy Ghost teacheth; comparing spiritual things with spiritual." 1 Corinthians 2:4, 10-13.

Throughout his ministry, Paul had looked to God for direct guidance. At the same time, he had been very careful to labor in harmony with the decisions of the general council at Jerusalem, and as a result the churches were "established in the faith, and increased in number daily." Acts 16:5. And now, notwithstanding the lack of sympathy shown him by some, he found comfort in the conscious-ness that he had done his duty in encouraging in his converts a spirit of loyalty, generosity, and brotherly love, as revealed on this occasion in the liberal contributions which he was enabled to place before the Jewish elders.

After the presentation of the gifts, Paul "declared particularly what things God had wrought among the Gentiles by his ministry." This recital of facts brought to the hearts of all, even of those who had been doubting, the conviction that the blessing of heaven had accompanied his labors. "When they heard it, they glorified the Lord." They felt that the methods of labor pursued by the apostle bore the signet of Heaven. The liberal contributions lying before them added weight to the testimony of the apostle concerning the faithfulness of the new churches established among the Gentiles. The men who, while numbered among those who were in charge of the work at Jerusalem, had urged that arbitrary measures of control be adopted, saw Paul's ministry in a new light and were convinced that their own course had been wrong, that they had been held in bondage by Jewish customs and traditions, and that the work of the gospel had been greatly hindered by their failure to recognize that the wall of partition between Jew and Gentile had been broken down by the death of Christ.

This was the golden opportunity for all the leading brethren to confess frankly that God had wrought through Paul, and that at times they had erred in permitting the reports of his enemies to arouse their jealousy and prejudice. But instead of uniting in an effort to do justice to the one who had been injured, they gave him counsel which showed that they still cherished a feeling that Paul should be held largely responsible for the existing prejudice. They did not stand nobly in his defense, endeavoring to show the disaf-fected ones where they were wrong, but sought to effect a compro-mise by counseling him to pursue a course which in their opinion would remove all cause for misapprehension.

"Thou seest, brother," they said, in response to his testimony, "how many thousands of Jews there are which believe; and they are all zealous of the law: and they are informed of thee, that thou teachest all the Jews which are among the Gentiles to forsake Moses, saying that they ought not to circumcise their children, neither to walk after the customs. What is it therefore? the multitude must needs come together: for they will hear that thou art come. Do therefore this that we say to thee: We have four men which have a vow on them; them take, and purify thyself with them, and be at charges with them, that they may shave their heads: and all may know that those things, whereof they were informed concerning thee, are nothing; but that thou thyself also walkest orderly, and keepest the law. As touching the Gentiles which believe, we have written and concluded that they observe no such thing, save only that they keep themselves from things offered to idols, and from blood, and from strangled, and from fornication."

The brethren hoped that Paul, by following the course suggested, might give a decisive contradiction to the false reports concerning him. They assured him that the decision of the former council concerning the Gentile converts and the ceremonial law, still held good. But the advice now given was not consistent with that decision. The Spirit of God did not prompt this instruction; it was the fruit of cowardice. The leaders of the church in Jerusalem knew that by non-conformity to the ceremonial law, Christians would bring upon themselves the hatred of the Jews and expose themselves to persecution. The Sanhedrin was doing its utmost to hinder the progress of the gospel. Men were chosen by this body to follow up the apostles, especially Paul, and in every possible way to oppose their work. Should the believers in Christ be condemned before the Sanhedrin as breakers of the law, they would suffer swift and severe punishment as apostates from the Jewish faith.

Many of the Jews who had accepted the gospel still cherished a regard for the ceremonial law and were only too willing to make unwise concessions, hoping thus to gain the confidence of their countrymen, to remove their prejudice, and to win them to faith in Christ as the world's Redeemer. Paul realized that so long as many of the leading members of the church at Jerusalem should continue to cherish prejudice against him, they would work constantly to counteract his influence. He felt that if by any reasonable concession he could win them to the truth he would remove a great obstacle to the success of the gospel in other places. But he was not authorized of God to concede as much as they asked.

When we think of Paul's great desire to be in harmony with his brethren, his tenderness toward the weak in the faith, his reverence for the apostles who had been with Christ, and for James, the brother of the Lord, and his purpose to become all things to all men so far as he could without sacrificing principle—when we think of all this, it is less surprising that he was constrained to deviate from the firm, decided course that he had hitherto followed. But instead of accomplishing the desired object, his efforts for conciliation only precipitated the crisis, hastened his predicted sufferings, and resulted in separating him from his brethren, depriving the church of one of its strongest pillars, and bringing sorrow to Christian hearts in every land.

On the following day Paul began to carry out the counsel of the elders. The four men who were under the Nazarite vow (Numbers 6), the term of which had nearly expired, were taken by Paul into the temple, "to signify the accomplishment of the days of purification, until that an offering should be offered for every one of them." Certain costly sacrifices for purification were yet to be offered.

Those who advised Paul to take this step had not fully considered the great peril to which he would thus be exposed. At this season, Jerusalem was filled with worshipers from many lands. As, in fulfillment of the commission given him by God, Paul had borne the gospel to the Gentiles, he had visited many of the world's largest cities, and he was well known to thousands who from foreign parts had come to Jerusalem to attend the feast. Among these were men whose hearts were filled with bitter hatred for Paul, and for him to enter the temple on a public occasion was to risk his life. For several days he passed in and out among the worshipers, apparently unnoticed; but before the close of the specified period, as he was talking with a priest concerning the sacrifices to be offered, he was recognized by some of the Jews from Asia.

With the fury of demons they rushed upon him, crying, "Men of Israel, help: This is the man, that teacheth all men everywhere against the people, and the law, and this place." And as the people responded to the call for help, another accusation was added—"and further brought Greeks also into the temple, and hath polluted this holy place."

By the Jewish law it was a crime punishable with death for an uncircumcised person to enter the inner courts of the sacred edifice. Paul had been seen in the city in company with Trophimus, an Ephesian, and it was conjectured that he had brought him into the temple. This he had not done; and being himself a Jew, his act in entering the temple was no violation of the law. But though the charge was wholly false, it served to arouse the popular prejudice.

As the cry was taken up and borne through the temple courts, the throngs gathered there were thrown into wild excitement. The news quickly spread through Jerusalem, "and all the city was moved, and the people ran together."

That an apostate from Israel should presume to profane the temple at the very time when thousands had come there from all parts of the world to worship, excited the fiercest passions of the mob. "They took Paul, and drew him out of the temple: and forthwith the doors were shut."

"As they went about to kill him, tidings came unto the chief captain of the band, that all Jerusalem was in an uproar." Claudius Lysias well knew the turbulent elements with which he had to deal, and he "immediately took soldiers and centurions, and ran down unto them: and when they saw the chief captain and the soldiers, they left beating of Paul." Ignorant of the cause of the tumult, but seeing that the rage of the multitude was directed against Paul, the Roman captain concluded that he must be a certain Egyptian rebel of whom he had heard, who had thus far escaped capture. He therefore "took him, and commanded him to be bound with two chains; and demanded who he was, and what he had done." At once many voices were raised in loud and angry accusation; "some cried one thing, some another, among the multitude: and when he could not know the certainty for the tumult, he commanded him to be carried into the castle. And when he came upon the stairs, so it was, that he was borne of the soldiers for the violence of the people. For the multitude of the people followed after, crying, Away with him."

In the midst of the tumult the apostle was calm and self-possessed. His mind was stayed upon God, and he knew that angels of heaven were about him. He felt unwilling to leave the temple without making an effort to set the truth before his countrymen. As he was about to be led into the castle he said to the chief captain, "May I speak unto thee?" Lysias responded, "Canst thou speak Greek? Art not thou that Egyptian, which before these days madest an uproar, and leddest out into the wilderness four thousand men that were murderers?" In reply Paul said, "I am a man which am a Jew of Tarsus, a city in Cilicia, a citizen of no mean city: and, I beseech thee, suffer me to speak unto the people."

The request was granted, and "Paul stood on the stairs, and beckoned with the hand unto the people." The gesture attracted their attention, while his bearing commanded respect. "And when there was made a great silence, he spake unto them in the Hebrew tongue, saying, Men, brethren, and fathers, hear ye my defense which I make now unto you." At the sound of the familiar Hebrew words, "they kept the more silence," and in the universal hush he continued:

"I am verily a man which am a Jew, born in Tarsus, a city in Cilicia, yet brought up in this city at the feet of Gamaliel, and taught according to the perfect manner of the law of the fathers, and was zealous toward God, as ye all are this day." None could deny the apostle's statements, as the facts that he referred to were well known to many who were still living in Jerusalem. He then spoke of his former zeal in persecuting the disciples of Christ, even unto death; and he narrated the circumstances of his conversion, telling his hearers how his own proud heart had been led to bow to the crucified Nazarene. Had he attempted to enter into argument with his opponents, they would have stubbornly refused to listen to his words; but the relation of his experience was attended with a convincing power that for the time seemed to soften and subdue their hearts.

He then endeavored to show that his work among the Gentiles had not been entered upon from choice. He had desired to labor for his own nation; but in that very temple the voice of God had spoken to him in holy vision, directing his course "far hence upon the Gentiles."

Hitherto the people had listened with close attention, but when Paul reached the point in his history where he was appointed Christ's ambassador to the Gentiles, their fury broke forth anew. Accustomed to look upon themselves as the only people favored by God, they were unwilling to permit the despised Gentiles to share the privileges which had hitherto been regarded as exclusively their own. Lifting their voices above the voice of the speaker, they cried, "Away with such a fellow from the earth: for it is not fit that he should live."

"As they cried out, and cast off their clothes, and threw dust into the air, the chief captain commanded him to be brought into the castle, and bade that he should be examined by scourging; that he might know wherefore they cried so against him.

"And as they bound him with thongs, Paul said unto the centurion that stood by, Is it lawful for you to scourge a man that is a Roman, and uncondemned? When the centurion heard that, he went and told the chief captain, saying, Take heed what thou doest: for this man is a Roman. Then the chief captain came, and said unto him, Tell me, art thou a Roman? He said, Yea. And the chief captain answered, With a great sum obtained I this freedom. And Paul said,

But I was freeborn. Then straightway they departed from him which should have examined him: and the chief captain also was afraid, after he knew that he was a Roman, and because he had bound him.

"On the morrow, because he would have known the certainty wherefore he was accused of the Jews, he loosed him from his bands, and commanded the chief priests and all their council to appear, and brought Paul down, and set him before them."

The apostle was now to be tried by the same tribunal of which he himself had been a member before his conversion. As he stood before the Jewish rulers, his bearing was calm, and his countenance revealed the peace of Christ. "Earnestly beholding the council," he said, "Men and brethren, I have lived in all good conscience before God until this day." Upon hearing these words, their hatred was kindled afresh; "and the high priest Ananias commanded them that stood by him to smite him on the mouth." At this inhuman command, Paul exclaimed, "God shall smite thee, thou whited wall: for sittest thou to judge me after the law, and commandest me to be smitten contrary to the law?" "They that stood by said, Revilest thou God's high priest?" With his usual courtesy Paul answered, "I wist not, brethren, that he was the high priest: for it is written, Thou shalt not speak evil of the ruler of thy people.

"But when Paul perceived that the one part were Sadducees, and the other Pharisees, he cried out in the council, Men and brethren, I am a Pharisee, the son of a Pharisee: of the hope and resurrection of the dead I am called in question.

"And when he had so said, there arose a dissension between the Pharisees and the Sadducees: and the multitude was divided. For the Sadducees say that there is no resurrection, neither angel, nor spirit: but the Pharisees confess both." The two parties began to dispute between themselves, and thus the strength of their opposition against Paul was broken. "The scribes that were of the Pharisees' part arose, and strove, saying, We find no evil in this man: but if a spirit or an angel hath spoken to him, let us not fight against God."

In the confusion that followed, the Sadducees were eagerly striving to gain possession of the apostle, that they might put him to death; and the Pharisees were as eager in striving to protect him. "The chief captain, fearing lest Paul should have been pulled in pieces of them, commanded the soldiers to go down, and to take him by force from among them, and to bring him into the castle."

Later, while reflecting on the trying experiences of the day, Paul began to fear that his course might not have been pleasing to God.

Could it be that he had made a mistake after all in visiting Jerusalem? Had his great desire to be in union with his brethren led to this disastrous result?

The position which the Jews as God's professed people occupied before an unbelieving world, caused the apostle intense anguish of spirit. How would those heathen officers look upon them?—claiming to be worshipers of Jehovah, and assuming sacred office, yet giving themselves up to the control of blind, unreasoning anger, seeking to destroy even their brethren who dared to differ with them in religious faith, and turning their most solemn deliberative council into a scene of strife and wild confusion. Paul felt that the name of his God had suffered reproach in the eyes of the heathen.

And now he was in prison, and he knew that his enemies, in their desperate malice, would resort to any means to put him to death. Could it be that his work for the churches was ended and that ravening wolves were to enter in now? The cause of Christ was very near to Paul's heart, and with deep anxiety he thought of the perils of the scattered churches, exposed as they were to the persecutions of just such men as he had encountered in the Sanhedrin council. In distress and discouragement he wept and prayed.

In this dark hour the Lord was not unmindful of His servant. He had guarded him from the murderous throng in the temple courts; He had been with him before the Sanhedrin council; He was with him in the fortress; and He revealed Himself to His faithful witness in response to the earnest prayers of the apostle for guidance. "The night following the Lord stood by him, and said, Be of good cheer, Paul: for as thou hast testified of Me in Jerusalem, so must thou bear witness also at Rome."

Paul had long looked forward to visiting Rome; he greatly desired to witness for Christ there, but had felt that his purposes were frustrated by the enmity of the Jews. He little thought, even now, that it would be as a prisoner that he would go.

While the Lord encouraged His servant, Paul's enemies were eagerly plotting his destruction. "And when it was day, certain of the Jews banded together, and bound themselves under a curse, saying that they would neither eat nor drink till they had killed Paul. And they were more than forty which had made this conspiracy." Here was a fast such as the Lord through Isaiah had condemned—a fast "for strife and debate, and to smite with the fist of wickedness." Isaiah 58:4.

The conspirators "came to the chief priests and elders, and said,

We have bound ourselves under a great curse, that we will eat nothing until we have slain Paul. Now therefore ye with the council signify to the chief captain that he bring him down unto you tomorrow, as though ye would inquire something more perfectly concerning him: and we, or ever he come near, are ready to kill him."

Instead of rebuking this cruel scheme, the priests and rulers eagerly agreed to it. Paul had spoken the truth when he compared Ananias to a whited sepulcher.

But God interposed to save the life of His servant. Paul's sister's son, hearing of the "lying in wait" of the assassins, "went and entered into the castle, and told Paul. Then Paul called one of the centurions unto him, and said, Bring this young man unto the chief captain: for he hath a certain thing to tell him. So he took him, and brought him to the chief captain, and said, Paul the prisoner called me unto him, and prayed me to bring this young man unto thee, who hath something to say unto thee."

Claudius Lysias received the youth kindly, and taking him aside, asked, "What is that thou hast to tell me?" The youth replied: "The Jews have agreed to desire thee that thou wouldest bring down Paul tomorrow into the council, as though they would inquire somewhat of him more perfectly. But do not thou yield unto them: for there lie in wait for him of them more than forty men, which have bound themselves with an oath, that they will neither eat nor drink till they have killed him: and now are they ready, looking for a promise from thee."

"The chief captain then let the young man depart, and charged him, See thou tell no man that thou hast showed these things to me."

Lysias at once decided to transfer Paul from his jurisdiction to that of Felix the procurator. As a people, the Jews were in a state of excitement and irritation, and tumults were of frequent occurrence. The continued presence of the apostle in Jerusalem might lead to consequences dangerous to the city and even to the commandant himself. He therefore "called unto him two centurions, saying, Make ready two hundred soldiers to go to Caesarea, and horsemen threescore and ten, and spearmen two hundred, at the third hour of the night; and provide them beasts, that they may set Paul on, and bring him safe unto Felix the governor."

No time was to be lost in sending Paul away. "The soldiers, as it was commanded them, took Paul, and brought him by night to Antipatris." From that place the horsemen went on with the prisoner to Caesarea, while the four hundred soldiers returned to Jerusalem.

The officer in charge of the detachment delivered his prisoner to Felix, also presenting a letter with which he had been entrusted by the chief captain:

"Claudius Lysias unto the most excellent governor Felix sendeth greeting. This man was taken of the Jews, and should have been killed of them: then came I with an army, and rescued him, having understood that he was a Roman. And when I would have known the cause wherefore they accused him, I brought him forth into their council: whom I perceived to be accused of questions of their law, but to have nothing laid to his charge worthy of death or of bonds. And when it was told me how that the Jews laid wait for the man, I sent straightway to thee, and gave commandment to his accusers also to say before thee what they had against him. Farewell."

After reading the communication, Felix inquired to what province the prisoner belonged, and being informed that he was of Cilicia, said: "I will hear thee . . . when thine accusers are also come. And he commanded him to be kept in Herod's judgment hall."

The case of Paul was not the first in which a servant of God had found among the heathen an asylum from the malice of the professed people of Jehovah. In their rage against Paul the Jews had added another crime to the dark catalogue which marked the history of that people. They had still further hardened their hearts against the truth and had rendered their doom more certain.

Few realize the full meaning of the words that Christ spoke when, in the synagogue at Nazareth, He announced Himself as the Anointed One. He declared His mission to comfort, bless, and save the sorrowing and the sinful; and then, seeing that pride and unbelief controlled the hearts of His hearers, He reminded them that in time past God had turned away from His chosen people because of their unbelief and rebellion, and had manifested Himself to those in heathen lands who had not rejected the light of heaven. The widow of Sarepta and Naaman the Syrian had lived up to all the light they had; hence they were accounted more righteous than God's chosen people who had backslidden from Him and had sacrificed principle to convenience and worldly honor.

Christ told the Jews at Nazareth a fearful truth when He declared that with backsliding Israel there was no safety for the faithful messenger of God. They would not know his worth or appreciate his labors. While the Jewish leaders professed to have great zeal for the honor of God and the good of Israel, they were enemies of both. By precept and example they were leading the people farther and farther from obedience to God—leading them where He could not be their defense in the day of trouble.

The Saviour's words of reproof to the men of Nazareth applied, in the case of Paul, not only to the unbelieving Jews, but to his own brethren in the faith. Had the leaders in the church fully surrendered their feeling of bitterness toward the apostle, and accepted him as one specially called of God to bear the gospel to the Gentiles, the Lord would have spared him to them. God had not ordained that Paul's labors should so soon end, but He did not work a miracle to counteract the train of circumstances to which the course of the leaders in the church at Jerusalem had given rise.

The same spirit is still leading to the same results. A neglect to appreciate and improve the provisions of divine grace has deprived the church of many a blessing. How often would the Lord have prolonged the work of some faithful minister, had his labors been appreciated! But if the church permits the enemy of souls to pervert the understanding, so that they misrepresent and misinterpret the words and acts of the servant of Christ; if they allow themselves to stand in his way and hinder his usefulness, the Lord sometimes removes from them the blessing which He gave.

Satan is constantly working through his agents to dishearten and destroy those whom God has chosen to accomplish a great and good work. They may be ready to sacrifice even life itself for the advancement of the cause of Christ, yet the great deceiver will suggest to their brethren doubts concerning them which, if entertained, would undermine confidence in their integrity of character, and thus cripple their usefulness. Too often he succeeds in bringing upon them, through their own brethren, such sorrow of heart that God graciously interposes to give His persecuted servants rest. After the hands are folded upon the pulseless breast, when the voice of warning and encouragement is silent, then the obdurate may be aroused to see and prize the blessings they have cast from them. Their death may accomplish that which their life has failed to do.

39

The Trial at Caesarea

This chapter is based on Acts 24

Five days after Paul's arrival at Caesarea his accusers came from Jerusalem, accompanied by Tertullus, an orator whom they had engaged as their counsel. The case was granted a speedy hearing. Paul was brought before the assembly, and Tertullus "began to accuse him." Judging that flattery would have more influence upon the Roman governor than the simple statements of truth and justice, the wily orator began his speech by praising Felix: "Seeing that by thee we enjoy great quietness, and that very worthy deeds are done unto his nation by thy providence, we accept it always, and in all places, most noble Felix, with all thankfulness."

Tertullus here descended to barefaced falsehood; for the character of Felix was base and contemptible. It was said of him, that "in the practice of all kinds of lust and cruelty, he exercised the power of a king with the temper of a slave."—Tacitus, *History, ch. 5, par. 9. Those who heard Tertullus knew that his flattering words were untrue, but their desire to secure the condemnation of Paul was stronger than their love of truth.*

In his speech, Tertullus charged Paul with crimes which, if proved, would have resulted in his conviction for high treason against the government. "We have found this man a pestilent fellow," declared the orator, "and a mover of sedition among all the Jews throughout the world, and a ringleader of the sect of the Nazarenes: who also hath gone about to profane the temple." Tertullus then stated that Lysias, the commandant of the garrison at Jerusalem, had violently taken Paul from the Jews when they were about to judge him by their ecclesiastical law, and had thus forced them to bring the matter before Felix. These statements were made with the design of inducing the procurator to deliver Paul over to the Jewish court. All the charges were vehemently supported by the Jews present, who made no effort to conceal their hatred of the prisoner.

Felix had sufficient penetration to read the disposition and character of Paul's accusers. He knew from what motive they had flattered him, and he saw also that they had failed to substantiate their charges against Paul. Turning to the accused, he beckoned to him to answer for himself. Paul wasted no words in compliments, but simply stated that he could the more cheerfully defend himself before Felix, since the latter had been so long a procurator, and therefore had so good an understanding of the laws and customs of the Jews. Referring to the charges brought against him, he plainly showed that not one of them was true. He declared that he had caused no disturbance in any part of Jerusalem, nor had he profaned the sanctuary. "They neither found me in the temple disputing with any man," he said, "neither raising up the people, neither in the synagogues, nor in the city: neither can they prove the things whereof they now accuse me."

While confessing that "after the way which they call heresy" he had worshiped the God of his fathers, he asserted that he had always believed "all things which are written in the law and in the prophets;" and that in harmony with the plain teaching of the Scriptures, he held the faith of the resurrection of the dead. And he further declared that the ruling purpose of his life was to "have always a conscience void of offense toward God, and toward men."

In a candid, straightforward manner he stated the object of his visit to Jerusalem, and the circumstances of his arrest and trial: "Now after many years I came to bring alms to my nation, and offerings. Whereupon certain Jews from Asia found me purified in the temple, neither with multitude, nor with tumult. Who ought to have been here before thee, and object, if they had aught against me. Or else let these same here say, if they have found any evil doing in me, while I stood before the council, except it be for this one voice, that I cried standing among them, Touching the resurrection of the dead I am called in question by you this day."

The apostle spoke with earnestness and evident sincerity, and his words carried with them a weight of conviction. Claudius Lysias, in his letter to Felix, had borne a similar testimony in regard to Paul's conduct. Moreover, Felix himself had a better knowledge of the Jewish religion than many supposed. Paul's plain statement of the facts in the case enabled Felix to understand still more clearly the motives by which the Jews were governed in attempting to convict the apostle of sedition and treasonable conduct. The governor would not gratify them by unjustly condemning a Roman citizen, neither would he give him up to them to be put to death without a fair trial. Yet Felix knew no higher motive than self-interest, and he was controlled by love of praise and a desire for promotion. Fear of offending the Jews held him back from doing full justice to a man whom he knew to be innocent. He therefore decided to suspend the trial until Lysias should be present, saying, "When Lysias the chief captain shall come down, I will know the uttermost of your matter."

The apostle remained a prisoner, but Felix commanded the centurion who had been appointed to keep Paul, "to let him have liberty," and to "forbid none of his acquaintance to minister or come unto him."

It was not long after this that Felix and his wife, Drusilla, sent for Paul in order that in a private interview they might hear from him "concerning the faith in Christ." They were willing and even eager to listen to these new truths—truths which they might never hear again and which, if rejected, would prove a swift witness against them in the day of God.

Paul regarded this as a God-given opportunity, and faithfully he improved it. He knew that he stood in the presence of one who had power to put him to death or to set him free; yet he did not address Felix and Drusilla with praise or flattery. He knew that his words would be to them a savor of life or of death, and, forgetting all selfish considerations, he sought to arouse them to a sense of their peril.

The apostle realized that the gospel had a claim upon whoever might listen to his words; that one day they would stand either among the pure and holy around the great white throne, or with those to whom Christ would say, "Depart from Me, ye that work iniquity." Matthew 7: 23. He knew that he must meet every one of his hearers before the tribunal of heaven and must there render an account, not only for all that he had said and done, but for the motive and spirit of his words and deeds.

So violent and cruel had been the course of Felix that few had ever before dared even to intimate to him that his character and conduct were not faultless. But Paul had no fear of man. He plainly declared his faith in Christ, and the reasons for that faith, and was thus led to speak particularly of those virtues essential to Christian character, but of which the haughty pair before him were so strikingly destitute.

He held up before Felix and Drusilla the character of God—His righteousness, justice, and equity, and the nature of His law. He clearly showed that it is man's duty to live a life of sobriety and temperance, keeping the passions under the control of reason, in conformity to God's law, and preserving the physical and mental powers in a healthy condition. He declared that there would surely come a day of judgment when all would be rewarded according to the deeds done in the body, and when it would be plainly revealed that wealth, position, or titles are powerless to gain for man the favor of God or to deliver him from the results of sin. He showed that this life is man's time of preparation for the future life. Should he neglect present privileges and opportunities he would suffer an eternal loss; no new probation would be given him.

Paul dwelt especially upon the far-reaching claims of God's law. He showed how it extends to the deep secrets of man's moral nature and throws a flood of light upon that which has been concealed from the sight and knowledge of men. What the hands may do or the tongue may utter—what the outer life reveals—but imperfectly shows man's moral character. The law searches his thoughts, motives, and purposes. The dark passions that lie hidden from the sight of men, the jealousy, hatred, lust, and ambition, the evil deeds meditated upon in the dark recesses of the soul, yet never executed for want of opportunity—all these God's law condemns.

Paul endeavored to direct the minds of his hearers to the one great Sacrifice for sin. He pointed to the sacrifices that were shadows of good things to come, and then presented Christ as the antitype of all those ceremonies—the object to which they pointed as the only source of life and hope for fallen man. Holy men of old were saved by faith in the blood of Christ. As they saw the dying agonies of the sacrificial victims they looked across the gulf of ages to the Lamb of God that was to take away the sin of the world.

God justly claims the love and obedience of all His creatures. He has given them in His law a perfect standard of right. But many forget their Maker and choose to follow their own way in opposition to His will. They return enmity for love that is as high as heaven and as broad as the universe. God cannot lower the requirements of His law to meet the standard of wicked men; neither can man in his own power meet the demands of the law. Only by faith in Christ can the sinner be cleansed from guilt and be enabled to render obedience to the law of his Maker.

Thus Paul, the prisoner, urged the claims of the divine law upon Jew and Gentile, and presented Jesus, the despised Nazarene, as the Son of God, the world's Redeemer.

The Jewish princess well understood the sacred character of that law which she had so shamelessly transgressed, but her prejudice against the Man of Calvary steeled her heart against the word of life. But Felix had never before listened to the truth, and as the Spirit of God sent conviction to his soul, he became deeply agitated.

Conscience, now aroused, made her voice heard, and Felix felt that Paul's words were true. Memory went back over the guilty past. With terrible distinctness there came up before him the secrets of his early life of profligacy and bloodshed, and the black record of his later years. He saw himself licentious, cruel, rapacious. Never before had the truth been thus brought home to his heart. Never before had his soul been so filled with terror. The thought that all the secrets of his career of crime were open before the eye of God, and that he must be judged according to his deeds, caused him to tremble with dread.

But instead of permitting his convictions to lead him to repentance, he sought to dismiss these unwelcome reflections. The interview with Paul was cut short. "Go thy way for this time," he said; "when I have a convenient season, I will call for thee."

How wide the contrast between the course of Felix and that of the jailer of Philippi! The servants of the Lord were brought in bonds to the jailer, as was Paul to Felix. The evidence they gave of being sustained by a divine power, their rejoicing under suffering and disgrace, their fearlessness when the earth was reeling with the earthquake shock, and their spirit of Christlike forgiveness, sent conviction to the jailer's heart, and with trembling he confessed his sins and found pardon. Felix trembled, but he did not repent. The jailer joyfully welcomed the Spirit of God to his heart and to his home; Felix bade the divine Messenger depart. The one chose to become a child of God and an heir of heaven; the other cast his lot with the workers of iniquity.

For two years no further action was taken against Paul, yet he remained a prisoner. Felix visited him several times and listened attentively to his words. But the real motive for this apparent friendliness was a desire for gain, and he intimated that by the payment of a large sum of money Paul might secure his release. The apostle, however, was of too noble a nature to free himself by a bribe. He was not guilty of any crime, and he would not stoop to commit a wrong in order to gain freedom. Furthermore, he was himself too poor to pay such a ransom, had he been disposed to do so, and he would not, in his own behalf, appeal to the sympathy and generosity of his converts. He also felt that he was in the hands of God, and he would not interfere with the divine purposes respecting himself.

Felix was finally summoned to Rome because of gross wrongs committed against the Jews. Before leaving Caesarea in answer to this summons, he thought to "show the Jews a pleasure" by allowing Paul to remain in prison. But Felix was not successful in his attempt to regain the confidence of the Jews. He was removed from office in disgrace, and Porcius Festus was appointed to succeed him, with headquarters at Caesarea.

A ray of light from heaven had been permitted to shine upon Felix, when Paul reasoned with him concerning righteousness, temperance, and a judgment to come. That was his heaven-sent opportunity to see and to forsake his sins. But he said to the messenger of God, "Go thy way for this time; when I have a convenient season, I will call for thee." He had slighted his last offer of mercy. Never was he to receive another call from God.

40

Paul Appeals to Caesar

This chapter is based on Acts 25:1-12

When Festus was come into the province, after three days he ascended from Caesarea to Jerusalem. Then the high priest and the chief of the Jews informed him against Paul, and besought him, and desired favor against him, that he would send for him to Jerusalem." In making this request they purposed to waylay Paul along the road to Jerusalem and murder him. But Festus had a high sense of the responsibility of his position, and courteously declined to send for Paul. "It is not the manner of the Romans," he declared, "to deliver any man to die, before that he which is accused have the accusers face to face, and have license to answer for himself concerning the crime laid against him." He stated that "he himself would depart shortly" for Caesarea. "Let them there . . . which among you are able, go down with me, and accuse this man, if there be any wickedness in him."

This was not what the Jews wanted. They had not forgotten their former defeat at Caesarea. In contrast with the calm bearing and forcible arguments of the apostle, their own malignant spirit and baseless accusations would appear in the worst possible light. Again they urged that Paul be brought to Jerusalem for trial, but Festus held firmly to his purpose of giving Paul a fair trial at Caesarea. God in His providence controlled the decision of Festus, that the life of the apostle might be lengthened.

Their purposes defeated, the Jewish leaders at once prepared to witness against Paul at the court of the procurator. Upon returning to Caesarea, after a few days' sojourn at Jerusalem, Festus "the next day sitting on the judgment seat commanded Paul to be brought." "The Jews which came down from Jerusalem stood round about, and laid many and grievous complaints against Paul, which they could not prove." Being on this occasion without a lawyer, the Jews preferred their charges themselves. As the trial proceeded, the accused with calmness and candor clearly showed the falsity of their statements.

Festus discerned that the question in dispute related wholly to Jewish doctrines, and that, rightly understood, there was nothing in the charges against Paul, could they be proved, that would render him subject to sentence of death, or even to imprisonment. Yet he saw clearly the storm of rage that would be created if Paul were not condemned or delivered into their hands. And so, "willing to do the Jews a pleasure," Festus turned to Paul, and asked if he was willing to go to Jerusalem under his protection, to be tried by the Sanhedrin.

The apostle knew that he could not look for justice from the people who by their crimes were bringing down upon themselves the wrath of God. He knew that, like the prophet Elijah, he would be safer among the heathen than with those who had rejected light from heaven and hardened their hearts against the gospel. Weary of strife, his active spirit could ill endure the repeated delays and wearing suspense of his trial and imprisonment. He therefore decided to exercise his privilege, as a Roman citizen, of appealing to Caesar.

In answer to the governor's question, Paul said: "I stand at Caesar's judgment seat, where I ought to be judged: to the Jews have I done no wrong, as thou very well knowest. For if I be an offender, or have committed anything worthy of death, I refuse not to die: but if there be none of these things whereof these accuse me, no man may deliver me unto them. I appeal unto Caesar."

Festus knew nothing of the conspiracies of the Jews to murder Paul, and he was surprised at this appeal to Caesar. However, the words of the apostle put a stop to the proceedings of the court. "Festus, when he had conferred with the council, answered, Hast thou appealed unto Caesar? unto Caesar shalt thou go."

Thus it was that once more, because of hatred born of bigotry and self-righteousness, a servant of God was driven to turn for protection to the heathen. It was this same hatred that forced the prophet Elijah to flee for succor to the widow of Sarepta; and that forced the heralds of the gospel to turn from the Jews to proclaim their message to the Gentiles. And this hatred the people of God living in this age have yet to meet. Among many of the professing followers of Christ there is the same pride, formalism, and selfishness, the same spirit of oppression, that held so large a place in the Jewish heart. In the future, men claiming to be Christ's representatives will take a course similar to that followed by the priests and rulers in their treatment of Christ and the apostles. In the great crisis through which they are soon to pass, the faithful servants of God will encounter the same hardness of heart, the same cruel determination, the same unyielding hatred.

All who in that evil day would fearlessly serve God according to the dictates of conscience, will need courage, firmness, and a knowledge of God and His word; for those who are true to God will be persecuted, their motives will be impugned, their best efforts misinterpreted, and their names cast out as evil. Satan will work with all his deceptive power to influence the heart and becloud the understanding, to make evil appear good, and good evil. The stronger and purer the faith of God's people, and the firmer their determination to obey Him, the more fiercely will Satan strive to stir up against them the rage of those who, while claiming to be righteous, trample upon the law of God. It will require the firmest trust, the most heroic purpose, to hold fast the faith once delivered to the saints.

God desires His people to prepare for the soon-coming crisis. Prepared or unprepared, they must all meet it; and those only who have brought their lives into conformity to the divine standard, will stand firm at that time of test and trial. When secular rulers unite with ministers of religion to dictate in matters of conscience, then it will be seen who really fear and serve God. When the darkness is deepest, the light of a godlike character will shine the brightest. When every other trust fails, then it will be seen who have an abiding trust in Jehovah. And while the enemies of truth are on every side, watching the Lord's servants for evil, God will watch over them for good. He will be to them as the shadow of a great rock in a weary land.

41

"Almost Thou Persuadest Me"

This chapter is based on Acts 25:13-27; 26

Paul had appealed to Caesar, and Festus could not do otherwise than send him to Rome. But some time passed before a suitable ship could be found; and as other prisoners were to be sent with Paul, the consideration of their cases also occasioned delay. This gave Paul opportunity to present the reasons of his faith before the principal men of Caesarea, and also before King Agrippa II, the last of the Herods.

"After certain days King Agrippa and Bernice came unto Caesarea to salute Festus. And when they had been there many days, Festus declared Paul's cause unto the king, saying, There is a certain man left in bonds by Felix: about whom, when I was at Jerusalem, the chief priests and the elders of the Jews informed me, desiring to have judgment against him." He outlined the circumstances that led to the prisoner's appeal to Caesar, telling of Paul's recent trial before him, and saying that the Jews had brought against Paul no accusation such as he had supposed they would bring, but "certain questions . . . of their own superstition, and of one Jesus, which was dead, whom Paul affirmed to be alive."

As Festus told his story, Agrippa became interested and said, "I would also hear the man myself." In harmony with his wish, a meeting was arranged for the following day. "And on the morrow, when Agrippa was come, and Bernice, with great pomp, and was entered into the place of hearing, with the chief captains, and principal men of the city, at Festus' commandment Paul was brought forth."

In honor of his visitors, Festus had sought to make this an occasion of imposing display. The rich robes of the procurator and his guests, the swords of the soldiers, and the gleaming armor of their commanders, lent brilliancy to the scene.

And now Paul, still manacled, stood before the assembled company. What a contrast was here presented! Agrippa and Bernice possessed power and position, and because of this they were favored by the world. But they were destitute of the traits of character that God esteems. They were transgressors of His law, corrupt in heart and life. Their course of action was abhorred by heaven.

The aged prisoner, chained to his soldier guard, had in his appearance nothing that would lead the world to pay him homage. Yet in this man, apparently without friends or wealth or position, and held a prisoner for his faith in the Son of God, all heaven was interested. Angels were his attendants. Had the glory of one of those shining messengers flashed forth, the pomp and pride of royalty would have paled; king and courtiers would have been stricken to the earth, as were the Roman guards at the sepulcher of Christ.

Festus himself presented Paul to the assembly with the words: "King Agrippa, and all men which are here present with us, ye see this man, about whom all the multitude of the Jews have dealt with me, both at Jerusalem, and also here, crying that he ought not to live any longer. But when I found that he had committed nothing worthy of death, and that he himself hath appealed to Augustus, I have determined to send him. Of whom I have no certain thing to write unto my lord. Wherefore I have brought him forth before you, and specially before thee, O King Agrippa, that, after examination had, I might have somewhat to write. For it seemeth to me unreasonable to send a prisoner, and not withal to signify the crimes laid against him."

King Agrippa now gave Paul liberty to speak for himself. The apostle was not disconcerted by the brilliant display or the high rank of his audience; for he knew of how little worth are worldly wealth and position. Earthly pomp and power could not for a moment daunt his courage or rob him of his self-control.

"I think myself happy, King Agrippa," he declared, "because I shall answer for myself this day before thee touching all the things whereof I am accused of the Jews: especially because I know thee to be expert in all customs and questions which are among the Jews: wherefore I beseech thee to hear me patiently."

Paul related the story of his conversion from stubborn unbelief to faith in Jesus of Nazareth as the world's Redeemer. He described the heavenly vision that at first had filled him with unspeakable terror, but afterward proved to be a source of the greatest consolation—a revelation of divine glory, in the midst of which sat enthroned He whom he had despised and hated, whose followers he was even then seeking to destroy. From that hour Paul had been a new man, a sincere and fervent believer in Jesus, made such by transforming mercy.

With clearness and power Paul outlined before Agrippa the

leading events connected with the life of Christ on earth. He testified that the Messiah of prophecy had already appeared in the person of Jesus of Nazareth. He showed how the Old Testament Scriptures had declared that the Messiah was to appear as a man among men, and how in the life of Jesus had been fulfilled every specification outlined by Moses and the prophets. For the purpose of redeeming a lost world, the divine Son of God had endured the cross, despising the shame, and had ascended to heaven triumphant over death and the grave.

Why, Paul reasoned, should it seem incredible that Christ should rise from the dead? Once it had thus seemed to him, but how could he disbelieve that which he himself had seen and heard? At the gate of Damascus he had verily looked upon the crucified and risen Christ, the same who had walked the streets of Jerusalem, died on Calvary, broken the bands of death, and ascended to heaven. As verily as had Cephas, James, John, or any others of the disciples, he had seen and talked with Him. The Voice had bidden him proclaim the gospel of a risen Saviour, and how could he disobey? In Damascus, in Jerusalem, throughout all Judea, and in the regions afar off, he had borne witness of Jesus the Crucified, showing all classes "that they should repent and turn to God, and do works meet for repentance.

"For these causes," the apostle declared, "the Jews caught me in the temple, and went about to kill me. Having therefore obtained help of God, I continue unto this day, witnessing both to small and great, saying none other things than those which the prophets and Moses did say should come: that Christ should suffer, and that He should be the first that should rise from the dead, and should show light unto the people, and to the Gentiles."

The whole company had listened spellbound to Paul's account of his wonderful experiences. The apostle was dwelling upon his favorite theme. None who heard him could doubt his sincerity. But in the full tide of his persuasive eloquence he was interrupted by Festus, who cried out, "Paul, thou art beside thyself; much learning doth make thee mad."

The apostle replied, "I am not mad, most noble Festus; but speak forth the words of truth and soberness. For the king knoweth of these things, before whom also I speak freely: for I am persuaded that none of these thing are hidden from him; for this thing was not done in a corner." Then, turning to Agrippa, he addressed him directly, "King Agrippa, believest thou the prophets? I know that thou believest."

Deeply affected, Agrippa for the moment lost sight of his surroundings and the dignity of his position. Conscious only of the truths which he had heard, seeing only the humble prisoner standing before him as God's ambassador, he answered involuntarily, "Almost thou persuadest me to be a Christian."

Earnestly the apostle made answer, "I would to God, that not only thou, but also all that hear me this day, were both almost, and altogether such as I am," adding, as he raised his fettered hands, "except these bonds."

Festus, Agrippa, and Bernice might in justice have worn the fetters that bound the apostle. All were guilty of grievous crimes. These offenders had that day heard the offer of salvation through the name of Christ. One, at least, had been almost persuaded to accept the grace and pardon offered. But Agrippa put aside the proffered mercy, refusing to accept the cross of a crucified Redeemer.

The king's curiosity was satisfied, and, rising from his seat, he signified that the interview was at an end. As the assembly dispersed, they talked among themselves, saying, "This man doeth nothing worthy of death or of bonds."

Though Agrippa was a Jew, he did not share the bigoted zeal and blind prejudice of the Pharisees. "This man," he said to Festus, "might have been set at liberty, if he had not appealed unto Caesar." But the case had been referred to that higher tribunal, and it was now beyond the jurisdiction of either Festus or Agrippa.

42

The Voyage and Shipwreck

This chapter is based on Acts 27; 28:1-10

At last Paul was on his way to Rome. "When it was determined," Luke writes, "that we should sail into Italy, they delivered Paul and certain other prisoners unto one named Julius, a centurion of Augustus' band. And entering into a ship of Adramyttium, we launched, meaning to sail by the coasts of Asia; one Aristarchus, a Macedonian of Thessalonica, being with us."

In the first century of the Christian Era traveling by sea was attended with peculiar hardship and peril. Mariners directed their course largely by the position of the sun and stars; and when these did not appear, and there were indications of storm, the owners of vessels were fearful of venturing into the open sea. During a portion of the year, safe navigation was almost impossible.

The apostle Paul was now called upon to endure the trying experiences that would fall to his lot as a prisoner in chains during the long and tedious voyage to Italy. One circumstance greatly lightened the hardship of his lot—he was permitted the companionship of Luke and Aristarchus. In his letter to the Colossians he afterward referred to the latter as his "fellow prisoner" (Colossians 4:10); but it was from choice that Aristarchus shared Paul's bondage, that he might minister to him in his afflictions.

The voyage began prosperously. The following day they cast anchor in the harbor of Sidon. Here Julius, the centurion, "courteously entreated Paul," and being informed that there were Christians in the place, "gave him liberty to go unto his friends to refresh himself." This permission was greatly appreciated by the apostle, who was in feeble health.

Upon leaving Sidon, the ship encountered contrary winds; and being driven from a direct course, its progress was slow. At Myra, in the province of Lycia, the centurion found a large Alexandrian ship, bound for the coast of Italy, and to this he immediately transferred his prisoners. But the winds were still contrary, and the ship's progress was difficult. Luke writes, "When we had sailed slowly many days, and scarce were come over against Cnidus, the wind not suffering us, we sailed under Crete, over against Salmone;

and, hardly passing it, came unto a place which is called the Fair Havens."

At Fair Havens they were compelled to remain for some time, waiting for favoring winds. Winter was approaching rapidly; "sailing was now dangerous;" and those in charge of the vessel had to give up hope of reaching their destination before the season for travel by sea should be closed for the year. The only question now to be decided was, whether to remain at Fair Havens, or attempt to reach a more favorable place in which to winter.

This question was earnestly discussed, and was finally referred by the centurion to Paul, who had won the respect of both sailors and soldiers. The apostle unhesitatingly advised remaining where they were. "I perceive," he said, "that this voyage will be with hurt and much damage, not only of the lading and ship, but also of our lives." But "the master and the owner of the ship," and the majority of passengers and crew, were unwilling to accept this counsel. Because the haven in which they had anchored "was not commodious to winter in, the more part advised to depart thence also, if by any means they might attain to Phenice, and there to winter; which is an haven of Crete, and lieth toward the southwest and northwest."

The centurion decided to follow the judgment of the majority. Accordingly, "when the south wind blew softly," they set sail from Fair Havens, in the hope that they would soon reach the desired harbor. "But not long after there arose . . . a tempestuous wind;" "the ship was caught, and could not bear up into the wind."

Driven by the tempest, the vessel neared the small island of Clauda, and while under its shelter the sailors made ready for the worst. The lifeboat, their only means of escape in case the ship should founder, was in tow and liable to be dashed in pieces any moment. Their first work was to hoist this boat on board. All possible precautions were then taken to strengthen the ship and prepare it to withstand the tempest. The scant protection afforded by the little island did not avail them long, and soon they were again exposed to the full violence of the storm.

All night the tempest raged, and notwithstanding the precautions that had been taken, the vessel leaked. "The next day they lightened the ship." Night came again, but the wind did not abate. The storm-beaten ship, with its shattered mast and rent sails, was tossed hither and thither by the fury of the gale. Every moment it seemed that the groaning timbers must give way as the vessel reeled and quivered under the tempest's shock. The leak increased rapidly, and passengers and crew worked continually at the pumps. There was not a moment's rest for any on board. "The third day," writes Luke, "we cast out with our own hands the tackling of the ship. And when neither sun nor stars in many days appeared, and no small tempest lay on us, all hope that we should be saved was then taken away."

For fourteen days they drifted under a sunless and starless heaven. The apostle, though himself suffering physically, had words of hope for the darkest hour, a helping hand in every emergency. He grasped by faith the arm of Infinite Power, and his heart was stayed upon God. He had no fears for himself; he knew that God would preserve him to witness at Rome for the truth of Christ. But his heart yearned with pity for the poor souls around him, sinful, degraded, and unprepared to die. As he earnestly pleaded with God to spare their lives, it was revealed to him that his prayer was granted.

Taking advantage of a lull in the tempest, Paul stood forth on the deck and, lifting up his voice, said: "Sirs, ye should have hearkened unto me, and not have loosed from Crete, and to have gained this harm and loss. And now I exhort you to be of good cheer: for there shall be no loss of any man's life among you, but of the ship. For there stood by me this night the angel of God, whose I am, and whom I serve, saying, Fear not, Paul; thou must be brought before Caesar: and, lo, God hath given thee all them that sail with thee. Wherefore, sirs, be of good cheer: for I believe God, that it shall be even as it was told me. Howbeit we must be cast upon a certain island."

At these words, hope revived. Passengers and crew roused from their apathy. There was much yet to be done, and every effort within their power must be put forth to avert destruction.

It was on the fourteenth night of tossing on the black, heaving billows, that "about midnight" the sailors, hearing the sound of breakers, "deemed that they drew near to some country; and sounded, and found it twenty fathoms: and when they had gone a little further, they sounded again, and found it fifteen fathoms. Then fearing," Luke writes, "lest we should have fallen upon rocks, they cast four anchors out of the stern, and wished for the day."

At break of day the outlines of the stormy coast were dimly visible, but no familiar landmarks could be seen. So gloomy was the outlook that the heathen sailors, losing all courage, "were about to flee out of the ship," and feigning to make preparations for casting "anchors out of the foreship," they had already let down the lifeboat, when Paul, perceiving their base design, said to the centurion and the soldiers, "Except these abide in the ship, ye cannot be saved." The soldiers immediately "cut off the ropes of the boat, and let her fall off" into the sea.

The most critical hour was still before them. Again the apostle spoke words of encouragement, and entreated all, both sailors and passengers, to take some food, saying, "This day is the fourteenth day that ye have tarried and continued fasting, having taken nothing. Wherefore I pray you to take some meat: for this is for your health: for there shall not a hair fall from the head of any of you."

"When he had thus spoken, he took bread, and gave thanks to God in presence of them all: and when he had broken it, he began to eat." Then that worn and discouraged company of two hundred and seventy-five souls, who but for Paul would have become desperate, joined with the apostle in partaking of food. "And when they had eaten enough, they lightened the ship, and cast out the wheat into the sea."

Daylight had now fully come, but they could see nothing by which to determine their whereabouts. However, "they discovered a certain creek with a shore, into the which they were minded, if it were possible, to thrust in the ship. And when they had taken up the anchors, they committed themselves unto the sea, and loosed the rudder bands, and hoisted up the mainsail to the wind, and made toward shore. And falling into a place where two seas met, they ran the ship aground; and the fore part stuck fast, and remained unmovable, but the hinder part was broken with the violence of the waves."

Paul and the other prisoners were now threatened by a fate more terrible than shipwreck. The soldiers saw that while endeavoring to reach land it would be impossible for them to keep their prisoners in charge. Every man would have all he could do to save himself. Yet if any of the prisoners were missing, the lives of those who were responsible for them would be forfeited. Hence the soldiers desired to put all the prisoners to death. The Roman law sanctioned this cruel policy, and the plan would have been executed at once, but for him to whom all alike were under deep obligation. Julius the centurion knew that Paul had been instrumental in saving the lives of all on board, and, moreover, convinced that the Lord was with him, he feared to do him harm. He therefore "commanded that they which could swim should cast themselves first into the sea, and get to land: and the rest, some on boards, and some on broken pieces of the ship. And so it came to pass, that they escaped all safe to land." When the roll was called, not one was missing.

The shipwrecked crew were kindly received by the barbarous people of Melita. "They kindled a fire," Luke writes, "and received us everyone, because of the present rain, and because of the cold." Paul was among those who were active in ministering to the comfort of others. Having gathered "a bundle of sticks," he "laid them on the fire," when a viper came forth "out of the heat, and fastened on his hand." The bystanders were horror-stricken; and seeing by his chain that Paul was a prisoner, they said to one another, "No doubt this man is a murderer, whom, though he hath escaped the sea, yet vengeance suffereth not to live." But Paul shook off the creature into the fire and felt no harm. Knowing its venomous nature, the people looked for him to fall down at any moment in terrible agony. "But after they had looked a great while, and saw no harm come to him, they changed their minds, and said that he was a god."

During the three months that the ship's company remained at Melita, Paul and his fellow laborers improved many opportunities to preach the gospel. In a remarkable manner the Lord wrought through them. For Paul's sake the entire shipwrecked company were treated with great kindness; all their wants were supplied, and upon leaving Melita they were liberally provided with everything needful for their voyage. The chief incidents of their stay are thus briefly related by Luke:

"In the same quarters were possessions of the chief man of the island, whose name was Publius; who received us, and lodged us three days courteously. And it came to pass, that the father of Publius lay sick of a fever and of a bloody flux: to whom Paul entered in, and prayed, and laid his hands on him, and healed him. So when this was done, others also, which had diseases in the island, came, and were healed: who also honored us with many honors; and when we departed, they laded us with such things as were necessary."

43

In Rome

This chapter is based on Acts 28:11-31 and the Epistle to Philemon

With the opening of navigation, the centurion and his prisoners set out on their journey to Rome. An Alexandrian ship, the "Castor and Pollux," had wintered at Melita on her way westward, and in this the travelers embarked. Though somewhat delayed by contrary winds, the voyage was safely accomplished, and the ship cast anchor in the beautiful harbor of Puteoli, on the coast of Italy.

In this place there were a few Christians, and they entreated the apostle to remain with them for seven days, a privilege kindly granted by the centurion. Since receiving Paul's epistle to the Romans, the Christians of Italy had eagerly looked forward to a visit from the apostle. They had not thought to see him come as a prisoner, but his sufferings only endeared him to them the more. The distance from Puteoli to Rome being but a hundred and forty miles, and the seaport being in constant communication with the metropolis, the Roman Christians were informed of Paul's approach, and some of them started to meet and welcome him.

On the eighth day after landing, the centurion and his prisoners set out for Rome. Julius willingly granted the apostle every favor which it was in his power to bestow; but he could not change his condition as a prisoner, or release him from the chain that bound him to his soldier guard. It was with a heavy heart that Paul went forward to his long-expected visit to the world's metropolis. How different the circumstances from those he had anticipated! How was he, fettered and stigmatized, to proclaim the gospel? His hopes of winning many souls to the truth in Rome, seemed destined to disappointment.

At last the travelers reach Appii Forum, forty miles from Rome. As they make their way through the crowds that throng the great thoroughfare, the gray-haired old man, chained with a group of hardened-looking criminals, receives many a glance of scorn and is made the subject of many a rude, mocking jest.

Suddenly a cry of joy is heard, and a man springs from the

passing throng and falls upon the prisoner's neck, embracing him with tears and rejoicing, as a son would welcome a long-absent father. Again and again is the scene repeated as, with eyes made keen by loving expectation, many discern in the chained captive the one who at Corinth, at Philippi, at Ephesus, had spoken to them the words of life.

As the warmhearted disciples eagerly flock around their father in the gospel, the whole company is brought to a standstill. The soldiers are impatient of delay, yet they have not the heart to interrupt this happy meeting; for they, too, have learned to respect and esteem their prisoner. In that worn, pain-stricken face, the disciples see reflected the image of Christ. They assure Paul that they have not forgotten him nor ceased to love him; that they are indebted to him for the joyful hope which animates their lives and gives them peace toward God. In the ardor of their love they would bear him upon their shoulders the whole way to the city, could they but have the privilege.

Few realize the significance of those words of Luke, that when Paul saw his brethren, "he thanked God, and took courage." In the midst of the weeping, sympathizing company of believers, who were not ashamed of his bonds, the apostle praised God aloud. The cloud of sadness that had rested upon his spirit was swept away. His Christian life had been a succession of trials, sufferings, and disappointments, but in that hour he felt abundantly repaid. With firmer step and joyful heart he continued on his way. He would not complain of the past, nor fear for the future. Bonds and afflictions awaited him, he knew; but he knew also that it had been his to deliver souls from a bondage infinitely more terrible, and he rejoiced in his sufferings for Christ's sake.

At Rome the centurion Julius delivered up his prisoners to the captain of the emperor's guard. The good account which he gave of Paul, together with the letter from Festus, caused the apostle to be favorably regarded by the chief captain, and, instead of being thrown into prison, he was permitted to live in his own hired house. Although still constantly chained to a soldier, he was at liberty to receive his friends and to labor for the advancement of the cause of Christ.

Many of the Jews who had been banished from Rome some years previously, had been allowed to return, so that large numbers were now to be found there. To these, first of all, Paul determined to present the facts concerning himself and his work, before his enemies should have opportunity to embitter them against him.

Three days after his arrival in Rome, therefore, he called together their leading men and in a simple, direct manner stated why he had come to Rome as a prisoner.

"Men and brethren," he said, "though I have committed nothing against the people, or customs of our fathers, yet was I delivered prisoner from Jerusalem into the hands of the Romans. Who, when they had examined me, would have let me go, because there was no cause of death in me. But when the Jews spake against it, I was constrained to appeal unto Caesar; not that I had aught to accuse my nation of. For this cause therefore have I called for you, to see you, and to speak with you: because that for the hope of Israel I am bound with this chain."

He said nothing of the abuse which he had suffered at the hands of the Jews, or of their repeated plots to assassinate him. His words were marked with caution and kindness. He was not seeking to win personal attention or sympathy, but to defend the truth and to maintain the honor of the gospel.

In reply, his hearers stated that they had received no charges against him by letters public or private, and that none of the Jews who had come to Rome had accused him of any crime. They also expressed a strong desire to hear for themselves the reasons of his faith in Christ. "As concerning this sect," they said, "we know that everywhere it is spoken against."

Since they themselves desired it, Paul bade them set a day when he could present to them the truths of the gospel. At the time appointed, many came together, "to whom he expounded and testified the kingdom of God, persuading them concerning Jesus, both out of the law of Moses, and out of the prophets, from morning till evening." He related his own experience, and presented arguments from the Old Testament Scriptures with simplicity, sincerity, and power.

The apostle showed that religion does not consist in rites and ceremonies, creeds and theories. If it did, the natural man could understand it by investigation, as he understands worldly things. Paul taught that religion is a practical, saving energy, a principle wholly from God, a personal experience of God's renewing power upon the soul.

He showed how Moses had pointed Israel forward to Christ as that Prophet whom they were to hear; how all the prophets had testified of Him as God's great remedy for sin, the guiltless One who was to bear the sins of the guilty. He did not find fault with their observance of forms and ceremonies, but showed that while they maintained the ritual service with great exactness, they were rejecting Him who was the antitype of all that system.

Paul declared that in his unconverted state he had known Christ, not by personal acquaintance, but merely by the conception which he, in common with others, cherished concerning the character and work of the Messiah to come. He had rejected Jesus of Nazareth as an impostor because He did not fulfill this conception. But now Paul's views of Christ and His mission were far more spiritual and exalted, for he had been converted. The apostle asserted that he did not present to them Christ after the flesh. Herod had seen Christ in the days of His humanity; Annas had seen Him; Pilate and the priests and rulers had seen Him; the Roman soldiers had seen Him. But they had not seen Him with the eye of faith; they had not seen Him as the glorified Redeemer. To apprehend Christ by faith, to have a spiritual knowledge of Him, was more to be desired than a personal acquaintance with Him as He appeared on the earth. The communion with Christ which Paul now enjoyed was more intimate, more enduring, than a mere earthly and human companionship.

As Paul spoke of what he knew, and testified of what he had seen, concerning Jesus of Nazareth as the hope of Israel, those who were honestly seeking for truth were convinced. Upon some minds, at least, his words made an impression that was never effaced. But others stubbornly refused to accept the plain testimony of the Scriptures, even when presented to them by one who had the special illumination of the Holy Spirit. They could not refute his arguments, but they refused to accept his conclusions.

Many months passed by after Paul's arrival in Rome, before the Jews of Jerusalem appeared in person to present their accusations against the prisoner. They had been repeatedly thwarted in their designs; and now that Paul was to be tried before the highest tribunal of the Roman Empire, they had no desire to risk another defeat. Lysias, Felix, Festus, and Agrippa had all declared their belief in his innocence. His enemies could hope for success only in seeking by intrigue to influence the emperor in their favor. Delay would further their object, as it would afford them time to perfect and execute their plans, and so they waited for a while before preferring their charges in person against the apostle.

In the providence of God this delay resulted in the furtherance of the gospel. Through the favor of those who had Paul in charge, he was permitted to dwell in a commodious house, where he could meet freely with his friends and also present the truth daily to those who came to hear. Thus for two years he continued his labors, "preaching the kingdom of God, and teaching those things which concern the Lord Jesus Christ, will all confidence, no man forbidding him."

During this time the churches that he had established in many lands were not forgotten. Realizing the dangers that threatened the converts to the new faith, the apostle sought so far as possible to meet their needs by letters of warning and practical instruction. And from Rome he sent out consecrated workers to labor not only for these churches, but in fields that he himself had not visited. These workers, as wise shepherds, strengthened the work so well begun by Paul; and the apostle, kept informed of the condition and dangers of the churches by constant communication with them, was enabled to exercise a wise supervision over all.

Thus, while apparently cut off from active labor, Paul exerted a wider and more lasting influence than if he had been free to travel among the churches as in former years. As a prisoner of the Lord, he had a firmer hold upon the affections of his brethren; and his words, written by one under bonds for the sake of Christ, commanded greater attention and respect than they did when he was personally with them. Not until Paul was removed from them, did the believers realize how heavy were the burdens he had borne in their behalf. Heretofore they had largely excused themselves from responsibility and burden bearing because they lacked his wisdom, tact, and indomitable energy; but now, left in their inexperience to learn the lessons they had shunned, they prized his warnings, counsels, and instructions as they had not prized his personal work. And as they learned of his courage and faith during his long imprisonment they were stimulated to greater fidelity and zeal in the cause of Christ.

Among Paul's assistants at Rome were many of his former companions and fellow workers. Luke, "the beloved physician," who had attended him on the journey to Jerusalem, through the two years' imprisonment at Caesarea, and upon his perilous voyage to Rome, was with him still. Timothy also ministered to his comfort. Tychicus, "a beloved brother, and a faithful minister and fellow servant in the Lord," stood nobly by the apostle. Demas and Mark were also with him. Aristarchus and Epaphras were his "fellow prisoners." Colossians 4:7-14.

Since the earlier years of his profession of faith, Mark's Christian experience had deepened. As he had studied more closely the life and death of Christ he had obtained clearer views of the

Saviour's mission, its toils and conflicts. Reading in the scars in Christ's hands and feet the marks of His service for humanity, and the length to which self-abnegation leads to save the lost and perishing, Mark had become willing to follow the Master in the path of self-sacrifice. Now, sharing the lot of Paul the prisoner, he understood better than ever before that it is infinite gain to win Christ, infinite loss to win the world and lose the soul for whose redemption the blood of Christ was shed. In the face of severe trial and adversity, Mark continued steadfast, a wise and beloved helper of the apostle.

Demas, steadfast for a time, afterward forsook the cause of Christ. In referring to this, Paul wrote, "Demas hath forsaken me, having loved this present world." 2 Timothy 4:10. For worldly gain, Demas bartered every high and noble consideration. How short-sighted the exchange! Possessing only worldly wealth or honor, Demas was poor indeed, however much he might proudly call his own; while Mark, choosing to suffer for Christ's sake, possessed eternal riches, being accounted in heaven an heir of God and a joint heir with His Son.

Among those who gave their hearts to God through the labors of Paul in Rome was Onesimus, a pagan slave who had wronged his master, Philemon, a Christian believer in Colosse, and had escaped to Rome. In the kindness of his heart, Paul sought to relieve the poverty and distress of the wretched fugitive and then endeavored to shed the light of truth into his darkened mind. Onesimus listened to the words of life, confessed his sins, and was converted to the faith of Christ.

Onesimus endeared himself to Paul by his piety and sincerity, no less than by his tender care for the apostle's comfort, and his zeal in promoting the work of the gospel. Paul saw in him traits of character that would render him a useful helper in missionary labor, and he counseled him to return without delay to Philemon, beg his forgiveness, and plan for the future. The apostle promised to hold himself responsible for the sum of which Philemon had been robbed. Being about to dispatch Tychicus with letters to various churches in Asia Minor, he sent Onesimus with him. It was a severe test for this servant thus to deliver himself up to the master he had wronged; but he had been truly converted, and he did not turn aside from his duty.

Paul made Onesimus the bearer of a letter to Philemon, in which, with his usual tact and kindness, the apostle pleaded the cause of the repentant slave and expressed a desire to retain his services in the future. The letter began with an affectionate greeting to Philemon as a friend and fellow laborer:

"Grace to you, and peace, from God our Father and the Lord Jesus Christ. I thank my God, making mention of thee always in my prayers, hearing of thy love and faith, which thou hast toward the Lord Jesus, and toward all saints; that the communication of thy faith may become effectual by the acknowledging of every good thing which is in you in Christ Jesus." The apostle reminded Philemon that every good purpose and trait of character which he possessed was due to the grace of Christ; this alone made him different from the perverse and the sinful. The same grace could make the debased criminal a child of God and a useful laborer in the gospel.

Paul might have urged upon Philemon his duty as a Christian; but he chose rather the language of entreaty: "As Paul the aged, and now also a prisoner of Jesus Christ, I beseech thee for my son Onesimus, whom I have begotten in my bonds; which in time past was to thee unprofitable, but now profitable to thee and to me."

The apostle asked Philemon, in view of the conversion of Onesimus, to receive the repentant slave as his own child, showing him such affection that he would choose to dwell with his former master, "not now as a servant, but above a servant, a brother beloved." He expressed his desire to retain Onesimus as one who could minister to him in his bonds as Philemon himself would have done, though he did not desire his services unless Philemon should of his own accord set the slave free.

The apostle well knew the severity which masters exercised toward their slaves, and he knew also that Philemon was greatly incensed because of the conduct of his servant. He tried to write to him in a way that would arouse his deepest and tenderest feelings as a Christian. The conversion of Onesimus had made him a brother in the faith, and any punishment inflicted on this new convert would be regarded by Paul as inflicted on himself.

Paul voluntarily proposed to assume the debt of Onesimus in order that the guilty one might be spared the disgrace of punishment, and might again enjoy the privileges he had forfeited. "If thou count me therefore a partner," he wrote to Philemon, "receive him as myself. If he hath wronged thee, or oweth thee aught, put that on mine account; I Paul have written it with mine own hand, I will repay it."

How fitting an illustration of the love of Christ for the repentant sinner! The servant who had defrauded his master had nothing with which to make restitution. The sinner who has robbed God of years of service has no means of canceling the debt. Jesus interposes between the sinner and God, saying, I will pay the debt. Let the sinner be spared; I will suffer in his stead.

After offering to assume the debt of Onesimus, Paul reminded Philemon how greatly he himself was indebted to the apostle. He owed him his own self, since God had made Paul the instrument of his conversion. Then, in a tender, earnest appeal, he besought Philemon that as he had by his liberalities refreshed the saints, so he would refresh the spirit of the apostle by granting him this cause of rejoicing. "Having confidence in thy obedience," he added, "I wrote unto thee, knowing that thou wilt also do more than I say."

Paul's letter to Philemon shows the influence of the gospel upon the relation between master and servant. Slave-holding was an established institution throughout the Roman Empire, and both masters and slaves were found in most of the churches for which Paul labored. In the cities, where slaves often greatly outnumbered the free population, laws of terrible severity were regarded as necessary to keep them in subjection. A wealthy Roman often owned hundreds of slaves, of every rank, of every nation, and of every accomplishment. With full control over the souls and bodies of these helpless beings, he could inflict upon them any suffering he chose. If one of them in retaliation or self-defense ventured to raise a hand against his owner, the whole family of the offender might be inhumanly sacrificed. The slightest mistake, accident, or carelessness was often punished without mercy.

Some masters, more humane than others, were more indulgent toward their servants; but the vast majority of the wealthy and noble, given up without restraint to the indulgence of lust, passion, and appetite, made their slaves the wretched victims of caprice and tyranny. The tendency of the whole system was hopelessly degrading.

It was not the apostle's work to overturn arbitrarily or suddenly the established order of society. To attempt this would be to prevent the success of the gospel. But he taught principles which struck at the very foundation of slavery and which, if carried into effect, would surely undermine the whole system. "Where the Spirit of the Lord is, there is liberty," he declared. 2 Corinthians 3:17. When converted, the slave became a member of the body of Christ, and as such was to be loved and treated as a brother, a fellow heir with his master to the blessings of God and the privileges of the gospel.

On the other hand, servants were to perform their duties, "not with eyeservice, as men pleasers; but as the servants of Christ, doing the will of God from the heart." Ephesians 6:6.

Christianity makes a strong bond of union between master and slave, king and subject, the gospel minister and the degraded sinner who has found in Christ cleansing from sin. They have been washed in the same blood, quickened by the same Spirit; and they are made one in Christ Jesus.

44

Caesar's Household

The gospel has ever achieved its greatest success among the humbler classes. "Not many wise men after the flesh, not many mighty, not many noble, are called." 1 Corinthians 1:26. It could not be expected that Paul, a poor and friendless prisoner, would be able to gain the attention of the wealthy and titled classes of Roman citizens. To them vice presented all its glittering allurements and held them willing captives. But from among the toilworn, wantstricken victims of their oppression, even from among the poor slaves, many gladly listened to the words of Paul and in the faith of Christ found a hope and peace that cheered them under the hardships of their lot.

Yet while the apostle's work began with the humble and the lowly, its influence extended until it reached the very palace of the emperor.

Rome was at this time the metropolis of the world. The haughty Caesars were giving laws to nearly every nation upon the earth. King and courtier were either ignorant of the humble Nazarene or regarded Him with hatred and derision. And yet in less than two years the gospel found its way from the prisoner's lowly home into the imperial halls. Paul is in bonds as an evildoer; but "the word of God is not bound." 2 Timothy 2:9.

In former years the apostle had publicly proclaimed the faith of Christ with winning power, and by signs and miracles he had given unmistakable evidence of its divine character. With noble firmness he had risen up before the sages of Greece and by his knowledge and eloquence had put to silence the arguments of proud philosophy. With undaunted courage he had stood before kings and governors, and reasoned of righteousness, temperance, and judgment to come, until the haughty rulers trembled as if already beholding the terrors of the day of God.

No such opportunities were now granted the apostle, confined as he was to his own dwelling, and able to proclaim the truth to those only who sought him there. He had not, like Moses and Aaron, a divine command to go before the profligate king and in the name of the great I AM rebuke his cruelty and oppression. Yet it was at this very time, when its chief advocate was apparently cut off from public labor, that a great victory was won for the gospel; for from the very household of the king, members were added to the church.

Nowhere could there exist an atmosphere more uncongenial to Christianity than in the Roman court. Nero seemed to have obliterated from his soul the last trace of the divine, and even of the human, and to bear the impress of Satan. His attendants and courtiers were in general of the same character as himself—fierce, debased, and corrupt. To all appearance it would be impossible for Christianity to gain a foothold in the court and palace of Nero.

Yet in this case, as in so many others, was proved the truth of Paul's assertion that the weapons of his warfare were "mighty through God to the pulling down of strongholds," 2 Corinthians 10:4. Even in Nero's household, trophies of the cross were won. From the vile attendants of a viler king were gained converts who became sons of God. These were not Christians secretly, but openly. They were not ashamed of their faith.

And by what means was an entrance achieved and a firm footing gained for Christianity where even its admission seemed impossible? In his epistle to the Philippians, Paul ascribed to his own imprisonment his success in winning converts to the faith from Nero's household. Fearful lest it might be thought that his afflictions had impeded the progress of the gospel, he assured them: "I would ye should understand, brethren, that the things which happened unto me have fallen out rather unto the furtherance of the gospel." Philippians 1:12.

When the Christian churches first learned that Paul was to visit Rome, they looked forward to a signal triumph of the gospel in that city. Paul had borne the truth to many lands; he had proclaimed it in great cities. Might not this champion of the faith succeed in winning souls to Christ even in the metropolis of the world? But their hopes were crushed by the tidings that Paul had gone to Rome as a prisoner. They had confidently hoped to see the gospel, once established at this great center, extend rapidly to all nations and become a prevailing power in the earth. How great their disappointment! Human expectations had failed, but not the purpose of God.

Not by Paul's sermon's, but by his bonds, was the attention of the court attracted to Christianity. It was as a captive that he broke from so many souls the bonds that held them in the slavery of sin. Nor was this all. He declared: "Many of the brethren in the Lord, waxing confident by my bonds, are much more bold to speak the word without fear." Philippians 1:14.

Paul's patience and cheerfulness during his long and unjust

imprisonment, his courage and faith, were a continual sermon. His spirit, so unlike the spirit of the world, bore witness that a power higher than that of earth was abiding with him. And by his example, Christians were impelled to greater energy as advocates of the cause from the public labors of which Paul had been withdrawn. In these ways were the apostle's bonds influential, so that when his power and usefulness seemed cut off, and to all appearance he could do the least, then it was that he gathered sheaves for Christ in fields from which he seemed wholly excluded.

Before the close of that two years' imprisonment, Paul was able to say, "My bonds in Christ are manifest in all the palace, and in all other places," and among those who sent greetings to the Philippians he mentions chiefly them "that are of Caesar's household." Verse 13; 4:22.

Patience as well as courage has its victories. By meekness under trial, no less than by boldness in enterprise, souls may be won to Christ. The Christian who manifests patience and cheerfulness under bereavement and suffering, who meets even death itself with the peace and calmness of an unwavering faith, may accomplish for the gospel more than he could have effected by a long life of faithful labor. Often when the servant of God is withdrawn from active duty, the mysterious providence which our shortsighted vision would lament is designed by God to accomplish a work that otherwise would never have been done.

Let not the follower of Christ think, when he is no longer able to labor openly and actively for God and His truth, that he has no service to render, no reward to secure. Christ's true witnesses are never laid aside. In health and sickness, in life and death, God uses them still. When through Satan's malice the servants of Christ have been persecuted, their active labors hindered, when they have been cast into prison, or dragged to the scaffold or to the stake, it was that truth might gain a greater triumph. As these faithful ones sealed their testimony with their blood, souls hitherto in doubt and uncertainty were convinced of the faith of Christ and took their stand courageously for Him. From the ashes of the martyrs has sprung an abundant harvest for God.

The zeal and fidelity of Paul and his fellow workers, no less than the faith and obedience of these converts to Christianity, under circumstances so forbidding, rebuke slothfulness and lack of faith in the minister of Christ. The apostle and his associate workers might have argued that it would be vain to call to repentance and faith in Christ the servants of Nero, subjected, as they were, to fierce temptations, surrounded by formidable hindrances, and exposed to bitter opposition. Even should they be convinced of the truth, how could they render obedience? But Paul did not reason thus; in faith he presented the gospel to these souls, and among those who heard were some who decided to obey at any cost. Notwithstanding obstacles and dangers, they would accept the light, and trust God to help them let their light shine forth to others.

Not only were converts won to the truth in Caesar's household, but after their conversion they remained in that household. They did not feel at liberty to abandon their post of duty because their surroundings were no longer congenial. The truth had found them there, and there they remained, by their changed life and character testifying to the transforming power of the new faith.

Are any tempted to make their circumstances an excuse for failing to witness for Christ? Let them consider the situation of the disciples in Caesar's household—the depravity of the emperor, the profligacy of the court. We can hardly imagine circumstances more unfavorable to a religious life, and entailing greater sacrifice or opposition, than those in which these converts found themselves. Yet amidst difficulties and dangers they maintained their fidelity. Because of obstacles that seem insurmountable, the Christian may seek to excuse himself from obeying the truth as it is in Jesus; but he can offer no excuse that will bear investigation. Could he do this he would prove God unjust in that He had made for His children conditions of salvation with which they could not comply.

He whose heart is fixed to serve God will find opportunity to witness for Him. Difficulties will be powerless to hinder him who is determined to seek first the kingdom of God and His righteousness. In the strength gained by prayer and a study of the word, he will seek virtue and forsake vice. Looking to Jesus, the Author and Finisher of the faith, who endured the contradiction of sinners against Himself, the believer will willingly brave contempt and derision. And help and grace sufficient for every circumstances are promised by Him whose word is truth. His everlasting arms encircle the soul that turns to Him for aid. In His care we may rest safely, saying, "What time I am afraid, I will trust in Thee." Psalm 56:3. To all who put their trust in Him, God will fulfill His promise.

By His own example the Saviour has shown that His followers can be in the world and yet not of the world. He came not to partake of its delusive pleasures, to be swayed by its customs, and to follow its practices, but to do His Father's will, to seek and save the lost. With this object before him the Christian may stand uncontaminated in any surroundings. Whatever his station or circumstances, exalted or humble, he will manifest the power of true religion in the faithful performance of duty.

Not in freedom from trial, but in the midst of it, is Christian character developed. Exposure to rebuffs and opposition leads the follower of Christ to greater watchfulness and more earnest prayer to the mighty Helper. Severe trial endured by the grace of God develops patience, vigilance, fortitude, and a deep and abiding trust in God. It is the triumph of the Christian faith that it enables its followers to suffer and be strong; to submit, and thus to conquer; to be killed all the day long, and yet to live; to bear the cross, and thus to win the crown of glory.

45

Written From Rome

This chapter is based on the Epistles to the Colossians and the Philippians

The apostle Paul early in his Christian experience was given special opportunities to learn the will of God concerning the followers of Jesus. He was "caught up to the third heaven," "into paradise, and heard unspeakable words, which it is not lawful for a man to utter." He himself acknowledged that many "visions and revelations" had been given him "of the Lord." His understanding of the principles of gospel truth was equal to that of "the very chiefest apostles." 2 Corinthians 12:2, 4, 1, 11. He had a clear, full comprehension of "the breadth, and length, and depth, and height" of "the love of Christ, which passeth knowledge." Ephesians 3:18, 19.

Paul could not tell all that he had seen in vision; for among his hearers were some who would have misapplied his words. But that which was revealed to him enabled him to labor as a leader and a wise teacher, and also molded the messages that he in later years sent to the churches. The impression that he received when in vision was ever with him, enabling him to give a correct representation of Christian character. By word of mouth and by letter he bore a message that ever since has brought help and strength to the church of God. To believers today this message speaks plainly of the dangers that will threaten the church, and the false doctrines that they will have to meet.

The apostle's desire for those to whom he addressed his letters of counsel and admonition was that they should "be no more children, tossed to and fro, and carried about with every wind of doctrine;" but that they should all come into "the unity of the faith, and of the knowledge of the Son of God, unto a perfect man, unto the measure of the stature of the fullness of Christ." He entreated those who were followers of Jesus in heathen communities not to walk "as other Gentiles walk, in the vanity of their mind, having the understanding darkened, being alienated from the life of God . . . because of the blindness of their heart," but "circumspectly, not as fools, but as wise, redeeming the time." Ephesians 4:14, 13, 17,

18; 5:15, 16. He encouraged the believers to look forward to the time when Christ, who "loved the church, and gave Himself for it," would "present it to Himself a glorious church, not having spot, or wrinkle, or any such thing"—a church "holy and without blemish." Ephesians 5:25, 27.

These messages, written with a power not of man but of God, contain lessons which should be studied by all and which may with profit be often repeated. In them practical godliness is outlined, principles are laid down that should be followed in every church, and the way that leads to life eternal is made plain.

In his letter to "the saints and faithful brethren in Christ which are at Colosse," written while he was a prisoner in Rome, Paul makes mention of his joy over their steadfastness in the faith, tidings of which had been brought him by Epaphras, who, the apostle wrote, "declared unto us your love in the Spirit. For this cause," he continued, "we also, since the day we heard it, do not cease to pray for you, and to desire that ye might be filled with the knowledge of His will in all wisdom and spiritual understanding; that ye might walk worthy of the Lord unto all pleasing, being fruitful in every good work, and increasing in the knowledge of God; strengthened with all might, according to His glorious power, unto all patience and long-suffering with joyfulness."

Thus Paul put into words his desire for the Colossian believers. How high the ideal that these words hold before the follower of Christ! They show the wonderful possibilities of the Christian life and make it plain that there is no limit to the blessings that the children of God may receive. Constantly increasing in a knowledge of God, they may go on from strength to strength, from height to height in Christian experience, until by "His glorious power" they are made "meet to be partakers of the inheritance of the saints in light."

The apostle exalted Christ before his brethren as the One by whom God had created all things and by whom He had wrought out their redemption. He declared that the hand that sustains the worlds in space, and holds in their orderly arrangements and tireless activity all things throughout the universe of God, is the hand that was nailed to the cross for them. "By Him were all things created," Paul wrote, "that are in heaven, and that are in earth, visible and invisible, whether they be thrones, or dominions, or principalities, or powers: all things were created by Him, and for Him: and He is before all things, and by Him all things consist." "And you, that were sometime alienated and enemies in your mind by wicked works, yet now hath He reconciled in the body of His flesh through death, to present you holy and unblamable and unreprovable in His sight."

The Son of God stooped to uplift the fallen. For this He left the sinless worlds on high, the ninety and nine that loved Him, and came to this earth to be "wounded for our transgressions" and "bruised for our iniquities." Isaiah 53:5. He was in all things made like unto His brethren. He became flesh, even as we are. He knew what it meant to be hungry and thirsty and weary. He was sustained by food and refreshed by sleep. He was a stranger and a sojourner on the earth—in the world, but not of the world; tempted and tried as men and women of today are tempted and tried, yet living a life free from sin. Tender, compassionate, sympathetic, ever considerate of others, He represented the character of God. "The Word was made flesh, and dwelt among us, . . . full of grace and truth." John 1:14.

Surrounded by the practices and influences of heathenism, the Colossian believers were in danger of being drawn away from the simplicity of the gospel, and Paul, in warning them against this, pointed them to Christ as the only safe guide. "I would that ye knew," he wrote, "what great conflict I have for you, and for them at Laodicea, and for as many as have not seen my face in the flesh; that their hearts might be comforted, being knit together in love, and unto all riches of the full assurance of understanding, to the acknowledgment of the mystery of God, and of the Father, and of Christ; in whom are hid all the treasures of wisdom and knowledge.

"And this I say, lest any man should beguile you with enticing words. . . . As ye have therefore received Christ Jesus the Lord, so walk yet in Him: rooted and built up in Him, and stablished in the faith, as ye have been taught, abounding therein with thanksgiving. Beware lest any man spoil you through philosophy and vain deceit, after the tradition of men, after the rudiments of the world, and not after Christ. For in Him dwelleth all the fullness of the Godhead bodily. And ye are complete in Him, which is the head of all principality and power."

Christ had foretold that deceivers would arise, through whose influence "iniquity" should "abound," and "the love of many" should "wax cold." Matthew 24:12. He had warned the disciples that the church would be in more danger from this evil than from the persecution of her enemies. Again and again Paul warned the believers against these false teachers. This peril, above all others, they must guard against; for by receiving false teachers, they would open the door to errors by which the enemy would dim the spiritual perceptions and shake the confidence of those newly come to the faith of the gospel. Christ was the standard by which they were to test the doctrines presented. All that was not in harmony with His teachings they were to reject. Christ crucified for sin, Christ risen from the dead, Christ ascended on high—this was the science of salvation that they were to learn and teach.

The warnings of the word of God regarding the perils surrounding the Christian church belong to us today. As in the days of the apostles men tried by tradition and philosophy to destroy faith in the Scriptures, so today, by the pleasing sentiments of higher criticism, evolution, spiritualism, theosophy, and pantheism, the enemy of righteousness is seeking to lead souls into forbidden paths. To many the Bible is as a lamp without oil, because they have turned their minds into channels of speculative belief that bring misunderstanding and confusion. The work of higher criticism, in dissecting, conjecturing, reconstructing, is destroying faith in the Bible as a divine revelation. It is robbing God's word of power to control, uplift, and inspire human lives. By spiritualism, multitudes are taught to believe that desire is the highest law, that license is liberty, and that man is accountable only to himself.

The follower of Christ will meet with the "enticing words" against which the apostle warned the Colossian believers. He will meet with spiritualistic interpretations of the Scriptures, but he is not to accept them. His voice is to be heard in clear affirmation of the eternal truths of the Scriptures. Keeping his eyes fixed on Christ, he is to move steadily forward in the path marked out, discarding all ideas that are not in harmony with His teaching. The truth of God is to be the subject for his contemplation and meditation. He is to regard the Bible as the voice of God speaking directly to him. Thus he will find the wisdom which is divine.

The knowledge of God as revealed in Christ is the knowledge that all who are saved must have. This is the knowledge that works transformation of character. Received into the life, it will re-create the soul in the image of Christ. This is the knowledge that God invites His children to receive, beside which all else is vanity and nothingness.

In every generation and in every land the true foundation for character building has been the same—the principles contained in the word of God. The only safe and sure rule is to do what God says. "The statutes of the Lord are right," and "he that doeth these things shall never be moved." Psalms 19:8; 15:5. It was with the word of God that the apostles met the false theories of their day, saying, "Other foundation can no man lay than that is laid." 1 Corinthians 3:11.

At the time of their conversion and baptism the Colossian believers pledged themselves to put away beliefs and practices that had hitherto been a part of their lives, and to be true to their allegiance to Christ. In his letter, Paul reminded them of this, and entreated them not to forget that in order to keep their pledge they must put forth constant effort against the evils that would seek for mastery over them. "If ye then be risen with Christ," he said, "seek those things which are above, where Christ sitteth on the right hand of God. Set your affection on things above, not on things on the earth. For ye are dead, and your life is hid with Christ in God."

"If any man be in Christ, he is a new creature: old things are passed away; behold, all things are become new." 2 Corinthians 5:17. Through the power of Christ, men and women have broken the chains of sinful habit. They have renounced selfishness. The profane have become reverent, the drunken sober, the profligate pure. Souls that have borne the likeness of Satan have become transformed into the image of God. This change is in itself the miracle of miracles. A change wrought by the Word, it is one of the deepest mysteries of the Word. We cannot understand it; we can only believe, as declared by the Scriptures, it is "Christ in you, the hope of glory."

When the Spirit of God controls mind and heart, the converted soul breaks forth into a new song; for he realizes that in his experience the promise of God has been fulfilled, that his transgression has been forgiven, his sin covered. He has exercised repentance toward God for the violation of the divine law, and faith toward Christ, who died for man's justification. "Being justified by faith," he has "peace with God through our Lord Jesus Christ." Romans 5:1.

But because this experience is his, the Christian is not therefore to fold his hands, content with that which has been accomplished for him. He who has determined to enter the spiritual kingdom will find that all the powers and passions of unregenerate nature, backed by the forces of the kingdom of darkness, are arrayed against him. Each day he must renew his consecration, each day do battle with evil. Old habits, hereditary tendencies to wrong, will strive for the mastery, and against these he is to be ever on guard, striving in Christ's strength for victory.

"Mortify therefore your members which are upon the earth,"

Paul wrote to the Colossians; "in the which ye also walked some-time, when ye lived in them. But now ye also put off all these: anger, wrath, malice, blasphemy, filthy communication out of your mouth. . . . Put on therefore, as the elect of God, holy and beloved, bowels of mercies, kindness, humbleness of mind, meekness, long-suffering; forbearing one another, and forgiving one another, if any man have a quarrel against any: even as Christ forgave you, so also do ye. And above all these things put on charity, which is the bond of perfectness. And let the peace of God rule in your hearts, to the which also ye are called in one body; and be ye thankful."

The letter to the Colossians is filled with lessons of highest value to all who are engaged in the service of Christ, lessons that show the singleness of purpose and the loftiness of aim which will be seen in the life of him who rightly represents the Saviour. Renouncing all that would hinder him from making progress in the upward way or that would turn the feet of another from the narrow path, the believer will reveal in his daily life mercy, kindness, humility, meekness, forbearance, and the love of Christ.

The power of a higher, purer, nobler life is our great need. The world has too much of our thought, and the kingdom of heaven too little.

In his efforts to reach God's ideal for him, the Christian is to despair of nothing. Moral and spiritual perfection, through the grace and power of Christ, is promised to all. Jesus is the source of power, the fountain of life. He brings us to His word, and from the tree of life presents to us leaves for the healing of sin-sick souls. He leads us to the more throne of God, and puts into our mouth a prayer through which we are brought into close contact with Himself. In our behalf He sets in operation the all-powerful agencies of heaven. At every step we touch His living power.

God fixes no limit to the advancement of those who desire to be "filled with the knowledge of His will in all wisdom and spiritual understanding." Through prayer, through watchfulness, through growth in knowledge and understanding, they are to be " strength-ened with all might, according to His glorious power." Thus they are prepared to work for others. It is the Saviour's purpose that human beings, purified and sanctified, shall be His helping hand. For this great privilege let us give thanks to Him who "hath made us meet to be partakers of the inheritance of the saints in light: who hath delivered us from the power of darkness, and hath translated us into the kingdom of His dear Son."

Paul's letter to the Philippians, like the one to the Colossians, was written while he was a prisoner at Rome. The church at Philippi had sent gifts to Paul by the hand of Epaphroditus, whom Paul calls "my brother, and companion in labor, and fellow soldier, but your messenger, and he that ministered to my wants." While in Rome, Epaphroditus was sick, "nigh unto death: but God had mercy on him," Paul wrote, "and not on him only, but on me also, lest I should have sorrow upon sorrow." Hearing of the sickness of Epaphroditus, the believers at Philippi were filled with anxiety regarding him, and he decided to return to them. "He longed after you all," Paul wrote, "and was full of heaviness, because that ye had heard that he had been sick. . . . I sent him therefore the more carefully, that, when ye see him again, ye may rejoice, and that I may be the less sorrowful. Receive him therefore in the Lord with all gladness; and hold such in reputation: because for the work of Christ he was nigh unto death, not regarding his life, to supply your lack of service toward me."

By Epaphroditus, Paul sent the Philippian believers a letter, in which he thanked them for their gifts to him. Of all the churches, that of Philippi had been the most liberal in supplying Paul's wants. "Now ye Philippians know also," the apostle said in his letter, "that in the beginning of the gospel, when I departed from Macedonia, no church communicated with me as concerning giving and receiving, but ye only. For even in Thessalonica ye sent once and again unto my necessity. Not because I desire a gift: but I desire fruit that may abound to your account. But I have all, and abound: I am full, having received of Epaphroditus the things which were sent from you, an odor of a sweet smell, a sacrifice acceptable, well-pleasing to God."

"Grace be unto you, and peace, from God our Father, and from the Lord Jesus Christ. I thank my God upon every remembrance of you, always in every prayer of mine for you all making request with joy, for your fellowship in the gospel from the first day until now; being confident of this very thing, that He which hath begun a good work in you will perform it until the day of Jesus Christ: even as it is meet for me to think this of you all, because I have you in my heart; inasmuch as both in my bonds, and in the defense and confirmation of the gospel, ye all are partakers of my grace. For God is my record, how greatly I long after you all. . . . And this I pray, that your love may abound yet more and more in knowledge and in all judgment; that ye may approve things that are excellent; that ye may be sincere and without offense till the day of Christ;

being filled with the fruits of righteousness, which are by Jesus Christ, unto the glory and praise of God."

The grace of God sustained Paul in his imprisonment, enabling him to rejoice in tribulation. With faith and assurance he wrote to his Philippian brethren that his imprisonment had resulted in the furtherance of the gospel. "I would ye should understand, brethren," he declared, "that the things which happened unto me have fallen out rather unto the furtherance of the gospel; so that my bonds in Christ are manifest in all the palace, and in all other places; and many of the brethren in the Lord, waxing confident by my bonds, are much more bold to speak the word without fear."

There is a lesson for us in this experience of Paul's, for it reveals God's way of working. The Lord can bring victory out of that which may seem to us discomfiture and defeat. We are in danger of forgetting God, of looking at the things which are seen, instead of beholding by the eye of faith the things which are unseen. When misfortune or calamity comes, we are ready to charge God with neglect or cruelty. If He sees fit to cut off our usefulness in some line, we mourn, not stopping to think that thus God may be working for our good. We need to learn that chastisement is a part of His great plan and that under the rod of affliction the Christian may sometimes do more for the Master than when engaged in active service.

As their example in the Christian life, Paul pointed the Philippians to Christ, who, "being in the form of God, thought it not robbery to be equal with God: but made Himself of no reputation, and took upon Him the form of a servant, and was made in the likeness of men: and being found in a fashion as a man, He humbled Himself, and became obedient unto death, even the death of the cross."

"Wherefore, my beloved," he continued, "as ye have always obeyed, not as in my presence only, but now much more in my absence, work out your own salvation with fear and trembling. For it is God which worketh in you both to will and to do His good pleasure. Do all things without murmurings and disputings: that ye may be blameless and harmless, the sons of God, without rebuke, in the midst of a crooked and perverse nation, among whom ye shine as lights in the world; holding forth the word of life; that I may rejoice in the day of Christ, that I have not run in vain, neither labored in vain."

These words were recorded for the help of every striving soul. Paul holds up the standard of perfection and shows how it may be reached. "Work out your own salvation," he says, "for it is God which worketh in you."

The work of gaining salvation is one of copartnership, a joint operation. There is to be co-operation between God and the repentant sinner. This is necessary for the formation of right principles in the character. Man is to make earnest efforts to overcome that which hinders him from attaining to perfection. But he is wholly dependent upon God for success. Human effort of itself is not sufficient. Without the aid of divine power it avails nothing. God works and man works. Resistance of temptation must come from man, who must draw his power from God. On the one side there is infinite wisdom, compassion, and power; on the other, weakness, sinfulness, absolute helplessness.

God wishes us to have the mastery over ourselves. But He cannot help us without our consent and co-operation. The divine Spirit works through the powers and faculties given to man. Of ourselves, we are not able to bring the purposes and desires and inclinations into harmony with the will of God; but if we are "willing to be made willing," the Saviour will accomplish this for us, "Casting down imaginations, and every high thing that exalteth itself against the knowledge of God, and bringing into captivity every thought to the obedience of Christ." 2 Corinthians 10:5.

He who would build up a strong, symmetrical character, he who would be a well-balanced Christian, must give all and do all for Christ; for the Redeemer will not accept divided service. Daily he must learn the meaning of self-surrender. He must study the word of God, learning its meaning and obeying its precepts. Thus he may reach the standard of Christian excellence. Day by day God works with him, perfecting the character that is to stand in the time of final test. And day by day the believer is working out before men and angels a sublime experiment, showing what the gospel can do for fallen human beings.

"I count not myself to have apprehended," Paul wrote; "but this one thing I do, forgetting those things which are behind, and reaching forth unto those things which are before, I press toward the mark for the prize of the high calling of God in Christ Jesus."

Paul did many things. From the time that he gave his allegiance to Christ, his life was filled with untiring service. From city to city, from country to country, he journeyed, telling the story of the cross, winning converts to the gospel, and establishing churches. For these churches he had a constant care, and he wrote many letters of instruction to them. At times he worked at his trade to earn his daily bread. But in all the busy activities of his life, Paul never lost sight of one great purpose—to press toward the prize of his calling. One aim he kept steadfastly before him—to be faithful to the One who at the gate of Damascus had revealed Himself to him. From this aim nothing had power to turn him aside. To exalt the cross of Calvary—this was the all-absorbing motive that inspired his words and acts.

The great purpose that constrained Paul to press forward in the face of hardship and difficulty should lead every Christian worker to consecrate himself wholly to God's service. Worldly attractions will be presented to draw his attentions from the Saviour, but he is to press on toward the goal, showing to the world, to angels, and to men that the hope of seeing the face of God is worth all the effort and sacrifice that the attainment of this hope demands.

Though he was a prisoner, Paul was not discouraged. Instead, a note of triumph rings through the letters that he wrote from Rome to the churches. "Rejoice in the Lord alway," he wrote to the Philippians, "and again I say, Rejoice. . . . Be careful for nothing; but in everything by prayer and supplication with thanksgiving let your requests be made known unto God. And the peace of God, which passeth all understanding, shall keep your hearts and minds through Christ Jesus. Finally, brethren, whatsoever things are true, whatsoever things are honest, whatsoever things are just, whatsoever things are pure, whatsoever things are lovely, whatsoever things are of good report; if there be any virtue, and if there be any praise, think on these things."

"My God shall supply all your need according to His riches in glory by Christ Jesus. . . . The grace of our Lord Jesus Christ be with you all."

46

At Liberty

While Paul's labors in Rome were being blessed to the conversion of many souls and the strengthening and encouragement of the believers, clouds were gathering that threatened not only his own safety, but also the prosperity of the church. On his arrival in Rome he had been placed in charge of the captain of the imperial guards, a man of justice and integrity, by whose clemency he was left comparatively free to pursue the work of the gospel. But before the close of the two years' imprisonment, this man was replaced by an official from whom the apostle could expect no special favor.

The Jews were now more active than ever in their efforts against Paul, and they found an able helper in the profligate woman whom Nero had made his second wife, and who, being a Jewish proselyte, lent all her influence to aid their murderous designs against the champion of Christianity.

Paul could hope for little justice from the Caesar to whom he had appealed. Nero was more debased in morals, more frivolous in character, and at the same time capable of more atrocious cruelty, than any ruler who had preceded him. The reins of government could not have been entrusted to a more despotic ruler. The first year of his reign had been marked by the poisoning of his young stepbrother, the rightful heir to the throne. From one depth of vice and crime to another, Nero had descended, until he had murdered his own mother, and then his wife. There was no atrocity which he would not perpetrate, no vile act to which he would not stoop. In every noble mind he inspired only abhorrence and contempt.

The details of the iniquity practiced in his court are too degrading, too horrible, for description. His abandoned wickedness created disgust and loathing, even in many who were forced to share his crimes. They were in constant fear as to what enormities he would suggest next. Yet even such crimes as Nero's did not shake the allegiance of his subjects. He was acknowledged as the absolute ruler of the whole civilized world. More than this, he was made the recipient of divine honors and was worshiped as a god.

From the viewpoint of human judgment, Paul's condemnation before such a judge was certain. But the apostle felt that so long as he was loyal to God, he had nothing to fear. The One who in the past had been his protector could shield him still from the malice of the Jews and from the power of Caesar.

And God did shield His servant. At Paul's examination the charges against him were not sustained, and, contrary to the general expectation, and with a regard for justice wholly at variance with his character, Nero declared the prisoner guiltless. Paul's bonds were removed; he was again a free man.

Had his trial been longer deferred, or had he from any cause been detained in Rome until the following year, he would doubtless have perished in the persecution which then took place. During Paul's imprisonment the converts to Christianity had become so numerous as to attract the attention and arouse the enmity of the authorities. The anger of the emperor was especially excited by the conversion of members of his own household, and he soon found a pretext to make the Christians the objects of his merciless cruelty.

About this time a terrible fire occurred in Rome by which nearly one half of the city was burned. Nero himself, it was rumored, had caused the flames to be kindled, but to avert suspicion he made a pretense of great generosity by assisting the homeless and destitute. He was, however, accused of the crime. The people were excited and enraged, and in order to clear himself, and also to rid the city of a class whom he feared and hated, Nero turned the accusation upon the Christians. His device succeeded, and thousands of the followers of Christ—men, women, and children— were cruelly put to death.

From this terrible persecution Paul was spared, for soon after his release he had left Rome. This last interval of freedom he diligently improved in laboring among the churches. He sought to establish a firmer union between the Greek and the Eastern churches and to fortify the minds of the believers against the false doctrines that were creeping in to corrupt the faith.

The trials and anxieties that Paul had endured had preyed upon his physical powers. The infirmities of age were upon him. He felt that he was now doing his last work, and, as the time of his labor grew shorter, his efforts became more intense. There seemed to be no limit to his zeal. Resolute in purpose, prompt in action, strong in faith, he journeyed from church to church, in many lands, and sought by every means within his power to strengthen the hands of the believers, that they might do faithful work in winning souls to Jesus, and that in the trying times upon which they were even then entering, they might remain steadfast to the gospel, bearing faithful witness for Christ.

47

The Final Arrest

Paul's work among the churches after his acquittal at Rome, could not escape the observation of his enemies. Since the beginning of the persecution under Nero the Christians had everywhere been a proscribed sect. After a time the unbelieving Jews conceived the idea of fastening upon Paul the crime of instigating the burning of Rome. Not one of them thought for a moment that he was guilty; but they knew that such a charge, made with the faintest show of plausibility, would seal his doom. Through their efforts, Paul was again arrested, and hurried away to his final imprisonment.

On his second voyage to Rome, Paul was accompanied by several of his former companions; others earnestly desired to share his lot, but he refused to permit them thus to imperil their lives. The prospect before him was far less favorable than at the time of his former imprisonment. The persecution under Nero had greatly lessened the number of Christians in Rome. Thousands had been martyred for their faith, many had left the city, and those who remained were greatly depressed and intimidated.

Upon his arrival at Rome, Paul was placed in a gloomy dungeon, there to remain until his course should be finished. Accused of instigating one of the basest and most terrible of crimes against the city and the nation, he was the object of universal execration.

The few friends who had shared the burdens of the apostle, now began to leave him, some by desertion, and others on missions to the various churches. Phygellus and Hermogenes were the first to go. Then Demas, dismayed by the thickening clouds of difficulty and danger, forsook the persecuted apostle. Crescens was sent by Paul to the churches of Galatia, Titus to Dalmatia, Tychicus to Ephesus. Writing to Timothy of this experience, Paul said, "Only Luke is with me." 2 Timothy 4:11. Never had the apostle needed the ministrations of his brethren as now, enfeebled as he was by age, toil, and infirmities, and confined in the damp, dark vaults of a Roman prison. The services of Luke, the beloved disciple and faithful friend, were a great comfort to Paul and enabled him to communicate with his brethren and the world without.

In this trying time Paul's heart was cheered by frequent visits from Onesiphorus. This warmhearted Ephesian did all in his power to lighten the burden of the apostle's imprisonment. His beloved teacher was in bonds for the truth's sake, while he himself went free, and he spared himself no effort to make Paul's lot more bearable.

In the last letter that the apostle ever wrote, he speaks thus of this faithful disciple: "The Lord give mercy unto the house of Onesiphorus; for he oft refreshed me, and was not ashamed of my chain; but, when he was in Rome, he sought me out very diligently, and found me. The Lord grant unto him that he may find mercy of the Lord in that day." 2 Timothy I:16-18.

The desire for love and sympathy is implanted in the heart by God Himself. Christ, in His hour of agony in Gethsemane, longed for the sympathy of His disciples. And Paul, though apparently indifferent to hardship and suffering, yearned for sympathy and companionship. The visit of Onesiphorus, testifying to his fidelity at a time of loneliness and desertion, brought gladness and cheer to one who had spent his life in service for others.

48

Paul Before Nero

When Paul was summoned to appear before the emperor Nero for trial, it was with the near prospect of certain death. The serious nature of the crime charged against him, and the prevailing animosity toward Christians, left little ground for hope of a favorable issue.

Among the Greeks and Romans it was customary to allow an accused person the privilege of employing an advocate to plead in his behalf before courts of justice. By force of argument, by impassioned eloquence, or by entreaties, prayers, and tears, such an advocate often secured a decision in favor of the prisoner or, failing in this, succeeded in mitigating the severity of the sentence. But when Paul was summoned before Nero, no man ventured to act as his counsel or advocate; no friend was at hand even to preserve a record of the charges brought against him, or of the arguments that he urged in his own defense. Among the Christians at Rome there was not one who came forward to stand by him in that trying hour.

The only reliable record of the occasion is given by Paul himself, in his second letter to Timothy. "At my first answer," the apostle wrote, "no man stood with me, but all men forsook me: I pray God that it may not be laid to their charge. Notwithstanding the Lord stood with me, and strengthened me; that by me the preaching might be fully known, and that all the Gentiles might hear: and I was delivered out of the mouth of the lion." 2 Timothy 4:16, 17.

Paul before Nero—how striking the contrast! The haughty monarch before whom the man of God was to answer for his faith, had reached the height of earthly power, authority, and wealth, as well as the lowest depths of crime and iniquity. In power and greatness he stood unrivaled. There were none to question his authority, none to resist his will. Kings laid their crowns at his feet. Powerful armies marched at his command, and the ensigns of his navies betokened victory. His statue was set up in the halls of justice, and the decrees of senators and the decisions of judges were but the echo of his will. Millions bowed in obedience to his mandates. The name of Nero made the world tremble. To incur his displeasure was to lose property, liberty, life; and his frown was more to be dreaded than a pestilence.

Without money, without friends, without counsel, the aged prisoner stood before Nero—the countenance of the emperor bearing the shameful record of the passions that raged within; the face of the accused telling of a heart at peace with God. Paul's experience had been one of poverty, self-denial, and suffering. Notwithstanding constant misrepresentation, reproach, and abuse, by which his enemies had endeavored to intimidate him, he had fearlessly held aloft the standard of the cross. Like his Master, he had been a homeless wanderer, and like Him, he had lived to bless humanity. How could Nero, a capricious, passionate, licentious tyrant, understand or appreciate the character and motives of this son of God?

The vast hall was thronged by an eager, restless crowd that surged and pressed to the front to see and hear all that should take place. The high and the low were there, the rich and the poor, the learned and the ignorant, the proud and the humble, all alike destitute of a true knowledge of the way of life and salvation.

The Jews brought against Paul the old charges of sedition and heresy, and both Jews and Romans accused him of instigating the burning of the city. While these accusations were urged against him, Paul preserved an unbroken serenity. The people and the judges looked at him in surprise. They had been present at many trials and had looked upon many a criminal, but never had they seen a man wear a look of such holy calmness as did the prisoner before them. The keen eyes of the judges, accustomed to read the countenances of prisoners, searched Paul's face in vain for some evidence of guilt. When he was permitted to speak in his own behalf, all listened with eager interest.

Once more Paul has an opportunity to uplift before a wondering multitude the banner of the cross. As he gazes upon the throng before him,—Jews, Greeks, Romans, with strangers from many lands,—his soul is stirred with an intense desire for their salvation. He loses sight of the occasion, of the perils surrounding him, of the terrible fate that seems so near. He sees only Jesus, the Intercessor, pleading before God in behalf of sinful men. With more than human eloquence and power, Paul presents the truths of the gospel. He points his hearers to the sacrifice made for the fallen race. He declares that an infinite price has been paid for man's redemption. Provision has been made for him to share the throne of God. By angel messengers, earth is connected with heaven, and all the deeds of men, whether good or evil, are open to the eye of Infinite Justice.

Thus pleads the advocate of truth. Faithful among the faithless, loyal among the disloyal, he stands as God's representative, and his voice is as a voice from heaven. There is no fear, no sadness, no discouragement in word or look. Strong in a consciousness of innocence, clothed in the panoply of truth, he rejoices that he is a son of God. His words are as a shout of victory above the roar of battle. He declares the cause to which he has devoted his life, to be the only cause that can never fail. Though he may perish, the gospel will not perish. God lives, and His truth will triumph.

Many who that day looked upon him "saw his face as it had been the face of an angel." Acts 6:15.

Never before had that company listened to words like these. They struck a cord that vibrated in the hearts of even the most hardened. Truth, clear and convincing, overthrew error. Light shone into the minds of many who afterward gladly followed its rays. The truths spoken on that day were destined to shake nations and to live through all time, influencing the hearts of men when the lips that had uttered them should be silent in a martyr's grave.

Never before had Nero heard the truth as he heard it on this occasion. Never before had the enormous guilt of his own life been so revealed to him. The light of heaven pierced the sin-polluted chambers of his soul, and he trembled with terror at the thought of a tribunal before which he, the ruler of the world, would finally be arraigned, and his deeds receive their just award. He feared the apostle's God, and he dared not pass sentence upon Paul, against whom no accusation had been sustained. A sense of awe restrained for a time his bloodthirsty spirit.

For a moment, heaven was opened to the guilty and hardened Nero, and its peace and purity seemed desirable. That moment the invitation of mercy was extended even to him. But only for a moment was the thought of pardon welcomed. Then the command was issued that Paul be taken back to his dungeon; and as the door closed upon the messenger of God, the door of repentance closed forever against the emperor of Rome. No ray of light from heaven was ever again to penetrate the darkness that enveloped him. Soon he was to suffer the retributive judgments of God.

Not long after this, Nero sailed on his infamous expedition to Greece, where he disgraced himself and his kingdom by contempt-ible and debasing frivolity. Returning to Rome with great pomp, he surrounded himself with his courtiers and engaged in scenes of revolting debauchery. In the midst of this revelry a voice of tumult in the streets was heard. A messenger dispatched to learn the cause, returned with the appalling news that Galba, at the head of an army, was marching rapidly upon Rome, that insurrection had already broken out in the city, and that the streets were filled with an enraged mob, which, threatening death to the emperor and all his supporters, was rapidly approaching the palace.

In this time of peril, Nero had not, like the faithful Paul, a powerful and compassionate God on whom to rely. Fearful of the suffering and possible torture he might be compelled to endure at the hands of the mob, the wretched tyrant thought to end his life by his own hand, but at the critical moment his courage failed. Completely unmanned, he fled ignominiously from the city and sought shelter at a countryseat a few miles distant, but to no avail. His hiding place was soon discovered, and as the pursuing horsemen drew near, he summoned a slave to his aid and inflicted on himself a mortal wound. Thus perished the tyrant Nero, at the early age of thirty-two.

49

Paul's Last Letter

This chapter is based on the Second Epistle to Timothy

From the judgment hall of Caesar, Paul returned to his cell, realizing that he had gained for himself only a brief respite. He knew that his enemies would not rest until they had compassed his death. But he knew also that for a time truth had triumphed. To have proclaimed a crucified and risen Saviour before the vast crowd who had listened to him, was in itself a victory. That day a work had begun which would grow and strengthen, and which Nero and all other enemies of Christ would seek in vain to hinder or destroy.

Sitting day after day in his gloomy cell, knowing that at a word or a nod from Nero his life might be sacrificed, Paul thought of Timothy and determined to send for him. To Timothy had been committed the care of the church at Ephesus, and he had therefore been left behind when Paul made his last journey to Rome. Paul and Timothy were bound together by an affection unusually deep and strong.

Since his conversion, Timothy had shared Paul's labors and sufferings, and the friendship between the two had grown stronger, deeper, and more sacred, until all that a son could be to a loved and honored father, Timothy was to the aged, toilworn apostle. It is little wonder that in his loneliness and solitude, Paul longed to see him.

Under the most favorable circumstances several months must pass before Timothy could reach Rome from Asia Minor. Paul knew that his life was uncertain, and he feared that Timothy might arrive too late to see him. He had important counsel and instruction for the young man, to whom so great responsibility had been entrusted; and while urging him to come without delay, he dictated the dying testimony that he might not be spared to utter. His soul filled with loving solicitude for his son in the gospel and for the church under his care, Paul sought to impress Timothy with the importance of fidelity to his sacred trust.

Paul began his letter with the salutation: "To Timothy, my dearly beloved son: Grace, mercy, and peace, from God the Father and Christ Jesus our Lord. I thank God, whom I serve from my forefathers with pure conscience, that without ceasing I have remembrance of thee in my prayers night and day."

The apostle then urged upon Timothy the necessity of steadfastness in the faith. "I put thee in remembrance," he wrote, "that thou stir up the gift of God, which is in thee by the putting on of my hands. For God hath not given us the spirit of fear; but of power, and of love, and of a sound mind. Be not thou therefore ashamed of the testimony of our Lord, nor of me His prisoner: but be thou partaker of the afflictions of the gospel according to the power of God." Paul entreated Timothy to remember that he had been called "with a holy calling" to proclaim the power of Him who had "brought life and immortality to light through the gospel: whereunto," he declared, "I am appointed a preacher, and an apostle, and a teacher of the Gentiles. For the which cause I also suffer these things: nevertheless I am not ashamed: for I know whom I have believed, and am persuaded that He is able to keep that which I have committed unto Him against that day."

Through his long term of service, Paul had never faltered in his allegiance to his Saviour. Wherever he was—whether before scowling Pharisees, or Roman authorities; before the furious mob at Lystra, or the convicted sinners in the Macedonian dungeon; whether reasoning with the panic-stricken sailors on the shipwrecked vessel, or standing alone before Nero to plead for his life—he had never been ashamed of the cause he was advocating. The one great purpose of his Christian life had been to serve Him whose name had once filled him with contempt; and from this purpose no opposition or persecution had been able to turn him aside. His faith, made strong by effort and pure by sacrifice, upheld and strengthened him.

"Thou therefore, my son," Paul continued, "be strong in the grace that is in Christ Jesus. And the things that thou hast heard of me among many witnesses, the same commit thou to faithful men, who shall be able to teach others also. Thou therefore endure hardness, as a good soldier of Jesus Christ."

The true minister of God will not shun hardship or responsibility. From the Source that never fails those who sincerely seek for divine power, he draws strength that enables him to meet and overcome temptation, and to perform the duties that God places upon him. The nature of the grace that he receives, enlarges his capacity to know God and His Son. His soul goes out in longing desire to do acceptable service for the Master. And as he advances in the Christian pathway he becomes "strong in the grace that is in

Christ Jesus." This grace enables him to be a faithful witness of the things that he has heard. He does not despise or neglect the knowledge that he has received from God, but commits this knowledge to faithful men, who in their turn teach others.

In this his last letter to Timothy, Paul held up before the younger worker a high ideal, pointing out the duties devolving on him as a minister of Christ. "Study to show thyself approved unto God," the apostle wrote, "a workman that needeth not to be ashamed, rightly dividing the word of truth." "Flee also youthful lusts: but follow righteousness, faith, charity, peace, with them that call on the Lord out of a pure heart. But foolish and unlearned questions avoid, knowing that they do gender strifes. And the servant of the Lord must not strive; but be gentle unto all men, apt to teach, patient, in meekness instructing those that oppose themselves; if God peradventure will give them repentance to the acknowledging of the truth."

The apostle warned Timothy against the false teachers who would seek to gain entrance into the church. "This know also," he declared, "that in the last days perilous times shall come. For men shall be lovers of their own selves, covetous, boasters, proud, blasphemers, disobedient to parents, unthankful, unholy; . . . having a form of godliness, but denying the power thereof: from such turn away."

"Evil men and seducers shall wax worse and worse," he continued, "deceiving, and being deceived. But continue thou in the things which thou hast learned and hast been assured of, knowing of whom thou hast learned them; and that from a child thou hast known the Holy Scriptures, which are able to make thee wise unto salvation. . . . All Scripture is given by inspiration of God, and is profitable for doctrine, for reproof, for correction, for instruction in righteousness: that the man of God may be perfect, throughly furnished unto all good works." God has provided abundant means for successful warfare against the evil that is in the world. The Bible is the armory where we may equip for the struggle. Our loins must be girt about with truth. Our breastplate must be righteousness. The shield of faith must be in our hand, the helmet of salvation on our brow; and with the sword of the Spirit, which is the word of God, we are to cut our way through the obstructions and entanglements of sin.

Paul knew that there was before the church a time of great peril. He knew that faithful, earnest work would have to be done by those left in charge of the churches; and he wrote to Timothy, "I charge thee therefore before God, and the Lord Jesus Christ, who shall judge the quick and the dead at His appearing and His kingdom; Preach the word; be instant in season, out of season; reprove, rebuke, exhort with all long-suffering and doctrine."

This solemn charge to one so zealous and faithful as was Timothy is a strong testimony to the importance and responsibility of the work of the gospel minister. Summoning Timothy before the bar of God, Paul bids him preach the word, not the sayings and customs of men; to be ready to witness for God whenever opportunity should present itself—before large congregations and private circles, by the way and at the fireside, to friends and to enemies, whether in safety or exposed to hardship and peril, reproach and loss.

Fearing that Timothy's mild, yielding disposition might lead him to shun an essential part of his work, Paul exhorted him to be faithful in reproving sin and even to rebuke with sharpness those who were guilty of gross evils. Yet he was to do this "with all long-suffering and doctrine." He was to reveal the patience and love of Christ, explaining and enforcing his reproofs by the truths of the word.

To hate and reprove sin, and at the same time to show pity and tenderness for the sinner, is a difficult attainment. The more earnest our own efforts to attain to holiness of heart and life, the more acute will be our perception of sin and the more decided our disapproval of any deviation from the right. We must guard against undue severity toward the wrongdoer, but we must also be careful not to lose sight of the exceeding sinfulness of sin. There is need of showing Christlike patience and love for the erring one, but there is also danger of showing so great toleration for his error that he will look upon himself as undeserving of reproof, and will reject it as uncalled for and unjust.

Ministers of the gospel sometimes do great harm by allowing their forbearance toward the erring to degenerate into toleration of sins and even participation in them. Thus they are led to excuse and palliate that which God condemns, and after a time they become so blinded as to commend the very ones whom God commands them to reprove. He who has blunted his spiritual perceptions by sinful leniency toward those whom God condemns, will erelong commit a greater sin by severity and harshness toward those whom God approves.

By the pride of human wisdom, by contempt for the influence of the Holy Spirit, and by disrelish for the truths of God's word, many who profess to be Christians, and who feel competent to teach others, will be led to turn away from the requirements of God. Paul declared to Timothy, "The time will come when they will not endure sound doctrine; but after their own lusts shall they heap to themselves teachers, having itching ears; and they shall turn away their ears from the truth, and shall be turned unto fables."

The apostle does not here refer to the openly irreligious, but to the professing Christians who make inclination their guide, and thus become enslaved by self. Such are willing to listen to those doctrines only that do not rebuke their sins or condemn their pleasure-loving course. They are offended by the plain words of the faithful servants of Christ and choose teachers who praise and flatter them. And among professing ministers there are those who preach the opinions of men instead of the word of God. Unfaithful to their trust, they lead astray those who look to them for spiritual guidance.

In the precepts of His holy law, God has given a perfect rule of life; and He has declared that until the close of time this law, unchanged in a single jot or tittle, is to maintain its claim upon human beings. Christ came to magnify the law and make it honorable. He showed that it is based upon the broad foundation of love to God and love to man, and that obedience to its precepts comprises the whole duty of man. In His own life He gave an example of obedience to the law of God. In the Sermon on the Mount He showed how its requirements extend beyond the outward acts and take cognizance of the thoughts and intents of the heart.

The law, obeyed, leads men to deny "ungodliness and worldly lusts," and to "live soberly, righteously, and godly, in this present world." Titus 2:12. But the enemy of all righteousness has taken the world captive and has led men and women to disobey the law. As Paul foresaw, multitudes have turned from the plain, searching truths of God's word and have chosen teachers who present to them the fables they desire. Many among both ministers and people are trampling under their feet the commandments of God. Thus the Creator of the world is insulted, and Satan laughs in triumph at the success of his devices.

With the growing contempt for God's law there is an increasing distaste for religion, an increase of pride, love of pleasure, disobedience to parents, and self-indulgence; and thoughtful minds everywhere are anxiously inquiring, What can be done to correct these alarming evils? The answer is found in Paul's exhortation to Timothy, "Preach the word." In the Bible are found the only safe principles of action. It is a transcript of the will of God, an expression of divine wisdom. It opens to man's understanding the great problems of life, and to all who heed its precepts it will prove an unerring guide, keeping them from wasting their lives in misdirected effort.

God has made known His will, and it is folly for man to question that which has gone out of His lips. After Infinite Wisdom has spoken, there can be no doubtful questions for man to settle, no wavering possibilities for him to adjust. All that is required of him is a frank, earnest concurrence in the expressed will of God. Obedience is the highest dictate of reason as well as of conscience.

Paul continued his charge: "Watch thou in all things, endure afflictions, do the work of an evangelist, make full proof of thy ministry." Paul was about to finish his course, and he desired Timothy to take his place, guarding the church from the fables and heresies by which the enemy, in various ways, would endeavor to lead them from the simplicity of the gospel. He admonished him to shun all temporal pursuits and entanglements that would prevent him from giving himself wholly to his work for God; to endure with cheerfulness the opposition, reproach, and persecution to which his faithfulness would expose him; to make full proof of his ministry by employing every means within his reach of doing good to those for whom Christ died.

Paul's life was an exemplification of the truths he taught, and herein lay his power. His heart was filled with a deep, abiding sense of his responsibility, and he labored in close communion with Him who is the fountain of justice, mercy, and truth. He clung to the cross of Christ as his only guarantee of success. The love of the Saviour was the undying motive that upheld him in his conflicts with self and in his struggles against evil as in the service of Christ he pressed forward against the unfriendliness of the world and the opposition of his enemies.

What the church needs in these days of peril is an army of workers who, like Paul, have educated themselves for usefulness, who have a deep experience in the things of God, and who are filled with earnestness and zeal. Sanctified, self-sacrificing men are needed; men who will not shun trial and responsibility; men who are brave and true; men in whose hearts Christ is formed "the hope of glory," and who with lips touched with holy fire will "preach the word." For want of such workers the cause of God languishes, and fatal errors, like a deadly poison, taint the morals and blight the hopes of a large part of the human race.

As the faithful, toilworn standard-bearers are offering up their lives for the truth's sake, who will come forward to take their place? Will our young men accept the holy trust at the hands of their fathers? Are they preparing to fill the vacancies made by the death of the faithful? Will the apostle's charge be heeded, the call to duty be heard, amidst the incitements to selfishness and ambition that allure the youth?

Paul concluded his letter with personal messages to different ones and again repeated the urgent request that Timothy come to him soon, if possible before the winter. He spoke of his loneliness, caused by the desertion of some of his friends and the necessary absence of others; and lest Timothy should hesitate, fearing that the church at Ephesus might need his labors, Paul stated that he had already dispatched Tychicus to fill the vacancy.

After speaking of the scene of his trial before Nero, the desertion of his brethren, and the sustaining grace of a covenant-keeping God, Paul closed his letter by commending his beloved Timothy to the guardianship of the Chief Shepherd, who, though the undershepherds might be stricken down, would still care for His flock.

50

Condemned to Die

During Paul's final trial before Nero, the emperor had been so strongly impressed with the force of the apostle's words that he deferred the decision of the case, neither acquitting nor condemning the accused servant of God. But the emperor's malice against Paul soon returned. Exasperated by his inability to check the spread of the Christian religion, even in the imperial household, he determined that as soon as a plausible pretext could be found, the apostle should be put to death. Not long afterward Nero pronounced the decision that condemned Paul to a martyr's death. Inasmuch as a Roman citizen could not be subjected to torture, he was sentenced to be beheaded.

Paul was taken in a private manner to the place of execution. Few spectators were allowed to be present; for his persecutors, alarmed at the extent of his influence, feared that converts might be won to Christianity by the scenes of his death. But even the hardened soldiers who attended him listened to his words and with amazement saw him cheerful and even joyous in the prospect of death. To some who witnessed his martyrdom, his spirit of forgiveness toward his murderers and his unwavering confidence in Christ till the last, proved a savor of life unto life. More than one accepted the Saviour whom Paul preached, and erelong fearlessly sealed their faith with their blood.

Until his latest hour the life of Paul testified to the truth of his words to the Corinthians: "God, who commanded the light to shine out of darkness, hath shined in our hearts, to give the light of the knowledge of the glory of God in the face of Jesus Christ. But we have this treasure in earthen vessels, that the excellency of the power may be of God, and not of us. We are troubled on every side, yet not distressed; we are perplexed, but not in despair; persecuted, but not forsaken; cast down, but not destroyed; always bearing about in the body the dying of the Lord Jesus, that the life also of Jesus might be made manifest in our body." 2 Corinthians 4:6-10. His sufficiency was not in himself, but in the presence and agency of the divine Spirit that filled his soul and brought every thought into subjection to the will of Christ. The prophet declares, "Thou wilt keep him in perfect peace, whose mind is stayed on Thee:

because he trusteth in Thee." Isaiah 26:3. The heaven-born peace expressed on Paul's countenance won many a soul to the gospel.

Paul carried with him the atmosphere of heaven. All who associated with him felt the influence of his union with Christ. The fact that his own life exemplified the truth he proclaimed, gave convincing power to his preaching. Here lies the power of truth. The unstudied, unconscious influence of a holy life is the most convincing sermon that can be given in favor of Christianity. Argument, even when unanswerable, may provoke only opposition; but a godly example has a power that it is impossible wholly to resist.

The apostle lost sight of his own approaching sufferings in his solicitude for those whom he was about to leave to cope with prejudice, hatred, and persecution. The few Christians who accompanied him to the place of execution he endeavored to strengthen and encourage by repeating the promises given for those who are persecuted for righteousness' sake. He assured them that nothing would fail of all that the Lord had spoken concerning His tried and faithful children. For a little season they might be in heaviness through manifold temptations; they might be destitute of earthly comforts; but they could encourage their hearts with the assurance of God's faithfulness, saying, "I know whom I have believed, and am persuaded that He is able to keep that which I have committed unto Him." 2 Timothy 1:12. Soon the night of trial and suffering would end, and then would dawn the glad morning of peace and perfect day.

The apostle was looking into the great beyond, not with uncertainty or dread, but with joyous hope and longing expectation. As he stands at the place of martyrdom he sees not the sword of the executioner or the earth so soon to receive his blood; he looks up through the calm blue heaven of that summer day to the throne of the Eternal.

This man of faith beholds the ladder of Jacob's vision, representing Christ, who has connected earth with heaven, and finite man with the infinite God. His faith is strengthened as he calls to mind how patriarchs and prophets have relied upon the One who is his support and consolation, and for whom he is giving his life. From these holy men who from century to century have borne testimony for their faith, he hears the assurance that God is true. His fellow apostles, who, to preach the gospel of Christ, went forth to meet religious bigotry and heathen superstition, persecution, and contempt, who counted not their lives dear unto themselves that they might bear aloft the light of the cross amidst the dark mazes of infidelity—these he hears witnessing to Jesus as the Son of God, the Saviour of the world. From the rack, the stake, the dungeon, from dens and caves of the earth, there falls upon his ear the martyr's shout of triumph. He hears the witness of steadfast souls, who, though destitute, afflicted, tormented, yet bear fearless, solemn testimony for the faith, declaring, "I know whom I have believed." These, yielding up their lives for the faith, declare to the world that He in whom they have trusted is able to save to the uttermost.

Ransomed by the sacrifice of Christ, washed from sin in His blood, and clothed in His righteousness, Paul has the witness in himself that his soul is precious in the sight of his Redeemer. His life is hid with Christ in God, and he is persuaded that He who has conquered death is able to keep that which is committed to His trust. His mind grasps the Saviour's promise, "I will raise him up at the last day." John 6:40. His thoughts and hopes are centered on the second coming of his Lord. And as the sword of the executioner descends and the shadows of death gather about the martyr, his latest thought springs forward, as will his earliest in the great awakening, to meet the Life-giver, who shall welcome him to the joy of the blest.

Well-nigh a score of centuries have passed since Paul the aged poured out his blood as a witness for the word of God and the testimony of Jesus Christ. No faithful hand recorded for the generations to come the last scenes in the life of this holy man, but Inspiration has preserved for us his dying testimony. Like a trumpet peal his voice has rung out through all the ages since, nerving with his own courage thousands of witnesses for Christ and wakening in thousands of sorrow-stricken hearts the echo of his own triumphant joy: "I am now ready to be offered, and the time of my departure is at hand. I have fought a good fight, I have finished my course, I have kept the faith: henceforth there is laid up for me a crown of righteousness, which the Lord, the righteous Judge, shall give me at that day: and not to me only, but unto all them also that love His appearing." 2 Timothy 4:6-8.

51

A Faithful Under-Shepherd

This chapter is based on the First Epistle of Peter

Little mention is made in the book of Acts of the later work of the apostle Peter. During the busy years of ministry that followed the outpouring of the Spirit on the Day of Pentecost, he was among those who put forth untiring efforts to reach the Jews who came to Jerusalem to worship at the time of the annual festivals.

As the number of believers multiplied in Jerusalem and in other places visited by the messengers of the cross, the talents possessed by Peter proved of untold value to the early Christian church. The influence of his testimony concerning Jesus of Nazareth extended far and wide. Upon him had been laid a double responsibility. He bore positive witness concerning the Messiah before unbelievers, laboring earnestly for their conversion; and at the same time he did a special work for believers, strengthening them in the faith of Christ.

It was after Peter had been led to self-renunciation and entire reliance upon divine power, that he received his call to act as an undershepherd. Christ had said to Peter, before his denial of Him, "When thou art converted, strengthen thy brethren." Luke 22:32. These words were significant of the wide and effectual work which this apostle was to do in the future for those who should come to the faith. For this work, Peter's own experience of sin and suffering and repentance had prepared him. Not until he had learned his weakness, could he know the believer's need of dependence on Christ. Amid the storm of temptation he had come to understand that man can walk safely only as in utter self-distrust he relies upon the Saviour.

At the last meeting of Christ with His disciples by the sea, Peter, tested by the thrice-repeated question, "Lovest thou Me?" (John 21:15-17), had been restored to his place among the Twelve. His work had been appointed him; he was to feed the Lord's flock. Now, converted and accepted, he was not only to seek to save those without the fold, but was to be a shepherd of the sheep.

Christ mentioned to Peter only one condition of service —

"Lovest thou Me?" This is the essential qualification. Though Peter might possess every other, yet without the love of Christ he could not be a faithful shepherd over the flock of God. Knowledge, benevolence, eloquence, zeal— all are essential in the good work; but without the love of Christ in the heart, the work of the Christian minister is a failure.

The love of Christ is not a fitful feeling, but a living principle, which is to be made manifest as an abiding power in the heart. If the character and deportment of the shepherd is an exemplification of the truth he advocates, the Lord will set the seal of His approval to the work. The shepherd and the flock will become one, united by their common hope in Christ.

The Saviour's manner of dealing with Peter had a lesson for him and his brethren. Although Peter had denied his Lord, the love which Jesus bore him had never faltered. And as the apostle should take up the work of ministering the word to others, he was to meet the transgressor with patience, sympathy, and forgiving love. Remembering his own weakness and failure, he was to deal with the sheep and lambs committed to his care as tenderly as Christ had dealt with him.

Human beings, themselves given to evil, are prone to deal untenderly with the tempted and the erring. They cannot read the heart; they know not its struggle and its pain. Of the rebuke that is love, of the blow that wounds to heal, of the warning that speaks hope, they have need to learn.

Throughout his ministry, Peter faithfully watched over the flock entrusted to his care, and thus proved himself worthy of the charge and responsibility given him by the Saviour. Ever he exalted Jesus of Nazareth as the Hope of Israel, the Saviour of mankind. He brought his own life under the discipline of the Master Worker. By every means within his power he sought to educate the believers for active service. His godly example and untiring activity inspired many young men of promise to give themselves wholly to the work of the ministry. As time went on, the apostle's influence as an educator and leader increased; and while he never lost his burden to labor especially for the Jews, yet he bore his testimony in many lands and strengthened the faith of multitudes in the gospel.

In the later years of his ministry, Peter was inspired to write to the believers "scattered throughout Pontus, Galatia, Cappadocia, Asia, and Bithynia." His letters were the means of reviving the courage and strengthening the faith of those who were enduring trial and affliction, and of renewing to good works those who through manifold temptations were in danger of losing their hold upon God. These letters bear the impress of having been written by one in whom the sufferings of Christ and also His consolation had been made to abound; one whose entire being had been transformed by grace, and whose hope of eternal life was sure and steadfast.

At the very beginning of his first letter the aged servant of God ascribed to his Lord a tribute of praise and thanksgiving. "Blessed be the God and Father of our Lord Jesus Christ," he exclaimed, "which according to His abundant mercy hath begotten us again unto a lively hope by the resurrection of Jesus Christ from the dead, to an inheritance incorruptible, and undefiled, and that fadeth not away, reserved in heaven for you, who are kept by the power of God through faith unto salvation ready to be revealed in the last time."

In this hope of a sure inheritance in the earth made new, the early Christians rejoiced, even in times of severe trial and affliction. "Ye greatly rejoice," Peter wrote, "though now for a season, if need be, ye are in heaviness through manifold temptations: that the trial of your faith, being much more precious than of gold that perisheth, though it be tried with fire, might be found unto praise and honor and glory at the appearing of Jesus Christ: whom having not seen, ye love; in whom, though now ye see Him not, . . . ye rejoice with joy unspeakable and full of glory: receiving the end of your faith, even the salvation of your souls."

The apostle's words were written for the instruction of believers in every age, and they have a special significance for those who live at the time when "the end of all things is at hand." His exhortations and warnings, and his words of faith and courage, are needed by every soul who would maintain his faith "steadfast unto the end." Hebrews 3:14.

The apostle sought to teach the believers how important it is to keep the mind from wandering to forbidden themes or from spending its energies on trifling subjects. Those who would not fall a prey to Satan's devices, must guard well the avenues of the soul; they must avoid reading, seeing, or hearing that which will suggest impure thoughts. The mind must not be left to dwell at random upon every subject that the enemy of souls may suggest. The heart must be faithfully sentineled, or evils without will awaken evils within, and the soul will wander in darkness. "Gird up the loins of your mind," Peter wrote, "be sober, and hope to the end for the grace that is to be brought unto you at the revelation of Jesus Christ; . . . not fashioning yourselves according to the former lusts in your ignorance: but as He which hath called you is holy, so be ye holy in all manner of conversation; because it is written, Be ye holy; for I am holy."

"Pass the time of your sojourning here in fear: forasmuch as ye know that ye were not redeemed with corruptible things, as silver and gold, from your vain conversation received by tradition from your fathers; but with the precious blood of Christ, as of a Lamb without blemish and without spot: who verily was foreordained before the foundation of the world, but was manifest in these last times for you, who by Him do believe in God, that raised Him up from the dead, and gave Him glory; that your faith and hope might be in God."

Had silver and gold been sufficient to purchase the salvation of men, how easily might it have been accomplished by Him who says, "The silver is Mine, and the gold is Mine." Haggai 2:8. But only by the precious blood of the Son of God could the transgressor be redeemed. The plan of salvation was laid in sacrifice. The apostle Paul wrote, "Ye know the grace of our Lord Jesus Christ, that, though He was rich, yet for your sakes He became poor, that ye through His poverty might be rich." 2 Corinthians 8:9. Christ gave Himself for us that He might redeem us from all iniquity. And as the crowning blessing of salvation, "the gift of God is eternal life through Jesus Christ our Lord." Romans 6:23.

"Seeing ye have purified your souls in obeying the truth through the Spirit unto unfeigned love of the brethren," Peter continued, "see that ye love one another with a pure heart fervently." The word of God—the truth—is the channel through which the Lord manifests His Spirit and power. Obedience to the word produces fruit of the required quality—"unfeigned love of the brethren." This love is heaven-born and leads to high motives and unselfish actions.

When truth becomes an abiding principle in the life, the soul is "born again, not of incorruptible seed, but of incorruptible, by the word of God, which liveth and abideth forever." This new birth is the result of receiving Christ as the Word of God. When by the Holy Spirit divine truths are impressed upon the heart, new conceptions are awakened, and the energies hitherto dormant are aroused to co-operate with God.

Thus it had been with Peter and his fellow disciples. Christ was the revealer of truth to the world. By Him the incorruptible seed—the word of God—was sown in the hearts of men. But many of the most precious lessons of the Great Teacher were spoken to those who did not then understand them. When, after His ascension, the

Holy Spirit brought His teachings to the remembrance of the disciples, their slumbering senses awoke. The meaning of these truths flashed upon their minds as a new revelation, and truth, pure and unadulterated, made a place for itself. Then the wonderful experience of His life became theirs. The Word bore testimony through them, the men of His appointment, and they proclaimed the mighty truth, "The Word was made flesh, and dwelt among us, . . . full of grace and truth." "And of His fullness have all we received, and grace for grace." John 1:14, 16.

The apostles exhorted the believers to study the Scriptures, through a proper understanding of which they might make sure work for eternity. Peter realized that in the experience of every soul who is finally victorious there would be scenes of perplexity and trial; but he knew also that an understanding of the Scriptures would enable the tempted one to bring to mind promises that would comfort the heart and strengthen faith in the Mighty One.

"All flesh is as grass," he declared, "and all the glory of man as the flower of grass. The grass withereth, and the flower thereof falleth away: but the word of the Lord endureth forever. And this is the word which by the gospel is preached unto you. Wherefore laying aside all malice, and all guile, and hypocrisies, and envies, and all evilspeakings, as newborn babes, desire the sincere milk of the word, that ye may grow thereby: if so be ye have tasted that the Lord is gracious."

Many of the believers to whom Peter addressed his letters, were living in the midst of heathen, and much depended on their remaining true to the high calling of their profession. The apostle urged upon them their privileges as followers of Christ Jesus. "Ye are a chosen generation," he wrote, "a royal priesthood, an holy nation, a peculiar people; that ye should show forth the praises of Him who hath called you out of darkness into His marvelous light: which in time past were not a people, but are now the people of God: which had not obtained mercy, but now have obtained mercy.

"Dearly beloved, I beseech you as strangers and pilgrims, abstain from fleshly lusts, which war against the soul; having your conversation honest among the Gentiles: that, whereas they speak against you as evildoers, they may by your good works, which they shall behold, glorify God in the day of visitation."

The apostle plainly outlined the attitude that believers should sustain toward the civil authorities: "Submit yourselves to every ordinance of man for the Lord's sake: whether it be to the king, as supreme; or unto governors, as unto them that are sent by him for the punishment of evildoers, and for the praise of them that do well. For so is the will of God, that with well-doing ye may put to silence the ignorance of foolish men: as free, and not using your liberty for a cloak of maliciousness, but as the servants of God. Honor all men. Love the brotherhood. Fear God. Honor the king."

Those who were servants were advised to remain subject to their masters "with all fear; not only to the good and gentle, but also to the froward. For this is thankworthy," the apostle explained, "if a man for conscience toward God endure grief, suffering wrongfully. For what glory is it, if, when ye be buffeted for your faults, ye shall take it patiently? but if, when ye do well, and suffer for it, ye take it patiently, this is acceptable with God. For even hereunto were ye called: because Christ also suffered for us, leaving us an example, that ye should follow His steps: who did no sin, neither was guile found in His mouth: who, when He was reviled, reviled not again; when He suffered, He threatened not; but committed Himself to Him that judgeth righteously: who His own self bare our sins in His own body on the tree, that we, being dead to sins, should live unto righteousness: by whose stripes ye were healed. For ye were as sheep going astray; but are now returned unto the Shepherd and Bishop of your souls."

The apostle exhorted the women in the faith to be chaste in conversation and modest in dress and deportment. "Whose adorning," he counseled, "let it not be that outward adorning of plaiting the hair, and of wearing of gold, or of putting on of apparel; but let it be the hidden man of the heart, in that which is not corruptible, even the ornament of a meek and quiet spirit, which is in the sight of God of great price."

The lesson applies to believers in every age. "By their fruits ye shall know them." Matthew 7:20. The inward adorning of a meek and quiet spirit is priceless. In the life of the true Christian the outward adorning is always in harmony with the inward peace and holiness. "If any man will come after Me," Christ said, "let him deny himself, and take up his cross, and follow Me." Matthew 16:24. Self-denial and sacrifice will mark the Christian's life. Evidence that the taste is converted will be seen in the dress of all who walk in the path cast up for the ransomed of the Lord.

It is right to love beauty and to desire it; but God desires us to love and seek first the highest beauty, that which is imperishable. No outward adorning can compare in value or loveliness with that "meek and quiet spirit," the "fine linen, white and clean" (Revelation 19:14), which all the holy ones of earth will wear. This apparel will make them beautiful and beloved here, and will hereafter be their badge of admission to the palace of the King. His promise is, "They shall walk with Me in white: for they are worthy." Revelation 3:4.

Looking forward with prophetic vision to the perilous times into which the church of Christ was to enter, the apostle exhorted the believers to steadfastness in the face of trial and suffering. "Beloved," he wrote, "think it not strange concerning the fiery trial which is to try you."

Trial is part of the education given in the school of Christ, to purify God's children from the dross of earthliness. It is because God is leading His children that trying experiences come to them. Trials and obstacles are His chosen methods of discipline, and His appointed conditions of success. He who reads the hearts of men knows their weaknesses better than they themselves can know them. He sees that some have qualifications which, if rightly directed, could be used in the advancement of His work. In His providence He brings these souls into different positions and varied circumstances, that they may discover the defects that are concealed from their own knowledge. He gives them opportunity to overcome these defects and to fit themselves for service. Often He permits the fires of affliction to burn, that they may be purified.

God's care for His heritage is unceasing. He suffers no affliction to come upon His children but such as is essential for their present and eternal good. He will purify His church, even as Christ purified the temple during His ministry on earth. All that He brings upon His people in test and trial comes that they may gain deeper piety and greater strength to carry forward the triumphs of the cross.

There had been a time in Peter's experience when he was unwilling to see the cross in the work of Christ. When the Saviour made known to the disciples His impending sufferings and death, Peter exclaimed, "Be it far from Thee, Lord: this shall not be unto Thee." Matthew 16:22. Self-pity, which shrank from fellowship with Christ in suffering, prompted Peter's remonstrance. It was to the disciple a bitter lesson, and one which he learned but slowly, that the path of Christ on earth lay through agony and humiliation. But in the heat of the furnace fire he was to learn its lesson. Now, when his once active form was bowed with the burden of years and labors, he could write, "Beloved, think it not strange concerning the fiery trial which is to try you, as though some strange thing happened unto you: but rejoice, inasmuch as ye are partakers of

Christ's sufferings; that, when His glory shall be revealed, ye may be glad also with exceeding joy."

Addressing the church elders regarding their responsibilities as undershepherds of Christ's flock, the apostle wrote: "Feed the flock of God which is among you, taking the oversight thereof, not by constraint, but willingly; not for filthy lucre, but of a ready mind; neither as being lords over God's heritage, but being ensamples to the flock. And when the Chief Shepherd shall appear, ye shall receive a crown of glory that fadeth not away."

Those who occupy the position of undersheperds are to exercise a watchful diligence over the Lord's flock. This is not to be a dictatorial vigilance, but one that tends to encourage and strengthen and uplift. Ministry means more than sermonizing; it means earnest, personal labor. The church on earth is composed of erring men and women, who need patient, painstaking effort that they may be trained and disciplined to work with acceptance in this life, and in the future life to be crowned with glory and immortality. Pastors are needed—faithful shepherds—who will not flatter God's people, nor treat them harshly, but who will feed them with the bread of life—men who in their lives feel daily the converting power of the Holy Spirit and who cherish a strong, unselfish love toward those for whom they labor.

There is tactful work for the undershepherd to do as he is called to meet alienation, bitterness, envy, and jealousy in the church, and he will need to labor in the spirit of Christ to set things in order. Faithful warnings are to be given, sins rebuked, wrongs made right, not only by the minister's work in the pulpit, but by personal labor. The wayward heart may take exception to the message, and the servant of God may be misjudged and criticized. Let him then remember that "the wisdom that is from above is first pure, then peaceable, gentle, and easy to be entreated, full of mercy and good fruits, without partiality, and without hypocrisy. And the fruit of righteousness is sown in peace of them that make peace." James 3:17, 18.

The work of the gospel minister is "to make all men see what is the fellowship of the mystery, which from the beginning of the world hath been hid in God." Ephesians 3:9. If one entering upon this work chooses the least self-sacrificing part, contenting himself with preaching, and leaving the work of personal ministry for someone else, his labors will not be acceptable to God. Souls for whom Christ died are perishing for want of well-directed, personal labor; and he has mistaken his calling who, entering upon the ministry, is unwilling to do the personal work that the care of the flock demands.

The spirit of the true shepherd is one of self-forgetfulness. He loses sight of self in order that he may work the works of God. By the preaching of the word and by personal ministry in the homes of the people, he learns their needs, their sorrows, their trials; and, co-operating with the great Burden Bearer, he shares their afflictions, comforts their distresses, relieves their soul hunger, and wins their hearts to God. In this work the minister is attended by the angels of heaven, and he himself is instructed and enlightened in the truth that maketh wise unto salvation.

In connection with his instruction to those in positions of trust in the church, the apostle outlined some general principles that were to be followed by all who were associated in church fellowship. The younger members of the flock were urged to follow the example of their elders in the practice of Christlike humility: "Likewise, ye younger, submit yourselves unto the elder. Yea, all of you be subject one to another, and be clothed with humility: for God resisteth the proud, and giveth grace to the humble. Humble yourselves therefore under the mighty hand of God, that He may exalt you in due time: casting all your care upon Him; for He careth for you. Be sober, be vigilant; because your adversary the devil, as a roaring lion, walketh about, seeking whom he may devour: whom resist steadfast in the faith."

Thus Peter wrote to the believers at a time of peculiar trial to the church. Many had already become partakers of Christ's sufferings, and soon the church was to undergo a period of terrible persecution. Within a few brief years many those who had stood as teachers and leaders in the church were to lay down their lives for the gospel. Soon grievous wolves were to enter in, not sparing the flock. But none of these things were to bring discouragement to those whose hopes were centered in Christ. With words of encouragement and good cheer Peter directed the minds of the believers from present trials and future scenes of suffering "to an inheritance incorruptible, and undefiled, and that fadeth not away." "The God of all grace," he fervently prayed, "who hath called us unto His eternal glory by Christ Jesus, after that ye have suffered awhile, make you perfect, stablish, strengthen, settle you. To Him be glory and dominion for ever and ever. Amen."

52

Steadfast Unto the End

This chapter is based on the Second Epistle of Peter

In the second letter addressed by Peter to those who had obtained "like precious faith" with himself, the apostle sets forth the divine plan for the development of Christian character. He writes:

"Grace and peace be multiplied unto you through the knowledge of God, and of Jesus our Lord, according as His divine power hath given unto us all things that pertain unto life and godliness, through the knowledge of Him that hath called us to glory and virtue: whereby are given unto us exceeding great and precious promises: that by these ye might be partakers of the divine nature, having escaped the corruption that is in the world through lust.

"And beside this, giving all diligence, add to your faith virtue; and to virtue knowledge; and to knowledge temperance; and to temperance patience; and to patience godliness; and to godliness brotherly kindness; and to brotherly kindness charity. For if these things be in you, and abound, they make you that ye shall neither be barren nor unfruitful in the knowledge of our Lord Jesus Christ."

These words are full of instruction, and strike the keynote of victory. The apostle presents before the believers the ladder of Christian progress, every step of which represents advancement in the knowledge of God, and in the climbing of which there is to be no standstill. Faith, virtue, knowledge, temperance, patience, godliness, brotherly kindness, and charity are the rounds of the ladder. We are saved by climbing round after round, mounting step after step, to the height of Christ's ideal for us. Thus He is made unto us wisdom, and righteousness, and sanctification, and redemption.

God has called His people to glory and virtue, and these will be manifest in the lives of all who are truly connected with Him. Having become partakers of the heavenly gift, they are to go unto perfection, being "kept by the power of God through faith." 1 Peter 1:5. It is the glory of God to give His virtue to His children. He desires to see men and women reaching the highest standard; and when by faith they lay hold of the power of Christ, when they plead His unfailing promises, and claim them as their own, when with an importunity that will not be denied they seek for the power of the Holy Spirit, they will be made complete in Him.

Having received the faith of the gospel, the next work of the believer is to add to his character virtue, and thus cleanse the heart and prepare the mind for the reception of the knowledge of God. This knowledge is the foundation of all true education and of all true service. It is the only real safeguard against temptation; and it is this alone that can make one like God in character. Through the knowledge of God and of His Son Jesus Christ, are given to the believer "all things that pertain unto life and godliness." No good gift is withheld from him who sincerely desires to obtain the righteousness of God.

"This is life eternal," Christ said, "that they might know Thee the only true God, and Jesus Christ, whom Thou hast sent." John 17:3. And the prophet Jeremiah declared: "Let not the wise man glory in his wisdom, neither let the mighty man glory in his might, let not the rich man glory in his riches: but let him that glorieth glory in this, that he understandeth and knoweth Me, that I am the Lord which exercise loving-kindness, judgment, and righteousness, in the earth: for in these things I delight, saith the Lord." Jeremiah 9:23, 24. Scarcely can the human mind comprehend the breadth and depth and height of the spiritual attainments of him who gains this knowledge.

None need fail of attaining, in his sphere, to perfection of Christian character. By the sacrifice of Christ, provision has been made for the believer to receive all things that pertain to life and godliness. God calls upon us to reach the standard of perfection and places before us the example of Christ's character. In His humanity, perfected by a life of constant resistance of evil, the Saviour showed that through co-operation with Divinity, human beings may in this life attain to perfection of character. This is God's assurance to us that we, too, may obtain complete victory.

Before the believer is held out the wonderful possibility of being like Christ, obedient to all the principles of the law. But of himself man is utterly unable to reach this condition. The holiness that God's word declares he must have before he can be saved is the result of the working of divine grace as he bows in submission to the discipline and restraining influences of the Spirit of truth. Man's obedience can be made perfect only by the incense of Christ's righteousness, which fills with divine fragrance every act of obedience. The part of the Christian is to persevere in overcoming every fault. Constantly he is to pray to the Saviour to heal the disorders of his sin-sick soul. He has not the wisdom or the strength to overcome; these belong to the Lord, and He bestows them on those who in humiliation and contrition seek Him for help.

The work of transformation from unholiness to holiness is a continuous one. Day by day God labors for man's sanctification, and man is to co-operate with Him, putting forth persevering efforts in the cultivation of right habits. He is to add grace to grace; and as he thus works on the plan of addition, God works for him on the plan of multiplication. Our Saviour is always ready to hear and answer the prayer of the contrite heart, and grace and peace are multiplied to His faithful ones. Gladly He grants them the blessings they need in their struggle against the evils that beset them.

There are those who attempt to ascend the ladder of Christian progress; but as they advance they begin to put their trust in the power of man, and soon lose sight of Jesus, the Author and Finisher of their faith. The result is failure— the loss of all that has been gained. Sad indeed is the condition of those who, becoming weary of the way, allow the enemy of souls to rob them of the Christian graces that have been developing in their hearts and lives. "He that lacketh these things," declares the apostle, "is blind, and cannot see afar off, and hath forgotten that he was purged from his old sins."

The apostle Peter had had a long experience in the things of God. His faith in God's power to save had strengthened with the years, until he had proved beyond question that there is no possibility of failure before the one who, advancing by faith, ascends round by round, ever upward and onward, to the topmost round of the ladder that reaches even to the portals of heaven.

For many years Peter had been urging upon the believers the necessity of a constant growth in grace and in a knowledge of the truth; and now, knowing that soon he would be called to suffer martyrdom for his faith, he once more drew attention to the precious privileges within the reach of every believer. In the full assurance of his faith the aged disciple exhorted his brethren to steadfastness of purpose in the Christian life. "Give diligence," he pleaded, "to make your calling and election sure: for if ye do these things, ye shall never fall: for so an entrance shall be ministered unto you abundantly into the everlasting kingdom of our Lord and Saviour Jesus Christ." Precious assurance! Glorious is the hope before the believer as he advances by faith toward the heights of Christian perfection!

"I will not be negligent," the apostle continued, "to put you always in remembrance of these things, though ye know them, and be established in the present truth. Yea, I think it meet, as long as I am in this tabernacle, to stir you up by putting you in remembrance; knowing that shortly I must put off this my tabernacle, even as our Lord Jesus Christ hath showed me. Moreover I will endeavor that ye may be able after my decease to have these things always in remembrance."

The apostle was well qualified to speak of the purposes of God concerning the human race; for during the earthly ministry of Christ he had seen and heard much that pertained to the kingdom of God. "We have not followed cunningly devised fables," he reminded the believers, "when we made known unto you the power and coming of our Lord Jesus Christ, but were eyewitnesses of His majesty. For He received from God the Father honor and glory, when there came such a voice to Him from the excellent glory, This is My beloved Son, in whom I am well pleased. And this voice which came from heaven we heard, when we were with Him in the holy mount."

Yet convincing as was this evidence of the certainty of the believers' hope, there was another still more convincing in the witness of prophecy, through which the faith of all might be confirmed and securely anchored. "We have also," Peter declared, "a more sure word of prophecy; whereunto ye do well that ye take heed, as unto a light that shineth in a dark place, until the day dawn, and the daystar arise in your hearts: knowing this first, that no prophecy of the Scripture is of any private interpretation. For the prophecy came not in old time by the will of man: but holy men of God spake as they were moved by the Holy Ghost."

While exalting the "sure word of prophecy" as a safe guide in times of peril, the apostle solemnly warned the church against the torch of false prophecy, which would be uplifted by "false teachers," who would privily bring in "damnable heresies, even denying the Lord." These false teachers, arising in the church and accounted true by many of their brethren in the faith, the apostle compared to "wells without water, clouds that are carried with a tempest; to whom the mist of darkness is reserved forever." "The latter end is worse with them," he declared, "than the beginning. For it had been better for them not to have known the way of righteousness, than, after they have known it, to turn from the holy commandment delivered unto them."

Looking down through the ages to the close of time, Peter was inspired to outline conditions that would exist in the world just prior to the second coming of Christ. "There shall come in the last days scoffers," he wrote, "walking after their own lusts, and saying,

Where is the promise of His coming? for since the fathers fell asleep, all things continue as they were from the beginning of the creation." But "when they shall say, Peace and safety; then sudden destruction cometh upon them." 1 Thessalonians 5:3. Not all, however, would be ensnared by the enemy's devices. As the end of all things earthly should approach, there would be faithful ones able to discern the signs of the times. While a large number of professing believers would deny their faith by their works, there would be a remnant who would endure to the end.

Peter kept alive in his heart the hope of Christ's return, and he assured the church of the certain fulfillment of the Saviour's promise, "If I go and prepare a place for you, I will come again, and receive you unto Myself." John 14:3. To the tried and faithful ones the coming might seem long delayed, but the apostle assured them: "The Lord is not slack concerning His promise, as some men count slackness; but is long-suffering to usward, not willing that any should perish, but that all should come to repentance. But the day of the Lord will come as a thief in the night; in the which the heavens shall pass away with a great noise, and the elements shall melt with fervent heat, the earth also and the works that are therein shall be burned up.

"Seeing then that all these things shall be dissolved, what manner of persons ought ye to be in all holy conversation and godliness, looking for and hasting unto the coming of the day of God, wherein the heavens being on fire shall be dissolved, and the elements shall melt with fervent heat? Nevertheless we, according to His promise, look for new heavens and a new earth, wherein dwelleth righteousness.

"Wherefore, beloved, seeing that ye look for such things, be diligent that ye may be found of Him in peace, without spot, and blameless. And account that the long-suffering of our Lord is salvation; even as our beloved brother Paul also according to the wisdom given unto him hath written unto you. . . . Ye therefore, beloved, seeing ye know these things before, beware lest ye also, being led away with the error of the wicked, fall from your own steadfastness. But grow in grace, and in the knowledge of our Lord and Saviour Jesus Christ."

In the providence of God, Peter was permitted to close his ministry in Rome, where his imprisonment was ordered by the emperor Nero about the time of Paul's final arrest. Thus the two veteran apostles, who for many years had been widely separated in their labors, were to bear their last witness for Christ in the world's metropolis, and upon its soil to shed their blood as the seed of a vast harvest of saints and martyrs.

Since his reinstatement after his denial of Christ, Peter had unflinchingly braved danger and had shown a noble courage in preaching a crucified, risen, and ascended Saviour. As he lay in his cell he called to mind the words that Christ had spoken to him: "Verily, verily, I say unto thee, When thou wast young, thou girdedst thyself, and walkedst whither thou wouldest: but when thou shalt be old, thou shalt stretch forth thy hands, and another shall gird thee, and carry thee whither thou wouldest not." John 21:18. Thus Jesus had made known to the disciple the very manner of his death, and even foretold the stretching of his hands upon the cross.

Peter, as a Jew and a foreigner, was condemned to be scourged and crucified. In prospect of this fearful death, the apostle remembered his great sin in denying Jesus in the hour of His trial. Once so unready to acknowledge the cross, he now counted it a joy to yield up his life for the gospel, feeling only that, for him who had denied his Lord, to die in the same manner as his Master died was too great an honor. Peter had sincerely repented of that sin and had been forgiven by Christ, as is shown by the high commission given him to feed the sheep and lambs of the flock. But he could never forgive himself. Not even the thought of the agonies of the last terrible scene could lessen the bitterness of his sorrow and repentance. As a last favor he entreated his executioners that he might be nailed to the cross with his head downward. The request was granted, and in this manner died the great apostle Peter.

53

John the Beloved

John is distinguished above the other apostles as "the disciple whom Jesus loved." John 21:20. He seems to have enjoyed to a pre-eminent degree the friendship of Christ, and he received many tokens of the Saviour's confidence and love. He was one of the three permitted to witness Christ's glory upon the mount of transfiguration and His agony in Gethsemane, and it was to his care that our Lord confided His mother in those last hours of anguish upon the cross.

The Saviour's affection for the beloved disciple was returned with all the strength of ardent devotion. John clung to Christ as the vine clings to the stately pillar. For his Master's sake he braved the dangers of the judgment hall and lingered about the cross, and at the tidings that Christ had risen, he hastened to the sepulcher, in his zeal out-stripping even the impetuous Peter.

The confiding love and unselfish devotion manifested in the life and character of John present lessons of untold value to the Christian church. John did not naturally possess the loveliness of character that his later experience revealed. By nature he had serious defects. He was not only proud, self-assertive, and ambitious for honor, but impetuous, and resentful under injury. He and his brother were called "sons of thunder." Evil temper, the desire for revenge, the spirit of criticism, were all in the beloved disciple. But beneath all this the divine Teacher discerned the ardent, sincere, loving heart. Jesus rebuked this self-seeking, disappointed his ambitions, tested his faith. But He revealed to him that for which his soul longed—the beauty of holiness, the transforming power of love.

The defects in John's character came strongly to the front on several occasions during his personal association with the Saviour. At one time Christ sent messengers before Him into a village of the Samaritans, requesting the people to prepare refreshments for Him and His disciples. But when the Saviour approached the town, He appeared to be desirous of passing on toward Jerusalem. This aroused the envy of the Samaritans, and instead of inviting Him to tarry with them, they withheld the courtesies which they would have given to a common wayfarer. Jesus never urges His presence upon any, and the Samaritans lost the blessing which would have been granted them had they solicited Him to be their guest.

[539, 540]

The disciples knew that it was the purpose of Christ to bless the Samaritans by His presence; and the coldness, jealousy, and disrespect shown to their Master filled them with surprise and indignation. James and John especially were aroused. That He whom they so highly reverenced should be thus treated, seemed to them a wrong too great to be passed over without immediate punishment. In their zeal they said, "Lord, wilt Thou that we command fire to come down from heaven, and consume them, even as Elias did?" referring to the destruction of the Samaritan captains and their companies sent out to take the prophet Elijah. They were surprised to see that Jesus was pained by their words, and still more surprised as His rebuke fell upon their ears: "Ye know not what manner of spirit ye are of. For the Son of man is not come to destroy men's lives, but to save them." Luke 9:54-56.

It is no part of Christ's mission to compel men to receive Him. It is Satan, and men actuated by his spirit, who seek to compel the conscience. Under a pretense of zeal for righteousness, men who are confederated with evil angels sometimes bring suffering upon their fellow men in order to convert them to their ideas of religion; but Christ is ever showing mercy, ever seeking to win by the revealing of His love. He can admit no rival in the soul, nor accept of partial service; but He desires only voluntary service, the willing surrender of the heart under the constraint of love.

On another occasion James and John presented through their mother a petition requesting that they might be permitted to occupy the highest positions of honor in Christ's kingdom. Notwithstanding Christ's repeated instruction concerning the nature of His kingdom, these young disciples still cherished the hope for a Messiah who would take His throne and kingly power in accordance with the desires of men. The mother, coveting with them the place of honor in this kingdom for her sons, asked, "Grant that these my two sons may sit, the one on Thy right hand, and the other on the left, in Thy kingdom."

But the Saviour answered, "Ye know not what ye ask. Are ye able to drink of the cup that I shall drink of, and to be baptized with the baptism that I am baptized with?" They recalled His mysterious words pointing to trial and suffering, yet answered confidently, "We are able." They would count it highest honor to prove their loyalty by sharing all that was to befall their Lord.

"Ye shall drink indeed of My cup, and be baptized with the baptism that I am baptized with," Christ declared— before Him a cross instead of a throne, two malefactors His companions at His right hand and at His left. James and John were to be sharers with their Master in suffering—the one, destined to swift-coming death by the sword; the other, longest of all the disciples to follow his Master in labor and reproach and persecution. "But to sit on My right hand, and on My left," He continued, "is not Mine to give, but it shall be given to them for whom it is prepared of My Father." Matthew 20:21-23.

Jesus understood the motive that prompted the request and thus reproved the pride and ambition of the two disciples: "The princes of the Gentiles exercise dominion over them, and they that are great exercise authority upon them. But it shall not be so among you: but whosoever will be great among you, let him be your minister; and whosoever will be chief among you, let him be your servant: even as the Son of man came not to be ministered unto, but to minister, and to give His life a ransom for many." Matthew 20:25-28.

In the kingdom of God, position is not gained through favoritism. It is not earned, nor is it received through an arbitrary bestowal. It is the result of character. The crown and the throne are the tokens of a condition attained—tokens of self-conquest through the grace of our Lord Jesus Christ.

Long afterward, when John had been brought into sympathy with Christ through the fellowship of His sufferings, the Lord Jesus revealed to him what is the condition of nearness to His kingdom. "To him that overcometh," Christ said, "will I grant to sit with Me in My throne, even as I also overcame, and am set down with My Father in His throne." Revelation 3:21. The one who stands nearest to Christ will be he who has drunk most deeply of His spirit of self-sacrificing love,—love that "vaunteth not itself, is not puffed up, . . . seeketh not her own, is not easily provoked, thinketh no evil" (1 Corinthians 13:4, 5),—love that moves the disciple, as it moved our Lord, to give all, to live and labor and sacrifice even unto death, for the saving of humanity.

At another time during their early evangelistic labors, James and John met one who, while not an acknowledged follower of Christ, was casting out devils in His name. The disciples forbade the man to work and thought they were right in doing this. But when they laid the matter before Christ, He reproved them, saying, "Forbid him not: for there is no man which shall do a miracle in My name, that can lightly speak evil of Me." Mark 9:39. None who showed themselves in any way friendly to Christ were to be repulsed. The disciples must not indulge a narrow, exclusive spirit, but must manifest the same far-reaching sympathy which they had seen in their Master. James and John had thought that in checking this man they had in view the Lord's honor; but they began to see that they were jealous for their own. They acknowledged their error and accepted the reproof.

The lessons of Christ, setting forth meekness and humility and love as essential to growth in grace and a fitness for His work, were of the highest value to John. He treasured every lesson and constantly sought to bring his life into harmony with the divine pattern. John had begun to discern the glory of Christ—not the worldly pomp and power for which he had been taught to hope, but "the glory as of the Only Begotten of the Father, full of grace and truth." John 1:14.

The depth and fervor of John's affection for his Master was not the cause of Christ's love for him, but the effect of that love. John desired to become like Jesus, and under the transforming influence of the love of Christ he did become meek and lowly. Self was hid in Jesus. Above all his companions, John yielded himself to the power of that wondrous life. He says, "The life was manifested, and we have seen it." "And of His fullness have all we received, and grace for grace." 1 John 1:2; John 1:16. John knew the Saviour by an experimental knowledge. His Master's lessons were graven on his soul. When he testified of the Saviour's grace, his simple language was eloquent with the love that pervaded his whole being.

It was John's deep love for Christ which led him always to desire to be close by His side. The Saviour loved all the Twelve, but John's was the most receptive spirit. He was younger than the others, and with more of the child's confiding trust he opened his heart to Jesus. Thus he came more into sympathy with Christ, and through him the Saviour's deepest spiritual teaching was communicated to the people.

Jesus loves those who represent the Father, and John could talk of the Father's love as no other of the disciples could. He revealed to his fellow men that which he felt in his own soul, representing in his character the attributes of God. The glory of the Lord was expressed in his face. The beauty of holiness which had transformed him shone with a Christlike radiance from his countenance. In adoration and love he beheld the Saviour until likeness to Christ and fellowship with Him became his one desire, and in his character was reflected the character of his Master.

"Behold," he said, "what manner of love the Father hath bestowed upon us, that we should be called the sons of God. . . . Beloved, now are we the sons of God, and it doth not yet appear what we shall be: but we know that, when He shall appear, we shall be like Him; for we shall see Him as He is." 1 John 3:1, 2.

54

A Faithful Witness

This chapter is based on the Epistles of John

After the ascension of Christ, John stands forth as a faithful, earnest laborer for the Master. With the other disciples he enjoyed the outpouring of the Spirit on the Day of Pentecost, and with fresh zeal and power he continued to speak to the people the words of life, seeking to lead their thoughts to the Unseen. He was a powerful preacher, fervent, and deeply in earnest. In beautiful language and with a musical voice he told of the words and works of Christ, speaking in a way that impressed the hearts of those who heard him. The simplicity of his words, the sublime power of the truths he uttered, and the fervor that characterized his teachings, gave him access to all classes.

The apostle's life was in harmony with his teachings. The love for Christ which glowed in his heart led him to put forth earnest, untiring labor for his fellow men, especially for his brethren in the Christian church.

Christ had bidden the first disciples love one another as He had loved them. Thus they were to bear testimony to the world that Christ was formed within, the hope of glory. "A new commandment I give unto you," He had said, "That ye love one another; as I have loved you, that ye also love one another." John 13:34. At the time when these words were spoken, the disciples could not understand them; but after they had witnessed the sufferings of Christ, after His crucifixion and resurrection, and ascension to heaven, and after the Holy Spirit had rested on them at Pentecost, they had a clearer conception of the love of God and of the nature of that love which they must have for one another. Then John could say to his fellow disciples:

"Hereby perceive we the love of God, because He laid down His life for us: and we ought to lay down our lives for the brethren."

After the descent of the Holy Spirit, when the disciples went forth to proclaim a living Saviour, their one desire was the salvation of souls. They rejoiced in the sweetness of communion with saints. They were tender, thoughtful, self-denying, willing to make any sacrifice for the truth's sake. In their daily association with one another, they revealed the love that Christ had enjoined upon them. By unselfish words and deeds they strove to kindle this love in other hearts.

Such a love the believers were ever to cherish. They were to go forward in willing obedience to the new commandment. So closely were they to be united with Christ that they would be enabled to fulfill all His requirements. Their lives were to magnify the power of a Saviour who could justify them by His righteousness.

But gradually a change came. The believers began to look for defects in others. Dwelling upon mistakes, giving place to unkind criticism, they lost sight of the Saviour and His love. They became more strict in regard to outward ceremonies, more particular about the theory than the practice of the faith. In their zeal to condemn others, they overlooked their own errors. They lost the brotherly love that Christ had enjoined, and, saddest of all, they were unconscious of their loss. They did not realize that happiness and joy were going out of their lives and that, having shut the love of God out of their hearts, they would soon walk in darkness.

John, realizing that brotherly love was waning in the church, urged upon believers the constant need of this love. His letters to the church are full of this thought. "Beloved, let us love one another," he writes; "for love is of God; and everyone that loveth is born of God, and knoweth God. He that loveth not knoweth not God; for God is love. In this was manifested the love of God toward us, because that God sent His only-begotten Son into the world, that we might live through Him. Herein is love, not that we loved God, but that He loved us, and sent His Son to be the propitiation for our sins. Beloved, if God so loved us, we ought also to love one another."

Of the special sense in which this love should be manifested by believers, the apostle writes: "A new commandment I write unto you, which thing is true in Him and in you: because the darkness is past, and the true light now shineth. He that saith he is in the light, and hateth his brother, is in darkness even until now. He that loveth his brother abideth in the light, and there is none occasion of stumbling in him. But he that hateth his brother is in darkness, and walketh in darkness, and knoweth not whither he goeth, because that darkness hath blinded his eyes." "This is the message that ye heard from the beginning, that we should love one another." "He that loveth not his brother abideth in death. Whosoever hateth his brother is a murderer: and ye know that no murderer hath eternal life abiding in him. Hereby perceive we the love of God, because

He laid down His life for us: and we ought to lay down our lives for the brethren."

It is not the opposition of the world that most endangers the church of Christ. It is the evil cherished in the hearts of believers that works their most grievous disaster and most surely retards the progress of God's cause. There is no surer way of weakening spirituality than by cherishing envy, suspicion, faultfinding, and evil surmising. On the other hand, the strongest witness that God has sent His Son into the world is the existence of harmony and union among men of varied dispositions who form His church. This witness it is the privilege of the followers of Christ to bear. But in order to do this, they must place themselves under Christ's command. Their characters must be conformed to His character and their wills to His will.

"A new commandment I give unto you," Christ said, "That ye love one another; as I have loved you, that ye also love one another." John 13:34. What a wonderful statement; but, oh, how poorly practiced! In the church of God today brotherly love is sadly lacking. Many who profess to love the Saviour do not love one another. Unbelievers are watching to see if the faith of professed Christians is exerting a sanctifying influence upon their lives; and they are quick to discern the defects in character, the inconsistencies in action. Let Christians not make it possible for the enemy to point to them and say, Behold how these people, standing under the banner of Christ, hate one another. Christians are all members of one family, all children of the same heavenly Father, with the same blessed hope of immortality. Very close and tender should be the tie that binds them together.

Divine love makes its most touching appeals to the heart when it calls upon us to manifest the same tender compassion that Christ manifested. That man only who has unselfish love for his brother has true love for God. The true Christian will not willingly permit the soul in peril and need to go unwarned, uncared for. He will not hold himself aloof from the erring, leaving them to plunge farther into unhappiness and discouragement or to fall on Satan's battleground.

Those who have never experienced the tender, winning love of Christ cannot lead others to the fountain of life. His love in the heart is a constraining power, which leads men to reveal Him in the conversation, in the tender, pitiful spirit, in the uplifting of the lives of those with whom they associate. Christian workers who succeed in their efforts must know Christ; and in order to know Him, they must know His love. In heaven their fitness as workers is measured by their ability to love as Christ loved and to work as He worked.

"Let us not love in word," the apostle writes, "but in deed and in truth." The completeness of Christian character is attained when the impulse to help and bless others springs constantly from within. It is the atmosphere of this love surrounding the soul of the believer that makes him a savor of life unto life and enables God to bless his work.

Supreme love for God and unselfish love for one another —this is the best gift that our heavenly Father can bestow. This love is not an impulse, but a divine principle, a permanent power. The unconsecrated heart cannot originate or produce it. Only in the heart where Jesus reigns is it found. "We love Him, because He first loved us." In the heart renewed by divine grace, love is the ruling principle of action. It modifies the character, governs the impulses, controls the passions, and ennobles the affections. This love, cherished in the soul, sweetens the life and sheds a refining influence on all around.

John strove to lead the believers to understand the exalted privileges that would come to them through the exercise of the spirit of love. This redeeming power, filling the heart, would control every other motive and raise its possessors above the corrupting influences of the world. And as this love was allowed full sway and became the motive power in the life, their trust and confidence in God and His dealing with them would be complete. They could then come to Him in full confidence of faith, knowing that they would receive from Him everything needful for their present and eternal good. "Herein is our love made perfect," he wrote, "that we may have boldness in the day of judgment: because as He is, so are we in this world. There is no fear in love; but perfect love casteth out fear." "And this is the confidence that we have in Him, that, if we ask anything according to His will, He heareth us: and if we know that He hear us, . . . we know that we have the petitions that we desired of Him."

"And if any man sin, we have an advocate with the Father, Jesus Christ the righteous: and He is the propitiation for our sins: and not for ours only, but also for the sins of the whole world." "If we confess our sins, He is faithful and just to forgive us our sins, and to cleanse us from all unrighteousness." The conditions of obtaining mercy from God are simple and reasonable. The Lord does not require us to do some grievous thing in order to gain forgiveness. We need not make long and wearisome pilgrimages, or perform painful penances, to commend our souls to the God of heaven or to expiate our transgression. He that "confesseth and forsaketh" his sin "shall have mercy." Proverbs 28:13.

In the courts above, Christ is pleading for His church —pleading for those for whom He has paid the redemption price of His blood. Centuries, ages, can never lessen the efficacy of His atoning sacrifice. Neither life nor death, height nor depth, can separate us from the love of God which is in Christ Jesus; not because we hold Him so firmly, but because He holds us so fast. If our salvation depended on our own efforts, we could not be saved; but it depends on the One who is behind all the promises. Our grasp on Him may seem feeble, but His love is that of an elder brother; so long as we maintain our union with Him, no one can pluck us out of His hand.

As the years went by and the number of believers grew, John labored with increasing fidelity and earnestness for his brethren. The times were full of peril for the church. Satanic delusions existed everywhere. By misrepresentation and falsehood the emissaries of Satan sought to arouse opposition against the doctrines of Christ, and in consequence dissensions and heresies were imperiling the church. Some who professed Christ claimed that His love released them from obedience to the law of God. On the other hand, many taught that it was necessary to observe the Jewish customs and ceremonies; that a mere observance of the law, without faith in the blood of Christ, was sufficient for salvation. Some held that Christ was a good man, but denied His divinity. Some who pretended to be true to the cause of God were deceivers, and in practice they denied Christ and His gospel. Living themselves in transgression, they were bringing heresies into the church. Thus many were being led into the mazes of skepticism and delusion.

John was filled with sadness as he saw these poisonous errors creeping into the church. He saw the dangers to which the church was exposed, and he met the emergency with promptness and decision. The epistles of John breathe the spirit of love. It seems as if he wrote with a pen dipped in love. But when he came in contact with those who were breaking the law of God, yet claiming that they were living without sin, he did not hesitate to warn them of their fearful deception.

Writing to a helper in the gospel work, a woman of good repute and wide influence, he said: "Many deceivers are entered into the world, who confess not that Jesus Christ is come in the flesh. This is a deceiver and an antichrist. Look to yourselves, that we lose not those things which we have wrought, but that we receive a full reward. Whosoever transgresseth, and abideth not in the doctrine of

Christ, hath not God. He that abideth in the doctrine of Christ, he hath both the Father and the Son. If there come any unto you, and bring not this doctrine, receive him not into your house, neither bid him Godspeed: for he that biddeth him Godspeed is partaker of his evil deeds.''

We are authorized to hold in the same estimation as did the beloved disciple those who claim to abide in Christ while living in transgression of God's law. There exist in these last days evils similar to those that threatened the prosperity of the early church; and the teachings of the apostle John on these points should be carefully heeded. "You must have charity," is the cry heard everywhere, especially from those who profess sanctification. But true charity is too pure to cover an unconfessed sin. While we are to love the souls for whom Christ died, we are to make no compromise with evil. We are not to unite with the rebellious and call this charity. God requires His people in this age of the world to stand for the right as unflinchingly as did John in opposition to soul-destroying errors.

The apostle teaches that while we should manifest Christian courtesy we are authorized to deal in plain terms with sin and sinners; that this is not inconsistent with true charity. "Whosoever committeth sin," he writes, "transgresseth also the law: for sin is the transgression of the law. And ye know that He was manifested to take away our sins; and in Him is no sin. Whosoever abideth in Him sinneth not: whosoever sinneth hath not seen Him, neither known Him."

As a witness for Christ, John entered into no controversy, no wearisome contention. He declared what he knew, what he had seen and heard. He had been intimately associated with Christ, had listened to His teachings, had witnessed His mighty miracles. Few could see the beauties of Christ's character as John saw them. For him the darkness had passed away; on him the true light was shining. His testimony in regard to the Saviour's life and death was clear and forcible. Out of the abundance of a heart overflowing with love for the Saviour he spoke; and no power could stay his words.

"That which was from the beginning," he declared, "which we have heard, which we have seen with our eyes, which we have looked upon, and our hands have handled, of the Word of life; . . . that which we have seen and heard declare we unto you, that ye also may have fellowship with us: and truly our fellowship is with the Father, and with His Son Jesus Christ."

So may every true believer be able, through his own experience, to "set to his seal that God is true." John 3:33. He can bear witness to that which he has seen and heard and felt of the power of Christ.

55

Transformed by Grace

In the life of the disciple John true sanctification is exemplified. During the years of his close association with Christ, he was often warned and cautioned by the Saviour; and these reproofs he accepted. As the character of the Divine One was manifested to him, John saw his own deficiencies, and was humbled by the revelation. Day by day, in contrast with his own violent spirit, he beheld the tenderness and forbearance of Jesus, and heard His lessons of humility and patience. Day by day his heart was drawn out to Christ, until he lost sight of self in love for his Master. The power and tenderness, the majesty and meekness, the strength and patience, that he saw in the daily life of the Son of God, filled his soul with admiration. He yielded his resentful, ambitious temper to the molding power of Christ, and divine love wrought in him a transformation of character.

In striking contrast to the sanctification worked out in the life of John is the experience of his fellow disciple, Judas. Like his associate, Judas professed to be a disciple of Christ, but he possessed only a form of godliness. He was not insensible to the beauty of the character of Christ; and often, as he listened to the Saviour's words, conviction came to him, but he would not humble his heart or confess his sins. By resisting the divine influence he dishonored the Master whom he professed to love. John warred earnestly against his faults; but Judas violated his conscience and yielded to temptation, fastening upon himself more securely his habits of evil. The practice of the truths that Christ taught was at variance with his desires and purposes, and he could not bring himself to yield his ideas in order to receive wisdom from heaven. Instead of walking in the light, he chose to walk in darkness. Evil desires, covetousness, revengeful passions, dark and sullen thoughts, were cherished until Satan gained full control of him.

John and Judas are representatives of those who profess to be Christ's followers. Both these disciples had the same opportunities to study and follow the divine Pattern. Both were closely associated with Jesus and were privileged to listen to His teaching. Each possessed serious defects of character; and each had access to the divine grace that transforms character. But while one in humility was learning of Jesus, the other revealed that he was not a doer of the word, but a hearer only. One, daily dying to self and overcoming sin, was sanctified through the truth; the other, resisting the transforming power of grace and indulging selfish desires, was brought into bondage to Satan.

Such transformation of character as is seen in the life of John is ever the result of communion with Christ. There may be marked defects in the character of an individual, yet when he becomes a true disciple of Christ, the power of divine grace transforms and sanctifies him. Beholding as in a glass the glory of the Lord, he is changed from glory to glory, until he is like Him whom he adores.

John was a teacher of holiness, and in his letters to the church he laid down unerring rules for the conduct of Christians. "Every man that hath this hope in him," he wrote, "purifieth himself, even as He is pure." "He that saith he abideth in Him ought himself also so to walk, even as He walked." 1 John 3:3; 2:6. He taught that the Christian must be pure in heart and life. Never should he be satisfied with an empty profession. As God is holy in His sphere, so fallen man, through faith in Christ, is to be holy in his sphere.

"This is the will of God," the apostle Paul wrote, "even your sanctification." 1 Thessalonians 4:3. The sanctification of the church is God's object in all His dealings with His people. He has chosen them from eternity, that they might be holy. He gave His Son to die for them, that they might be sanctified through obedience to the truth, divested of all the littleness of self. From them Her requires a personal work, a personal surrender. God can be honored by those who profess to believe in Him, only as they are conformed to His image and controlled by His Spirit. Then, as witnesses for the Saviour, they may make known what divine grace has done for them.

True sanctification comes through the working out of the principle of love. "God is love; and he that dwelleth in love dwelleth in God, and God in him." 1 John 4:16. The life of him in whose heart Christ abides, will reveal practical godliness. The character will be purified, elevated, ennobled, and glorified. Pure doctrine will blend with works of righteousness; heavenly precepts will mingle with holy practices.

Those who would gain the blessing of sanctification must first learn the meaning of self-sacrifice. The cross of Christ is the central pillar on which hangs the "far more exceeding and eternal weight of glory." "If any man will come after Me," Christ says, "let him deny himself, and take up his cross, and follow Me." 2 Corinthians 4:17; Matthew 16:24. It is the fragrance of our love for our fellow men that reveals our love for God. It is patience in service that brings rest to the soul. It is through humble, diligent, faithful toil that the welfare of Israel is promoted. God upholds and strengthens the one who is willing to follow in Christ's way.

Sanctification is not the work of a moment, an hour, a day, but of a lifetime. It is not gained by a happy flight of feeling, but is the result of constantly dying to sin, and constantly living for Christ. Wrongs cannot be righted nor reformations wrought in the character by feeble, intermittent efforts. It is only by long, persevering effort, sore discipline, and stern conflict, that we shall overcome. We know not one day how strong will be our conflict the next. So long as Satan reigns, we shall have self to subdue, besetting sins to overcome; so long as life shall last, there will be no stopping place, no point which we can reach and say, I have fully attained. Sanctification is the result of lifelong obedience.

None of the apostles and prophets ever claimed to be without sin. Men who have lived the nearest to God, men who would sacrifice life itself rather than knowingly commit a wrong act, men whom God has honored with divine light and power, have confessed the sinfulness of their nature. They have put no confidence in the flesh, have claimed no righteousness of their own, but have trusted wholly in the righteousness of Christ.

So will it be with all who behold Christ. The nearer we come to Jesus, and the more clearly we discern the purity of His character, the more clearly shall we see the exceeding sinfulness of sin, and the less shall we feel like exalting ourselves. There will be a continual reaching out of the soul after God, a continual, earnest, heartbreaking confession of sin and humbling of the heart before Him. At every advance step in our Christian experience our repentance will deepen. We shall know that our sufficiency is in Christ alone and shall make the apostle's confession our own: "I know that in me (that is, in my flesh,) dwelleth no good thing." "God forbid that I should glory, save in the cross of our Lord Jesus Christ, by whom the world is crucified unto me, and I unto the world." Romans 7:18; Galatians 6:14.

Let the recording angels write the history of the holy struggles and conflicts of the people of God; let them record their prayers and tears; but let not God be dishonored by the declaration from human lips, "I am sinless; I am holy." Sanctified lips will never give utterance to such presumptuous words.

The apostle Paul had been caught up to the third heaven and had seen and heard things that could not be uttered, and yet his unassuming statement is: "Not as though I had already attained, either were already perfect: but I follow after." Philippians 3:12. Let the angels of heaven write of Paul's victories in fighting the good fight of faith. Let heaven rejoice in his steadfast tread heavenward, and that, keeping the prize in view, he counts every other consideration dross. Angels rejoice to tell his triumphs, but Paul makes no boast of his attainments. The attitude of Paul is the attitude that every follower of Christ should take as he urges his way onward in the strife for the immortal crown.

Let those who feel inclined to make a high profession of holiness look into the mirror of God's law. As they see its far-reaching claims, and understand its work as a discerner of the thoughts and intents of the heart, they will not boast of sinlessness. "If we," says John, not separating himself from his brethren, "say that we have no sin, we deceive ourselves, and the truth is not in us." "If we say that we have not sinned, we make Him a liar, and His word is not in us." "If we confess our sins, He is faithful and just to forgive us our sins, and to cleanse us from all unrighteousness." 1 John 1:8, 10, 9.

There are those who profess holiness, who declare that they are wholly the Lord's, who claim a right to the promises of God, while refusing to render obedience to His commandments. These transgressors of the law claim everything that is promised to the children of God; but this is presumption on their part, for John tells us that true love for God will be revealed in obedience to all His commandments. It is not enough to believe the theory of truth, to make a profession of faith in Christ, to believe that Jesus is no impostor, and that the religion of the Bible is no cunningly devised fable. "He that saith, I know Him, and keepeth not His commandments," John wrote, "is a liar, and the truth is not in him. But whoso keepeth His word, in him verily is the love of God perfected: hereby know we that we are in Him." "He that keepeth His commandments dwelleth in Him, and He in him." 1 John 2:4, 5; 3:24.

John did not teach that salvation was to be earned by obedience; but that obedience was the fruit of faith and love. "Ye know that He was manifested to take away our sins," he said, "and in Him is no sin. Whosoever abideth in Him sinneth not: whosoever sinneth hath not seen Him, neither known Him." 1 John 3:5, 6. If we abide in Christ, if the love of God dwells in the heart, our feelings, our thoughts, our actions, will be in harmony with the will of God. The sanctified heart is in harmony with the precepts of God's law.

There are many who, though striving to obey God's commandments, have little peace or joy. This lack in their experience is the result of a failure to exercise faith. They walk as it were in a salt land, a parched wilderness. They claim little, when they might claim much; for there is no limit to the promises of God. Such ones do not correctly represent the sanctification that comes through obedience to the truth. The Lord would have all His sons and daughters happy, peaceful, and obedient. Through the exercise of faith the believer comes into possession of these blessings. Through faith, every deficiency of character may be supplied, every defilement cleansed, every fault corrected, every excellence developed.

Prayer is heaven's ordained means of success in the conflict with sin and the development of Christian character. The divine influences that come in answer to the prayer of faith will accomplish in the soul of the suppliant all for which he pleads. For the pardon of sin, for the Holy Spirit, for a Christlike temper, for wisdom and strength to do His work, for any gift He has promised, we may ask; and the promise is, "Ye shall receive."

It was in the mount with God that Moses beheld the pattern of that wonderful building that was to be the abiding place of His glory. It is in the mount with God—in the secret place of communion—that we are to contemplate His glorious ideal for humanity. In all ages, through the medium of communion with heaven, God has worked out His purpose for His children, by unfolding gradually to their minds the doctrines of grace. His manner of imparting truth is illustrated in the words, "His going forth is prepared as the morning." Hosea 6:3. He who places himself where God can enlighten him, advances, as it were, from the partial obscurity of dawn to the full radiance of noonday.

True sanctification means perfect love, perfect obedience, perfect conformity to the will of God. We are to be sanctified to God through obedience to the truth. Our conscience must be purged from dead works to serve the living God. We are not yet perfect; but it is our privilege to cut away from the entanglements of self and sin, and advance to perfection. Great possibilities, high and holy attainments, are placed within the reach of all.

The reason many in this age of the world make no greater advancement in the divine life is because they interpret the will of God to be just what they will to do. While following their own desires, they flatter themselves that they are conforming to God's will. These have no conflicts with self. There are others who for a time are successful in the struggle against their selfish desire for pleasure and ease. They are sincere and earnest, but grow weary of protracted effort, of daily death, of ceaseless turmoil. Indolence seems inviting, death to self repulsive; and they close their drowsy eyes and fall under the power of temptation instead of resisting it.

The directions laid down in the word of God leave no room for compromise with evil. The Son of God was manifested that He might draw all men unto Himself. He came not to lull the world to sleep, but to point out the narrow path in which all must travel who reach at last the gates of the City of God. His children must follow where He has led the way; at whatever sacrifice of ease or selfish indulgence, at whatever cost of labor or suffering, they must maintain a constant battle with self.

The greatest praise that men can bring to God is to become consecrated channels through whom He can work. Time is rapidly passing into eternity. Let us not keep back from God that which is His own. Let us not refuse Him that which, though it cannot be given with merit, cannot be denied without ruin. He asks for a whole heart; give it to Him; it is His, both by creation and by redemption. He asks for your intellect; give it to Him; it is His. He asks for your money; give it to Him; it is His. "Ye are not your own, for ye are bought with a price." 1 Corinthians 6: 19, 20. God requires the homage of a sanctified soul, which has prepared itself, by the exercise of the faith that works by love, to serve Him. He holds up before us the highest ideal, even perfection. He asks us to be absolutely and completely for Him in this world as He is for us in the presence of God.

"This is the will of God" concerning you, "even your sanctification." 1 Thessalonians 4:3. Is it your will also? Your sins may be as mountains before you; but if you humble your heart and confess your sins, trusting in the merits of a crucified and risen Saviour, He will forgive and will cleanse you from all unrighteousness. God demands of you entire conformity to His law. This law is the echo of His voice saying to you, Holier, yes, holier still. Desire the fullness of the grace of Christ. Let your heart be filled with an intense longing for His righteousness, the work of which God's word declares is peace, and its effect quietness and assurance forever.

As your soul yearns after God, you will find more and still more of the unsearchable riches of His grace. As you contemplate these riches you will come into possession of them and will reveal the merits of the Saviour's sacrifice, the protection of His righteousness, the fullness of His wisdom, and His power to present you before the Father "without spot, and blameless." 2 Peter 3:14.

56

Patmos

More than half a century had passed since the organization of the Christian church. During that time the gospel message had been constantly opposed. Its enemies had never relaxed their efforts, and had at last succeeded in enlisting the power of the Roman emperor against the Christians.

In the terrible persecution that followed, the apostle John did much to confirm and strengthen the faith of the believers. He bore a testimony which his adversaries could not controvert and which helped his brethren to meet with courage and loyalty the trials that came upon them. When the faith of the Christians would seem to waver under the fierce opposition they were forced to meet, the old, tried servant of Jesus would repeat with power and eloquence the story of the crucified and risen Saviour. He steadfastly maintained his faith, and from his lips came ever the same glad message: "That which was from the beginning, which we have heard, which we have seen with our eyes, which we have looked upon, and our hands have handled, of the Word of life; . . . that which we have seen and heard declare we unto you.: 1 John 1:1-3.

John lived to be very old. He witnessed the destruction of Jerusalem and the ruin of the stately temple. The last survivor of the disciples who had been intimately connected with the Saviour, his message had great influence in setting forth the fact that Jesus was the Messiah, the Redeemer of the world. No one could doubt his sincerity, and through his teachings many were led to turn from unbelief.

The rulers of the Jews were filled with bitter hatred against John for his unwavering fidelity to the cause of Christ. They declared that their efforts against the Christians would avail nothing so long as John's testimony kept ringing in the ears of the people. In order that the miracles and teachings of Jesus might be forgotten, the voice of the bold witness must be silenced.

John was accordingly summoned to Rome to be tried for his faith. Here before the authorities the apostle's doctrines were misstated. False witnesses accused him of teaching seditious heresies. By these accusations his enemies hoped to bring about the disciple's death.

John answered for himself in a clear and convincing manner,

and with such simplicity and candor that his words had a powerful effect. His hearers were astonished at his wisdom and eloquence. But the more convincing his testimony, the deeper was the hatred of his opposers. The emperor Domitian was filled with rage. He could neither dispute the reasoning of Christ's faithful advocate, nor match the power that attended his utterance of truth; yet he determined that he would silence his voice.

John was cast into a caldron of boiling oil; but the Lord preserved the life of His faithful servant, even as He preserved the three Hebrews in the fiery furnace. As the words were spoken, Thus perish all who believe in that deceiver, Jesus Christ of Nazareth, John declared, My Master patiently submitted to all that Satan and his angels could devise to humiliate and torture Him. He gave His life to save the world. I am honored in being permitted to suffer for His sake. I am a weak, sinful man. Christ was holy, harmless, undefiled. He did no sin, neither was guile found in His mouth.

These words had their influence, and John was removed from the caldron by the very men who had cast him in.

Again the hand of persecution fell heavily upon the apostle. By the emperor's decree John was banished to the Isle of Patmos, condemned "for the word of God, and for the testimony of Jesus Christ." Revelation 1:9. Here, his enemies thought, his influence would no longer be felt, and he must finally die of hardship and distress.

Patmos, a barren, rocky island in the Aegean Sea, had been chosen by the Roman government as a place of banishment for criminals; but to the servant of God this gloomy abode became the gate of heaven. Here, shut away from the busy scenes of life, and from the active labors of former years, he had the companionship of God and Christ and the heavenly angels, and from them he received instruction for the church for all future time. The events that would take place in the closing scenes of this earth's history were outlined before him; and there he wrote out the visions he received from God. When his voice could no longer testify to the One whom he loved and served, the messages given him on that barren coast were to go forth as a lamp that burneth, declaring the sure purpose of the Lord concerning every nation on the earth.

Among the cliffs and rocks of Patmos, John held communion with his Maker. He reviewed his past life, and at thought of the blessings he had received, peace filled his heart. He had lived the life of a Christian, and he could say in faith, "We know that we have passed from death unto life." 1 John 3:14. Not so the emperor who had banished him. He could look back only on fields of warfare and carnage, on desolated homes, on weeping widows and orphans, the fruit of his ambitious desire for pre-eminence.

In his isolated home John was able to study more closely than ever before the manifestations of divine power as recorded in the book of nature and in the pages of inspiration. To him it was a delight to meditate on the work of creation and to adore the divine Architect. In former years his eyes had been greeted by the sight of forest-covered hills, green valleys, and fruitful plains; and in the beauties of nature it had ever been his delight to trace the wisdom and skill of the Creator. He was now surrounded by scenes that to many would appear gloomy and uninteresting; but to John it was otherwise. While his surroundings might be desolate and barren, the blue heavens that bent above him were as bright and beautiful as the skies above his loved Jerusalem. In the wild, rugged rocks, in the mysteries of the deep, in the glories of the firmament, he read important lessons. All bore the message of God's power and glory.

All around him the apostle beheld witnesses to the Flood that had deluged the earth because the inhabitants ventured to transgress the law of God. The rocks thrown up from the great deep and from the earth by the breaking forth of the waters, brought vividly to his mind the terrors of that awful outpouring of God's wrath. In the voice of many waters—deep calling unto deep—the prophet heard the voice of the Creator. The sea, lashed to fury by the merciless winds, represented to him the wrath of an offended God. The mighty waves, in their terrible commotion, restrained within limits appointed by an invisible hand, spoke of the control of an infinite Power. And in contrast he realized the weakness and folly of mortals, who, though but worms of the dust, glory in their supposed wisdom and strength, and set their hearts against the Ruler of the universe, as if God were altogether such a one as themselves. By the rocks he was reminded of Christ, the Rock of his strength, in whose shelter he could hide without fear. From the exiled apostle on rocky Patmos there went up the most ardent longing of soul after God, the most fervent prayers.

The history of John affords a striking illustration of the way in which God can use aged workers. When John was exiled to the Isle of Patmos, there were many who thought him to be past service, an old and broken reed, ready to fall at any time. But the Lord saw fit to use him still. Though banished from the scenes of his former labor, he did not cease to bear witness to the truth. Even in Patmos he made friends and converts. His was a message of joy, proclaiming a risen Saviour who on high was interceding for His people until He should return to take them to Himself. And it was after John had grown old in the service of his Lord that he received more communications from heaven than he had received during all the former years of his life.

The most tender regard should be cherished for those whose life interest has been bound up with the work of God. These aged workers have stood faithful amid storm and trial. They may have infirmities, but they still possess talents that qualify them to stand in their place in God's cause. Though worn, and unable to bear the heavier burdens that younger men can and should carry, the counsel they can give is of the highest value.

They may have made mistakes, but from their failures they have learned to avoid errors and dangers, and are they not therefore competent to give wise counsel? They have borne test and trial, and though they have lost some of their vigor, the Lord does not lay them aside. He gives them special grace and wisdom.

Those who have served their Master when the work went hard, who endured poverty and remained faithful when there were few to stand for truth, are to be honored and respected. The Lord desires the younger laborers to gain wisdom, strength, and maturity by association with these faithful men. Let the younger men realize that in having such workers among them they are highly favored. Let them give them an honored place in their councils.

As those who have spent their lives in the service of Christ draw near to the close of their earthly ministry, they will be impressed by the Holy Spirit to recount the experiences they have had in connection with the work of God. The record of His wonderful dealings with His people, of His great goodness in delivering them from trial, should be repeated to those newly come to the faith. God desires the old and tried laborers to stand in their place, doing their part to save men and women from being swept downward by the mighty current of evil, He desires them to keep the armor on till He bids them lay it down.

In the experience of the apostle John under persecution, there is a lesson of wonderful strength and comfort for the Christian. God does not prevent the plottings of wicked men, but He causes their devices to work for good to those who in trial and conflict maintain their faith and loyalty. Often the gospel laborer carries on his work amid storms of persecution, bitter opposition, and unjust reproach. At such times let him remember that the experience to be gained in the furnace of trial and affliction is worth all the pain it costs. Thus

God brings His children near to Him, that He may show them their weakness and His strength. He teaches them to lean on Him. Thus He prepares them to meet emergencies, to fill positions of trust, and to accomplish the great purpose for which their powers were given them.

In all ages God's appointed witnesses have exposed themselves to reproach and persecution for the truth's sake. Joseph was maligned and persecuted because he preserved his virtue and integrity. David, the chosen messenger of God, was hunted like a beast of prey by his enemies. Daniel was cast into a den of lions because he was true to his allegiance to heaven. Job was deprived of his worldly possessions, and so afflicted in body that he was abhorred by his relatives, and friends; yet he maintained his integrity. Jeremiah could not be deterred from speaking the words that God had given him to speak; and his testimony so enraged the king and princes that he was cast into a loathsome pit. Stephen was stoned because he preached Christ and Him crucified. Paul was imprisoned, beaten with rods, stoned, and finally put to death because he was a faithful messenger for God to the Gentiles. And John was banished to the Isle of Patmos "for the word of God, and for the testimony of Jesus Christ."

These examples of human steadfastness bear witness to the faithfulness of God's promises—of His abiding presence and sustaining grace. They testify to the power of faith to withstand the powers of the world. It is the work of faith to rest in God in the darkest hour, to feel, however sorely tried and tempest-tossed, that our Father is at the helm. The eye of faith alone can look beyond the things of time to estimate aright the worth of the eternal riches.

Jesus does not present to His followers the hope of attaining earthly glory and riches, of living a life free from trial. Instead He calls upon them to follow Him in the path of self-denial and reproach. He who came to redeem the world was opposed by the united forces of evil. In an unpitying confederacy, evil men and evil angels arrayed themselves against the Prince of Peace. His every word and act revealed divine compassion, and His unlikeness to the world provoked the bitterest hostility.

So it will be with all who will live godly in Christ Jesus. Persecution and reproach await all who are imbued with the Spirit of Christ. The character of the persecution changes with the times, but the principle—the spirit that underlies it—is the same that has slain the chosen of the Lord ever since the days of Abel.

In all ages Satan has persecuted the people of God. He has

tortured them and put them to death, but in dying they became conquerors. They bore witness to the power of One mightier than Satan. Wicked men may torture and kill the body, but they cannot touch the life that is hid with Christ in God. They can incarcerate men and women in prison walls, but they cannot bind the spirit.

Through trial and persecution the glory—the character— of God is revealed in His chosen ones. The believers in Christ, hated and persecuted by the world, are educated and disciplined in the school of Christ. On earth they walk in narrow paths; they are purified in the furnace of affliction. They follow Christ through sore conflicts; they endure self- denial and experience bitter disappointments; but thus they learn the guilt and woe of sin, and they look upon it with abhorrence. Being partakers of Christ's sufferings, they can look beyond the gloom to the glory, saying, "I reckon that the sufferings of this present time are not worthy to be compared with the glory which shall be revealed in us." Romans 8:18.

57

The Revelation

In the days of the apostles the Christian believers were filled with earnestness and enthusiasm. So untiringly did they labor for their Master that in a comparatively short time, notwithstanding fierce opposition, the gospel of the kingdom was sounded to all the inhabited parts of the earth. The zeal manifested at this time by the followers of Jesus has been recorded by the pen of inspiration for the encouragement of believers in every age. Of the church at Ephesus, which the Lord Jesus used as a symbol of the entire Christian church in the apostolic age, the faithful and true Witness declared:

"I know thy works, and thy labor, and thy patience, and how thou canst not bear them which are evil: and thou hast tried them which say they are apostles, and are not, and hast found them liars: and hast borne, and hast patience, and for My name's sake hast labored, and hast not fainted." Revelation 2:2, 3.

At the first the experience of the church at Ephesus was marked with childlike simplicity and fervor. The believers sought earnestly to obey every word of God, and their lives revealed an earnest, sincere love for Christ. They rejoiced to do the will of God because the Saviour was in their hearts as an abiding presence. Filled with love for their Redeemer, their highest aim was to win souls to Him. They did not think of hoarding the precious treasure of the grace of Christ. They felt the importance of their calling; and, weighted with the message, "On earth peace, good will toward men," they burned with desire to carry the glad tidings of salvation to earth's remotest bounds. And the world took knowledge of them that they had been with Jesus. Sinful men, repentant, pardoned, cleansed, and sanctified, were brought into partnership with God through His Son.

The members of the church were united in sentiment and action. Love for Christ was the golden chain that bound them together. They followed on to know the Lord more and still more perfectly, and in their lives were revealed the joy and peace of Christ. They visited the fatherless and widows in their affliction, and kept themselves unspotted from the world, realizing that a failure to do this would be a contradiction of their profession and a denial of their Redeemer.

In every city the work was carried forward. Souls were con-

[578, 579]

verted, who in their turn felt that they must tell of the inestimable treasure they had received. They could not rest till the light which had illumined their minds was shining upon others. Multitudes of unbelievers were made acquainted with the reasons of the Christian's hope. Warm, inspired personal appeals were made to the erring, to the outcast, and to those who, while professing to know the truth, were lovers of pleasure more than lovers of God.

But after a time the zeal of the believers began to wane, and their love for God and for one another grew less. Coldness crept into the church. Some forgot the wonderful manner in which they had received the truth. One by one the old standard-bearers fell at their post. Some of the younger workers, who might have shared the burdens of these pioneers, and thus have been prepared for wise leadership, had become weary of oft-repeated truths. In their desire for something novel and startling they attempted to introduce new phases of doctrine, more pleasing to many minds, but not in harmony with the fundamental principles of the gospel. In their self-confidence and spiritual blindness they failed to discern that these sophistries would cause many to question the experiences of the past, and would thus lead to confusion and unbelief.

As these false doctrines were urged, differences sprang up, and the eyes of many were turned from beholding Jesus as the Author and Finisher of their faith. The discussion of unimportant points of doctrine, and the contemplation of pleasing fables of man's invention, occupied time that should have been spent in proclaiming the gospel. The masses that might have been convicted and converted by a faithful presentation of the truth were left unwarned. Piety was rapidly waning, and Satan seemed about to gain the ascendancy over those who claimed to be followers of Christ.

It was at this critical time in the history of the church that John was sentenced to banishment. Never had his voice been needed by the church as now. Nearly all his former associates in the ministry had suffered martyrdom. The remnant of believers was facing fierce opposition. To all outward appearance the day was not far distant when the enemies of the church of Christ would triumph.

But the Lord's hand was moving unseen in the darkness. In the providence of God, John was placed where Christ could give him a wonderful revelation of Himself and of divine truth for the enlightenment of the churches.

In exiling John, the enemies of truth had hoped to silence forever the voice of God's faithful witness; but on Patmos the disciple received a message, the influence of which was to continue to strengthen the church till the end of time. Though not released from the responsibility of their wrong act, those who banished John became instruments in the hands of God to carry out Heaven's purpose; and the very effort to extinguish the light placed the truth in bold relief.

It was on the Sabbath that the Lord of glory appeared to the exiled apostle. The Sabbath was as sacredly observed by John on Patmos as when he was preaching to the people in the towns and cities of Judea. He claimed as his own the precious promises that had been given regarding that day. "I was in the Spirit on the Lord's day," John writes, "and heard behind me a great voice, as of a trumpet, saying, I am Alpha and Omega, the first and the last. . . . And I turned to see the voice that spake with me. And being turned, I saw seven golden candlesticks; and in the midst of the seven candlesticks One like unto the Son of man." Revelation 1:10-13.

Richly favored was this beloved disciple. He had seen his Master in Gethsemane, His face marked with the blood drops of agony, His "visage . . . marred more than any man, and His form more than the sons of men." Isaiah 52:14. He had seen Him in the hands of the Roman soldiers, clothed with an old purple robe and crowned with thorns. He had seen Him hanging on the cross of Calvary, the object of cruel mockery and abuse. Now John is once more permitted to behold his Lord. But how changed is His appearance! He is no longer a Man of Sorrows, despised and humiliated by men. He is clothed in a garment of heavenly brightness. "His head and His hairs" are "white like wool, as white as snow; and His eyes . . . as a flame of fire; and His feet like unto fine brass, as if they burned in a furnace." Revelation 1:14, 15, 17. His voice is like the music of many waters. His countenance shines as the sun. In His hand are seven stars, and out of His mouth issues a sharp two-edged sword, an emblem of the power of His word. Patmos is made resplendent with the glory of the risen Lord.

"And when I saw Him," John writes, "I fell at His feet as dead. And He laid His right hand upon me, saying unto me, Fear not." Verse 17.

John was strengthened to live in the presence of his glorified Lord. Then before his wondering vision were opened the glories of heaven. He was permitted to see the throne of God and, looking beyond the conflicts of earth, to behold the white-robed throng of the redeemed. He heard the music of the heavenly angels and the triumphant songs of those who had overcome by the blood of the Lamb and the word of their testimony. In the revelation given to him there was unfolded scene after scene of thrilling interest in the experience of the people of God, and the history of the church foretold to the very close of time. In figures and symbols, subjects of vast importance were presented to John, which he was to record, that the people of God living in his age and in future ages might have an intelligent understanding of the perils and conflicts before them.

This revelation was given for the guidance and comfort of the church throughout the Christian dispensation. Yet religious teachers have declared that it is a sealed book and its secrets cannot be explained. Therefore many have turned from the prophetic record, refusing to devote time and study to its mysteries. But God does not wish His people to regard the book thus. It is "the revelation of Jesus Christ, which God gave unto Him, to show unto His servants things which must shortly come to pass." "Blessed is he that readeth," the Lord declares, "and they that hear the words of this prophecy, and keep those things which are written therein: for the time is at hand." Verses 1, 3. "I testify unto every man that heareth the words of the prophecy of this book, If any man shall add unto these things, God shall add unto him the plagues that are written in this book: and if any man shall take away from the words of the book of this prophecy, God shall take away his part out of the book of life, and out of the Holy City, and from the things which are written in this book. He which testifieth these things saith, Surely I come quickly." Revelation 22:18-20.

In the Revelation are portrayed the deep things of God. The very name given to its inspired pages, "the Revelation," contradicts the statement that this is a sealed book. A revelation is something revealed. The Lord Himself revealed to His servant the mysteries contained in this book, and He designs that they shall be open to the study of all. Its truths are addressed to those living in the last days of this earth's history, as well as to those living in the days of John. Some of the scenes depicted in this prophecy are in the past, some are now taking place; some bring to view the close of the great conflict between the powers of darkness and the Prince of heaven, and some reveal the triumphs and joys of the redeemed in the earth made new.

Let none think, because they cannot explain the meaning of every symbol in the Revelation, that it is useless for them to search this book in an effort to know the meaning of the truth it contains. The One who revealed these mysteries to John will give to the diligent searcher for truth a foretaste of heavenly things. Those whose hearts are open to the reception of truth will be enabled to understand its teachings, and will be granted the blessing promised to those who "hear the words of this prophecy, and keep those things which are written therein."

In the Revelation all the books of the Bible meet and end. Here is the complement of the book of Daniel. One is a prophecy; the other a revelation. The book that was sealed is not the Revelation, but that portion of the prophecy of Daniel relating to the last days. The angel commanded, "But thou, O Daniel, shut up the words, and seal the book, even to the time of the end." Daniel 12:4.

It was Christ who bade the apostle record that which was to be opened before him. "What thou seest, write in a book," He commanded, "and send it unto the seven churches which are in Asia; unto Ephesus, and unto Smyrna, and unto Pergamos, and unto Thyatira, and unto Sardis, and unto Philadelphia, and unto Laodicea." "I am He that liveth, and was dead; and, behold, I am alive for evermore. . . . Write the things which thou hast seen, and the things which are, and the things which shall be hereafter; the mystery of the seven stars which thou sawest in My right hand, and the seven golden candlesticks. The seven stars are the angels of the seven churches: and the seven candlesticks which thou sawest are the seven churches." Revelation 1:11, 18-20.

The names of the seven churches are symbolic of the church in different periods of the Christian Era. The number 7 indicates completeness, and is symbolic of the fact that the messages extend to the end of time, while the symbols used reveal the condition of the church at different periods in the history of the word.

Christ is spoken of as walking in the midst of the golden candlesticks. Thus is symbolized His relation to the churches. He is in constant communication with His people. He knows their true state. He observes their order, their piety, their devotion. Although He is high priest and mediator in the sanctuary above, yet He is represented as walking up and down in the midst of His churches on the earth. With untiring wakefulness and unremitting vigilance, He watches to see whether the light of any of His sentinels is burning dim or going out. If the candlesticks were left to mere human care, the flickering flame would languish and die; but He is the true watchman in the Lord's house, the true warden of the temple courts. His continued care and sustaining grace are the source of life and light.

Christ is represented as holding the seven stars in His right hand. This assures us that no church faithful to its trust need fear coming to nought, for not a star that has the protection of Omnipotence can be plucked out of the hand of Christ.

"These things saith He that holdeth the seven stars in His right hand." Revelation 2:1. These words are spoken to the teachers in the church—those entrusted by God with weighty responsibilities. The sweet influences that are to be abundant in the church are bound up with God's ministers, who are to reveal the love of Christ. The stars of heaven are under His control. He fills them with light. He guides and directs their movements. If He did not do this, they would become fallen stars. So with His ministers. They are but instruments in His hands, and all the good they accomplish is done through His power. Through them His light is to shine forth. The Saviour is to be their efficiency. If they will look to Him as He looked to the Father they will be enabled to do His work. As they make God their dependence, He will give them His brightness to reflect to the world.

Early in the history of the church the mystery of iniquity foretold by the apostle Paul began its baleful work; and as the false teachers concerning whom Peter had warned the believers, urged their heresies, many were ensnared by false doctrines. Some faltered under trial and were tempted to give up the faith. At the time when John was given this revelation, many had lost their first love of gospel truth. But in His mercy God did not leave the church to continue in a backslidden state. In a message of infinite tenderness He revealed His love for them and His desire that they should make sure work for eternity. "Remember," He pleaded, "from whence thou art fallen, and repent, and do the first works." Verse 5.

The church was defective and in need of stern reproof and chastisement, and John was inspired to record messages of warning and reproof and entreaty to those who, losing sight of the fundamental principles of the gospel, should imperil their hope of salvation. But always the words of rebuke that God finds it necessary to send are spoken in tender love and with the promise of peace to every penitent believer. "Behold, I stand at the door, and knock," the Lord declares; "if any man hear My voice, and open the door, I will come in to him, and will sup with him, and he with Me." Revelation 3:20.

And for those who in the midst of conflict should maintain their faith in God, the prophet was given the words of commendation and promise: "I know thy works: behold, I have set before thee an open door, and no man can shut it: for thou hast a little strength, and hast kept My word, and hast not denied My name." "Because thou hast kept the word of My patience, I also will keep thee from the hour of temptation, which shall come upon all the world, to try them that dwell upon the earth." The believers were admonished: "Be watchful, and strengthen the things which remain, that are ready to die." "Behold, I come quickly: hold that fast which thou hast, that no man take thy crown." Verses 8, 10, 2, 11.

It was through one who declared himself to be a "brother, and companion in tribulation" (Revelation 1:9), that Christ revealed to His church the things that they must suffer for His sake. Looking down through long centuries of darkness and superstition, the aged exile saw multitudes suffering martyrdom because of their love for the truth. But he saw also that He who sustained His early witnesses would not forsake His faithful followers during the centuries of persecution that they must pass through before the close of time. "Fear none of those things which thou shalt suffer," the Lord declared; "behold, the devil shall cast some of you into prison, that ye may be tried; and ye shall have tribulation: . . . be thou faithful unto death, and I will give thee a crown of life." Revelation 2:10.

And to all the faithful ones who were striving against evil, John heard the promises made: "To him that overcometh will I give to eat of the tree of life, which is in the midst of the Paradise of God." "He that overcometh, the same shall be clothed in white raiment; and I will not blot out his name out of the book of life, but I will confess his name before My Father, and before His angels." "To him that overcometh will I grant to sit with Me in My throne, even as I also overcame, and am set down with My Father in His throne." Verse 7; 3:5, 21.

John saw the mercy, the tenderness, and the love of God blending with His holiness, justice, and power. He saw sinners finding a Father in Him of whom their sins had made them afraid. And looking beyond the culmination of the great conflict, he beheld upon Zion "them that had gotten the victory . . . stand on the sea of glass, having the harps of God," and singing "the song of Moses" and the Lamb. Revelation 15:2, 3.

The Saviour is presented before John under the symbols of "the Lion of the tribe of Judah" and of "a Lamb as it had been slain." Revelation 5:5, 6. These symbols represent the union of omnipotent power and self-sacrificing love. The Lion of Judah, so terrible to the rejectors of His grace, will be the Lamb of God to the obedient and faithful. The pillar of fire that speaks terror and wrath to the transgressor of God's law is a token of light and mercy and deliverance to those who have kept His commandments. The arm strong to smite the rebellious will be strong to deliver the loyal. Everyone who is faithful will be saved. "He shall send His angels with a great sound of a trumpet, and they shall gather together His elect from the four winds, from one end of heaven to the other." Matthew 24:31.

In comparison with the millions of the world, God's people will be, as they have ever been, a little flock; but if they stand for the truth as revealed in His word, God will be their refuge. They stand under the broad shield of Omnipotence. God is always a majority. When the sound of the last trump shall penetrate the prison house of the dead, and the righteous shall come forth with triumph, exclaiming, "O death, where is thy sting? O grave, where is thy victory?" (1 Corinthians 15:55)—standing then with God, with Christ, with the angels, and with the loyal and true of all ages, the children of God will be far in the majority.

Christ's true disciples follow Him through sore conflicts, enduring self-denial and experiencing bitter disappointment; but this teaches them the guilt and woe of sin, and they are led to look upon it with abhorrence. Partakers of Christ's sufferings, they are destined to be partakers of His glory. In holy vision the prophet saw the ultimate triumph of God's remnant church. He writes:

"I saw as it were a sea of glass mingled with fire: and them that had gotten the victory . . . stand on the sea of glass, having the harps of God. And they sing the song of Moses the servant of God, and the song of the Lamb, saying, Great and marvelous are Thy works, Lord God Almighty; just and true are Thy ways, Thou King of saints." Revelation 15:2, 3.

"And I looked, and, lo, a Lamb stood on the Mount Sion, and with Him a hundred forty and four thousand, having His Father's name written in their foreheads." Revelation 14:1. In this world their minds were consecrated to God; they served Him with the intellect and with the heart; and now He can place His name "in their foreheads." "And they shall reign for ever and ever." Revelation 22:5. They do not go in and out as those who beg a place. They are of that number to whom Christ says, "Come, ye blessed of My Father, inherit the kingdom prepared for you from the foundation of the world." He welcomes them as His children, saying, "Enter thou into the joy of thy Lord." Matthew 25:34, 21.

"These are they which follow the Lamb withersoever He goeth. These were redeemed from among men, being the first fruits unto God and to the Lamb." Revelation 14:4. The vision of the prophet pictures them as standing on Mount Zion, girt for holy service, clothed in white linen, which is the righteousness of the saints. But all who follow the Lamb in heaven must first have followed Him on earth, not fretfully or capriciously, but in trustful, loving, willing obedience, as the flock follows the shepherd.

"I heard the voice of harpers harping with their harps: and they sung as it were a new song before the throne: ... and no man could learn that song but the hundred and forty and four thousand, which were redeemed from the earth.... In their mouth was found no guile: for they are without fault before the throne of God." Verses 2-5.

"And I John saw the Holy City, New Jerusalem, coming down from God out of heaven, prepared as a bride adorned for her husband." "Her light was like unto a stone most precious, even like a jasper stone, clear as crystal; and had a wall great and high, and had twelve gates, and at the gates twelve angels, and names written thereon, which are the names of the twelve tribes of the children of Israel." "The twelve gates were twelve pearls; every several gate was of one pearl: and the street of the city was pure gold, as it were transparent glass. And I saw no temple therein: for the Lord God Almighty and the Lamb are the temple of it." Revelation 21:2, 11, 12, 21, 22.

"And there shall be no more curse: but the throne of God and of the Lamb shall be in it; and His servants shall serve Him: and they shall see His face; and His name shall be in their foreheads. And there shall be no night there; and they need no candle, neither light of the sun; for the Lord God giveth them light." Revelation 22:3-5.

"He showed me a pure river of water of life, clear as crystal, proceeding out of the throne of God and of the Lamb. In the midst of the street of it, and on either side of the river, was there the tree of life, which bare twelve manner of fruits, and yielded her fruit every month: and the leaves of the tree were for the healing of the nations." "Blessed are they that do His commandments, that they may have right to the tree of life, and may enter in through the gates into the city." Verses 1, 2, 14.

"And I heard a great voice out of heaven saying,

"Behold, the tabernacle of God is with men,
And He will dwell with them,
And they shall be His people,
And God Himself shall be with them,
And be their God." Revelation 21:3.

58

The Church Triumphant

More than eighteen centuries have passed since the apostles rested from their labors, but the history of their toils and sacrifices for Christ's sake is still among the most precious treasures of the church. This history, written under the direction of the Holy Spirit, was recorded in order that by it the followers of Christ in every age might be impelled to greater zeal and earnestness in the cause of the Saviour.

The commission that Christ gave to the disciples, they fulfilled. As these messengers of the cross went forth to proclaim the gospel, there was such a revelation of the glory of God as had never before been witnessed by mortal man. By the co-operation of the divine Spirit, the apostles did a work that shook the world. To every nation was the gospel carried in a single generation.

Glorious were the results that attended the ministry of the chosen apostles of Christ. At the beginning of their ministry some of them were unlearned men, but their consecration to the cause of their Master was unreserved, and under His instruction they gained a preparation for the great work committed to them. Grace and truth reigned in their hearts, inspiring their motives and controlling their actions. Their lives were hid with Christ in God, and self was lost sight of, submerged in the depths of infinite love.

The disciples were men who knew how to speak and pray sincerely, men who could take hold of the might of the Strength of Israel. How closely they stood by the side of God, and bound their personal honor to His throne! Jehovah was their God. His honor was their honor. His truth was their truth. Any attack made upon the gospel was as if cutting deep into their souls, and with every power of their being they battled for the cause of Christ. They could hold forth the word of life because they had received the heavenly anointing. They expected much, and therefore they attempted much. Christ had revealed Himself to them, and to Him they looked for guidance. Their understanding of truth and their power to withstand opposition were proportionate to their conformity to God's will. Jesus Christ, the wisdom and power of God, was the theme of every discourse. His name—the only name given under heaven whereby men can be saved—was by them exalted. As they proclaimed the completeness of Christ, the risen Saviour, their words moved hearts, and men and women were won to the gospel. Multitudes who had reviled the Saviour's name and despised His power now confessed themselves disciples of the Crucified.

Not in their own power did the apostles accomplish their mission, but in the power of the living God. Their work was not easy. The opening labors of the Christian church were attended by hardship and bitter grief. In their work the disciples constantly encountered privation, calumny, and persecution; but they counted not their lives dear unto themselves and rejoiced that they were called to suffer for Christ. Irresolution, indecision, weakness of purpose, found no place in their efforts. They were willing to spend and be spent. The consciousness of the responsibility resting on them purified and enriched their experience, and the grace of heaven was revealed in the conquests they achieved for Christ. With the might of omnipotence God worked through them to make the gospel triumphant.

Upon the foundation that Christ Himself had laid, the apostles built the church of God. In the Scriptures the figure of the erection of a temple is frequently used to illustrate the building of the church. Zechariah refers to Christ as the Branch that should build the temple of the Lord. He speaks of the Gentiles as helping in the work: "They that are far off shall come and build in the temple of the Lord;" and Isaiah declares, "The sons of strangers shall build up thy walls." Zechariah 6:12, 15; Isaiah 60:10.

Writing of the building of this temple, Peter says, "To whom coming, as unto a living stone, disallowed indeed of men, but chosen of God, and precious, ye also, as lively stones, are built up a spiritual house, an holy priesthood, to offer up spiritual sacrifices, acceptable to God by Jesus Christ." 1 Peter 2:4, 5.

In the quarry of the Jewish and the Gentile world the apostles labored, bringing out stones to lay upon the foundation. In his letter to the believers at Ephesus, Paul said, "Now therefore ye are no more strangers and foreigners, but fellow citizens with the saints, and of the household of God; and are built upon the foundation of the apostles and prophets, Jesus Christ Himself being the Chief Cornerstone; in whom all the building fitly framed together groweth unto an holy temple in the Lord: in whom ye also are builded together for an habitation of God through the Spirit." Ephesians 2:19-22.

And to the Corinthians he wrote: "According to the grace of God which is given unto me, as a wise master builder, I have laid the foundation, and another buildeth thereon. But let every man take heed how he buildeth thereupon. For other foundation can no man lay than that is laid, which is Jesus Christ. Now if any man build upon this foundation gold, silver, precious stones, wood, hay, stubble; every man's work shall be made manifest: for the day shall declare it, because it shall be revealed by fire; and the fire shall try every man's work of what sort it is." 1 Corinthians 3:10-13.

The apostles built upon a sure foundation, even the Rock of Ages. To this foundation they brought the stones that they quarried from the world. Not without hindrance did the builders labor. Their work was made exceedingly difficult by the opposition of the enemies of Christ. They had to contend against the bigotry, prejudice, and hatred of those who were building upon a false foundation. Many who wrought as builders of the church could be likened to the builders of the wall in Nehemiah's day, of whom it is written: "They which builded on the wall, and they that bare burdens, with those that laded, everyone with one of his hands wrought in the work, and with the other hand held a weapon." Nehemiah 4:17.

Kings and governors, priests and rulers, sought to destroy the temple of God. But in the face of imprisonment, torture, and death, faithful men carried the work forward; and the structure grew, beautiful and symmetrical. At times the workmen were almost blinded by the mists of superstition that settled around them. At times they were almost overpowered by the violence of their opponents. But with unfaltering faith and unfailing courage they pressed on with the work.

One after another the foremost of the builders fell by the hand of the enemy. Stephen was stoned; James was slain by the sword; Paul was beheaded; Peter was crucified; John was exiled. Yet the church grew. New workers took the place of those who fell, and stone after stone was added to the building. Thus slowly ascended the temple of the church of God.

Centuries of fierce persecution followed the establishment of the Christian church, but there were never wanting men who counted the work of building God's temple dearer than life itself. Of such it is written: "Others had trial of cruel mockings and scourgings, yea, moreover of bonds and imprisonment: they were stoned, they were sawn asunder, were tempted, were slain with the sword: they wandered about in sheepskins and goatskins; being destitute, afflicted, tormented; (of whom the world was not worthy:) they wandered in deserts, and in mountains, and in dens and caves of the earth." Hebrews 11:36-38.

The enemy of righteousness left nothing undone in his effort to stop the work committed to the Lord's builders. But God "left not Himself without witness." Acts 14:17. Workers were raised up who ably defended the faith once delivered to the saints. History bears record to the fortitude and heroism of these men. Like the apostles, many of them fell at their post, but the building of the temple went steadily forward. The workmen were slain, but the work advanced. The Waldenses, John Wycliffe, Huss and Jerome, Martin Luther and Zwingli, Cranmer, Latimer, and Knox, the Huguenots, John and Charles Wesley, and a host of others brought to the foundation material that will endure throughout eternity. And in later years those who have so nobly endeavored to promote the circulation of God's word, and those who by their service in heathen lands have prepared the way for the proclamation of the last great message— these also have helped to rear the structure.

Through the ages that have passed since the days of the apostles, the building of God's temple has never ceased. We may look back through the centuries and see the living stones of which it is composed gleaming like jets of light through the darkness of error and superstition. Throughout eternity these precious jewels will shine with increasing luster, testifying to the power of the truth of God. The flashing light of these polished stones reveals the strong contrast between light and darkness, between the gold of truth and the dross of error.

Paul and the other apostles, and all the righteous who have lived since then, have acted their part in the building of the temple. But the structure is not yet complete. We who are living in this age have a work to do, a part to act. We are to bring to the foundation material that will stand the test of fire—gold, silver, and precious stones, "polished after the similitude of a palace." Psalm 144:12. To those who thus build for God, Paul speaks words of encouragement and warning: "If any man's work abide which he hath built thereupon, he shall receive a reward. If any man's work shall be burned, he shall suffer loss: but he himself shall be saved; yet so as by fire." 1 Corinthians 3:14, 15. The Christian who faithfully presents the word of life, leading men and women into the way of holiness and peace, is bringing to the foundation material that will endure, and in the kingdom of God he will be honored as a wise builder.

Of the apostles it is written, "They went forth, and preached everywhere, the Lord working with them, and confirming the word with signs following." Mark 16:20. As Christ sent forth His disciples, so today He sends forth the members of His church. The same power that the apostles had is for them. If they will make God their strength, He will work with them, and they shall not labor in vain. Let them realize that the work in which they are engaged is one upon which the Lord has placed His signet. God said to Jeremiah, "Say not, I am a child: for thou shalt go to all that I shall send thee, and whatsoever I command thee thou shalt speak. Be not afraid of their faces: for I am with thee to deliver thee." Then the Lord put forth His hand and touched His servant's mouth, saying, "Behold, I have put My words in thy mouth." Jeremiah 1:7-9. And He bids us go forth to speak the words He gives us, feeling His holy touch upon our lips.

Christ has given to the church a sacred charge. Every member should be a channel through which God can communicate to the world the treasures of His grace, the unsearchable riches of Christ. There is nothing that the Saviour desires so much as agents who will represent to the world His Spirit and His character. There is nothing that the world needs so much as the manifestation through humanity of the Saviour's love. All heaven is waiting for men and women through whom God can reveal the power of Christianity.

The church is God's agency for the proclamation of truth, empowered by Him to do a special work; and if she is loyal to Him, obedient to all His commandments, there will dwell within her the excellency of divine grace. If she will be true to her allegiance, if she will honor the Lord God of Israel, there is no power that can stand against her.

Zeal for God and His cause moved the disciples to bear witness to the gospel with mighty power. Should not a like zeal fire our hearts with a determination to tell the story of redeeming love, of Christ and Him crucified? It is the privilege of every Christian, not only to look for, but to hasten the coming of the Saviour.

If the church will put on the robe of Christ's righteousness, withdrawing from all allegiance with the world, there is before her the dawn of a bright and glorious day. God's promise to her will stand fast forever. He will make her an eternal excellency, a joy of many generations. Truth, passing by those who despise and reject it, will triumph. Although at times apparently retarded, its progress has never been checked. When the message of God meets with opposition, He gives it additional force, that it may exert greater influence. Endowed with divine energy, it will cut its way through the strongest barriers and triumph over every obstacle.

What sustained the Son of God during His life of toil and sacrifice? He saw the results of the travail of His soul and was satisfied. Looking into eternity, He beheld the happiness of those who through His humiliation had received pardon and everlasting life. His ear caught the shout of the redeemed. He heard the ransomed ones singing the song of Moses and the Lamb.

We may have a vision of the future, the blessedness of heaven. In the Bible are revealed visions of the future glory, scenes pictured by the hand of God, and these are dear to His church. By faith we may stand on the threshold of the eternal city, and hear the gracious welcome given to those who in this life co-operate with Christ, regarding it as an honor to suffer for His sake. As the words are spoken, "Come, ye blessed of My Father," they cast their crowns at the feet of the Redeemer, exclaiming, "Worthy is the Lamb that was slain to receive power, and riches, and wisdom, and strength, and honor, and glory, and blessing. . . . Honor, and glory, and power, be unto Him that sitteth upon the throne, and unto the Lamb for ever and ever." Matthew 25:34; Revelation 5:12, 13.

There the redeemed greet those who led them to the Saviour, and all unite in praising Him who died that human beings might have the life that measures with the life of God. The conflict is over. Tribulation and strife are at an end. Songs of victory fill all heaven as the ransomed ones take up the joyful strain, Worthy, worthy is the Lamb that was slain, and lives again, a triumphant conqueror.

"I beheld, and, lo, a great multitude, which no man could number, of all nations, and kindreds, and people, and tongues, stood before the throne, and before the Lamb, clothed with white robes, and palms in their hands; and cried with a loud voice, saying, Salvation to our God which sitteth upon the throne, and unto the Lamb." Revelation 7:9, 10.

"These are they which came out of great tribulation, and have washed their robes, and made them white in the blood of the Lamb. Therefore are they before the throne of God, and serve Him day and night in His temple: and He that sitteth on the throne shall dwell among them. They shall hunger no more, neither thirst any more; neither shall the sun light on them, nor any heat. For the Lamb which is in the midst of the throne shall feed them, and shall lead them unto living fountains of waters: and God shall wipe away all tears from their eyes." "And there shall be no more death, neither sorrow, nor crying, neither shall there be any more pain: for the former things are passed away." Revelation 7:14-17; 21:4.

INDEXES

Index to Scripture References